Jewish Liturgy

prayer and synagogue service through the ages

Jewish Liturgy

prayer and synagogue service through the ages

Raphael Posner

Uri Kaploun

Shalom Cohen

Editors

LEON AMIEL PUBLISHER
New York - Paris

KETER PUBLISHING HOUSE JERUSALEM LTD.

Administration and Co-ordination: Hayyim Schneid
Design and Execution: Murray Bloom
Illustration Research: Peretz Hein
Nechama Unterman

Published in the Western Hemisphere by
LEON AMIEL PUBLISHER
New York – Paris

ISBN 0–8148 – 0596–5
Library of Congress Catalog Card Number 74–12586

Distributed in the rest of the world by
KETER PUBLISHING HOUSE JERUSALEM LTD.
P.O. Box 7145, Jerusalem, Israel

ISBN 0–7065 – 1414–9
Cat. No. 25086

Set, printed and bound by Keterpress Enterprises, Jerusalem
Printed in Israel

contents

FOREWORD

The Book of Exodus relates that when the Children of Israel stood at the Sea of Reeds after their miraculous delivery from Egypt, they saw the Egyptian hosts bearing down on them. Pharaoh had had yet another change of heart. At this point "they were sore afraid, and the Children of Israel cried out unto the Lord." The waters parted: the Jews marched forward into history. A midrashic homily on this episode remarks that the Jews "adopted the skill of their forefathers, Abraham, Isaac and Jacob," the veritable masters of prayer; their descendants, like them, saw only one way to cope with the threat of impending disaster, and cried out to the Lord. Like their fathers, they too prayed.

Nor is it only in times of disaster that Jews have learned to pray. When "Jacob went out from Beer-sheba, . . . and lay down in that place to sleep, and he dreamed, and behold a ladder set up on the earth, and the top of it reached to heaven, and behold the angels of God ascending and descending on it"—this ladder, says the *Zohar*, is prayer. On this ladder the mortal may grope his way upward, and on this ladder the very heavens may be drawn down earthward.

And indeed it is fair to say that Judaism is unimaginable without prayer. Judaism has always taught that finite man has direct access to the infinite Creator simply by talking to Him. There is no need for intermediaries. This doctrine has been constant in Judaism throughout the ages and in all trends, from the Bible to this day. Something, though, has changed over these three millennia. The amorphous instinct that impelled the Children of Israel to utter their prayer at the Sea of Reeds gradually assumed a tangible form, as regards content, style, and time. Certain forms of prayer crystallized, and liturgical texts were committed to writing—with varying degrees of uniformity—and came to be recited at fixed times.

Lest the form become an end in itself, the rabbis of the centuries always taught—as did Baḥya ibn Pakuda in his classic *Duties of the Heart*—that a prayer without devotion is "a body without a soul, a shell without a kernel." The most sublime prayer can be hardly worth saying unless it is accompanied by a due measure of devout concentration, or *kavvanah*, to call it by its Hebrew name. Though ignorance of the meaning of the prayers does not necessarily rule out the possibility of *kavvanah*—for God "knows the heart of man"—understanding the prayers most certainly contributes to it. This is true not only for the meaning of the actual words used in prayer, but also for its history, its original settings, its format, and what may be called the techniques of prayer. Indeed, knowing *about* the prayers may well be as important as knowing the prayers, for such knowledge gives an intimacy to the act of praying.

It is *about* prayer that this book tells. It presents the history and structure of the prayer services and of the individual prayers; it discusses various attitudes to prayer, and describes the ways in which Jews pray. It is not the hundredth, nor even the thousandth work to be written about the prayer book, which is itself one of the most reprinted books in the Jewish library. Yet it will have justified its appearance if it helps even one reader to achieve the ideal articulated nearly 900 years ago by Judah Halevi: "The tongue agrees with the thought, and does not overstep its bounds. It does not speak in prayer in a mere mechanical way, like the starling or the parrot, but utters every word thoughtfully and attentively."

I PRAYER: THE IDEA

in the Bible
in rabbinic thought
in medieval thought
in the Kabbalah
in Ḥasidism
swaying in prayer
in modern thought

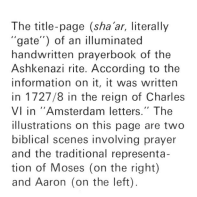

The title-page (*sha'ar*, literally "gate") of an illuminated handwritten prayerbook of the Ashkenazi rite. According to the information on it, it was written in 1727/8 in the reign of Charles VI in "Amsterdam letters." The illustrations on this page are two biblical scenes involving prayer and the traditional representation of Moses (on the right) and Aaron (on the left).

IN THE BIBLE

The concept of prayer in the Bible is based on the conviction that God hears what human beings say to Him and answers them. In a sense it is a corollary of the biblical doctrine that man was created "in the image of God," which implies, inter alia, fellowship with God. Although the biblical idea of prayer has an intellectual base, it is essentially emotional in character. It is an expression of man's quest for the Divine and his longing to unburden his soul before God. Hence prayer takes many forms: petition, expostulation, confession, meditation, recollection, thanksgiving, praise, adoration, and intercession. For the purpose of classification, praise should be distinguished from prayer in the narrower, supplicatory sense, and spontaneous prayer from liturgical prayer. But the source is the same; in its irresistible outpouring, the human heart merges all categories in an indivisible "I-Thou" relationship. Thus prayer and praise may intermingle, and supplication and thanksgiving follow in close succession. Indeed, many scriptural passages might be called para-prayers—they seem to hover between discourse and entreaty, meditation and petition, or expostulation and entreaty. Some scholars estimate that there are 85 prayers in the Bible, apart from 60 complete Psalms and 14 parts of Psalms that can be so termed; five Psalms are specifically called prayers. But such liturgical statistics depend on the definition given to prayer.

Terminology. The variegated character of biblical prayer has given rise to many names for prayer and the act of praying. The rabbis of the Talmud noted that "prayer is called by ten different expressions;" on closer examination even more can be found. The most common word for prayer is *tefillah,* and the corresponding verb is *hitpallel.* The root of this word, *pll,* has been explained to mean "to cut oneself," and to refer to the primitive pagan custom of slashing oneself in a frenzy during worship. This etymology is not only hypothetical, but wholly irrelevant to the biblical situation. It was the idol-worshipers who cut themselves and the verb used is *va-yitgodedu;* the Torah forbids such practices. In Scripture the root *pll* signifies "to interpose, judge, hope." These meanings are eminently suited to the biblical conception of prayer as intercession and self-scrutiny leading to hope. Other terms are: *kara* ("to call" on the name of the Deity, i.e. worship); *za'ak* ("to cry out" for redress of wrongs); *shivva* ("to cry aloud" for help); *rinnah* ("ringing cry" of joy or sorrow); *darash* ("to seek" God); *bikkesh penei . . .* ("to seek the face of" God); *sha'al* ("to inquire"); *nasa* ("to lift up"); *paga* ("to encounter," i.e. to appease, gain favor); *hitḥannen* ("to seek favor," i.e. beseech); *shafakh lev* ("to pour out one's heart"); and *si'aḥ* ("complaint").

The Character of Prayer. Despite its multifaceted character, biblical prayer is essentially a simple human reaction. The rabbis called it "the service in the heart," an expression which has its roots in biblical thought. But the needs of man are so numerous and complex that prayer inevitably came to reflect the vast range of human moods, fears, hopes, feelings, desires, and aspirations. In the patriarchal age a simple invocation, a calling upon the name of the Lord, would suffice. The approach to God at this stage was marked by spontaneity, directness, and familiarity. God was near. Yet the future was veiled in mystery; man was often undecided how to act. Hence the request for a sign or oracle addressed directly to God, or indirectly through a priest or prophet. From this stratum grew the noble prayers for understanding and guidance; such as these examples from the Books of Numbers, Kings and Psalms respectively:

> The Lord bless you and keep you!
> The Lord deal kindly and graciously with you!
> The Lord bestow his favor upon you and grant you peace!

> And Solomon said: 'Thou hast shown unto Thy servant David my father great kindness, according as he walked before Thee in truth, and in righteousness, and in uprightness of heart with Thee; and Thou hast kept for him this great kindness, that Thou hast given him a son to sit on his throne, as it is this day. And now, O Lord my God, Thou hast made Thy servant king instead of David my father; and I am but a little child; I know not how to go out or come in. And Thy servant is in the midst of

"Last Prayer," an oil painting by Samuel Hirschenberg, 1897. The contemplative mood and the lighted candle seem to suggest that the prayer is that recited before retiring. However, both the *tallit* the subject is wearing and that lying on the table indicate that the scene is in the *bet ha-midrash*.

Thy people which Thou hast chosen, a great people, that cannot be numbered nor counted for multitude. Give Thy servant therefore an understanding heart to judge Thy people, that I may discern between good and evil; for who is able to judge this Thy great people?

Teach me, O Lord, the way of Thy statutes;
And I will keep it at every step.
Give me understanding, that I keep Thy law
And observe it with my whole heart.
Make me to tread in the path of Thy commandments;
For therein do I delight.
Incline my heart unto Thy testimonies,
And not to covetousness.
Turn away mine eyes from beholding vanity,
And quicken me in Thy ways.
Confirm Thy word unto Thy servant,
Which pertaineth unto the fear of Thee.
Turn away my reproach which I dread;
For Thine ordinances are good.
Behold, I have longed after Thy precepts;
Quicken me in Thy righteousness.

But in emergency man does not merely want to know the future; he seeks to determine it by entreating God's help. Thus the patriarch Abraham prayed for the salvation of Sodom; his servant for the success of his matrimonial mission; Jacob for essential material needs; Moses for forgiveness for erring Israel; Joshua for divine help in the hour of defeat; King Hezekiah for deliverance from Sennacherib; and the prophets for all the possible needs of Israel—material, spiritual, individual and communal. Solomon's dedication prayer at the consecration of the Temple includes almost every type of prayer—adoration, thanksgiving, petition and confession.

And he said: "O Lord, the God of Israel, there is no God like Thee, in heaven above, or on earth beneath; who keepest covenant and mercy with Thy servants, that walk before Thee with all their heart.

Now therefore, O Lord, the God of Israel, keep with Thy servant David my father that which Thou hast promised him, saying: There shall not fail thee a man in My sight to sit on the throne of Israel, if only thy children take heed to their way, to walk before Me as thou hast walked before Me.

Whatever prayer and supplication be made by any man of all Thy people Israel—every man knowing the plague of his own heart, and spreading forth his hands toward this house—then hear Thou in heaven Thy dwelling-place, and forgive, and do, and render unto every man according to all his ways, whose heart Thou knowest—for Thou, Thou only, knowest the hearts of all the children of men—that they may fear Thee all the days that they live in the land which Thou gavest unto our fathers."

Prayer also strikes the universal note so often echoed by the prophets. The spectrum of biblical prayer thus ranges from the simplest material needs to the highest spiritual yearnings, transcending, like prophecy, the horizon of history and reaching to the realm of eschatology.

There was an early relationship between sacrifice and prayer, which persisted until the destruction of the Second Temple. The sacrifice suggested man's submission to the will of God; the prayer often provided a commentary on the offering. But the two are not necessarily linked. It is noteworthy that the sacrificial regulations make no liturgical provisions (except for the Day

of Atonement); but actually the offerings were themselves a dramatic form of prayer. Contrariwise, prayer could replace sacrifice. In the synagogue, prayer—accompanied by Scripture reading and exposition—entirely took the place of altar offerings.

Examples of prayers of intercession have already been cited. The existence of an intercessor, however, whether prophet, priest, king, or national leader, does not point to the need for an intermediary in worship: "The Lord is near to all who call upon Him in truth." The intercessor is one who, by his innate spiritual attributes, lends weight to the entreaty. The ultimate criterion still remains not the worthiness of the pleader but of those for whom he is pleading. At the same time, in the talmudic period, some men were renowned for their capacity to pray and to have their prayers answered, so that great scholars, less gifted in this direction, would ask these saints to pray on their behalf.

Place, Time, and Manner. Prayer, unlike sacrifice, could be offered up anywhere, but, in the Bible, there was always a natural tendency to prefer sites which had been sanctified by their associations with the holy, such as Shiloh or Gibeon. Eventually the Temple at Jerusalem became the major place of prayer; those who could not be there physically at least turned toward it when worshiping. In time to come, according to the prophets, the Temple would be a house of prayer for all nations. In the meantime, the synagogue, which presumably had its origin during the Babylonian exile—originally as a place of assembly—became a house of prayer. Day and night, the Heavenly Father could be entreated, but the need for regularity brought about a synchronization of the times of prayer and of sacrifice; morning worship corresponded to the morning oblation, and the afternoon service to the late afternoon sacrifice. Nightfall provided yet another occasion for worship, so that prayers came to be offered thrice daily. This is indicated in at least two biblical passages, although in the Book of Chronicles reference is made to twice-daily prayers. The seven times mentioned in Psalms presumably mean "often" or "constantly."

Although no particular gestures are prescribed in the Bible in connection with prayer, certain postures developed naturally to lend emphasis to the content of the prayer: standing, which is normative; kneeling; prostration; head bowed; hands stretched out or uplifted; face between knees; and sitting. More important accompaniments of prayer were fasting, mourning, and weeping—but the ultimate criterion remained earnestness of heart.

Three attitudes of prayer. A statue of Daniel, considered by the rabbis of the Talmud as an archetype of supplicant. This statue is by Bernini and was executed in 1655–57. It stands in St. Maria del Papolo in Rome. Herman Struck's (1876–1944) etching of the ḥasid praying at the Western Wall conveys quite a different, more subdued atmosphere, one caught by Arielli's post-1967 photograph of a soldier at the same place.

Originally prayer was undoubtedly spontaneous and personal; the eventual rise of liturgical patterns and musical renderings is discussed in the chapters which follow. As will be seen, forerunners of later liturgical forms may be found in the Pentateuch, while sophisticated choral and instrumental features are frequently alluded to in the Psalms. Other biblical books, such as Nehemiah, include elements such as a prayer before the reading of the Torah, a doxology, and a review of God's dealings with Israel leading to a confession and a pledge.

Answer to Prayer. That prayer is answered is an accepted biblical verity—but Scripture is no less emphatic that not all prayers are answered. Ritual is not enough, while hypocritical worship is an abomination; and there are occasions when intercession is forbidden. It is at this point that the biblical concept of prayer is seen in its true inwardness. Paganism regarded worship as a form of magic, whereby the deity could be compelled to fulfill the worshiper's wishes; the moral element was wholly absent. In biblical faith the divine response is essentially linked to ethical and spiritual values. Man, as it were, answers his own prayer, and fundamentally the answer is a significant change of spirit and outlook. Abraham learned the lesson of faith; Moses became his people's deliverer; Isaiah was transformed into a prophet. Indeed, prayer and prophecy were probably closely correlated, the former providing spiritual soil in which the revelatory seed took root. In many instances prayer assumes a tempestuous character, but the storm always resolves itself in newfound faith and peace. At times, moreover, God answers before He is appealed to, for not only does man beseech God: God also seeks man. The I-Thou relationship is reciprocal.

In sum, the Bible conceives of prayer as a spiritual bridge between man and God. It is a great instrument of human regeneration and salvation, worthy even of martyrdom. Rooted in faith and moral integrity, it banishes fear and asks, in its noblest formulations, only the blessing of divine favor. Clothed in language of simple beauty, it is imbued with religious love and a sense of sweet fellowship with God. Both the Christian and Muslim liturgies have been profoundly influenced by the spirit, thought, and forms of biblical prayer.

IN RABBINIC THOUGHT

On the biblical verse "And serve Him with all your heart," the rabbis commented: "What is service in the heart?—This is prayer." In this context service (*avodah*) is connected with the Temple and its worship, for which prayer is seen as a substitute. On the other hand, the dictum of Rabbi Eleazar that prayer is dearer to God than good works and sacrifices, though hyperbolic, may nonetheless be intended to express the real superiority of prayer. Possibly, the tension in this matter is to be perceived in the two reasons given for the daily statutory prayers. According to one opinion, these were established by the patriarchs: Abraham, Isaac and Jacob each ordained one of the three daily services—for morning, afternoon, and night. Another view has it that they correspond to the regular offerings in Temple times.

The obligation of offering up prayer, though supported by a scriptural verse, is considered to be of rabbinic authority, not biblical. In all ages, in addition to the three statutory services and private prayers of various kinds, public prayers were offered in times of distress, such as prayers for rain in times of drought.

Indeed, prayer stands so high in the world of values that one rabbinic homily has it that God Himself prays. The question of the content of His prayers, and to whom they could be addressed, is resolved by the suggestion that He prays to Himself—that His mercy might overcome His judgment. Nevertheless, the study of the Torah occupies a higher rung than prayer, and some scholars, whose main occupation was study, prayed only periodically. One rabbi who spent more time than was usual on his prayers was even rebuked by one of his colleagues for neglecting eternal life (which is the result of Torah study) to engage in temporal existence.

Valuable as private prayer might be, the rabbis of the Talmud vied with each other in creating homilies which taught the superior value of communal prayer—a subject which is discussed in Chapter III.

Proper Forms of Prayer. Not every prayer is valid. A prayer for God to change the past, for instance, is a "vain prayer." The impossibility of God's answering every prayer addressed to Him

"Psalmist," an oil by Ben-Zion (1897–). The artist, who is known for his unconventional interpretation of biblical themes, has succeeded in creating something of the mood of the Book of Psalms. The activity of playing the lyre is offset by the expression of absolute serenity and trust on the face of the "Psalmist."

is acknowledged in the classical account of the high priest's prayer on the Day of Atonement, before the rainy season, that the prayers of the travelers who required dry weather should not be allowed to enter God's presence because the farmers need rain. The rabbis taught that a man should not only pray for himself but should also keep others in mind, using the plural form "grant us" rather than the singular "grant me." Furthermore, they taught, if a man needs something for himself but prays to God to grant that very thing to his neighbor who also needs it, the unselfishness of his prayer causes God to grant him his wish first.

In praising God, man should be circumspect, using only the standard forms of praise based on Scripture and established for use in prayer, since the theological import of the prayers is such that the supplicant could inadvertently utter a heresy. Prayers of thanksgiving, particularly in the form of the benediction, are repeatedly enjoined by the rabbis, as well as praise of God for His wondrous works and for the beings He has created. Both the notion and the structure of the commonest liturgical forms are discussed in Chapter II.

A man should never despair of offering supplication to God, "even if a sharp sword is resting upon his neck." Rabbi Judah discussed the addressing of prayers directly to God with a metaphor. If a human being is in trouble and wishes to invoke the aid of his patron he must first stand at the door and call out to a servant or a member of the patron's family, and he may or may not be allowed to enter. But it is otherwise with God. God says, "When a man is in trouble, he should not cry out to the angel Michael or to the angel Gabriel but to Me, and I will answer immediately." Rabbi Johanan's teaching appears to differ. "When one petitions for his needs in Aramaic, the ministering angels do not heed him, for they do not understand that language." Possibly a distinction is to be drawn between the angels' bringing man's prayers to God, and intercession as such, with the angels as intermediaries between man and God.

Kavvanah. Prayer should be offered with proper concentration on the words uttered in God's presence. Rabbi Eliezer said: "He that makes his prayer a fixed task, his prayer is not supplication." So, too, Rabbi Simeon ben Nethanel said: "... and when thou prayest make not thy prayer a fixed form, but [a plea for] mercies and supplications before God." One classic way of avoiding the deadening familiarity of a "fixed form" was to recite a new prayer each day. When Rabbi Eliezer was asked by his disciples to teach them the ways of life that they might learn them and thereby attain the life of the world to come, part of his reply was: "When you pray, know before Whom you stand."

In rabbinic literature the term used to denote a state of mental concentration and devotion at prayer and during the performance of *mitzvot* is *kavvanah* (literally "direction"). Although the demand for *kavvanah* as an obligatory component of prayer is not explicitly mentioned in the Torah, praying, by its very definition, must be offered with *kavvanah,* which in addition is clearly referred to by the prophets. Isaiah, for instance, condemns those who "with their mouth and with their lips do honor Me, but have removed their heart far from Me."

The Talmud too attaches considerable importance to *kavvanah* in prayer. It is related that the pious men of ancient times used to wait an hour before prayer to achieve a state of *kavvanah* and another hour after prayer in order to emerge from it. However, from the discussion in the Mishnah and the Gemara, it is clear that the rabbis, keenly aware of the "problem" of prayer, were by no means unanimous in their interpretation of what proper *kavvanah* should be. Later medieval authors distinguished between the preparation for *kavvanah* which precedes prayer and the achievement of *kavvanah* during prayer itself, while repeatedly stressing the importance of both. Maimonides ruled as a matter of *halakhah* (which was not, however, agreed with by later codifiers) that "since prayer without *kavvanah* is no prayer at all, if one has prayed without *kavvanah* he has to pray again with *kavvanah.* Should one feel preoccupied or overburdened, or should one have just returned from a voyage, one must delay one's prayer until one can once again pray with *kavvanah* ... True *kavvanah* implies freedom from all extraneous thoughts, and complete awareness of the fact that one stands before the Divine Presence." The moral philosopher Bahya ibn Paquda of the 11th century remarks that prayer without concentration is like a body with-

out a soul, or a husk without a kernel. And in the same spirit the *Shulḥan Arukh* states: "Better a little supplication with *kavvanah,* than a great deal without it."

Many talmudic decisions relating to *kavvanah* were modified in the course of time. Thus, although the Mishnah states that a bridegroom is not required to read the *Shema* on his wedding night (because he would not be able to achieve a proper degree of concentration), it was later ruled that "since nowadays we do not pray with proper attention in any case" he is obliged to do so. Similarly, "even if one did not recite the *Amidah* with *kavvanah,* it is not necessary to repeat it," since it is assumed that the *kavvanah* of the repetition would be no better.

IN MEDIEVAL THOUGHT

Although medieval Jewish thinkers profoundly considered major theological problems, there is surprisingly little discussion in their writings of the intellectual difficulties involved in prayer. One of the few discussions as to why prayer should be necessary, since God knows man's needs, is that of Joseph Albo of the 14th century. Albo believes that the act of turning to God in prayer is itself one of the conditions upon which God's help depends, just as it depends on other forms of human effort. True to his doctrine of theological negation, Maimonides only permits the mention, in the standard liturgy, of those terms designating the divine attributes which were ordained by the prophets. Similarly, he is opposed to the indiscriminate writing of hymns. In spite of the talmudic statement that the obligation to pray is of rabbinic origin, Maimonides observes that this only applies to the frequency, form, and times, of prayer, but that it is a duty of biblical authority for a Jew to pray daily. As was mentioned above, the need for adequate concentration in prayer is particularly emphasized by medieval Jewish thinkers, forming part of their general tendency to stress the inwardness of religious life.

IN THE KABBALAH

Perhaps the best-known kabbalistic statement on prayer is the

comment in the *Zohar,* the basic kabbalistic text, on the wondrous ladder of Jacob's dream, whose feet stood on earth and whose head reached to the very heavens. "This ladder," says the *Zohar,* "is prayer."

At the same time, the kabbalists stress the difficulty of petitionary prayer to a God who is unchanging. They advance the view that prayer cannot, in fact, be offered to God as He is in Himself (the infinite *Ein Sof*), but only to God as He is manifested in the ten divine potencies (the *sefirot*). God Himself is, therefore, not entreated directly to show mercy, for example, but prayer is directed to God as He is manifested in the *sefirah* or attribute of lovingkindness. As a result of the power of man's prayer, this potency might function on earth. The mystical nature of kabbalistic prayer and the dangers of setting up the *sefirot* as divine intermediaries were the topic of much subsequent debate. The kabbalists, in fact, substituted for the older doctrine of *kavvanah* the concept of particular intentions (*kavvanot*), that is, meditations on the realm of *sefirot*. Instead

This 1928 book illustration, after a painting by J.L. Gerome (Paris, 1824–1904), gives the decided impression of humility and supplication in prayer. Batya Lishansky's (1900–) wooden sculpture, "Jewish Refugee with Sefer Torah" executed in 1945, conveys inner turmoil and intense devotion. Both attitudes have their place in Jewish prayer.

of concentrating on the plain meaning of the prayers, the kabbalist dwells on the realm of divine potencies and directs his mind, when reciting the words, to the supernal mysteries which govern and are controlled by them. Some kabbalists were thus known as *mekhavvenim* (that is, those who meditate on the *kavvanot*), and guides to *kavvanot* were written.

With the correct *kavvanot* it is considered possible to achieve a state of *devekut,* which can perhaps best be translated as "communion with God." Usually the kabbalists emphasize clearly that the communion achieved by the living mystic during prayer is transitory and incomplete in its nature. Only after death can a man hope that his soul will reach a complete and permanent state of *devekut* with God (usually by way of communion with the tenth and lowest of the divine emanations, the *Shekhinah*), and the final state of bliss will not be achieved until the redemption, after the coming of the Messiah, when all righteous Jews will live together in the state of *devekut*. This, the most conservative attitude, is expressed in the *Zohar* several times (although other concepts are found in it too), and was widely accepted by the writers of kabbalistic ethical literature in the 16th to the 18th centuries, in Safed and Eastern Europe.

In most kabbalistic writings, there is a connection between the state of *devekut* and prophecy, which is the outcome of such union between man and God. The patriarchs, Moses, and the prophets were described as people who achieved a lasting state of *devekut*. When *devekut* is achieved, *Ru'aḥ ha-Kodesh* ("The Holy Spirit") comes into contact with the mystic and gives him superhuman spiritual abilities. The idea of *devekut* as the highest spiritual achievement in religious life was popularized by the writers of kabbalistic ethical literature, so that numerous people who were not mystics became familiar with this concept.

IN ḤASIDISM

The last phase of this development was reached with the ḥasidic movement, where *devekut* became not only the supreme achievement of religious life, but also its starting point. *Devekut,* according to Ḥasidism, should be the believer's constant state of mind, even while he is dealing with everyday necessities of life and not only during the high points of prayer and religious activity. It has been said that "the metamorphosis which took place in the meaning of *kavvanot* at the advent of Ḥasidism, and more explicitly after the Great Maggid, Dov Baer of Mezhirech, consists in this—that an originally intellectual effort of meditation and contemplation had become an intensely emotional and highly enthusiastic act." In Ḥasidism, prayer is a mystical encounter with the Divine, the heart leaping in ecstasy to its Source. Violent movements in prayer were, thus, not unusual; some ḥasidic groups even encouraged their followers to turn somersaults during their prayers. Many ḥasidic groups, otherwise strictly conformist, disregarded the laws governing prayer at fixed times, on the grounds that these interfere with the need for adequate preparation, and with the spontaneity which is part of prayer's essence.

Prayer is frequently seen in Ḥasidism as man's most important religious activity. Shneur Zalman of Lyady, the founder of the intellectual Ḥabad sect in Ḥasidism, wrote: "For although the forms of the prayers and the duty of praying three times a day are rabbinic, the idea of prayer is the founda-

Prayer is not just for the synagogue or the Western Wall. Wherever man is, that is the right place. These settlers at Kefar Eẓion in 1943 had serious security problems. But at the turn of the day they devoted themselves to the *Minḥah* service. Isidor Kaufmann (1853–1921) obviously knew the rabbinic evaluation of study as an act of prayer. Perhaps that is why his Jew studying is enveloped in the *tallit*.

tion of the whole Torah. This means that man knows God, recognizing His greatness and His splendor with a serene and whole mind, and an understanding heart. Man should reflect on these ideas until his rational soul is awakened to love God, to cleave to Him and to His Torah, and to desire His commandments." In Ḥabad Ḥasidism, the true meaning of prayer is contemplation on the kabbalistic scheme whereby God's infinite light proceeds through the whole chain of being, from the highest sphere to the lowest. Man should reflect on this until his heart is moved in rapture, but he should not engage in prayer for the sake of the pleasure such rapture will bring him; he must take care not to confuse authentic ecstasy with artificial spiritual titillation.

SWAYING IN PRAYER

During the Middle Ages, the practice of swaying during prayer is mentioned in various texts. The *Zohar* sees swaying in Torah study as indicating the difference between Israel and the nations. "This thing alone is sufficient to distinguish the holy souls of Israel from the souls of heathen people. The souls of Israel have been hewn from the Holy Lamp, as it is written, 'The spirit of man is the lamp of the Lord.' Now once this lamp has been kindled from the supernal Torah, the light upon it never ceases for an instant. So when an Israelite has said one word of Torah, a light is kindled and he cannot keep still, but sways to and fro like the flame of a wick." Judah Halevi also refers to the custom as practiced during the study of the Torah, but makes no mention of prayer. The codifier Moses Isserles, quoting earlier authorities, does mention the custom in connection with prayer, but other authorities disagree. A biblical source to justify the practice was found in Psalms: "All my bones shall say, 'Lord, who is like unto Thee?'" The explanation given by one ingenious writer, that swaying during study and prayer was intended to afford the body exercise, is incredibly banal.

IN MODERN THOUGHT

The early liturgical reformers in the 19th century were much concerned about such questions as prayers for the restoration of sacrifices or the return to Zion, and whether prayer might be recited in the vernacular. These subjects are taken up in later chapters. Very few challenges, however, were presented to the idea of prayer as such in its traditional understanding. It was only in the 20th century that Jewish thinkers began to consider the basic philosophical problems surrounding prayer. Petitionary prayer was felt to be especially difficult in the light of scientific views regarding cause and effect, and a definite move may be discerned away from the idea of prayer as a means of influencing God and toward its function as a way to affect man's attitudes. One of the leaders of the Reform movement at the beginning of the century put it as follows: "Self-expression before God in prayer has thus a double effect: it strengthens faith in God's love and kindness, as well as in His all-wise and all-bountiful prescience. But it also chastens the desires and feelings of man, teaching him to banish from his heart all thoughts of self-seeking and sin, and to raise himself toward the purity and the freedom of the divine will and demand."

However, other modern thinkers have adopted a more existentialist attitude toward prayer. They see it as a human need which is beyond theological or scientific consistency. This approach is, of course, based on the fact that the object of prayer, God, is beyond proof; one either believes in God or one does not. Once the believer believes, the problems of prayer are not so crucial and may even appear to be unreal. The idea of utilizing prayer as a sort of do-it-yourself psychiatric treatment, which was often suggested during the early part of the 20th century, seems to have been completely rejected. The tendency today is towards finding a value in prayer for itself, as a dialogue (or monologue) between man and God.

It was perhaps unavoidable that prayer, because of the prime importance it has enjoyed in Jewish thought, should become "established." The invention of printing tended to create a uniform text and the development of the synagogue, particularly in the Ashkenazi world, gave a fixed form which seemed to discourage the "heart" and spontaneity that the ancient rabbis stressed so much, and which make praying the experience it should be. Ḥasidism definitely intended to correct this state

of affairs when it developed the *shtibl* and did away with salaried cantors and officials. However, Ḥasidism was the product of a specific mode of life in Eastern Europe, and although it has made some notable advances in the Western Jewish world, it has not become the mass movement it was in its birthplace. In modern Israel, a definite tendency has developed towards a prayer service, led by one of the congregants, in which communal singing and participation play a great part. Of course, the danger here is that one enjoys the singing and mistakes it for an act of prayer.

The ability to pray and the attitude to prayer depend, to a great extent, on the society in which the person lives and the education he receives. Many modern Jewish philosophers have bewailed modern man's inability to pray, but this is, of course, a direct result of the technology-oriented modern world and the pace of modern life which hardly allows the "hours" the ancient pietists used to devote to preparing for prayer. Further, the language of prayer, Hebrew, makes the effort difficult for the non-Hebrew speaker since he insists that he understand and "believe in" his prayers. "Modern prayer," except in progressive congregations, has not really become widely accepted, and even in those communities where it is tried, it too tends to become established.

However, it has also been suggested that perhaps too much is being expected of prayer and that modern man is demanding "instant uplift" to start at the commencement of the service and last till the end. The range of emotions and thoughts within the classical prayer texts is so wide that there is generally something for everybody, and every situation, and perhaps the ancients were satisfied to reach a high point only every so often, and considered it worthwhile, for the sake of that experience of *devekut*, to invest a prodigious amount of effort.

II Genres of Prayer

Benedictions

Psalms

Piyyut

שאו שערים ראשיכם

והנשאו פתחי עולם ויבא מלך הכבוד

ספר תהילים

מסודר כפי ימי
השבועה על הסדר
והאומרו בכל יום
מובטח לו שהוא בן
עולם הבא

פה ק"ק פראג

תחת ממשלת אדוננו המיוחס
פאוד הקיסר לעאפאלדוס יר"ה

בשנת תכ"ח לפ"ק

Because of the importance of Psalms in the Jewish liturgy, many prayerbooks included the whole text. In this prayerbook from Prague (1668), the title page is not extant, but this is the title page of the Book of Psalms which was included in it.

Although prayer should be spontaneous and from the heart, there must, obviously, be some fixed forms. Even the most patriotic army must march in step, and even the most inspired poet must crystallize his insights into some kind of pattern. On the other hand, not everybody is capable of articulating his own prayers, which does not mean that he does not want or need to pray.

The discipline of prayer is expressed both in the times fixed for daily devotions and in the forms in which they should be uttered. Now the existence of forms need not jeopardize the spontaneity of prayer since these forms are, generally speaking, not so specific as to prevent the supplicant from infusing them with his own emotions. Furthermore, there is certainly no objection to the supplicant's adding his own personal prayers to the officially sanctioned forms.

Foremost among these classical forms are the benedictions. These are frequently supplemented by the inclusion of Psalms, and occasionally embellished by the artfully contrived poetic compositions known as *piyyutim*. It is with these three genres of prayer—the benediction, the Psalm, and the *piyyut*—that the present chapter deals.

BENEDICTIONS

The formulas of blessing or thanksgiving that figure prominently in public and private prayer are commonly known in English as benedictions, a word that stems from Latin roots meaning to speak well, or to bless.

Individual benedictions are to be found scattered throughout the various books of the Bible. Thus the servant of Abraham, overwhelmed with gratitude for the Divine Providence that has led him to find a bride worthy of his master's son Isaac, exclaims: "Blessed be the Lord, God of my master Abraham, Who hath not forsaken His mercy and His truth toward my master." Post-biblical literature has likewise preserved instances of benedictions pronounced in direct response to the events of the day. Following the victory of the Maccabees over the invading Syrian officer Nicanor in 161 B.C.E., the people declared: "Blessed be He Who has kept His holy place undefiled." And according to the Apocryphal Book of Enoch, each time that personage beheld the wonders of nature he "blessed the Lord of Glory, Who had made mighty and glorious wonders to show the greatness of His work to the angels and to spirits and to men, that they might praise His work and all His creation."

The institution and formulation of the benedictions as we know them today derive variously—according to the ascriptions of the Talmud—from the sages of old, or from the 120 Elders who led the restored community in Ereẓ Israel at the time of Ezra, following the Babylonian exile, or from their successors, "the Men of the Great Synagogue" of the Second Temple period. Though modern scholars tend to question the historical authenticity of these ascriptions, they regard them as indicating an awareness of the high antiquity of the benedictions.

Recent scholars hold that the various benedictions originated in different congregations and localities. The formulas which were ultimately adopted universally are thus conceived as selections and combinations based on local customs and traditions. An alternative school of thought has attempted to establish a definite date for the formulation of each benediction and to reconstruct a hypothetical "original" wording. Such attempts are unconvincing, when confronted with the indications which suggest that different formulas were in use simultaneously. The eighteen benedictions of the *Amidah* prayer, for example, have some parallel in a prayer recorded in the Apocryphal Book of Ecclesiasticus. There, too, a series of benedictions prays for the ingathering of the exiles, the salvation of Israel, and the restoration of God's glory to Zion and the Temple. Reminiscent, too, of these series are accounts in the Mishnah of the eight benedictions recited by the High Priest on the Day of Atonement, and the order of service conducted by the priests in the Temple every morning.

By the end of the Second Temple period, in the first century C.E., certain "orders of benedictions" had become the generally accepted custom in most communities. Prominent among these were the seven benedictions which comprise the *Amidah* for Sabbaths and festivals, the nine for Rosh Ha-Shanah, and most likely also the 18 benedictions for the weekday *Amidah*. The

The seven benedictions form a central part of the marriage ceremony. This page from the *Rothchild Miscellany*, Italy, c. 1470 contains the marriage benedictions and the illustration of a groom placing the ring on the finger of his bride under the supervision of a rabbi. The dove in the initial-word panel is symbolic of the love which it is hoped will reign in this union.

number and contents of the benedictions recited before and after the *Shema,* and the first three benedictions of the Grace after Meals, were also standardized about this time. The redaction of the regular, prescribed prayers and benedictions under Rabban Gamaliel II at Jabneh at the end of the first century C.E. gave official sanction to what had been in essence the prevailing custom for a considerable time, and probably established the order and content of the benedictions. The formulas then established did not, however, become the only authoritative versions. Indeed, many alternative formulations of the same benedictions are known from talmudic sources dating from the succeeding four centuries, and some of these are in use in different rites to the present day. At the earliest, prayers were written down by the end of the talmudic period, late in the fifth century C.E. Even then the order of prayer was still relatively flexible, for while the general outline and the motifs of the prayers and benedictions were well defined, their recital was colored by a degree of improvisation. This was seen as a safeguard against mechanical prayer. Thus some *amoraim* were singled out for praise by their talmudic contemporaries because they recited a new prayer or a new benediction every day. At the same time, it was during the talmudic period that the requirements for the wording of each benediction were fixed in increasing detail, and various subsidiary motifs were laid down as mandatory components of some of them.

The Benediction Formula. The fixed wording is known in Hebrew as *matbe'a,* which literally means "coin." The implication is that a particular benediction or prayer, if phrased in the authoritatively sanctioned manner, is being tendered in acceptable currency.

There are three types of formulas for benedictions, all of them opening with the words *Barukh attah Adonai,* which mean "Blessed art Thou, O Lord." The first type of benediction is known in Hebrew as *matbe'a kaẓar,* the short formula, in which the standard opening phrase is followed by a few words of praise specific to the occasion. Thus the benediction over bread, which concludes: *ha-moẓi leḥem min ha-areẓ,* blesses Him "Who brings forth bread from the earth." The second type is the *matbe'a arokh,* or long formula, in which the three standard opening words are followed by a more elaborate text, which in turn needs to be rounded off by a concluding formula of benediction. An example is the first paragraph of the Grace after Meals, in which the description of the Creator as the provider of sustenance is concluded by the benediction formula *Barukh attah Adonai, ha-zan et ha-kol* ("Blessed art Thou, O Lord, Who feedest all").

The third type of benediction forms part of a series—*berakhah ha-semukhah la-ḥavertah,* or contiguous blessings. In these cases, the opening formula is used for the first benediction in each series, and the conclusion of the series is also phrased in the benediction style. The second paragraph of the Grace after Meals, for instance, begins with the phrase *Nodeh lekha* ("We thank Thee") and ends with the benediction *Barukh attah Adonai, al ha-areẓ ve-al ha-mazon* ("Blessed art Thou, O Lord, for the land and for the food"). Since most of the obligatory prayers, such as the *Amidah* and the benedictions preceding and following the *Shema,* consist respectively of a series of blessings, the form occurring most frequently in the synagogue service is

וצונו על המילה:
ברוך אתה יי אלהינו מלך העולם
אשר קדשנו במצותיו וצונו להכניסו
בבריתו של אברהם אבינו
כשם שנכנס לברית כן יכנס

This manuscript illustration depicts the circumcision and the blessing which the father of the child recites on that occasion. Along with the benedictions, the Psalms form a major part of Jewish prayer. In the picture opposite, some elderly folk are reciting the Book of Psalms at the Western Wall. Psalm-reciters can usually be found there during the whole day and night.

the third, in which the benediction formula is used only as a conclusion.

In a discussion on this subject the Talmud quotes Rav as saying that every benediction must include the name of God, and Rabbi Johanan as saying that each benediction must also mention the attribute of God's kingship. Accordingly, in the first two kinds of benedictions the standard opening formula of three words is followed by the phrase *Eloheinu melekh ha-olam,* meaning "our God, King of the Universe." However, this description of God in His attribute of sovereignty (*malkhut* in Hebrew) never occurs in the third type, the contiguous blessings, nor does it appear in the *Amidah,* and probably did not become customary at all before the second century C.E. Its introduction may have been motivated by a desire to stress the exclusive kingship of God, as a protest against the Roman cult of emperor worship.

The standard benediction pattern *Barukh attah Adonai* occurs only twice in the Bible, and was not widely used until the fourth century B.C.E. Other formulas such as *Hodu la-Adonai* ("Praise God") or *Odekha Adonai* ("I will thank Thee, O Lord") are more commonly found in the Bible, as is the phrase *Barukh attah,* not followed by the name of God. The same applies to surviving documents of the late Second Temple period, such as the Dead Sea Scrolls. The extent to which some of the above-mentioned terms were then used interchangeably was dramatically demonstrated by the discovery in 1947 of a scroll of the non-biblical Thanksgiving Psalms, in which the phrase *Odekha Adonai* was struck out by the scribe and replaced by what is now the standard benediction formula. The Dead Sea Scrolls, when quoting benedictions, likewise use the divine names *Adonai* and *El* interchangeably.

It was not by mere chance that the Talmud ultimately chose the formula which includes both the Tetragrammaton and the direct address of God in the second person. This combination reflects the personal and even intimate relationship of the worshiper with God. It also ensures that supplications and petitions (such as those which constitute the intermediary benedictions of the *Amidah*) invariably conclude with words of praise. Thus the request for forgiveness concludes: "Blessed art Thou . . . Who dost abundantly forgive."

Nevertheless, the ultimate crystallization of the benediction formula retains an anomalous vestige of its two divergent sources. On the one hand, as has been seen, the standard opening phrase—"Blessed art Thou"—addresses God directly in the second person. On the other hand, an alternative biblical formula—this one in the third person—maintained its hold as a parallel prototype: "Blessed be God Who [performed a certain beneficient act]." There is no substantive difference between the second and third person forms, but the juxtaposition of direct address to God and a sequel in the third person created a syntactical paradox which has exercised commentators and theologians down to this day. Some thinkers explain this juxtaposition homiletically as indicating God's dual relation to man—being simultaneously near and transcendent. On the practical level of translation, since English syntax does not tolerate such transitions from second to third person, the benedictions are sometimes rendered consistently in the second person.

The binding nature of the benediction pattern was qualified by the talmudic sages in two significant respects. Firstly, while it is always obligatory in the prescribed prayers, its use is precluded in spontaneous prayers. In the words of the Talmud: "He who recites a superfluous benediction is considered to have transgressed the biblical prohibition: 'Thou shalt not take the name of the Lord thy God in vain.'" Secondly, the sages ruled that the concluding words of praise did not necessarily have to be pronounced in Hebrew. It is apparent from a talmudic debate mentioned above that a benediction could be recited in the vernacular and did not have to be an exact translation of the Hebrew formula. Thus a certain shepherd named Benjamin is quoted as having substituted the formal Hebrew text of the Grace after Meals by his own artless prayer in Aramaic: "Blessed be God, the master of this bread." The rabbis deemed this sufficient.

The Term Barukh. Surprisingly, a certain ambiguity and difficulty of translation surrounds the common Hebrew word *barukh,* which introduces all benedictions, and which provides the root for the Hebrew word for benediction, viz. *berakhah.* The plural form, *berakhot,* is also the name of the tractate in the Talmud which discusses the subject of benedictions.

The conventional translation of *barukh* is "blessed," but its etymology is disputed. Its three root letters, which also constitute the Hebrew word for knee, seem to have originally signified bending the knee in prayerful obeisance. It is in this sense, apparently, that this root is used in the opening words of the Psalmist's call to prayer: "Let us bow down and bend the knee; let us kneel before the Lord our Maker." A conflicting view maintains that the word originally signified bestowing a gift, since this is what is evidently intended by the verb in the biblical statement that "the Lord had blessed Abraham in all things."

Both views can be reconciled once *barukh* is understood as a homonym which expresses a reciprocal relationship. On the one hand, man can use the word *barukh* in addressing God to express feelings of thanksgiving, reverence, love and praise. Indeed, the phrase *barukh Adonai,* in this sense of man blessing God, occurs 24 times in the Bible. At the same time, *barukh* describes man's status as a beneficiary on whom God bestows His material and spiritual gifts. The person upon whom the divine blessing rests is thus called *berukh Adonai,* "blessed of the Lord."

Types of Benedictions. Maimonides distinguishes three kinds of benedictions according to their content: those recited before and after the enjoyment of a pleasure, such as eating; those preceding the performance of certain *mitzvot,* or religious duties, such as hearing the *shofar;* and those which are forms of thanksgiving and praise. The morning benedictions which express man's gratitude for awakening in possession of all his faculties were originally of this type. (To these categories Abudarham, a 14th-century exegete, adds a fourth: those recited in the daily prayers.) Many of the benedictions in these three categories, though obligatory and therefore couched in the characteristic formulas, are essentially of a private character. Accordingly, no *minyan,* or quorum, is required for their recital; they are uttered by the individual in private prayer. An exception is the Grace after Meals which, when said in company, is preceded by an invitation to those present to offer their thanks in unison.

Every benediction recited before the performance of a *mitzvah* begins with a standard formula, and proceeds to refer to the specific *mitzvah* about to be performed. For example, before affixing a *mezuzah* scroll to one's doorpost: "Blessed art Thou, O Lord—the King of the Universe, Who has sanctified us through His precepts and commanded us to affix the *mezuzah.*" A similar formula is used before the performance of commandments which are of post-biblical, rabbinic origin, since such commandments are implied in the biblical injunction to observe the teaching of the sages.

The actual benediction over a *mitzvah* (say, "Who has commanded us to kindle the Ḥanukkah lights") is sometimes followed by further benedictions. In this case, the second benediction concludes with the words: "Who performed miracles for our fathers in days of old at this season." When a seasonal *mitzvah* is performed for the first time in the year, the *She-heḥeyanu* benediction is further added. This applies—to pursue the same example—to the first night of Ḥanukkah, when three benedictions in all are recited.

No benedictions are said after the observance of *mitzvot,* unless they involve public reading from the Scriptures. Examples are the synagogal readings from the Torah and from the Prophets, and the reading of the *Hallel* portion of the Psalms even by an individual—on prescribed festive occasions. It is further recorded that the scholars of ancient Ereẓ Israel used to recite a benediction, which has since fallen into disuse, on removing the *tefillin.*

At the opposite end of the spectrum, there are certain *mitzvot* which are never even introduced by a benediction. Some commentators have suggested that these *mitzvot* fall into two categories: those which involve no action, such as leaving the corner of one's field unharvested for the poor, and those whose performance is possible only in undesirable circumstances, such as divorce, or the return of stolen goods. In the case of other *mitzvot,* such as the giving of alms, the reason for the absence of a benediction is not readily apparent, and there is no general agreement regarding the determining principles. One ingenious explanation which would apply to this case, is that offered by the aforementioned Abudraham. This scholar points out that certain commandments lapse and remain unfulfilled in any given case if the intended beneficiary does not cooperate (for example) by accepting the charity which is proffered to him. A blessing made at the prescribed time—that is, immediately before the performance of the *mitzvah*—would then have been said in vain. In practice, custom on the matter seems to have varied as late as geonic times, in the early Middle Ages.

A variety of special occasions, unconnected with *mitzvot,* call for the recitation of a benediction. Thus a special benediction is to be pronounced on witnessing an awesome natural phenomenon such as an electrical storm, or on visiting a site in Ereẓ Israel where a miracle was once performed. A certain benediction articulates the gratitude of an individual recently saved from danger, and another is recited on hearing glad tidings—such as of rain after a drought—which will benefit the hearer and others as well. And, by the same token, for a person hearing grievous tidings an appropriate benediction is prescribed.

With regard to function, the last-mentioned category of benedictions differs from the other two. While the benedictions over food are evidently intended to sanctify the physical act of taking nourishment, and those recited before *mitzvot* serve to prevent the performance of the *mitzvah* in a mechanical, routine manner, the recital of the so-called "blessings of praise" is practically an end in itself. In the words of Maimonides, their main purpose is "to make us remember our Creator at all times."

Indeed, Rabbi Meir went so far as to declare it to be the duty of every Jew to recite 100 benedictions daily, a custom which, according to one tradition, had been instituted by King David a thousand years earlier. And, in a similar vein, the observation by Maimonides on the "blessings of praise" may well be taken more widely to illuminate the educational function served by the benedictions in general: to transmute every mundane occurrence into a religious experience.

PSALMS

"That man whose soul yearns to cleave to the Blessed One, let him cleave to the Book of Psalms," wrote a 17th-century kabbalist, and the sages taught that King David himself prayed that his hymns should be read in Israel's houses of prayer.

That wish of "the sweet singer of Israel" was ultimately granted, though only by gradual stages extending over the centuries. The superscriptions of some of the Psalms testify that they already served a liturgical purpose in Temple times. Thus the heading of Psalm 100, *Mizmor le-Todah,* implies a recitation to accompany the offering of the *todah* sacrifice. In the talmudic period, early in the Common Era, the statutory prayers included no Psalms whatsoever on Sabbaths and weekdays, and the only Psalms recited as part of the liturgy were the *Hallel* passages of thanksgiving on the three Pilgrim Festivals, Ḥanukkah, and the New Moon.

This situation may give a misleading impression of the considerable importance with which the Psalms were invested by the talmudic rabbis. In the first place, it is possible that in

A page from a psalter from the early 19th century, donated to the Great Synagogue in Paris by Baron Rothschild of London in 1879. The illustration depicts King David both as the monarch and the Psalmist. Another depiction of King David, this time accompanied by a duo of angels, is the engraving in the Holy Bible published by the Society of Divines in London, 1793. The rays of light which are common to both scenes presumably represent the divine inspiration which rested on the Psalmist.

some regions the Psalms were read in a triennial cycle, corresponding to the weekly reading of the Pentateuch and the Prophets, which was then also completed in the Palestinian synagogues every three years. (Such a practice would explain the comparison made by the rabbis between the Five Books of Moses and the five books of Psalms, and the effort made to equalize the number of Psalms with the pericopes or weekly portions of the Pentateuch.) In the second place, though not then prominent in the liturgy, the Psalms were so much the subject of the rabbis' homilies and preaching, that there is not a single chapter of Psalms—indeed hardly a single verse—which is not expounded somewhere in the Talmud and Midrash.

Statutory Prayers. Increasingly the Psalms found their way into the liturgy too. In fact some half of the 150 Psalms were eventually incorporated in the various statutory services, partly, at least, as a result of popular demand. For example, on the Daily Psalm, which is today a veteran fixture in the prayer book, a post-talmudic tractate reports that "the people have adopted the custom of including it." With regard to the choice of Psalm 136—which mentions the Exodus from Egypt—as the Psalm for Passover, the same tractate likewise comments that "the people have adopted the custom of reciting this Psalm, though it is not the best choice."

In this absorption of the Psalms into the liturgy, every talmudic reference to their recitation—whether as acts of individual piety or as part of the Temple service—became regarded as a justification for making them part of the statutory service. To this class belong the Daily Psalm mentioned above, and the introductory hymns of praise in the morning service, which are known in Hebrew as *Pesukei de-Zimra*. These consisted originally of the last six chapters of the Psalter alone—the Hallelujah Psalms. Whereas the Talmud mentions their recitation as an act of especial piety, the above-quoted post-talmudic tractate calls them simply "the six daily Psalms" which were already part of the statutory service. Both these passages, it will be noted, understand the term *Pesukei de-Zimra* as embracing only those six Psalms. However, as the next step in the inclusion of the Psalms in the liturgy, and on the principle that the Sabbaths and festivals afford the worshiper more leisure than usual, the Ashkenazi rite adds nine and the Sephardi rite 14 further Psalms.

The same process may be discerned with regard to the Daily Psalms. These are first mentioned in the Midrash as "the Psalms which the Levites used to sing in the Temple." At their second appearance, already noted, they are already part of the daily prayers, "the people having adopted the custom." Once transferred from the Temple to the synagogue, the custom was extended to include special Psalms for every festival.

In like manner, other individual Psalms were added in the course of time to various stages of the daily service, and to the services for various festive or penitential occasions. Among these additions are two whole groups: Psalms 104 and the 15 Songs of Degrees which, from the 12th century, were included in the Sabbath afternoon service during the winter months, and

Hau - du la-dau-noj, kir - u wisch-mau, hau-di - u wo-am - mim a - li - lau-ssow.

the most recent addition of all, and one that spread with remarkable rapidity—Psalms 95 to 99 and Psalm 20, for the Inauguration of the Sabbath. The latter inclusion was the work of the kabbalists of Safed in the 16th century. By 1630, one writer noted this as a novelty, but praised it as "a good and beautiful custom." Since that time, these six Psalms have become standard in all Ashkenazi services, symbolizing the workaday week of six days, and serving as a foil and a prologue to *Lekhah Dodi,* the lyrical welcome to the Sabbath Queen.

The Psalms, however, did not enter the statutory service only as individual chapters or as continuous cycles. Some 250 verses were also incorporated singly. In fact certain prayers consist exclusively of a mosaic of single verses selected from perhaps a score of different chapters. Two such passages, which precede the six complete Psalms of the daily *Pesukei de-Zimra,* take their names from their opening words: *Romemu* and *Yehi Khevod.* Both consist almost entirely of verses from Psalms, representing between them all of the five books into which Psalms is divided. Only the second book is not represented in the *Yehi Khevod.* The Yemenite rite remedies this omission by including one verse from the second book, and this version is thus probably the original one, already mentioned in the post-talmudic tractate *Soferim.* This circumstance highlights the way in which the rite of the Yemenite Jews—isolated as if in a cocoon for long centuries—furnishes the curious researcher with a peek into the probable state of the liturgy in its near pristine state.

Non-Statutory Prayers. It can be safely said that there is no special or non-statutory service that does not include one or more Psalms. This is true in the case of the introduction to the Grace after Meals, the prayers during drought and before going on a journey, the night prayer before retiring to rest, the prayers for and by the sick, the burial service, the prayers in the house of mourning, the memorial service for the dead, and the service at the consecration of a tombstone. This practice has also been followed in all forms of service added in recent years, such as the thanksgiving of a woman after childbirth, the consecration of a house, and the prayers recited on Israel's Independence Day.

Quite apart from services of whatever kind, the recital of the whole Book of Psalms as an act of piety is widespread, whether by saintly individuals, or by groups of unlearned people. But this reflects only one aspect of the universality of its appeal. Thomas Carlyle maintained that the Psalms of David "struck tones that were an echo of the sphere-harmonies," while on the more mundane level of content and mood, worshipers of whatever temperament have each managed to find in it their own spiritual niche. For this Book includes hymns of God's providence and majesty, songs lauding Zion and the

The music is that of a simple psalmody from a book called *Der Frankfurter Kantor,* Frankfort-on-Main, 1930. It is, however, unlikely that the man reciting psalms in a quiet corner at the Western Wall is using that melody. He is performing this devotion quietly to himself as part of his daily routine. The luxurious page from the 13th-century Spanish *Hamilton Siddur* is from the end of the festive *Hallel* service which is completely composed of psalms. The key words are formed of painted zoomorphic and anthropomorphic letters.

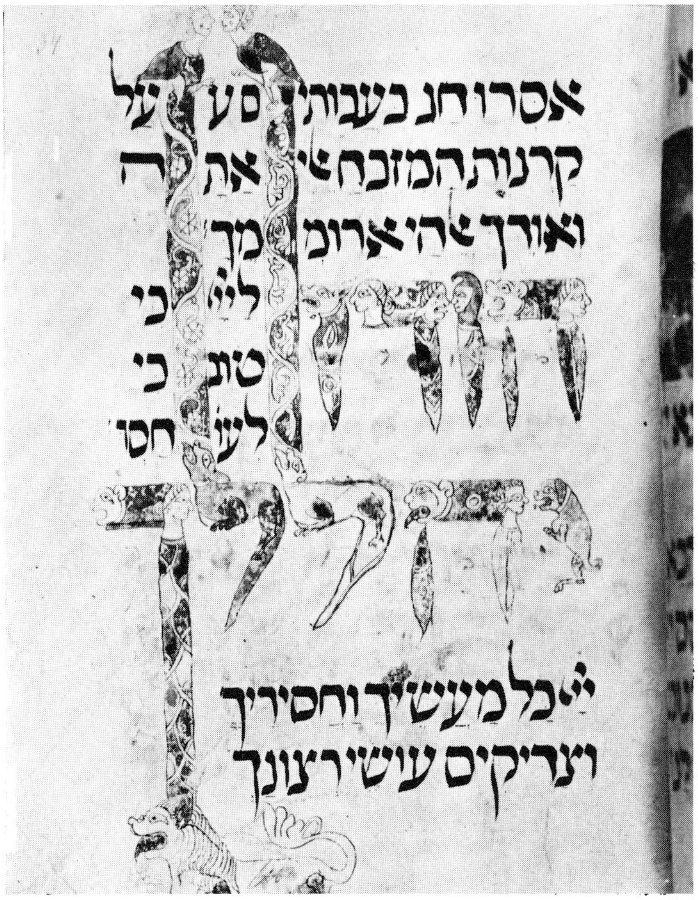

Torah, poems of pedagogic intent, and laments both individual and national. The last-mentioned Psalms are often coupled with pleas for divine help, which sometimes conclude as "Psalms of confidence," that is, with an expression of the worshiper's absolute certainty that his prayers will be heard.

For very sound reasons, then, the Book of Psalms has been published in hundreds of pocket editions, and often appears in its entirety as an addendum to the prayer book. Prayers have been composed to be recited before and after the reading of each of the five books, as well as for the midnight reading on Hoshana Rabba, which specifically mention their parallelism with the Five Books of Moses. In many communities it is customary to complete the Psalms in the course of a month by a daily selection of several chapters after the morning service. Some pious folk do the same on a weekly basis. In many countries, "fraternities of reciters of Psalms" (*ḥevrot Tehillim*) have been formed for these purposes, and visitors to Israel today will find two groups of Jerusalemites chanting the whole Book of Psalms daily at the Western Wall.

Musical Rendition. Considerable scholarly ingenuity has been expended in an effort to reconstruct the instrumental and vocal setting of the Psalms in ancient times. This is no easy task. For example, the superscriptions of many of the Psalms are so baffling in their obscurity that they appear to some investigators to be vestiges of the technical jargon of various guilds of singers and musicians who jealously (and successfully) guarded their professional secrets—until they themselves disappeared from history. One such term has been variously interpreted to be a cue-word identifying a particular tune, the name of an obsolete wind instrument, or a choreographic direction.

It is evident that certain Psalms were rendered in responsorial fashion, or antiphonally. Thus the simple recurring response *ki le-olam ḥasdo* ("for His mercy endures forever") that appears in various Psalms may have been sung to an equally simple melody, by the levitical choir or by the public, after the more elaborate rendition of the first part of the verse by a soloist or by the choir. Such arrangements are discussed in the Talmud, and further documented by textual variants recently found in the Qumran caves.

The majority of the melodies existing today follow the pattern which musicologists call psalmody, that is, a simple melodic curve of two waves corresponding to the structure of the majority of the verses of the Psalms, which have two parallel clauses. This basic grid shows sufficient flexibility to accommodate verses of any number of words, and even verses of three clauses instead of the more typical two. It also serves as a point of departure for florid elaboration which is ad-libbed by the worshiper according to his individual taste and regional traditions.

Within the framework of the psalmody, the melody used may be plaintive or joyous, festive or exultant, depending partly on the contents of the particular Psalm and partly on the occasion. The daily weekday reading in the synagogue or in private devotions is the simplest, and most closely follows the principle of psalmody. With the increasing festiveness of the occasion—a Sabbath, a festival, or a wedding—the melodies tend to become more elaborate, especially when their rendition is left to the *ḥazzan*. Since not every family, however, can muster such virtuosity, the simplest psalmodic melodies retain their traditional place in home rituals, such as the *Hallel* sung at the *Seder* service on Passover.

Some communities are particularly rich in Psalm melodies, such as those of Morocco, Tunisia, Cochin, Syria, Turkey,

הודו לה׳ כי טוב
תהלים (קי״ז ב׳) קי״ח א
קריאה לחזן לנענועים בהלל
לפי נוסח יהודי ג׳רבה (תוניס)
הוקלט: מפי פנחס כהן בתפילה בביה״כ
ברכיה, הושענה רבה תשט״ו, 7.10.1955
Parlando

The music is the way the Jews of Djerba (Tunisia) sang one of the refrains in the *Hallel* service. It was recorded on Hoshanna Rabba, 1955. That festive day takes its name from the large number of *piyyutim* called *hoshanot* which are recited in the synagogue. The page from the *Rothschild Miscellany* depicts various Sukkot scenes, and is the first page of the section for Hoshanna Rabba.

Italy, and the "Portuguese communities" of Western Europe. In Yemen, groups of Psalms used to be sung artistically at the prayer meetings called *ashmorot* at dawn on the Sabbath, very similar to the singing of hymns by Near Eastern congregations in the *bakkashot* services. However, whereas in group performance a Psalm is traditionally sung in unison, Yemenite group singing is distinguished by a polyphony that can strike the unaccustomed Western ear as discordant.

Among the Ashkenazi communities hardly any true psalmodies have survived. Instead, Psalm singers around the world have unabashedly adopted the favorite melodies of their respective environments with the versatility of a chameleon. Among Ḥasidim, verses of Psalms have been set to the melodies of numerous cultures, and in Israel today a whole genre of popular song has evolved, in which a verse from the Psalms (or another biblical source) is set to a lively rhythmic melody, creating a kind of pseudo-ḥasidic pop. In the ordered *ḥazzanut* of the 19th century in Western Europe, the Psalms (together with the prayers in general) were set to music often as showpieces for the synagogue's choir, somewhat in the manner of an Anglican anthem. In Reform Judaism, the text was sometimes paraphrased as a rhymed poem in Western meters, which then followed the stylistic precedents of the Protestant chorale, and even utilized its tunes. Showing a different bias, Psalm 126 (*Shir ha-Ma'alot*) that introduces the Grace after Meals is nowadays sung in certain circles to the measured tones of *Hatikvah*. In the Antipodes, somewhat less reverently, it may be heard to the tune of *Waltzing Matilda*.

PIYYUT

If the benedictions constitute the supports of the ladder of prayer, and the Psalms are its rungs of ascent, then the *piyyut* may be imagined as the intricately carved ornamentation which makes that ascent an aesthetically pleasing experience.

For the *piyyut* is a lyrical composition intended to embellish an obligatory prayer or a religious ceremony. In a wider sense, *piyyut* means the totality of hymns composed in various genres of Hebrew liturgical poetry from the early centuries of the Common Era until the beginning of the Haskalah in the 1770s. In ancient times, the *piyyutim* were intended to replace most of the set versions of prayer, thus ensuring variety within the obligatory prayers, mainly on Sabbaths and festivals. In a later period, when the prayers became fixed, passages of these hymns were interspersed at certain points within the set pattern of the prayers. Most of this very extensive poetic literature is devoted to the adornment of the liturgy of the major festivals. During the early Oriental period in the history of the *piyyut,* liturgical compositions were also produced in great abundance for regular Sabbaths, for the minor fast days, and even for weekdays. The standard prayers were likewise adorned with special sets of *piyyutim* for private occasions, such as weddings, circumcisions, and mourning.

History of the Piyyut. *Piyyut* literature appeared in Ereẓ Israel while the various versions of the statutory prayers were crystallizing. Though the evidence from this period is limited, texts of ancient *piyyutim* are to be found scattered in talmudic sources, and those which were apparently composed at this early stage were absorbed into the established versions of the

various rites of prayer. These ancient segments, dating from "the period of the anonymous *piyyut,*" can be recognized by their lofty style and characteristic rhythm; they did not as yet use rhyme. The ancient compositions are known from various sources, but especially from the Cairo *Genizah,* an unbelievably rich storehouse of ancient manuscripts discovered in 1753 in the attic of the medieval Ezra Synagogue at Fostat, or Old Cairo.

The earliest *paytan* (composer of *piyyutim*) known to us by name is Yose ben Yose, who lived in Ereẓ Israel in approximately the sixth century or even earlier. His works retain the above-mentioned characteristics of the form: they do not employ rhyme, even though something similar to rhyme can be seen in his composition for the *Musaf* service of Rosh Ha-Shanah, where similar words are employed as line endings. The most important of his countrymen, who were evidently active before Ereẓ Israel was conquered by the Arabs in 636 C.E., are Yannai, Simeon ben Megas, Eleazar ben Kallir, Ḥaduta ben Abraham, Joshua ha-Kohen, and Joseph ben Nisan from Shaveh Kiryatayim. During their period, the structural framework of most of the classical types of *piyyut* was finally standardized.

Even after Ereẓ Israel was conquered by the Arabs, and until the beginning of the 11th century, all the great *paytanim* worked in the East. Outstanding among those of Ereẓ Israel are Phinehas ben Jacob ha-Kohen from Kafra at the beginning of the period, and Samuel ha-Shelishi ben Hoshana at its close. Now, for the first time, *paytanim* from the Diaspora begin to appear, such as Solomon Suleiman ben 'Amr al-Sanjari, Nisi al-Nahrawani, Saadiah Gaon and Joseph al-Bardani. Toward the end of the period, in the tenth and 11th centuries, creative activities spread to North Africa. The direct continuation of Oriental *piyyut* was in Spain, which from the middle of the tenth century was the home of several generations of great composers, including Joseph ibn Abitur, Solomon ibn Gabirol, Isaac ibn Ghayyat, Moses ibn Ezra, Judah Halevi, and Abraham ibn Ezra.

On European soil, the first examples of *piyyut* literature had already appeared in southern Italy, which was under Byzantine rule, in the second half of the ninth century. Only a few hymns from among the creations of the early Italian *paytanim*—Silano, Shephatiah, and his son Amittai—are now extant, but even these testify to an extensive and consolidated literary activity, which is partly original and in part influenced by the compositions of Ereẓ Israel. In the tenth century, the work of the *paytanim* of southern Italy became in turn a basis for the development of *piyyut* in central and northern Italy. The liturgical poets working there, headed by Solomon ben Judah ha-Bavli, created a precedent for Central European *piyyut,* whose major representatives henceforth worked in Italy, Ashkenaz (now Germany), France and Byzantine Greece. The impressive development of the *piyyut* in Germany may be largely attributed to the activity of a number of great *paytanim* in the tenth and 11th centuries, such as Moses ben Kalonymus, Meshullam ben Kalonymus (both of Italian extraction), Simeon ben Isaac, and Meir Isaac. Ashkenazi or Western

These two pages from medieval manuscript prayerbooks are *piyyutim* which are said on various festive occasions. The illustrated initial word marks a *piyyut* to be recited in the evening service for Shemini Aẓeret (Simḥat Torah) and is from a South German *maḥzor* dated 1459. The zoomorphic figures illustrating the Passover *piyyut* are of uncertain date but were a common feature of manuscript illustration.

piyyut continued to develop in the succeeding centuries.

Though creativity in the realm of *piyyut* did not cease in Central Europe, Northern Africa, or the East until the beginning of the Haskalah in the 18th century, the 13th century marks the beginning of the decline; later *paytanim,* despite their often impressive output, failed to create works of stature. Although some of their poetry was included in local prayer rites, most of it has been excluded from the generally accepted prayer books.

Types of Piyyut. *Piyyutim* can be divided according to their liturgical purpose into a number of categories, differing in their histories, structures, and distribution. The smaller groups include the *hoshanot,* which are the hymns composed to accompany the solemn processions in the synagogue during the morning prayers on the festival of Sukkot. In the early period of *piyyut* supplementary hymns were composed for obligatory prayers such as these, but not for religious ceremonies, except for the Grace after Meals, and even in that case they were probably intended for use only at communal festive meals or at meals accompanying special religious occasions. The funeral service is another example of a religious ceremony which was furnished in the early period with its own special hymns. These are called *ashkavot*. Later, the Spanish *paytanim* developed new types of hymns for private devotions and for a wide variety of domestic religious ceremonies. The most familiar examples are *zemirot,* which are hymns sung by the family at the Sabbath table, and *havdalot,* which are poems to accompany the Sabbath at its departure.

KEROVOT. However, the earliest and most important types of *piyyut* are the *kerovah* and the *yoẓer*. The former is designed for inclusion in the *Amidah* prayer, while the latter is an addendum to the benedictions before and after the *Shema* in the morning service and, occasionally, in the evening service.

The *kerovah* was evidently the dominant type of ancient *piyyut*. Among the *kerovot* of the major festivals, a number of special types of *piyyut* for different occasions are found. These include the *tekiata,* which supplements the *Amidah* of *Musaf* for Rosh Ha-Shanah; *Seder ha-Avodah,* which describes the sacrificial service on the Day of Atonement in the Temple, for the *Musaf* of that day; and the *azharot,* which allude to the 613 commandments of the Torah, for the *Musaf* of Shavuot. The *kerovot* for the fast days in general include *seliḥot,* or penitential prayers, while the *kerovot* composed specifically for Tish'ah be-Av include *kinot,* or dirges. *Seliḥot* were likewise composed for the penitential period during the month of Elul and between Rosh Ha-Shanah and the Day of Atonement. In time, *kerovot* were also produced in honor of bridegrooms, or to mark the death of important men.

YOẒEROT. The *yoẓer,* of composite origin, appeared later than the *kerovah,* enjoying wide circulation mainly in the second period of the Oriental *piyyut,* between the seventh and the 11th centuries. Certain *yoẓerot* gave the service of each Sabbath and each festival its own distinctive flavor, by incorporating the opening of that day's Torah reading or *haftarah* passage.

MA'ARAVOT. In many Ashkenazi communities, though never in the Sephardi rite, the *Ma'ariv* or evening service for festivals and red-letter Sabbaths is supplemented by the recitation of hymns called *ma'aravot* or *ma'arivim*. On the eve of Shavuot, for example, the special *piyyut* commemorates the bringing of the First Fruits to the Temple in ancient times, and from this ceremonial—*Bikkurim*—it takes its name, *Tosefet Bikkur*.

PIZMONIM. In modern Israel the word *pizmon* means the lyrics of a popular song. This term, which reached Hebrew from Greek by way of Aramaic, and primarily signifies adoration, originally referred to a certain kind of refrain in *piyyutim*. It later came to mean the whole hymn in which the refrain occurred, and ultimately was loosely used to mean poems and songs in general. In Spain the officiant who chanted the *pizmon* or refrain before the congregation was known as a *pizmanana*.

SELIḤOT. The word *seliḥah* means "forgiveness," and in the singular it is used to indicate a *piyyut* whose subject is a plea for forgiveness for sins. In the plural, the word is used for a special order of service consisting of non-statutory additional prayers which are recited on all fast days, on occasions of special intercession, and during the penitential season which begins before Rosh Ha-Shanah and concludes with the Day of Atonement.

The original form of one of today's *seliḥot* is to be found in the Mishnah, which gives the order of service for public fasts,

usually proclaimed during periods of drought. It provides, inter alia, for the addition of six benedictions to the usual eighteen of the daily *Amidah,* and gives the concluding formula before the actual blessing for each: "May He Who answered our father Abraham on Mt. Moriah answer you . . . , may He Who answered our fathers at the Red Sea . . . Joshua in Gilgal . . . Samuel at Mizpah . . . Elijah in Carmel . . . Jonah in the belly of the whale . . . David and his son Solomon . . . hearken to your plea."

The first mention of a distinct order of *seliḥot* occurs in a midrashic source which possibly dates to as early as the third century: "David knew that the Temple was destined to be destroyed and that the sacrificial system would be abolished as a result of Israel's iniquities, and David was distressed for Israel. With what would they effect atonement? And the Holy One, blessed be He, said: 'When troubles come upon Israel because of their iniquities, let them stand together before Me as one brotherhood and confess their iniquities before Me and recite before Me the order of *seliḥot,* and I will answer them.' And how did the Holy One, blessed be He, reveal this? . . . He revealed this in the verse: 'And the Lord passed before him' [and the verse proceeds to list the thirteen divine Attributes of Mercy which were communicated to Moses at Sinai]. This teaches that the Holy One, blessed be He, descended from the mist like a *sheli'aḥ ẓibbur* enveloped in his *tallit,* and stood before the Ark and revealed to Moses the order of *seliḥot.*"

It is not until the ninth century that such an order of *seliḥot* is found committed to writing—which it is in the *Seder* of Rav Amram Gaon. The two passages, "May He Who answered" and the scriptural verse referred to above, figure among the essential elements in it, as in all subsequent orders of *seliḥot.* This verse is the kernel of a petitionary prayer called *El Melekh Yoshev* ("God, King enthroned") which is the theme and refrain of the penitential services in all rites, and is thought to have originated in the sixth century.

The *seliḥot* were at first inserted, as is indicated by the Mishnah, after the sixth benediction of the *Amidah,* which is the request for forgiveness for sins. The Palestinian custom of reciting them separately after the *Amidah* prevailed, however, and became the almost universal practice, though the Italian and Roman rites retain the old custom.

Originally, *seliḥot* were recited only on fast days, whether statutory and annual, or proclaimed in particular times of trouble. Since God was just, the calamities of the time were the result of Israel's sins, and the evil could be averted by confession and asking forgiveness for those sins. The extension of reciting *seliḥot* during the penitential season is derived from the old custom of fasting on the six days before Rosh Ha-Shanah, when their recitation was connected with the fast. The practice of saying *seliḥot* was then extended over the Ten Days of Penitence, including the Day of Atonement, but not Rosh Ha-Shanah. Going one step further, the Sephardim are accustomed to recite similar prayers for the 40 days from the beginning of the month of Elul until the Day of Atonement, whereas the Ashkenazi custom is to commence reciting them on the Sunday before Rosh Ha-Shanah, or on the Sunday of the preceding week should Rosh Ha-Shanah fall on Monday or Tuesday. The service on the first day usually begins at midnight, and thereafter in the early hours before the morning prayers.

The *Nuremberg Maḥzor* (South Germany) contained the German prayer rite for the entire year. According to the colophon, the manuscript was written in 1331. In 1804 soldiers of Napoleon's army cut out 11 pages from the manuscript; 100 years later, five of them were re-discovered. Shown here is a large decorated initial-word panel for a *piyyut* for the first day of Passover.

In addition to the above-mentioned occasions, penitential hymns have been composed for semi-official voluntary fasts undertaken on certain dates by pious individuals. *Seliḥot* are also recited at their annual service by the members of the *ḥevra kaddisha*, or burial society, and by whole congregations to avert epidemics affecting children.

BAKKASHOT. The word *bakkashot* denotes a wide range of prayers in prose or verse, of the same type as *seliḥot*. A number of such hymns found at the beginning of the Sephardi prayer books from the 17th century onward are meant to be recited by congregants before dawn while waiting for the regular service to begin. This custom apparently originated in Safed among the followers of the kabbalist Isaac Luria, and from there spread to other communities. It is first mentioned in a letter dated 1603. Groups of Sephardim in Jerusalem called *Omerei Bakkashot* ("Sayers of Supplications") continue this practice every Sabbath from midnight until sunrise. These prayers were originally recited daily, but in the course of time, as a result of reduced attendance, they were confined to the Sabbath except during the month of Elul. At the approach of that month of penitence posters are to be seen today in certain of the old neighborhoods in Jerusalem, coaxing the Sephardi public to attend by means of florid appeals to traditions of group togetherness. These prayer fellowships are not to be confused with the Ashkenazi societies of *Shomerim la-Boker* ("Morning Watchers") which recite hymns on Monday and Thursday mornings before dawn.

The term *bakkashot* has often been applied arbitrarily to certain other hymns included in the service. Different anthologies of *bakkashot* exist, but all of them include the poem *Yedid Nefesh* by Eleazar Azikri. Each composition concludes with a selection of scriptural verses introduced by the words of a classical biblical prayer: "And Hannah prayed."

Although the singing of *bakkashot* is traditional in many communities, it evolved into an organized form of semi-religious activity only in Syria and Morocco. The melodies are extremely varied and include both sophisticated and popular idioms, and traditional tunes which have otherwise disappeared from contemporary cultures. In fact the musical factor is so prominent that it often tends to overshadow the basically religious purpose of the meeting. The singing of *bakkashot* may thus be considered as part religious concert and part prayer meeting, attended equally for religious, aesthetic, and social reasons.

The social upheavals of this century have left their mark even on the musical traditions of the singers of *bakkashot*. Thus, after the establishment of an important community of Aleppo Jews in Jerusalem at the beginning of the century, Aleppo *bakkashot* became a model for other Middle Eastern communities—but were themselves considerably modified by the participation of non-Aleppo singers from the neighborhood. The result was the generalized *bakkashot* style now common to several groups. In contrast, the wider distribution of Moroccan settlement in homogeneous immigrants' villages, especially after 1948, helped to preserve the purity of the distinctive Moroccan *bakkashot* tradition. Furthermore, the Aleppo repertoire is elastic, enabling a degree of choice in the hymns according to the occasion and the character of the audience. The Moroccan tradition, by contrast, is fixed.

Each *bakkashah* is performed antiphonally by two groups. Soloists or smaller groups take turns at singing the opening phrases, which may be a Psalm or the last verse of the preceding *piyyut*. The melodies are improvised, florid, and flexible enough to include the musical themes of the current Sabbath. The Moroccan congregations perform in the style of traditional Moroccan art music—a kind of vocal and instrumental suite. Since instruments are not permitted on the Sabbath, the singers compensate by adding their own vocal imitations of instrumental passages. However, when the Moroccan *bakkashot* are sung at weekday celebrations outside the synagogue, the appropriate instruments come into their own.

KINOT. The mournful moments of Jewish history are perhaps those best preserved. One reason must surely be the instinct which led the ancients to distill their woe in a poetic eulogy or lament. Such *kinot* were first spoken by a bereaved family or nation, and later recited over other calamities, such as oppressive edicts decreed upon a community or upon the people as a whole.

In Bible times, *kinot* were intoned and often composed by professional mourners of either sex. Several ancient dirges are preserved in the Bible, including David's lament, moving in its simplicity: "Saul and Jonathan, lovely and pleasant in their lives, and even in their death they were not divided." Also extant is an entire Book of Lamentations, attributed to Jeremiah, and bewailing in an alphabetical pattern of verses the destruction of Jerusalem and the exile of Israel. This biblical book is chanted by candlelight to a gently doleful melody in the synagogue on the Ninth of Av, the anniversary of the destruction of the Temple. These biblical passages are the forerunners of the dirges of later generations, of the Talmud and of the Middle Ages, when *kinot* were composed in the wake of public calamities, such as an earthquake in Tiberias, or of private grief, as in the case of the saintly Eleazar ben Judah of Worms, who wrote a rhymed elegy following the murder of his wife and two daughters during a pogrom in 1197.

The laments composed over the restrictive edicts of the Middle Ages were usually appended to those recited on the fast days, especially the Ninth of Av, whose dirges are collectively known in popular parlance as the *kinot*. One cycle of such poems is known as the Zionides, since they each start with the word Zion, as in Judah Halevi's oft-quoted lines: "Zion, dost thou not inquire after the peace of those bound to thee, the remnant of thy flocks, who yearn for thy peace?"

Some elegies have an alphabetical acrostic, or one indicating the name of the author, or both; some are also rhymed. Though many of the medieval compositions are preserved only in manuscript, hundreds of editions of the *kinot* have appeared, both with and without commentaries, since the first publication (in Cracow in 1585) of those recited on the fast days according to the Ashkenazi rite. An odd fate awaits many of these little books. Whereas all other prayer books for special occasions are stored away lovingly, ready for the corresponding festival in the coming year, certain Jerusalemites are accustomed to abandon their booklet of *kinot* at the conclusion of the Ninth of Av. For if the Messiah arrives and rebuilds the Temple within the forthcoming year, then the time for bewailing the Destruction will surely have passed.

TEḤINNOT. A distinctive *piyyut* form is the *teḥinnah*, a prayer of supplication which was originally associated with the voluntary private fasts observed on certain Mondays and Thursdays. The term was extended to refer to certain penitential *piyyutim* of the days of *seliḥot*. The *teḥinnah* is usually read quietly; its subject—the relationship between God and His people.

This relationship was also expressed in far less sophisticated style in the Yiddish prose equivalent of these prayers—the *tkhines*. These are homespun prayers of private supplication, outside the body of the liturgical canon, and varying in content according to the needs (or wants) of the hour. Mainly considered prayers for women, and often attributed to women authors, these supplications are characterized by sincerity, simplicity, and sentimentality. *Tkhines* are found as early as the 16th century in printed Yiddish texts, sometimes in prayer books with Yiddish translations. They were widely published in booklet form from the early 18th century, especially in Bohemia, Switzerland, Germany, Russia and Poland. Some editions are still reprinted today, while live vestiges of the *tkhines* are preserved in Yiddish (and other Jewish dialects) by pious matrons who recite them as they light the Sabbath candles.

Language and Style. In the period of the classical anonymous *piyyut,* writers followed the stylistic and lexical paths of the standard prayers: the vocabulary is mostly biblical, with a seasoning of the later linguistic bases of midrashic and talmudic Hebrew. The style of these early *piyyutim* is lucid, eschewing wordplay and rhetorical embellishment. With the work of Yannai in the sixth or seventh century, Hebrew sacral poetry became more expansive in its vocabulary and increasingly vague and flowery in its style. Thereafter, during the whole Oriental period of the *piyyut,* the early medieval composers drew on the whole Hebrew lexicon, with all its various strata, to such an extent that some of their early creations preserve ancient Hebrew words with no other mention in any of the classical sources. In addition, they adorned the *piyyut* with flamboyant idioms and words of their own creation. Their poetic innovations in language and form, which do not always conform to the classical rules of Hebrew grammar, gave their work a singular stylistic character. As to content, these *paytanim* (who are of the Kallir school, so called after its major representative, Eleazar ben Kallir) were fond of flavoring their works with an abundance of talmudic and midrashic material, often alluded to by contrived and cryptic wordplay. Some of their works thus became enigmatic, constituting difficult exegetical problems. Indeed, under their influence the *piyyut* became a species of crossword puzzle for medieval scholars—and modern antiquarians. This tradition grew, and reached its peak in the radically novel poetic works of Saadiah Gaon and his pupils in Babylonia, in the tenth and 11th centuries.

Such liberties were met with harsh criticism, especially by the 12th-century biblical commentator Ibn Ezra, himself a prolific *paytan*. In one tirade of especial acidity, he gives a foretaste of the wrath to come by choosing as his text—significantly—the following verses: "Be not rash with thy mouth, and let not thy heart be hasty to utter a word before God . . . for . . . a fool's voice [cometh] through a multitude of words." Ibn Ezra launches his attack as follows: "Everyone is obligated, when he prays, to guard the utterance of his lips and realize that he stands before the King, in whose hands are life and death. One is therefore forbidden to introduce into the prayers *piyyutim* of whose meaning he [the reader] is utterly ignorant, nor should he content himself with relying upon the author." He then proceeds to accuse Kallir of four failings: the inclusion in his poems of riddles and obscure allusions; the indiscriminate mixing of biblical and mishnaic Hebrew; his disdain for the dictates of Hebrew grammar; and the undue inclusion of midrashic and aggadic material.

Finally, having submitted a precious Kallirian phrase to merciless grammatical scrutiny, Ibn Ezra writes: "Why should we not follow the example of King Solomon, the wisest of men, whose prayer is explicitly clear? Everyone who knows Hebrew understands it, for it does not contain enigmas and allegories . . . Why should we not follow the example of the prescribed prayers, all of which are in pure Hebrew, instead of employing the dialects of the Medes, Persians, Greeks and Arabs?"

Ultimately, as a reaction to the Saadianic style of exaggerated innovations, Hebrew sacred poetry in Spain restricted itself to a clearly biblical framework of language and style, free of allusions to talmudic and midrashic material. The style of the Spanish *piyyutim* is impressively lucid, lyrical and flexible, approaching the style of contemporary secular poetry. The 11th-century poet and philosopher, Solomon ibn Gabirol, was

In ancient times, many prayerbooks contained the full text of the Passover *Haggadah*. This page, which shows one of the *piyyutim* for the Passover-night home ceremony, is from a 15th-century German manuscript which is known as the *Siddur of the Rabbi of Ruzhin*, so-called because it came into the possession of that ḥasidic rabbi.

instrumental in this process of chastening, and the earliest of the Spanish *paytanim* whose work appears to be entirely within the new stylistic framework is Isaac ibn Ghayyat. This change of attitude greatly influenced the *paytanim* of other lands, such as North Africa, Yemen, Ereẓ Israel, Babylonia, and Provence. And even though Italian and Ashkenazi poets generally remained faithful to the Kallir model, they were more restrained and moderate in their use of language and style. Poised between two traditions, the creations of the greatest of them reach impressive heights of beauty and flexibility.

Rhyme and Meter. Whereas the ancient anonymous *piyyut* did not employ rhyme, *paytanim* from the time of Yannai concentrated much more on rhyme than on rhythm. Those of the Kallir school attained great virtuosity in their techniques of toying with rhyme, and this lowered the level and content of their compositions, especially in the works of the more mediocre versifiers. The early anonymous *piyyut* was also unsophisticated in its use of rhythm. Its limited use characteristically divides each line into four feet, each of two or three stresses. A number of Eastern *paytanim* employed a peculiar rhythmic system which established an identical number of words or stresses in every line. This method is found in only a few works, and was used more widely by the early Central European *paytanim*, who also developed the traditions of rhyme of the early Kallir school.

It was the Spanish poets who introduced a precise method of rhythm. Though some of them dispensed with meter altogether, many drew on secular poetry for their quantitative approach to it, which was of Arabic origin, while the majority composed in a unique meter created in Spain for sacred poetry. This is mainly syllabic, assigning to each line a fixed number of syllables. Variegated rhyme schemes were also developed in Spain for liturgical as for secular poetry.

Acrostics. A literary technique utilized more frequently in the *piyyutim* than in the prayers in general is the acrostic, in which successive or alternating verses, or clusters of verses, begin with the letters of the alphabet in sequence. This tradition may be traced back to the Bible, which includes 14 alphabetizing compositions. In later usage the letters, syllables, or words are arranged in such a way that their combinations constitute phrases or even sentences independent of the meaning of the context. The significant letters or words may be all at the beginning, middle, or end of the respective words or lines in which they appear. Sometimes they combine to produce the alphabet, in order or reversed. In other variations, successive verses begin alternately with letters from either end of the alphabet.

Originally, the acrostic fulfilled several important functions. It simplified learning by heart and prevented mistakes, deletions, and additions. Furthermore, it often preserved the name of the author, together with that of his father, place of residence, and pseudonym, sometimes combined with blessings or verses from the Bible, all ingeniously woven into the *piyyut* in acrostic form.

One enterprising writer contrived to begin each word of his thousand-word opus with the letter *alef*—surely some kind of record. Needless to say, sustained alliteration and gimmickry of this kind not only defies mere considerations of smoothness and intelligibility, but involves literary acrobatics comparable to that of the Englishman who in the 19th century produced a primer containing stories made up of words of two letters only.

III Modes of Prayer

Orientation
Communal Prayer
The Language of Prayer
Musical Expression

The recitation of Psalms has always been considered an act of great piety. This prayerbook (Amsterdam, 1664) divides the Book of Psalms into daily portions so that the whole Book is recited in the course of the week—an act which, according to the title page, will ensure the reciter a share in the world-to-come. The printer was a Levite, and the two putti are pouring water on the hands of priests as the Levites do for the Priestly Blessing. The fish represent the zodiacal sign of the month in which the printer was born, and the two scenes at the bottom show biblical episodes in which Levites were involved.

סדר

מעמדות

מסודר כפי ימי השבוע על׳ הסדר
והאומרם בכל יום מובטח לו
שהוא בן העולם הבא :

עם תקון כיוב טעיות אשר נפלו בדפוסים :

נדפס

באמשטילרדם

בדפוס המשכיל היקר והנעלה והאלוף כמר
אורי ויב״ש בלא״א כה״רר
אהרן הלוי זלה״ה :

שנת לעשות כדת לפ״ק :

מעשה שכם

האומר לאביו

In future time, foretold Solomon, men the world over would address their prayers "toward the house which I have built for Thy name." David, his father, in a Psalm eloquent with the praise of his Creator, had declared: "I will give thanks unto the Lord with my whole heart, in the council of the upright, and in the congregation." Forever seeking the means to articulate his gratitude, he prayed: "O Lord, open Thou my lips, and my mouth shall declare Thy praise." And in the exuberant peroration to the Book of Psalms, David exclaimed: "Praise Him with the blast of the horn, praise Him with the psaltery and the harp. Praise Him with the timbrel and dance, praise Him with stringed instruments and the pipe."

These verses respectively set the four keynotes of the present chapter: the geographical orientation of the worshiper, communal prayer, the language of prayer, and the vocal and instrumental music in which worship finds expression.

ORIENTATION

God is Eternal, and God is Omnipresent. But just as the preferred times of worship are prescribed—for man is a creature of time, so the preferred places and directions of prayer are prescribed—for man is likewise a creature of space.

In particular, a specific direction is required for the recitation of the *Amidah*, namely, facing the Sanctuary of the Temple in Jerusalem. For Jews living in Europe this was eastward, and thus the term *mizraḥ* (the Hebrew word meaning east) came to mean the direction to be faced during prayer. It also designates the front wall of the synagogue where seats were reserved for the rabbi and other dignitaries. A further meaning of the term refers to the ornamental wall plaque which indicates the direction of prayer.

The custom of facing the Temple during prayer has biblical origins, beginning with Solomon's prayer at the dedication ceremony of the Temple, in which one of the recurring phrases refers to those who will "pray unto the Lord . . . toward the house which I have built for Thy name." The Bible also relates that Daniel prayed three times daily in his chamber, the windows of which were opened toward Jerusalem. The rule laid down in the Talmud prescribes that if one prays in the Diaspora, he should direct himself toward Ereẓ Israel, in Ereẓ Israel, to Jerusalem; in Jerusalem, toward the Temple; and in the Temple, toward the Holy of Holies. If a man is east of the Temple, he should turn westward; if in the west, eastward; in the south, northward; and if in the north, southward. Thus Jews the world over direct themselves in prayer toward one place. At least one Jew today takes this rule to its logical conclusion, and when he prays at the Western Wall—which is the retaining wall of the Temple Mount—this venerable worshiper directs himself somewhat to the left, bearing in mind the precise site in former days of the Holy of Holies.

That this orientation was practiced in ancient times is confirmed in most cases by excavations of early synagogues. Thus those uncovered at Miletus, Priene, and Aegina, all west of Ereẓ Israel, show an eastern orientation, as has been recorded too of Egyptian synagogues. Those houses of worship which stood north of Jerusalem and west of the Jordan River—at Bet Alfa, Capernaum, Hammath and Chorazin—all face southward, whereas ancient sanctuaries east of the Jordan, such as Val-Dokki, Umm al-Qanatir, Jarash and Dura-Europos, all face west. In the south, the synagogue excavated at Masada near the Dead Sea faces northwest to Jerusalem. In practice the directions frequently varied somewhat due to the terrain. Surprisingly, exceptions have been found in the synagogues at Khirbat Summaqa, a village on Mt. Carmel, and at Usifiyya, where the orientations are not toward Jerusalem. There is no satisfactory explanation for this divergence from the norm. In the early Christian church it was also customary to pray facing toward the Holy Land. For Islam too the original direction of prayer was toward Jerusalem, but this was subsequently changed by Muhammad in favor of Mecca.

The orientation toward Jerusalem was expressed architecturally in different ways. Excavations of ancient synagogues show that the earliest houses of worship had their entrances facing Jerusalem, and it was the portals, therefore, that indicated the sacred direction. However, the remains of the Dura-Europos synagogue on the Euphrates—more or less east of Ereẓ Israel—reveal that by the third century C.E. the doors

The wooden synagogue from Horb, southwest Germany, decorated and painted in 1735 by Eliezer Sussman. The lavish decorations, reminiscent of tapestry work, illustrate scenes from Jewish history and religious life. Jerusalem, Israel Museum.

Right: *Mizraḥ* panel presented to a German synagogue in 1833 on the occasion of a wedding. Jerusalem, Israel Museum.
Below: *Mizraḥ* panel, used to indicate the location of east, the direction of prayer, with the names of the Patriarchs and Moses, Aaron, David and Solomon on the Moorish arches. It is made of paper mounted on colored metal. North Africa, early 19th century. Paris, Musée d'Art Juif.

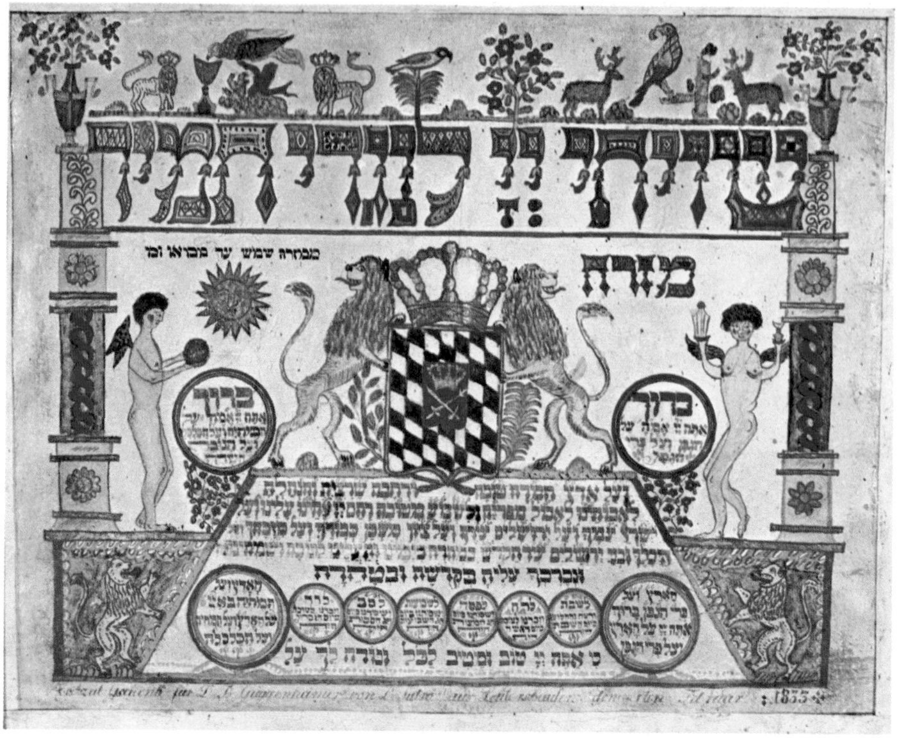

Left: *Mizraḥ* papercut from Eastern Europe, 19th century. Mishkan le-Omanut, Kibbutz Ein Harod.
Below: A *Mizraḥ* plaque, colored drawing on parchment, from Iran, 1855. It was also used in the home as an amulet. Tel Aviv, I. Einhorn Collection.

Right: The synagogue at Worms, reconstructed in 1961 from the 11th-century building destroyed by the Nazis in 1938. The smaller building on the right is the so-called "Rashi chapel," where, according to legend, the famous Bible and Talmud commentator conducted his school following the massacres of the First Crusade in his home-town Troyes, France. Worms, Kulturinstitute.
Below: The great synagogue in Florence, Italy, designed by a team of architects and completed in 1882. The elaborate decoration is Moorish in style. Photo Locci, Florence.

These two papercuts are *Shivviti* plaques, so called because of the central phrase, "I have put (*shivviti*) the Lord before me continually." Such plaques were attached to the cantor's lectern and intended to instill in him a prayerful attitude. Besides the verse cited, they also often contain other apposite biblical quotations, the name of the donor and the date of the donation. They also serve to indicate the correct direction to be faced in prayer. The upper example is from 18th-century Syria, while the lower is from Poland and dated 1882.

were on the eastern side and the opposite wall, in which a special niche had been made to place the Torah scrolls during worship, faced Jerusalem. In Ereẓ Israel the wall facing the Temple site was likewise changed from the side of entrance to the side of the ark in the fifth or sixth century. This change is already found in synagogues at Naaran near Jericho and at Bet Alfa. Worshipers came through the portals and immediately faced both the scrolls and Jerusalem. However, in those sanctuaries found in Hammath, Yafa in Galilee, and Eshtemoa in Judea, the sacred direction is properly south in the first two cases and north in the third while the entrance is from the eastern side. This may be in imitation of the biblical Tabernacle, which had its gates on the eastern side, or of Solomon's Temple, the portals of which were to the east. The precise reason, however, is not known. Maimonides, quoting a passage in Numbers in support of this practice, states that the doors of the synagogue should face east, while the Ark should be placed "in the direction in which people pray in that city," that is, toward Jerusalem. In codifying the law, the *Shulḥan Arukh* records the same rule, but to avoid the appearance of worshiping the sun by facing east, it recommends that one turn toward the southeast. If a person is unable to ascertain the points of the compass, he should direct his heart toward Jerusalem. This was also the opinion of the talmudic scholars Rabbi Tarfon and Rav Sheshet, who held that, since the Divine Presence is everywhere, the essential requirement is that one direct one's heart to God.

It is customary in traditional homes to mark the eastern wall in a distinctive manner to enable a guest to recite his prayers in the proper direction. Artistic wall plaques serving this purpose are usually inscribed with the word *mizraḥ*, and sometimes incorporate kabbalistic inscriptions, or pictures of holy places such as the Western Wall or the Tomb of Rachel, which are traditional sites of pilgrimage and prayer. On occasion, designers of such plaques have punningly used the verse: "From the rising of the sun unto the going down thereof, the Lord's name is to be praised." In the first place, the verse itself is appropriate, and secondly, the Hebrew word used for "rising" is *mizraḥ*, which means east, the traditional direction of prayer.

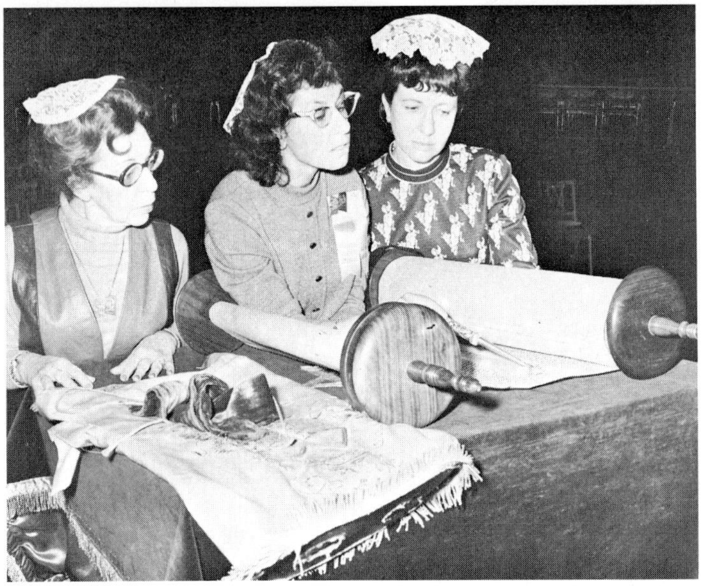

COMMUNAL PRAYER

The Minyan. Certain portions of the synagogue service and various other religious ceremonies can be performed only in the presence of at least ten males over 13 years of age. This quorum is called a *minyan,* from the Hebrew word for counting. Since Scripture refers to the group of ten spies who reported back to Moses as an *edah,* or community, the Talmud infers that ten or more men constitute a congregation. The Talmud also mentions the fact that Boaz "took ten men of the elders of the city" as witnesses of his purchase of land from Naomi and of his marriage with Ruth. Nearer the subject of prayer is the invocation in Psalms: "Bless ye God in full assemblies," which the Talmud understands as a reference to prayer with a quroum. Some relate the requirement of ten to Abraham's plea that God save Sodom if at least ten righteous men were found there. And on the basis of the verse in Psalms: "God standeth in the congregation of God," the Talmud explains that if ten men pray together the Divine Presence abides with them.

This quorum is necessary for the following sections of the synagogue service: the repetition of the *Amidah* with *Kedushah,* the public reading from the Torah and the Prophets, the priestly benediction, and the *Kaddish.* Most opinions also require a *minyan* for the recital of the *Barekhu* invocation, while others permit this to be said even if only six or seven males are present. The accepted custom in cases of emergency is to regard nine adults and a boy holding a Bible as a *minyan.* A quorum of ten was also necessary in certain rites—which have fallen into disuse—of comforting the mourners. The recital of the seven nuptial blessings, at wedding ceremonies and at the subsequent week-long festivities, requires a *minyan,* and the invocation preceding the Grace after Meals has an amplified version—"Let us bless our God of whose bounty we have eaten"—which is reserved for a meal of which ten men partake together.

Attendance at synagogue is strongly encouraged by the rabbis, to the extent that one talmudic teaching has it that "a man's prayer is only heard in the synagogue." And again: "One who has a synagogue in his city and does not attend it is called a bad neighbor." One sage went further, and attributed the longevity of Babylonian Jews to their regular attendance at synagogue. Another recommended that if one is unable to attend services, he should at least synchronize his private prayer with that of the congregation, thus joining them in a kind of metaphysical fellowship. Thus, over the years, the instinct to worship with a congregation became so ingrained in the Jewish consciousness, that a Yiddish saying claims that if only two Jews remained in the world, one would summon to synagogue, and the other would go there.

Nonetheless, strictly speaking, a quorum may be constituted in any clean place, and there is no need for a synagogue building (nor an officiating rabbi) to make possible the holding of divine services. In fact, world Jewry's best-known prayer location today is an open-air plaza—at the Western Wall—where ad hoc *minyanim* of total strangers spontaneously coalesce with amazing rapidity. Incidentally, this gives the services held there a spirit of unparalleled democracy, the suburban street-sweeper taking his turn at the congregational honors side by side with the local bank manager.

In talmudic times a community was regarded as having the status of a city if there were at least "ten idle men," that is, citizens not occupied by work or other duties, who could come to each synagogue service to make up the *minyan.* Indeed, Rabbi Johanan said: "When God comes to a synagogue and does not find a *minyan* there, He is wrathful, as it is written, 'Wherefore, when I came, was there no man? When I called, was there none to answer?'" In small traditional congregations, especially in Eastern Europe, whenever it was difficult to muster a *minyan* for daily services, it was customary to pay a few elderly or retired men to be present twice a day at the services. These people were known as "*minyan* men," and there are Diaspora congregations today that have had to resort to this means of maintaining a *minyan.*

The active participation of women in the prayer services is a comparatively recent phenomenon, started by Reform and later adopted by Reconstructionist and some Conservative congregations. The "Women's Lib" movement has had a definite influence on this trend. The ladies here were preparing for a special morning service at a Convention of the Women's League for Conservative Judaism. Although there are halakhic opinions permitting women by themselves (without men) to conduct services, the congregants in Isidor Kaufmann's scene of a ḥasidic synagogue would have found the idea horrifying.

In the Reform ritual women are counted in the quorum of ten persons to constitute a public prayer service since they have full religious equality with men. In 1973 the Rabbinical Assembly of America decided likewise that in Conservative congregations women could be counted in the quorum of ten. Notwithstanding, the decision as to whether to implement this in practice was to remain the prerogative of the individual congregational rabbi.

Children's Services. From its inception in early 19th-century Germany, Liberal Judaism sought a way to enable school-age youth of both sexes to participate actively in synagogue services. However, many young people had received insufficient home instruction in Jewish matters, and their inadequate knowledge of Hebrew precluded their understanding the prayers. Accordingly, special services were introduced in almost all Liberal congregations for children of school age. They are an abridged form of the order of prayer for adults, and typically include its central portions such as *Shema, Barekhu,* the *Amidah,* and *Aleinu.* The other prayers in children's services are composed in simple language, in the vernacular or in Hebrew, and on a level which is held to be psychologically relevant to the participants. Moreover, the opportunity to recite portions of the prayers before the assembled juvenile congregation serves as a preparation for active participation in adult services. Many Liberal congregations regularly hold children's services on Sabbath mornings or afternoons, or before religious school sessions, while Hebrew schools and summer camps commonly hold them at the daily assembly hours.

The institution of children's services has spread to most Conservative and to some Orthodox synagogues. The predominant Orthodox tradition, however, assumes that the child's attendance at regular prayer services with his parents is the best means to familiarize him with the liturgy and prepare him for more active participation after bar mitzvah. In many Orthodox synagogues, nonetheless, particularly in Israel, boys under 13 years of age are encouraged to lead those parts of the adult service that do not halakhically require majority, such as the Psalms of the *Pesukei de-Zimra.*

THE LANGUAGE OF PRAYER

Though scattered over all continents among speakers of 70 tongues, the Jewish people has continued throughout the ages to use Hebrew as the language of prayer. Deviations have been minor, and mostly in recent times.

This in itself is a remarkable phenomenon. It is even more remarkable when one considers that strictly according to the letter of the *halakhah,* prayer does not have to be offered in Hebrew. In the early centuries of this era, the Mishnah laid it down that the *Shema,* the *Amidah* and the Grace after Meals "may be recited in any language." At the same time, it is clear that Hebrew is not regarded merely as one language among many alternatives. Rather, there is an interesting halakhic ruling that whereas prayers may be offered in Hebrew even if the worshiper does not understand that language, they may be recited in the vernacular only if it is understood.

Another Mishnah enumerates a few passages of the Scriptural readings which it was obligatory to recite only in Hebrew. They amount in all to some 60 verses of the whole Bible, with the corollary that with the exception of those passages, it was permitted to read the Scriptural portions, which are an essential element of the liturgy, in the vernacular.

Despite this fact custom, as so often happens in Judaism, proved stronger than the letter of the law, and the rabbis waged a successful campaign for the predominance of Hebrew as

practically the sole medium of prayer. It is interesting to note that during the reign of Justinian in the mid-sixth century B.C.E., a conflict took place between those who, maintaining that they did not understand Hebrew, wished to have the Scriptures read in the synagogue in the prevalent vernacular (Latin or Greek) and those who insisted on the use of Hebrew only. The former appealed to the Emperor, who upheld their claim and issued a decree that the Scriptures should be read in the synagogue in Greek, Latin, or any other language understood by the congregation. That the temporal, non-Jewish power had to be invoked to establish this right speaks volumes for the force of custom which established Hebrew as the sole vehicle of prayer amongst Jews.

And it cannot be gainsaid that the granting of this unique status to Hebrew proved to be a long-term national blessing. It forged a spiritual link between the various Jewish communities in the far-flung Diaspora throughout the ages. It rendered it possible for any Jew, whatever his vernacular, and from whatever country he came, to join his coreligionists in prayer; no linguistic barrier prevents a Jew from Maine and a Jew from the Ukraine from joining in each other's communal worship. Moreover it was a powerful factor in keeping the Hebrew language alive. Innovations made in various communities during the Middle Ages whereby, for instance, the Book of Jonah was read on the Day of Atonement in Greek in some Greek-speaking countries in the 15th century, and the Book of Esther on Purim in Spanish, particularly for women, in the 16th century, struck no roots.

Samson Raphael Hirsch, doyen of German Jewish theologians in the 19th century, expresses the traditional attitude to the sole use of Hebrew as the language of prayer in the following words: "It is certainly not without reason that the scattered members of the House of Israel in all the lands of their dispersion everywhere retained for eighteen centuries the Hebrew divine worship, and nowhere associated the language of the land with their public worship, despite the fact that they had before them the legal declarations of the Sages. One must also consider how the continuity of the national institution of the *Avodah*

The Torah ark in the synagogue has always received a great deal of love and devotion. The synagogue of Rabbi Isaac Luria (known as the Ari; one of the greatest kabbalists) in Safed, was built towards the end of the 16th century but destroyed in the earthquake of 1837. Later it was rebuilt and the ark constructed in the fashion of European synagogues. The ark, albeit less elaborate, dominates Chaim Gliksberg's synagogue scene.

[Hirsch used this term for "communal prayer"] would be endangered if it were clothed in the language of the country. What would we do now if our fathers had adopted the old Germanic and Roman dialects as the language of our communal prayers? One has moreover to consider that Hebrew divine worship in the *Galut* [Diaspora] is a most important spiritual bond that still unites, in the Houses of God, the dispersed members of our nation in East and West, North and South."

The English rabbinical scholar Isidore Epstein expresses a related view as follows: "While private meditation and petition may be offered in any language, the language for *fixed* prayers must remain Hebrew. There is nothing exclusive about this insistence. The prayer for the universal Kingdom of God which forms the all-dominating theme and the highest content of Jewish prayer forbids such a thought. But just as the Jewish religion demands for its work and aims the maintenance of religious observances, it also requires the retention of the Hebrew language in prayers. Both serve to keep awake within the Jew the consciousness of the tasks laid upon him, alike as a son of Israel and as a member of the larger humanity."

Aramaic. Hebrew's nearest rival was Aramaic. During the formative period of the established Jewish liturgy (which is essentially from the first two pre-Christian centuries to the tenth century), Aramaic was largely the vernacular of the Jews of Ereẓ Israel and of Babylon. Firstly, Aramaic is a Semitic language cognate to Hebrew. Secondly, it was invested with a certain aura of sanctity, due not only to the fact that portions of the Bible (such as in Daniel and Ezra) are in Aramaic, as is the Talmud, but also to the fact that it became a religious duty to read through the weekly Scriptural portion "twice in the original and once in the Targum" (this being the authorized Aramaic translation of the Bible). As a result the temptation to employ the familiar Aramaic as the language of prayer became very powerful. As to the intriguing statement of Rabbi Johanan that "he who recites his prayers in Aramaic will receive no assistance from the ministering angels, since they do not understand Aramaic," it has been contended that this is to be regarded as part of the counterattack of the rabbis against this tendency.

Nevertheless Aramaic has found its niche, however obscure, in the traditional liturgy. It is an interesting fact that the four passages of the standard prayers which are in Aramaic, and which virtually constitute the total, all belong to different periods, and their inclusion was due in each case to different circumstances.

The first, and most important, is the *Kaddish,* which is discussed in Chapter V. The fact that originally it was a doxology recited after a talmudic or midrashic discourse which was itself delivered in Aramaic, and the affectionate and tenacious hold which this prayer exercised upon the sentiments of the people when it became *par excellence* the prayer of filial piety recited by mourners, combined to ensure its retention in its original language.

The second is the *Yekum Purkan* prayer, which in content is unique. A prayer for the welfare of the spiritual and semi-autonomous temporal leaders of the Jewish people during the centuries-long hegemony of Babylonian Jewry, it has something in common with the modern Prayer for the Royal Family or for the Government.

The beautiful *Berikh Shemeih* is the third of these Aramaic passages. It is recited as the Ark is opened, and was introduced in recent centuries under the influence of the kabbalists. It is an extract from the *Zohar* (which is entirely in Aramaic) as is the *Ke-gavna* prayer that appears in the ḥasidic liturgy for Friday night.

A fourth well-known Aramaic passage incorporated in the prayerbook is *Kol Nidrei*. Strictly speaking, this is not a prayer at all, but a legal formula for the absolution of vows which, like the *ketubbah,* the marriage contract, is couched in Aramaic legal terminology.

Aramaic has also been used to some extent in liturgical compositions apart from the statutory formulae. There are not many *piyyutim* extant in Aramaic; the best known is the *Akdamut* which is chanted before the reading of the Torah on Shavuot, and which is actually a poetic introduction to the enumeration of the traditional 613 commandments. (Ironically, this list itself is not read, except for its private recitation as part of the readings of the previous night's vigil.)

In the 16th century, what was almost a revival of Aramaic took place among the Safed school of mystics (of whom Isaac Luria, the "Ari", was the leading figure) as a result of the central role occupied among them by the *Zohar*. A considerable number of *zemirot*, or table hymns, were composed in Aramaic. One of these—*Yah Ribbon*, by Israel Najara, a disciple of Luria—has become a classic.

The Hebrew of the Prayers. The Talmud differentiates between biblical Hebrew (*leshon* Torah) and mishnaic Hebrew (*leshon ḥakhamim*) and it is noteworthy that despite the fact that the formulation of the prayers belongs entirely to the mishnaic and post-mishnaic period, the statutory prayers are almost without exception couched in the purest of biblical Hebrew, both in terminology and in syntax. This is classical literary Hebrew at its purest; the foreign loan words are few indeed, and even they appear in what may be called the secondary prayers. Post-biblical forms and phrases are almost non-existent.

This rigid adherence to classical biblical Hebrew in the liturgy disappears almost completely in the *piyyutim*, the poetic hymnal compositions which were added in the course of time to the statutory prayers. The early *paytanim* of Ereẓ Israel such as Yannai, Yose ben Yose, and especially Eleazar Kallir, and their successors in Ashkenazi Jewry, either predated the period of the development of Hebrew grammar which flourished in Spain and Provence, or were unaware of it.

In Chapter II, in the section on the language and style of the *piyyutim*, the consequent problems of intelligibility were discussed. True it is that a conscientious reader may well succeed in working out the identity of a biblical personage who is hinted at in two rare epithets; he may well detect the relevance of a sublime midrashic passage, even though the only clues provided are two or three cryptic alliterative allusions. But after all the arduous effort is over, the ordinary worshiper cannot but feel sympathy with much of Ibn Ezra's criticism, and would willingly forego ingenuity in favor of a more generous measure of intelligibility.

This hurdle does not have to be faced daily, however, because the tendency in most rites is to restrict these poetic additions to the statutory liturgy of the High Holy Days only.

It is by no means to be assumed that knowledge of Hebrew was so widespread before the dawn of the modern age that most Jews understood even the statutory prayers, but at least most could read and recite them, even if they did not understand quite what they were saying, and a simple unquestioning faith was an acceptable substitute for knowledge. Others could only recite the prayers by heart, and the repetition of the *Amidah* by the reader was specifically designed to enable even the least learned to discharge their religious obligations.

The Modern Period. The dawn of the modern age raised problems which did not obtrude in earlier times. Simple unquestioning faith in the efficacy of the mere recital of prayers, even if they were unintelligible, diminished as the rational spirit grew. The need was increasingly felt for understanding what one was saying if one was really to pray. Only in Israel, where Hebrew is the vernacular, did the problem not present itself.

In the Diaspora little progress has been made towards a solution, and the three trends of religious Judaism have attempted to deal with the problem in different ways. The one universal exception to the sole use of Hebrew is the "loyal prayer" for King or Government, which is invariably read,

The Aramaic text is a kabbalistic invocation for the Sabbath meals, originating from the 16th-century Safed school of kabbalists. Every *mitzvah* performed on earth has an effect on high, and the Sabbath meals are no exception. The curtain for the Torah ark from Bamberg, Bavaria, demonstrates a common use of the Hebrew letters. The last two lines of the text—which records the name of the donor—are a biblical quotation in which the letters with the indicators make up the date, 1809. The interior of the synagogue of the Polish town of Lancut is shown in a painting by Zygmunt Vogel.

almost as a demonstration of loyalty, in the vernacular. Apart from that the Orthodox community on the whole has retained Hebrew as the language of prayer and meets the difficulty of non-comprehension on the part of worshipers both by fostering the teaching of Hebrew, and by providing prayer books with a translation in the vernacular. Until recently, the conventional translations were severely literal, and often couched in the archaic cadences of pulpit English. Translators in recent years, in order to do justice to their texts, have tended to prefer lucid and judicious paraphrasing.

Apart from providing translations of Hebrew prayers, there is a tendency in Orthodox congregations in Western countries to either replace or supplement the Hebrew reading of what may perhaps be termed non-statutory passages by a reading in the vernacular. Passages so treated include, for example, *Berikh Shemeih,* and the second paragraph of *Aleinu*. The

The cantor performs an important function in the synagogue. Issachar Ryback (1897–1935) expresses this clearly in his "Prayer in the Synagogue." The detail from a 19th-century European illuminated Scroll of Esther shows a cantor about to ascend the *bimah* to read the Scroll on the festival of Purim. A much earlier depiction of a *ḥazzan* is that of the *Birds' Head Haggadah* which was copied in South Germany in the 13th century. Because of the prohibition against making graven images, the artist gave every figure a bird's head.

Conservative movement not only carries this tendency further but has introduced meditations or other extraneous passages in the vernacular into standard prayers for which Hebrew is retained.

It is the Reform Movement that has adopted the use of the vernacular in prayer to the greatest extent. The Union Prayer Book, published by the Central Conference of American Rabbis for the use of Reform congregations, is set out in the form of an English book, reading from left to right. Hebrew is reduced to a minimum, some of the Psalms and traditional prayers are given in English only, and even where the Hebrew is given on the opposite page, it is the English version that is recited during services. This version is not necessarily a translation. Paraphrases abound, as do free renditions which show little connection with the Hebrew equivalent.

In sum, this whole vexed question may perhaps be distilled into a simple choice—between (on the one hand) the obvious and praiseworthy demand for ready intelligibility and meaningfulness, and (on the other) the long-term benefits accruing from loyalty to a universal language for Jewish prayer, with its emphasis on the brotherhood of *all* of dispersed Israel, even if that language is not yet fully understood by all.

MUSICAL EXPRESSION

Music has accompanied Jewish worship from its very inception. The Book of Exodus already records the exultant song that Moses and the Israelites sang in praise of God after the crossing of the Red Sea. Indeed, the song of Moses' sister together with the womenfolk was accompanied by instrumental music and by dancing. "And Miriam the prophetess, the sister of Aaron, took a timbrel in her hand; and all the women went out after her with timbrels and with dances." In the First and Second Temples, centuries later, both singing and instrumental music adorned the divine service. And, as has been noted, many of the chapters of the Book of Psalms which were recited in the Temples seem to have been composed with a specific instrumental accompaniment in mind.

In 70 C.E., when the Second Temple was destroyed by the Romans, the disrupted worship there was replaced by the synagogue service. In the course of this transfer the refined instrumental art of the Levites was lost, since the sages prohibited the use of instruments in the synagogue service as a permanent reminder of the national calamity.

Though the pronouncements of the *halakhah* dealt thus harshly with instrumental music, the aggadic portions of the Talmud reveal many instances of a feeling for music. In the words of one well-known example: "A lyre was suspended over David's bed. When midnight neared, a northerly wind blew on it, whereupon it made music of itself." The link between the musical and the mystical also finds expression in references by the sages to the music of the angels. One midrashic source, for example, tells of the celestial songs which the ministering angels sing before the heavenly throne, in language rich in word music and vocal harmony. Beautiful as these harmonies may be, the Midrash goes on to say, it is a song from another source that is preferred by Him Who is to be praised. "Rabbi Ishmael said: 'Blessed is Israel—how much dearer are they to the Holy One than the ministering angels! For no sooner do the ministering angels wish to burst forth in song, than rivers of fire and mountains of flame encircle the Throne of Glory. But the Holy One says: Let every angel, cherub and seraph that I have created hold his peace—until I have listened to the song of praise of Israel, My children.'"

Though outsinging the heavenly hosts, the singers in the temporal world were denied—after the Destruction of the Temple—the use of instruments. Music accordingly became a strictly vocal art and, thus limited, underwent changes in style and form. Moreover, the musical skill of the levitic singers and their traditions, accumulated over generations, were not utilized in synagogue song, and their professional teaching and rules were never preserved in writing. Synagogue song was thus a new beginning in every respect, especially with regard to its spiritual basis.

In the new era, prayer took the place of sacrifice in securing atonement and grace. Levitical music had been an integral part of the order of sacrifices, but its nature can only be guessed at. It has been conjectured that since it was directed heavenwards rather than to a human audience, it probably strove to attain an objective and transcendental beauty—a hypothetical early form of art music. The task of synagogue song was a different one. It is by means of the spoken word that both the individual and the congregation appeal to God. Prayer, being "the service of the heart," has to express a broad scale of human feelings: joy, thanksgiving, and praise, side by side with supplication and contrition. All these emotions prompt the warm subjective expression afforded by song, rather than the more abstract beauty of instrumental music.

The human element in synagogue song found expression in styles which may be guessed at. These would need to be suited to a musically random assemblage of people, for the majority of whom artistically contrived and complicated tunes would be out of range. Such congregations had to be cemented together by a kind of music that was easily grasped and performed. The above conditions are fulfilled by three musical forms, which are the archetypes of synagogue song, and which have been preserved by the whole vast range of Jewish communities over the ages. These forms are: psalmody, which was discussed in an earlier chapter; the chanted public reading of the Torah, which is dealt with at a later stage; and the prayer melodies in general, especially as they are interpreted by the *sheliaḥ ẓibbur*, or prayer leader.

The Sheliaḥ Ẓibbur. At all public worship, services are led by an "envoy of the congregation" or, in Hebrew, *sheliaḥ ẓibbur*. This function includes the intoning aloud of certain prayers, especially their opening phrases or closing benedictions, thus enabling the congregation to proceed more or less in unison; the recitation of the *Kaddish* at various junctures in the services; and leading the congregation in responsive readings.

Although today this function is sometimes a professional one, in earlier days any member of a congregation could be called upon to lead his fellow-worshipers in prayer. It might be said that the gift of a fine voice almost obliged a congregant to accept the responsibility of serving as lay envoy. His voice alone, though, did not qualify him to serve in that capacity. The Code of Jewish Law lists several other qualifications: humility, acceptability to the congregation, knowledge of the laws governing prayer and of the correct pronunciation of the Hebrew text, proper dress, and a beard. The last requirement is often waived except for the High Holy Days, and in certain circles completely ignored. Apart from the recital of hymns and Psalms, such as the introductory *Pesukei de-Zimra* portion of the morning service, only a congregant beyond the age of bar mitzvah may officiate. And for the High Holy Days, a man with the responsibilities of a wife and children is preferred, so that his supplications will rise "from the very walls of his heart."

The Ḥazzan. A *sheliaḥ ẓibbur* with a trained voice, a knowledge of music, and a measure of creative virtuosity is commonly known as a *ḥazzan*. The word frequently occurs in talmudic sources. There, however, it denotes various types of communal officials, especially the *ḥazzan ha-keneset*. This functionary performed certain duties in the synagogue, such as bringing out the scrolls for the public reading of the Torah, and blowing a trumpet to announce the commencement of the Sabbath and festivals. His was an honored post. The Code of Theodosius (though defining Jews as "enemies of the Roman laws and of the supreme majesty") exempted the *ḥazzan* from taxes in 438, and 160 years later this privilege was endorsed by the relatively liberal Pope Gregory the Great.

The early *ḥazzan* was not regularly required to lead the services although, like any other congregant, he could do so on request. It was only during the period of the *geonim*, in the centuries preceding the Middle Ages, that the *ḥazzan* became the permanent *sheliaḥ ẓibbur*. Among the factors contributing to this change were the increasing complexity of the liturgy, a decline in the knowledge of Hebrew, and a desire to enhance the beauty of the service through its musical content. The *ḥazzan ha-keneset*, who had traditionally guarded the correct texts and selected new prayers, was a natural choice. Furthermore, as *piyyutim* increasingly found their way into the liturgy, this form of sung art-poetry demanded the expertise of a gifted soloist, especially when the singer himself was expected

An inventory of initial motifs of *Mi-Sinai* tunes: No. 2, earliest notation, 1783 (Aaron Beer); No. 3, earliest evidence, c.1800 (Jacob Goldstein); No. 4, earliest evidence, 1765 (Aaron Beer); No. 5, earliest notation, 1765 (Aaron Beer); No. 6, earliest notation, 1791 (Aaron Beer); No. 7, earliest notation, 1744 (Judah Elias of Hanover); No. 8, earliest evidence, 1782 (Aaron Beer). Nos. 1 and 9, conventional form notated by Hanoch Avenary. Aaron Beer (1739–1821) was a famous cantor, composer and collector who, from the age of 26, was chief cantor at a main Berlin synagogue. He made a habit of varying the tunes to discourage the congregation from joining in his singing.

to compose both text and tune. Under these circumstances, a lay precentor could hardly continue to suffice as prayer leader.

The professional recitation of the *piyyutim* was called *ḥizana* by the Arabic-speaking communities. Its Hebrew equivalent, *ḥazzanut* (or *ḥazzaniyyah* among Sephardi communities) came to designate the traditional form of chanting the whole service, or the repertoire and style of a particular soloist, or the profession of cantor. The assumption of the title *ḥazzan* by the singer probably took place during the ninth century. Since the function of *ḥazzanut* soon came to be passed on from father to son, it eventually belonged to an almost closed social class, where it was the custom for a young *ḥazzan* to marry the daughter of his master or of a colleague. This family orientation fostered the early training of talents and helped preserve local musical traditions.

Musical Tradition. It is difficult to imagine the musical character of early *ḥazzanut*. Attempts have been made, nonetheless, to demonstrate the features common to Oriental and European *ḥazzanim* today, with comparable gentile melodies taken as a control group. In addition, the tunes noted down by Obadiah the Norman proselyte in the early 12th century are available for comparison. In general, it may be said that *ḥazzanut* implies the free evolution of a melodic line, without reference to any system of harmony. For the *ḥazzan* must command a reasonable degree of musical inventiveness. He does not simply reproduce a preconceived piece of music, but edits the general outlines of a theme into final shape by improvisations of his own. In this way, for example, each stanza of a *piyyut* may develop as a new variation on a familiar traditional theme.

This feature is already found in the tunes notated by the above-mentioned Obadiah. The expressive elements which today are still characteristic of *ḥazzanut* are also to be discovered there, as too are the repetition of words and the pulsing trill around a single note that have remained the pride of the *ḥazzan* until this day.

To sum up, musical tradition in *ḥazzanut* means a melodic pattern to be followed, the choice of a scale appropriate to the mood required, and a stock of motifs to be arranged and rearranged in changing melodic structures. Pliable and versatile by its very nature, this ancient musical tradition cannot be confined to regular bar lines nor enclosed in a framework of symmetrical phrases. Its rhythm is as free as that of the Hebrew poetry of most ages.

Traditional Themes. The melodic conventions of venerable rabbis and *ḥazzanim* were handed down orally by their disciples. Scattered references to the music of certain prayer texts can be found in medieval compendia of liturgical practice, while other traditions are traceable as far back as the talmudic period, such as extending the singing of the Amen response, of the Priestly Blessing, and of *eḥad*, the last word of *Shema Yisrael*.

The efforts to consolidate an Ashkenazi tradition of sacred song were concentrated in the school of Jacob ben Moses Moellin of Mainz (died 1427), commonly called "the Maharil." Although a rabbi of scholarly renown, he also served as a *ḥazzan*. The musical usage taught by him was, on the one hand, a continuation of existing traditions accepted from former *ḥazzanim*, and on the other, his personal choice and example became normative. Indeed, they remained the established custom in Mainz until modern times. As a rule, testifies a disciple, the Maharil used to uphold local traditions: "Local custom should not be altered at any price, not even by unfamiliar melodies."

It is remarkable how elaborate and detailed the musical performance of the Maharil was. His disciple, Zalman of St. Goar, recorded many details with great care and transmitted to posterity a score without music, so to speak, of the most important parts of the liturgy. For example, in the service for the Ninth of Av, in commemoration of the destruction of the Temple, not only is the distribution of texts between congregation and cantor defined, but also what the latter had to sing in a loud, medium, or low voice, what in a mournful intonation, and where a cry of anguish was to be sent up. The pauses at the end of the verses and chapters are not forgotten, nor are the melodies which were to be drawn out. The music of the Day of Atonement is treated in a similar way.

Though the Maharil disapproved of hymns sung in the German vernacular, which were then in vogue in the same way as Ladino hymns are current among Sepharim to the present,

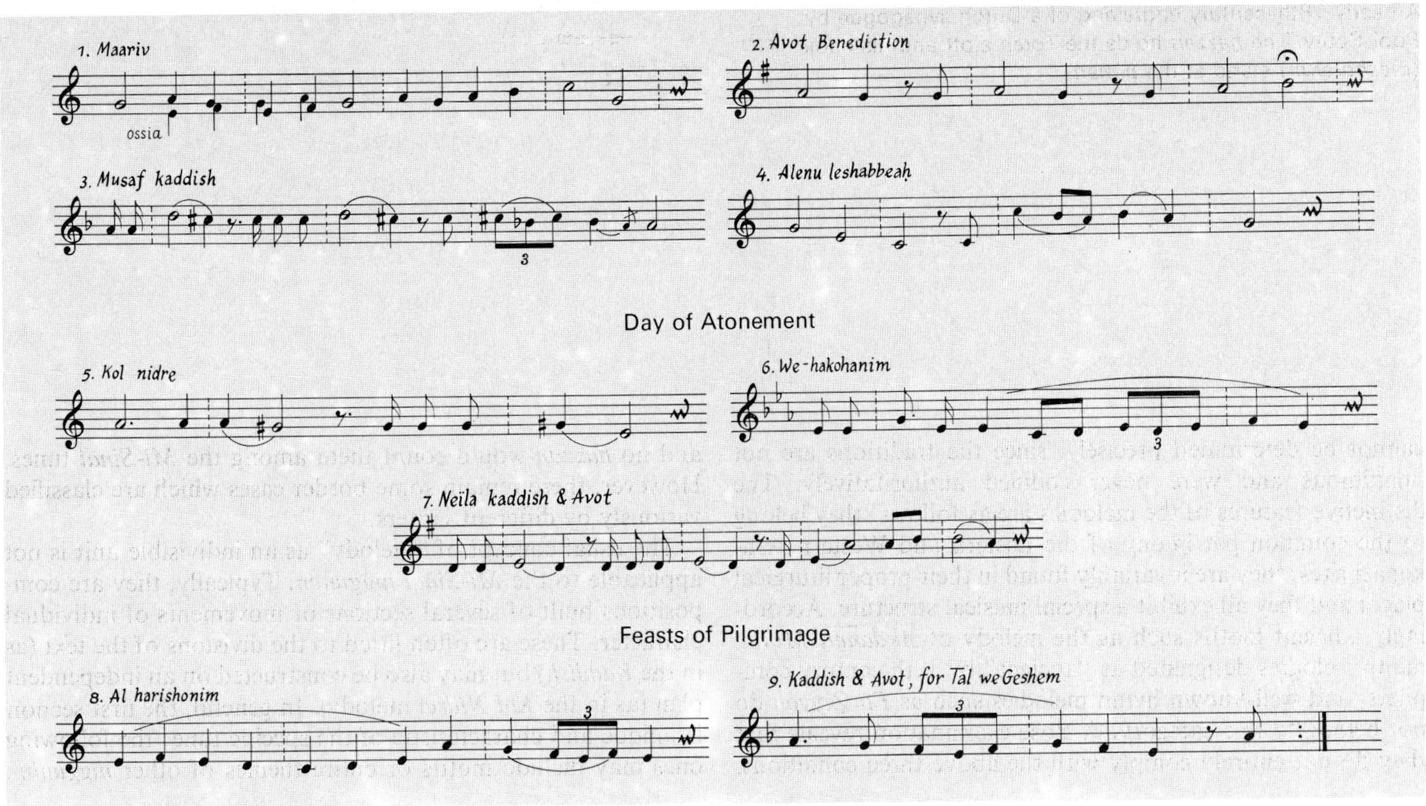

he stressed the importance of hymns as such. Moreover, unlike many other rabbis, he regarded melody as an essential of liturgical tradition. At the same time, his musical teachings are replete with mystical concepts (*kavvanot*). There are striking examples of their influence on melodic configuration, noted by contemporaries: "He used to greatly extend the tune at the word 'Thou,' obviously concentrating his mind on the divine faculty of 'Thou' known to all the adepts of mysticism."

Such musical suggestions of a hidden sense of the words were indicated by remarks in the various prayer books. Thus the *Maḥzor Hadrat Kodesh* (Venice, 1512) advises the *ḥazzan* to sing a certain passage "to a drawn-out and beautiful tune." The prayer *Nishmat Kol Ḥai* opens with the words: "The breath of every creature blesses Thy name," and the same manual accordingly assigns to it "a beautiful melody, since all the people of Israel are given an additional soul on the Sabbath." Other books attest the use of veritable leitmotifs, still current today, in the recitation of the Book of Esther when, for instance, the drinking vessels of Ahasuerus are mentioned to the tune of the Scroll of Lamentations, for they traditionally formed part of the booty from the despoiled Temple of Jerusalem. It was also an old custom to prolong the tune of *Barukh she-Amar* in the Morning Prayer. The German scribe Shimshon ben Eliezer recorded in the 14th century that he used to sing it as an orphan in Prague with such a sweet voice that he was given the nickname *Shimshon Barukh she-Amar*. Although directions for musical execution are found in the works of many authors, it is the Maharil who was made the legendary patron of Ashkenazi *ḥazzanut* and the composition of traditional melodies was ascribed to him. In particular, the so-called *Mi-Sinai* melodies were believed to go back to the authority of the Maharil, and in cantorial circles they are accordingly known as "the tunes of Rabbi Maharil."

MI-SINAI MELODIES. Prominent in the cantorial repertoire of Ashkenazi synagogues of both the East and West European rites are the *Mi-Sinai niggunim,* from the Hebrew meaning "melodies from Sinai." Their seemingly presumptuous title stems from a reverent analogy with certain authoritative ritual laws known collectively as *halakhah le-Mosheh mi-Sinai* ("laws transmitted to Moses at Sinai") which, though of hoary provenance, have no explicit biblical source.

These melodies are so hallowed by this vicarious authority, that no cantor would contemplate replacing them by any other, no matter how appealing. This status is reflected in their Eastern European name: *skarbowe niggunim,* from Polish and Hebrew words meaning "official tunes." Located at those points in the service where the liturgical and emotional elements join in equal force, the *Mi-Sinai* tunes may be called the heart of Ashkenazi synagogue song.

The family of *Mi-Sinai* tunes comprises about ten solemn compositions which are associated mainly with the prayers of the penitential period of the New Year. Their exact scope

An early 18th-century engraving of a Dutch synagogue by Pool-Sculy. The *ḥazzan* holds the Torah aloft and his choir (*meshorerim*) stand at the *bimah*.

cannot be determined precisely, since the traditions are not unanimous and were never codified authoritatively. The distinctive features of the melodies are as follows: they belong to the common patrimony of the Eastern and Western Ashkenazi rites; they are invariably found in their proper liturgical place; and they all exhibit a special musical structure. Accordingly, ancient motifs such as the melody of *Akdamut Millin,* many melodies designated as "ancient" by 19th-century compilers, and well-known hymn melodies such as *Eli Ẓiyyon* do not belong to this category. A close examination reveals that they do not entirely comply with the above three conditions, and no *ḥazzan* would count them among the *Mi-Sinai* tunes. However, there remain some border cases which are classified variously by different writers.

The usual concept of "melody" as an indivisible unit is not applicable to the *Mi-Sinai niggunim*. Typically, they are compositions built of several sections or movements of individual character. These are often fitted to the divisions of the text (as in the *Kaddish*) but may also be constructed on an independent plan (as in the *Kol Nidrei* melody). In general, the first section is unique and characteristic of the specific tune; the following ones may include motifs or entire themes of other *niggunim,*

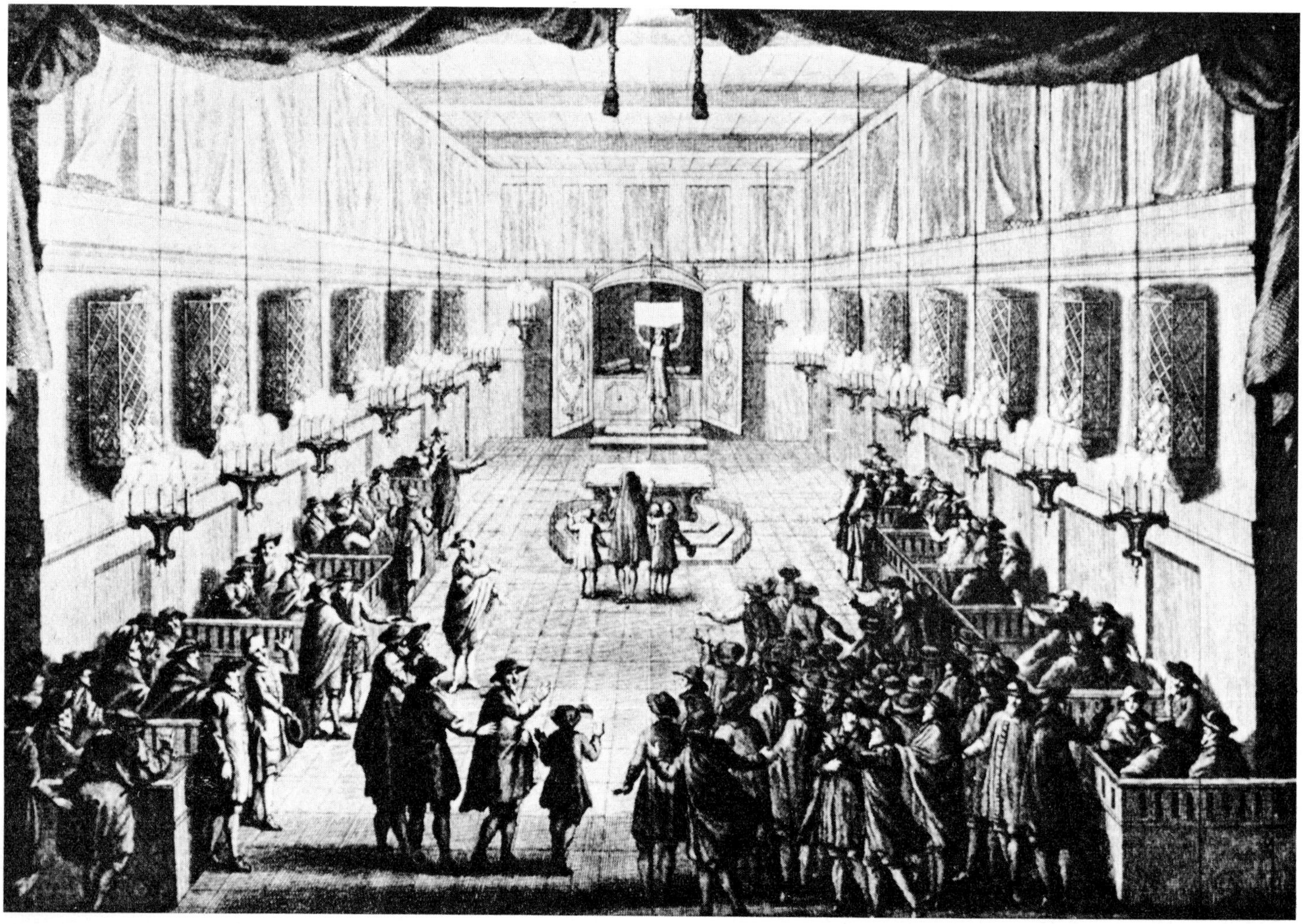

thereby creating a kind of family likeness among the members of the group. The order of the themes within each section is usually constant, distinguishing this music clearly from the more flexible *nusaḥ* style. This still allows for a certain plasticity of themes and motifs, which in turn allows for their easy adaptation to a wide range of texts. The performer is granted considerable liberty to shape the music by himself; tradition prescribes only the approximate layout and motivic profile—an idea or master plan which the singer must realize in sounds. This challenge to creative improvisation recalls principles governing Oriental music and exceeds by far the freedom of embellishment characteristic of older European art. One should therefore not expect to discover the archetype of any *Mi-Sinai* tune, for there exist only numerous realizations of a certain mental image. Other Oriental features are the free rhythm, which cannot be fitted without distortion to the regular bars beloved of Western ears, and the rich and fluent coloratura adorning it.

In East Ashkenazi tradition, the bond between music and text has been loosened: entire sections may be sung without words. Certain themes, preserved only in the earlier, Western notated documents, disappeared from common usage in Eastern Europe, and others replaced them in the established order. Alternatively, surviving themes or sections came to be repeated in order to provide sufficient musical accompaniment for the full text. This regressive evolution in the East was apparently caused by the early displacement of these communities from the birthplace and centers of *Mi-Sinai* song. The Western *ḥazzanim,* on the other hand, developed extensive and elaborate compositions from the original tunes. Such fantasias were in fashion from about 1750 to 1850. Basically, however, the *Mi-Sinai* melodies retained their identity in Jewish settlements as distant from each other as Eastern Russia and Northern France, south of the Carpathians, and Scandinavia or Britain.

There is no doubt that they antedate the great migrations from Central to Eastern Europe in the 15th century or even earlier. That the musical ideas and outlines of the *Mi-Sinai niggunim* originated in the Middle Ages can be concluded from musical evidence, from a few references in literature and, above all, from the fact that they are found in two Ashkenazi rites which separated early in their history. It may further be supposed that the sufferings of Crusader times made Ashkenazi Jewry ripe for expressing the feelings that emanate from out of the depths of these melodies. It is of interest that their character and profound musicality attracted gentile composers, such as Max Bruch (*Kol Nidrei,* op.47) and Maurice Ravel (*Kaddish,* 1914), while their confrontation with the idioms of contemporary music is demonstrated in A. Schoenberg's *Kol Nidrei,* which first appeared in 1938.

Nusaḥ. Let a visiting *ḥazzan* but deliver himself of the first phrase of his favorite overture for a festive occasion, and the seasoned congregants will immediately catalog his style: "a classical Galician *nusaḥ,*" "an obviously Lithuanian *nusaḥ,*" and the like.

The Hebrew word *nusaḥ* has many meanings. For a start, it signifies a prayer rite, that is, the order of prayers followed in a particular region. This meaning has two extensions in a musical context. On the one hand, a public reading of the Torah may be described as *nusaḥ Sepharad,* that is, the Sephardi version of melodic Bible-reading. On the other hand, the comment that "this cantor has a good *nusaḥ*" means that he renders the traditional tunes faithfully and in good taste.

The word, however, is also used as a technical term of synagogue music. In combinations such as *nusaḥ ha-tefillah, nusaḥ Yamim Nora'im,* and *nusaḥ Shabbat,* it denotes the specific musical mode to which a certain part of the liturgy is sung. The musical characteristics of these modes are defined in terms of the following elements. In the first place, each is based upon a particular series of notes, which may be a scale of less or more than eight notes. Secondly, each mode or *nusaḥ* contains a stock of characteristic motifs which undergo constant variation. Thirdly, these motifs are combined in a completely free order, forming an irregular pattern. And fourthly, each *nusaḥ,* as defined by the above-mentioned three elements, is always associated with a particular section of a specific holiday liturgy as, for instance, the *Musaf* prayer of the High Holy Days, the Morning Prayer on weekdays, and so on. It is worth noting

This detail from the 14th-century *"Sister" to the Golden Haggadah* clearly shows a cantor on the synagogue *bimah.* The Hebrew superscription which reads: "A man and the members of his family reciting the *Haggadah,*" is presumably a later, incorrect addition as there is no known custom for the family to recite the *Haggadah* in the synagogue, and it is unlikely that a person has a *bimah* at home. Furthermore, the family recitation of the *Haggadah* should take place at a table with the symbolic foods.

that the *nusaḥ*-principle is known both to European and to Oriental Jewish communities. On the assumption that it therefore antedates their current dispersion it may be regarded as a very old musical trait in synagogue song.

At the same time, the particular *nusaḥ* that evolves in any community inevitably bears the imprint of its cultural environment. Thus the Roman *nusaḥ* of certain periods is recognizably solemn and decorous; to the amateur the *nusaḥ* of an Oriental *ḥazzan* is barely distinguishable from an Arab dirge; while his German counterpart is predictably precise in the execution of his decidedly Teutonic rhythms. Dabblers in liturgical geography can enjoy the equivalent of a world trip by a visit to the Western Wall, where side by side scores of *ad hoc* congregations enjoy their own prayer services, each in the *nusaḥ* which they brought with them to Israel as part of their cultural baggage.

SHTAYGER. An important ingredient of the *nusaḥ* in Ashkenazi communities is the *shtayger,* a Yiddish term for the musical modes of traditional synagogue song. The *shtayger* are characterized by an order of intervals which is unusual in European music, and are named after the initial words of certain prayers sung to them, with some differences in nomenclature between East and West Ashkenazi usage. Originally these cantorial modes were conceived of as the Jewish parallel of the liturgical modes of the medieval European Church, and were accordingly described by early investigators in terms of Western octave scales. Increased knowledge of non-European modal structures, such as the Oriental *maqama* or Indian *raga,* later gave scholars the clue for understanding the nature of the *shtayger.* First, their "scales" need not be an octave repeating itself through the whole gamut; their tonal range may extend over less or more than eight notes; and the intervals may be altered in different octave pitches or in ascending and descending order. These include not only semitones but sometimes micro-intervals. Another characteristic is given by the specific location of the keynotes, which serve as resting points of the intermediary and final cadences, corresponding to the shorter and longer pauses in the text being sung. Furthermore, certain *shtayger* are characterized by a stock of motifs of their own. Singing according to a *shtayger* thus comes very close to Oriental concepts of modality.

One well-known *shtayger* appears not only in synagogue music but in folksong and ḥasidic melodies as well, and has accordingly been used for the musical characterization of the Jewish people by Mussorgsky, Anton Rubinstein, and other composers. Another *shtayger* resembles the natural minor scale, while a third is reminiscent of the so-called Gypsy scale. In the free compositions of individual cantors, modulation from one *shtayger* to another frequently occurs, and contributes much to the expressive power of the East Ashkenazi singing style.

Predictably, the use of *shtayger* melodies in art music raises certain problems, especially when their harmonization is attempted. Some convincing solutions have been found, as when the solo tune is allowed to display itself before a background of sustained chords.

Harmony. At various points in the liturgy, the cantor invites the congregation afresh to join him in worship. This collaboration is expressed musically in their alternating responses—as soloist and choir—according to a traditional division of the texts.

Very old practices of responsorial performance have been preserved, especially by the Sephardi communities. As indicated in the Talmud and also adopted by the Roman Church, the cantor may intone the first words of a chapter, whereupon the choir takes over, or they may alternate and respond to one another. Among the Sephardim the congregation is also accustomed to take up the key-words of the more important prayers from the mouth of the cantor. The division of tasks between solo and choir sometimes affects the melodic onfiguration. For example, if a particular prayer is sung to a *nusaḥ,* its original free rhythm may change into measured time when taken over by the congregation, while conversely, the *ḥazzan* may execute a simple pattern in elaborate coloraturas.

Many Ashkenazi communities provide the cantor with two assistants (known variously as *mezammerim, somekhim,* or *maftirim*) who flank him at the prayer desk and take over at certain points of the liturgy. At one time Ashkenazi *ḥazzanim* did likewise, with a view to the enrichment of their singing. According to convention, one of these assistants (or *meshorerim*) had to be a boy-descant, known as the singer, and the other an adult, known as the bass. It is not known when this custom was introduced; a picture in the so-called *Leipzig Maḥzor* of the 14th century may be regarded as the earliest representation of such a trio. The heyday of *ḥazzanut* with accompanying *meshorerim* was the 17th and 18th centuries, and it is only from the sources of this late period that its nature can be inferred. It appears that the assistants improvised an accompaniment of hummed chords, drones, and short figures, while in addition the singer intoned thirds and sixths, that is, tones harmonizing with the basic melody sung by the *ḥazzan.* In addition, both singer and bass had their solo parts—most often extended coloraturas to be performed while the cantor paused. Famous cantors traveled, with the *meshorerim* as part of their household, from one large center to another as guest prayer-leaders, while the less famed undertook such wanderings in search of a hoped-for permanent post. In the late baroque period, if not earlier, the traditional number of two assistants was supplemented by performers of distinctive tasks, including the *fistel* singer (falsetto), and specialists in the imitation of musical instruments, such as the *sayt-bass, fagot-bass,* and *fleyt-singer,* for strings, bassoon and flute respectively.

The use of musical instruments proper is attested in medieval Baghdad by the traveler Pethahiah of Regensburg, who visited there between 1175 and 1190. However, this was a rare exception and restricted to the half-holidays, since the ban on instrumental music in commemoration of the Destruction remained in force. It was only under the influence of later mystical movements, with their emphasis on joyful worship, that instruments were played in some 17th-century Ashkenazi synagogues before the entry of the Sabbath as a token of the joy of the day of rest. In general, however, vocal performances remained the basic characteristic of synagogue music. An incessant struggle took place in this field between the traditional claims of the older singing styles and the musical expression of spiritual tendencies that arose during the Middle Ages. This interplay of forces preserved Jewish liturgical music from the petrifaction typical of many other traditions of religious chant.

Later Ḥazzanut. In the course of the Middle Ages the status of *ḥazzanim* rose, and they enjoyed increasing salaries, longer tenure of office, and growing exemptions from communal taxation. The post of *ḥazzan,* already ancient then, has undergone very little change since that time, except that in Northern Europe it was occupied by eminent rabbis, such as the Maharil in medieval Mainz.

Indeed, prominent scholars had always lent their ideological support to the centrality in prayer which music enjoys. That this is often the case in practice—on a collective, congregational level—may be averred by anyone who has a memory of a traditional synagogue. Indeed, Israel Zangwill could have been describing communities in any continent when he depicted the atmosphere created by the synagogal melodies beloved of "the sons of the covenant," the members of an intimate conventicle in London's East End at the beginning of the century. "Their religious consciousness was largely a musical box: the thrill of the ram's horn, the cadenza of a psalmic phrase, the jubilance of a festival "Amen" and the sobriety of a workaday "Amen," the Passover melodies and the Pentecost, the minor keys of Atonement and the hilarious rhapsodies of Rejoicing, the plain chant of the Law and the more ornate intonation of the Prophets—all this was known and loved, and was far more important than the meaning of it all . . ."

On the individual, personal level, the role of music in prayer finds its classic expression in the 12th-century spiritual manual

entitled *Sefer Ḥasidim,* where a celebrated ascetic pietist counsels as follows: "When you pray, search for a melody which you find pleasant; you will then be able to concentrate, and your heart will respond to the words you utter."

On a mystical level, the Ḥasidim of the past two centuries have believed that the human heart has longings for God too deep to be expressed in words and for which melody is the only vehicle. Thus, for example, Rabbi Dov Baer of Lubavitch (1773–1827) develops the kabbalistic idea that the soul of Moses (the "Faithful Shepherd") embraced all the souls of his people, and since no two souls are exactly alike each person has his own particular melody by which he is drawn to the divine. Rabbi Dov Baer writes: "What is the nature of melody? There is a well-known saying that the Faithful Shepherd used to sing every kind of melody in his prayer. For his soul comprised the six hundred thousand souls of Israel, and only by means of song can each sould ascend to the root of the source whence she was hewn."

If this spiritual subjectivity is true of music in prayer in general, it is doubly self-evident in the case of East European *ḥazzanut*. For one of the ironclad rules of his profession grants the *ḥazzan* flexibility to sing just as the spirit moves him. Expression is the element which counts. As soon as the *ḥazzan*'s voice is heard, the prayer of the congregation subsides, and the mind completely identifies itself with the voice. Unlike the self-imposed restraint of the Western cantor, the aim is to generate an upsurge of religious feelings (*hit'orerut* in Hebrew) and a strong and immediate response. A striking instance of this emotional power is to be found in the chronicle of martyrdom entitled *Yeven Meẓulah,* in which the contemporary social historian Nathan Hannover tells of the surrender of four communities to the Tatars in 1648. When the *ḥazzan* Hirsch of Zywotow chanted the memorial prayer *El Male Raḥamim,* the whole congregation burst forth in tears, and even the compassion of the rough captors was stirred, until they released the Jews.

The impressive capacities of the singing of *ḥazzanut*—an original and self-sufficient style of music—are not easily described in precise technical terms. As has been said, the

Two famous cantors. A portrait of Jehiel Michael, the *ḥazzan* of the Ashkenazi community in Amsterdam in 1700, and a photograph of perhaps the most famous *ḥazzan* of all time, Josef (affectionately known as Yossele) Rosenblatt (1882–1933). The latter flourished in the Golden Age of *ḥazzanut*, between the two World Wars, and made many recordings. His compositions are still widely used in synagogue music and many cantors have copied his style.

expressive intention is overwhelming: it dissolves the form of the underlying poetic text past recognition; single words may be repeated over and over, in spite of halakhic prohibition; emotional exclamations intermingle; and long coloraturas expand certain syllables, in particular towering above the penultima at the end of compositions. These traits may appear exaggerated to a Western taste accustomed to classicist restraint, but they are capable of the most suggestive presentation of sentiments, mainly in the pitiful and lachrymose mood (the expression of joy being channeled mostly through imitations of foreign song). The *ḥazzan*'s voice plays on a variety of sound colors, complemented by a high falsetto, and favors techniques such as the gliding passage from tone to tone, slowly entering trills, and other characteristics of an advanced vocal culture.

With a musical diet as rich as this, East European Jewry—until the 19th century—remained immune to the advance of the times and kept its ears shut before art music, which had by then become available to the middle classes throughout Europe. Even outstanding musical talents could find an outlet only in synagogue song or, alternatively, in popular music making and entertaining. They thus had no option but to contribute their sometimes considerable gifts to the musical life of the community, which was deeply concerned with all matters of music. Within that responsive musical microcosm, synagogue song represented the highest level of art; the interest and knowledgeability of the public was focused on the solo performance of the *ḥazzan* and subjected it to both relentless criticism and unconditional adulation.

This was the East European community's spectator sport *par excellence;* and the celebrated *ḥazzan,* Pinchas Minkowski, recalling a professional visit to Odessa, perpetuated one of its high moments for posterity in his *Recollections:* "The Odessa community was not an ordinary one, but was split in two factions, accusers and defenders . . . When I had sung ancient melodies known to every listener, a dispute arose on the spot . . . as to whether my song was in the style of [Pitshe] Abrass or of Bachman, and people of venerable age also conjured Zalel up from his grave in Ereẓ Israel in order to pitch my singing against Zalel's . . ."

Like all good spectator sportsmen of whatever generation, these worshipers showed their affection for their folk-heroes by dubbing them with nicknames—usually Yiddish diminutives of their Hebrew names: Yossele Rosenblatt, Dovidl Brod, Pitshe Odesser ("the mite from Odessa"), and the like. Pride in one's local *ḥazzan* takes many forms. Even today many a surreptitious clockwatcher, after having been pewbound for hours at the mercy of a longwinded virtuoso, may be heard on a Rosh Ha-Shanah afternoon proudly telling a worshiper from a rival synagogue that *his* service was so melodious that it lasted until 2.30 p.m.

Ironically, the growing popularity of the *ḥazzan* made him in the course of time the most controversial communal official. His dual role of religious representative and artistic performer inevitably gave rise to tensions, which persist in modern times. Leading rabbis never tired of castigating *ḥazzanim* for the needless repetition of words and for extending their chanting of the prayers with the sole purpose of displaying the beauty of their voices. At the same time, many communities gave priority to vocal quality and musical skill over the traditional requirements of learning and piety. It once happened that an irate congregant took to task the saintly *rebbe* of Gur for appointing as *sheliaḥ ẓibbur* an individual with a singularly cacophonous voice. Retorted the *ẓaddik*: "The Code of Jewish Law prescribes that a *ḥazzan* should be characterized by scholarship, piety, virtue, sincerity—and a pleasant voice. Now, my friend, is it fair to expect one man to be blessed with *all* the necessary virtues?

THE WINDS OF CHANGE. Inexorably, the emancipation of European Jewry in the 19th century changed the style and content of synagogue music. Traditional melodies which had hitherto been transmitted, like some hallowed incantation, by word of mouth only, were now for the first time set down in musical notation, with prescribed harmonies to be sung by *ḥazzan* and choir. Daringly new melodies were composed, which betrayed the influence of contemporary European trends and techniques, notably those of Rossini. The pioneer in this field was Solomon Sulzer, chief *ḥazzan* in Vienna from 1825 to 1890, whose singing won the admiration of Schubert and Liszt. Sulzer was closely followed by Samuel Naumbourg of Paris, Louis Lewandowski of Berlin, Hirsch Weintraub of Koenigsberg, Moritz Deutsch of Breslau, Abraham Baer of Goteborg, Sweden, and many others.

The ḥasidic movement, where the *rebbe* led the congregation in informal prayer, remained uninfluenced by this development. Indeed, the joyful tunes of the Ḥasidim gradually became popular with many non-ḥasidic Orthodox communities.

Also apart from this development was the Reform movement, but for different reasons. In the first place, the introduction of the organ and of mixed choirs radically changed cantorial music. Hebrew and German prayer texts were chanted to German chorale tunes, which replaced the traditional melodies. Furthermore, Isaac M. Wise, architect of American Jewish Reform, substituted the plain reading of the liturgy for the office of *ḥazzan*. Only a few Reform congregations retained *ḥazzanim* (of whom Alois Kaiser was one), who endeavored to develop a distinctive tradition of American synagogue music. In reaction to these changes, classical reform in the United States was modified at the turn of the century under the dual impact of the Zionist movement and East European immigration. A demand was made that the traditional forms of worship be restored. In line with this trend, two *ḥazzanim* who became professors, the composer A. W. Binder at the Jewish Institute of Religion and the celebrated musicologist A. Z. Idelsohn at the Hebrew Union College, reintroduced traditional liturgy and music into Reform rabbinical studies.

The period from the end of the 19th century until World War II has been described as the Era of Golden *Ḥazzanut*. Cantorial music had a singular appeal to the Jewish masses, who would fill the synagogues to overflowing in order to hear an outstanding *ḥazzan*. Improved communications enabled leading *ḥazzanim* to tour Jewish communities on a far greater scale than previously, thereby increasing their reputations, sometimes to legendary proportions. Indeed, in the popular estimation they were equated with the great operatic tenors of the time, whose style they grew to imitate. Non-Jews too were attracted to the synagogues to hear famous *ḥazzanim*, and Gershon Sirota was invited annually to sing for the czar.

The *hazzan* (whose name was Kantor) and his choir from the town of Kolo, in central Poland. The town was occupied by the Germans on September 15, 1939 and the 5,000 strong Jewish community subsequently destroyed. This photograph was taken before World War II.

Following the mass emigration of Jews from Eastern Europe to the United States during this period, great *hazzanim* like Sirota, Josef Rosenblatt, Mordecai Herschman and Zavel Kwartin made concert tours in America, where all of them, except Sirota, remained. There they were able to command prodigious salaries and fees for concerts and High Holy Day services.

A major factor in building up the reputations and perpetuating the fame of the great *hazzanim* was the development of sound recordings, beginning with the first cantorial disk made by Sirota in 1903. Furthermore, lesser *hazzanim* adopted the style and melodies of the great cantors which they learnt from the records, and the singing of famous musical compositions became a leading attraction of synagogue services. In the post-war period prominent *hazzanim* included Moshe Koussevitzky and his brothers Jacob, Simchah and David, Leib Glanz, Israel Alter, Moshe Ganchoff, Pierre Pinchik, Leibele Waldman, Shalom Katz and, in the younger generation, Moshe Stern. Some, such as Richard Tucker and Jan Peerce, also achieved international fame as operatic tenors, but retained their contact with the synagogue through recordings and High Holyday and Passover services.

In Israel the development of *hazzanut* has not kept pace with the United States. However, the regular radio programs devoted to both Ashkenazi and Sephardi *hazzanut* have a large following. Request programs are popular, as too are live concerts featuring ethnic and regional traditions of *hazzanut*. Producers of television programs with a religious slant frequently employ *hazzanut*, whether for straightforward singing, or for the evocation of a particular mood. Many of the world's leading *hazzanim* have sung in Israel, and a cantorial conference was held there in 1968. *Hazzanim* serve in the chaplaincy corps of the Israel army, but only the large towns employ *hazzanim* on a regular basis. Moreover, a number of successful soloists have been attracted to the United States, Great Britain and South Africa, where the financial rewards are much greater.

Most major Jewish communities in the world now have professional associations of *hazzanim* and several bulletins and journals are regularly published. An important factor in assuring the future development of *hazzanut* is the growth of cantorial training schools, in the U.S. (at Yeshiva University, the Jewish Theological Seminary, and the Hebrew Union College), in Great Britain (at Jews' College), and in Israel (at the Selah Seminary in Tel Aviv, and elsewhere).

Synagogal Choirs. It was following a choral and instrumental overture that Solomon pronounced his memorable prayer of dedication on the completion of the First Temple, "when the trumpeters and singers were as one, to make one sound to be heard in praising and thanking the Lord, and when they lifted up their voice with the trumpets and cymbals and instruments of music, and praised the Lord."

The music which a thousand years later accompanied public worship, during the latter days of the Second Temple, early in the Common Era, is described in the Talmud. This information is presumably valid for earlier times as well. The chorus consisted of a minimum of 12 adult singers, though it could be enlarged, and the number of musicians equaled that of the singers. The choristers passed through a period of training from the age of 25 to 30 and usually performed their Temple service between the ages of 30 and 50. Though young Levites often joined the choir to "add sweetness to the sound," they were not permitted to stand on the same platform as the adult Levites. Women were excluded from the Temple service. They took a leading part in secular music, however. The question as to the comparative importance of the vocal and instrumental part of the service was discussed by the rabbis in the Talmud. During the period of the Second Temple the importance of the instrumental part of the service, always secondary, declined further. There was a large number of singers in contrast to a smaller number of instrumentalists, and non-Levites were permitted to play, though singing in the Temple remained the privilege of the Levites.

Choral singing is again mentioned a century later, during the period of the Babylonian exile. The second-century mishnaic scholar, Nathan ha-Bavli, in his vivid description of the induction of the exilarch, relates that the Sabbath service was conducted throughout by a *hazzan* and a male choir consisting of young men with sweet voices, who chanted verses responsively. In the view of most authorities, the post-Destruction rabbinic

In Israel it is customary to celebrate the Simḥat Torah with Torah processions also on the night following the festival. This picture, taken in 1969, shows Jews of Bukharan origin celebrating the *hakkafot* in informal street dancing. The detail from the early 15th-century Italian *Schocken Haggadah* illustrates the biblical verse (Exodus 15:20): "And Miriam the prophetess, the sister of Aaron, took a timbrel in her hand, and all the women went out after her with timbrels and with dances."

ban on music did not apply to music in the synagogue, except for the prohibition of instrumental music. Hai Gaon, the gaon of Pumbedita who died in 1038, states specifically that the ban referred only to Arabian love songs, while it is possible to infer that Maimonides, several generations later, permitted a choir at all religious feasts.

The modern synagogue choir, the invention of a much later period, owes its origin to the spirit of the Italian Renaissance. Leone Modena at the beginning of the 17th century founded the first artistic choir in synagogal history, a choir of six to eight voices in the Ferrara synagogue, which he conducted "according to the relation of voices to each other, based on that science." The innovation met with strong opposition but was upheld after a rabbinical assembly had approved it. The outstanding Jewish choral composer of the period was Salamone Rossi, who attempted far-reaching reforms in synagogal music, setting the Psalms and prayers for chorus and solos.

The choir, which has in modern times become an integral part of many synagogues, Orthodox, Conservative, and Reform, has nevertheless been the subject of much controversy. The ḥasidic movement with its belief in music as a form of communion with God avoided an organized choir, preferring the spontaneous outpouring of congregational singing. Reform Judaism, on the other hand, not only developed choral music but introduced female and even gentile singers into the chorus, with instrumental accompaniment usually provided by an organ. To these latter developments, Orthodoxy was vehemently opposed. Indeed, when first introduced, the "Chorshul"—the Orthodox synagogue with a male choir and no instrumental accompaniment—was also opposed and even derided in certain Orthodox circles. Undaunted, the urbanized taste of the newly emancipated "Jewish European" disposed of the traditional homely trio consisting of the cantor and his two assistant singers. The improvised accompaniment of the latter was to be replaced by harmonies of regular structure, and their solo coloraturas were to be clipped as eccentricities of an outmoded taste. Likewise, the boisterous chorus of the entire congregation, a moving experience with ancient roots, was to be silenced, and substituted by well-rehearsed part singing. The polished choral scores composed by Sulzer for the Vienna Seitenstettengassen Synagoge were soon in brisk demand, and during the 1830s and 1840s synagogue choirs were founded in Prague, Copenhagen, Breslau, Berlin, Dresden, London, and New York. Their growing popularity was due in no small part to the work of a number of cantors, musicians and choirmasters who endeavored to find a synthesis between hoary tradition and modern musical developments.

One of the classic subjects of controversy in liturgical matters between advocates of Orthodoxy and advocates of Reform was the question of gentile singers and female voices (Jewish or non-Jewish) in a synagogue choir. The question of gentile singers in a Jewish prayer service is not debated in traditional rabbinic literature; the question never arose. The responsa literature does deal with the question of inviting Christian musicians to entertain in a synagogue at a wedding, for making music in honor of bride and groom was regarded as a *mitzvah*. Many rabbinic authorities permit the entertainment of bride and groom by Christian musicians even on the Sabbath, although there are opposing opinions. Such special occasions of entertainment apart, no Orthodox rabbinic authority ever consented to gentile choir singers in a synagogue as part of the prayer service. Reform congregations, however, do not object to gentile choir members in the synagogue, and argue that the gentile singers do not conduct the service and are in no sense the "representatives of the congregation" (*sheliaḥ ẓibbur*) but merely help to beautify the service with their music. They argue further that the Talmud forbids Jews to respond "Amen" after hearing only part of a benediction recited by a Samaritan or gentile in case he did not recite the proper formula, but otherwise there is no objection to responding "Amen" after a valid blessing uttered by a gentile.

As to the question of female choristers, the talmudic warning against listening to a woman singing because it might lead to unchaste thoughts was understood by the rabbinic scholars to include the prohibition of female voices in a synagogue choir. In their responsa on this subject, the authorities consulted were accustomed to appeal to biblical texts which were thought to provide authoritative precedents for one contention or the

other. One favorite text concerned Miriam, who after the Crossing of the Red Sea led the womenfolk in a song of thanksgiving, while another involved Deborah who, following an Israelite victory over the Canaanites, led the people in an eloquent paean of divine praise.

The Organ. Although there are obscure late talmudic traditions identifying the *magrefeh,* an implement used in the Temple service, with the organ, very little is known about the use of the organ in the synagogue before its introduction by Reform Judaism in the 19th century. Giulio Morosini (also known as Samuel Nahmias, a pupil of Leone Modena who converted to Christianity) tells in his *Via della Fede* of the performance of the Jewish Academy of Music in the Spanish synagogue of Venice, at about 1628. On one occasion (the festival of Simḥat Torah) there was an organ among the instruments used, but the Venetian rabbis disapproved of it because of its close association with Christian worship. Another Italian source of the 17th century indicates however that the organ was not frowned upon by some Italian rabbis of this period. One such case is Abraham Joseph Solomon Graziano, the rabbi of Modena, who died in 1684, and whose leniency in certain matters aroused the opposition of his contemporaries. In glosses on the Shulḥan Arukh, he wrote: "... Jewish musicians should not be prevented from playing on the organ [to accompany] songs and praises performed [in honor of] God ..." He went on to suggest that the argument of *ḥukkot ha-goyim* ("customs of the gentiles") was not relevant: no competent rabbinic authority would forbid organ playing; only ignorant people would oppose it.

The existence of a synagogue organ in Prague in the late 17th and 18th centuries is indicated by several writers of the period. Its use seems to have been linked mainly with the musical "inauguration of the Sabbath," though a broadsheet published in 1716 gives evidence of other functions, revealing too the name of the Jewish builder of the "new organ" employed during the celebrations of the Jewish community of Prague in honor of the birth of Prince Leopold, son of the German emperor, Charles IV.

As with the trained choir, the organ was introduced by Reform Judaism into the synagogue services as part of its stress on the aesthetic aspects of Jewish worship. The controversies surrounding the use of the organ began when Israel Jacobson installed an organ in the temple he opened for his boys' school in Seesen in 1810. He also employed the organ in the services which were held in private homes in Berlin from the year 1815. The Hamburg Temple, which opened in 1818, likewise held services with organ accompaniment. From that time, this became the distinguishing feature of all Reform congregations. Of all the liturgical reforms introduced in the 19th century, none has proved to be as divisive as the introduction of the organ. The installation of an organ in a synagogue was usually followed by an exodus of the more traditionalist members, who organized services for themselves without organ accompaniment. As the shibboleth of Reform, the organ figured primarily in Germany and in America. French and Italian synagogues, not otherwise departing from traditional usage, introduced the organ without giving rise to controversy. For midweek wedding ceremonies, the organ is played in some modern Orthodox synagogues. Many American Conservative synagogues also play it on the Sabbath.

To justify their innovation, the Reformers published a collection of responsa, entitled *Nogah ha-Ẓedek* ("The Splendor of Justice") in 1818. The Orthodox replied in 1819 with a

responsa collection of their own: *Elleh Divrei ha-Berit* ("These are the Words of the Covenant"). Since then, a vast literature has accumulated around the subject, consisting mainly of restatements and reformulations of the arguments used in 1818 and 1819. Basically, three halakhic objections have been raised. Firstly, playing the organ on the Sabbath, even by a non-Jew, is prohibited "work"—if not biblically forbidden, at least falling into the rabbinic category of *shevut,* that is, occupations forbidden on Sabbaths and festivals. Secondly, as a sign of mourning for the destruction of the Temple, instrumental music in general is prohibited. Finally, the organ is so closely associated with worship in the Christian churches that it would be a case of the prohibited "imitation of gentile customs" (*ḥukkot ha-goyim*) to play it in the synagogue.

In reply, the Reform justification has taken the following form: In the first place, the Shulḥan Arukh permits the playing of music by a non-Jew on the Sabbath for the purpose of entertaining a wedding party. What is permitted for a wedding party, it is argued, should be permitted all the more for the enhancement of worship. Just as the rules of *shevut* did not apply to the Temple, so it is further contended, they should not apply to the synagogues which have taken its place. Secondly, the prohibition of music as a sign of mourning for the destruction of Jerusalem includes—in its original formulation—vocal no less than instrumental music. Yet tradition has obviously accepted vocal music for religious purposes. Reform is thus merely extending the compromise to instrumental music as well. Besides, instrumental music was used in some pre-modern synagogues, although not on the Sabbath; a synagogue in Prague even had an organ. As to the last objection, the Reformers pointed out that the organ is not universal in Christian worship. Since there can be Christian worship without an organ, it follows that the instrument is by no means "essential" to the worship. A certain rabbinic responsum had made a distinction between melodies which are an integral part of Christian worship and those which are not. The Reformers extended that distinction to musical instruments as well. In addition, they claimed that instrumental music in the church itself is a borrowing from the Temple, in which there was an implement called the *magrefah,* held by some to be an organ-like instrument.

While the use of the organ, particularly when played by non-Jewish musicians, has frequently led to the introduction of melodies alien to traditional Jewish worship, it has likewise led both to the stimulation of modern synagogue music and to a revival of old Jewish modes. One of its enthusiastic proponents, the philosopher Hermann Heymann Steinthal, wrote: "The organ has restored to us the old *ḥazzanut*. It will preserve it, and transmit it to our children." But Leopold Zunz, a friend of the organ, cautioned: "Unity is the sweetest harmony. It is, therefore, better to refrain from the use of the organ . . ., if that should be the sole cause for a serious split in the congregation."

Dance. Dancing is familiar as an expression of religious ecstasy from the biblical account of David's exultation when he brought the Ark of the Covenant from the provinces to Jerusalem. "And it was so, as the Ark of the Lord came into the city of David, that Michal the daughter of Saul looked out at the window,

Dance, for the Ḥasidim, is a form of worship. Tully Filmus' charcoal drawings capture the spirit of ecstasy which, apparently, does not suffer because of the separation of the sexes.

and saw king David leaping and dancing before the Lord, and she despised him in her heart." More specifically related to the notion of prayer are the exhortations in the Book of Psalms: "Praise God's name in the dance," and "Praise Him with timbrels and dance."

The classic instance of the dance in a religious context in Temple days has been preserved by the account given in the Mishnah of the celebration, during the festival of Sukkot, of the water-drawing festivities: "Whoever has not witnessed the rejoicing of the festival of the water-drawing has never seen joy. Men of piety and good deeds danced with torches in their hands, singing songs of joy and of praise, and the Levites made music with lyre and harp and cymbals and trumpets and countless other instruments."

From earliest times it was customary to welcome the Sabbath on Friday before sunset with processions and dancing. A modern revival of this custom may be seen by visitors to the Western Wall on any Friday at dusk. A hundred exuberant youths from a nearby yeshivah in the Jewish Quarter of the Old City, arranged in a phalanx, and with their rabbis in the vanguard, dance their way downhill from the Quarter to the Wall, their arms linked and singing lustily. In the 16th century, the kabbalists of the town of Safed used to likewise go out over the Galilean hills to welcome the mystic Queen Sabbath with the singing of Psalms and dancing. And on Saturday night they danced a farewell to the departing Queen. In the Yemenite Jewish communities, the Sabbath welcoming dances were performed on tiptoe, with tremulous movements of ankle and knee joints, the dancers working themselves up to religious ecstasy.

Many Oriental communities preserve dance forms that are peculiar to particular religious occasions, such as the circumcision ceremony. Perhaps the most exotic of all was that discovered by Benjamin II, a 19th-century explorer, in Alkush, in the mountains of Kurdistan, where pilgrims to this region in northern Iraq celebrated Shavuot at the tomb of the prophet Nahum. They first joined in the reading of the Book of Nahum and circled the shrine singing while women danced around the catafalque. Next morning, the men went to the summit of a nearby hill, symbolizing Mt. Sinai, where they read excerpts from the Torah, and then descended in warlike procession, clashing their weapons, thus simulating the great combat which will herald the coming of the Messiah. The women met the men with dancing and singing to the accompaniment of tambourines.

With the rise of Ḥasidism in Eastern Europe in the 18th century, dance assumed great importance for the Jewish masses. Israel Ba'al Shem Tov, the founder of Ḥasidism, used to dance to attain religious enthusiasm (*hitlahavut*) and communion with God (*devekut*). He taught his followers that "the dances of the Jew before his Creator are prayers," and quoted the Psalmist, "All my bones shall say: 'Lord, who is like unto Thee?'" Ḥasidic dance assumed the form of the circle, symbolic of the ḥasidic philosophy that "everyone is equal, each one being a link in the chain, the circle having no front or rear, no beginning or ending." The Ḥasidim would start their dancing in slow tempo, and as the music became faster they held arms upward and leapt in the air in an effort to reach ecstasy. The accompanying melodies were composed to brief texts from either the Bible or the Talmud. Naḥman of Bratslav, great-grandson of the Ba'al Shem Tov, believed that to dance in prayer was a sacred command, and he composed a prayer which he recited before dancing. He and certain other ḥasidic rabbis called for dancing on all festive occasions and even on the solemn days of the Ninth of Av, Rosh Ha-Shanah, and the Day of Atonement. Indeed, Naḥman requested his disciples to observe the anniversary of his death by studying a chapter of the Mishnah and dancing at his grave. The Bratslav Ḥasidim faithfully fulfilled his wish for generations at the cemetery in Uman in the Ukraine.

During the celebrations on Simḥat Torah among Ḥasidim, the usual processions with the scrolls would reach a climax in the *rebbe*'s own dance. Wrapped in a *tallit,* and with a Sefer Torah held high in his hands, the rabbi danced with spiritual ecstasy as the Ḥasidim sang and clapped hands in a circle around him. Ḥasidic dancing has influenced the celebrations at Jewish festivals generally, and has served as the basis and inspiration of choreography on Jewish themes in ballet.

IV Accessories of Prayer

covering the head
the tallit
tefillin
the sefer torah
the ark
the bimah

The elaborate title page of a prayerbook compiled by Jehiel Michal ben Abraham Epstein (died 1706). The *siddur*, which included a Yiddish translation as well as the laws and customs of prayer, was very popular and went through many printings. This one was printed in Offenbach, Germany, in 1791 but states proudly that it is like the "Amsterdam edition." Amsterdam was recognized for the outstanding quality of its printing.

Though it is one of the duties of the heart, even prayer resembles the vast majority of the more practical precepts in that it finds part of its expression in physical appurtenances. Thus, for example, the *halakhah* calls for the wearing of the *tallit* and the *tefillin* during certain prayer services. And let it not be thought that their corporeality is merely incidental to their spiritual function. Indeed, the Kabbalah sees in their use a demonstration of how the physical objects of the created universe—things as humdrum, as mundane, as seemingly godless as wool and leather—can be ennobled by the intention of the user. When a man uses these worldly objects reverently in his performance of the *mitzvot,* he reveals the divine spark so subtly concealed in them, and thus sublimates and elevates them. And in this way the physical objects which house the sparks are affirmed for the purpose for which they were first created.

Among these material objects are the tangible accessories of prayer. Some of these—head-covering, the *tallit,* the *tefillin,* and the *Sefer Torah,* together with its repository, the ark, and the *bimah* at which it is read—collectively form the subject of the present chapter.

COVERING THE HEAD

Jewish tradition requires men to cover the head as a sign of humility before God, and women, as evidence of modesty before men, although the Bible does not explicitly command either men or women to cover the head.

In Ancient Times. According to the description of the priestly garb in the Bible, the high priest wore a miter (*miẓnefet*), and the ordinary priests a hat (*migba'at*). It was generally considered a sign of mourning to completely cover the head and face, and in talmudic times, too, men expressed their sense of grief while mourning by covering their heads, as did Bar Kappara, for example, after the death of Rabbi Judah ha-Nasi. A mourner, a leper, and one on whom a ban had been pronounced, were in fact obliged to muffle their heads and faces, as was anyone who fasted in times of drought. This was considered an expression of awe before the Divine Presence, especially while praying or engaged in the study of mysticism. The headgear of scholars was an indication of their elevated position; some of them claimed that they never walked more than four cubits (about six feet) without a head covering. The custom was, however, restricted to dignified personages; young men doing so were considered presumptuous. Artistic representations, such as ancient Egyptian and Babylonian tablets or the murals of the third-century synagogue at Dura-Europos on the Euphrates, generally depict Israelites (and later Jews) without head covering. On the other hand, some rabbis believed that covering a child's head would ensure his piety in later years.

According to the Talmud, it was optional and a matter of custom for men to cover their heads. Palestinian custom, moreover, did not insist that the head be covered during the priestly benediction. French and Spanish rabbinical authorities during the Middle Ages followed this ruling, and regarded the covering of the head during prayer and the study of the Torah merely as a custom. Some of them prayed with a bare head themselves. Tractate *Soferim,* however, rules that a person who is improperly dressed and has no headgear may not act as the *ḥazzan* or as the reader of the Torah in the synagogue, and may not invoke the priestly benediction upon the congregation. Moreover, the covering of the head, as an expression of the "fear of God" (*yir'at shamayim*), and as a continuation of the practice of the Babylonian scholars, was gradually endorsed by the Ashkenazi rabbis. Even they stated, however, that it was merely a worthy custom, and that there was no injunction against praying with the head uncovered. The opinion of David Halevy of Ostrog (of the 17th century) is an exception. He declared that since Christians generally pray bareheaded, the Jewish prohibition to do so was based on the biblical injunction not to imitate heathen customs (*ḥukkat ha-goy*). In the course of time, traditional Jewry came to equate bareheadedness with unseemly lightmindedness and frivolity (*kallut rosh*) and therefore forbids it.

The Modern Period. The covering of the head has become one of the most hotly debated points of controversy between Reform and Orthodox Jewry. The latter regards the covering of the head, both outside and inside the synagogue, as a sign

These ladies of the ultra-Orthodox Me'ah She'arim quarter of Jerusalem were taking part in a demonstration protesting the conscription of women into the Israel army. Married women are required to cover their heads since the sight of their hair may entice men. Although many Orthodox women wear wigs, in this community the heads are shaved at marriage and the kerchief (known as *tikhel*) is worn. The custom of men covering their heads is of a more symbolic nature. The caps shown here are of the type worn in various Oriental Jewish communities, particularly that of Bukhara.

of allegiance to Jewish tradition, and demands the wearing at least of a skullcap (which in Hebrew is called a *kippah*, and in Yiddish a *yarmulka*). Worship with covered heads is also the accepted rule in Conservative synagogues. In Reform congregations, however, it is optional.

Women. In biblical times, women covered their heads with veils or scarves as a sign of chastity and modesty; the unveiling of a woman's hair, as in the case of a woman suspected of adultery, was considered a humiliation and punishment. In talmudic times, too, women always covered their hair. Some rabbis forbid the recital of any blessing in the presence of a bareheaded woman, and pious women over the centuries took care not to uncover their hair even in the privacy of their home. Although today women in certain Orthodox circles cover their hair all the time, it remains the general practice, including that of some Reform congregations, for women to cover their hair in synagogue. Accordingly, just as men visiting the Western Wall today are offered a skullcap, women as they approach are offered a headscarf.

THE TALLIT

Apart from the covering of the head, there are few restrictions on the garb of the worshiper, provided he is decently dressed. There are times, however, when the law prescribes the wearing of a *tallit*, the large rectangular prayer shawl whose corners bear the *ẓiẓit*, or fringes, as laid down in the Bible. "The Lord spoke to Moses as follows: Speak to the Israelite people and instruct them to make for themselves fringes on the corners of their garments throughout the ages; let them attach a cord of blue to the fringe at each corner. That shall be your fringe; look at it and recall all the commandments of the Lord and observe them, so that you do not follow your heart and eyes in your lustful urge. Thus you shall be reminded to observe all My commandments and to be holy to your God."

The Ẓiẓit. These *ẓiẓit* are tassels, or fringes, made of four white threads which are passed through small holes near the corners of the garment, and entwined and knotted in a particular way, each detail of their braiding having a symbolic connotation. The single colored thread at each corner was in ancient times processed with *tekhelet*, the dye extracted from a rare species of sea or land snail. Interestingly, dyed *ẓiẓit* were recently found in the Dead Sea Caves among the personal belongings of Bar Kokhba's freedom fighters of the second century. Laboratory tests, however, have proved almost beyond doubt that these were in fact colored with the dye extracted from the Indian indigo plant, which was introduced into Ereẓ Israel in Mishnaic times as a cheaper substitute—or counterfeit—for the costly, genuine *tekhelet* dye. The use of the blue thread

In Lazar Krestin's "In the Synagogue," the two boys are sharing one prayerbook. This painter (1868–1938) produced many scenes of Eastern European Jewish life. There it was customary for persons of substance to adorn their *tallitot* with silver neckpieces. In the one shown here—from 18th-century Poland—each square is inscribed with a word; together they make up a kabbalistic prayer to be recited before putting on the *tallit*, and the benediction. In Abraham Goldberg's painting, the lines of the *tallit* are essential for the prayerful attitude.

lapsed in post-Talmudic times as the secret of the dyeing process fell into oblivion.

The *tallit* which bears these tassels is usually white, and its minimum size is that which would suffice to clothe a toddler. It is made of wool, cotton or silk, though some authorities object to the use of the latter. Certain observant Jews prefer *tallitot* made of coarse bleached lamb's wool. Curiously, there are some Jews, emigrants from Russia, who after decades still treasure a barely-bleached coarse homespun *tallit*, which they had woven on a homemade undergound loom—a relic of the spiritual resistance movement which outlived the Stalinist regime.

In remembrance of the blue thread of the *ẓiẓit*, some *tallitot* have several blue stripes woven into the white material. Until recently, however, they had only black stripes, running in one direction, and arranged according to one of a number of traditional patterns. Frequently that part of the *tallit* which is worn around the neck and on the shoulders has a special collar of cloth sewn with silver threads (called an *atarah*, Hebrew for diadem), to mark the upper edge of the prayer shawl. Sometimes the benediction which is recited when putting on the *tallit* is woven in white over the entire area of the cloth.

Wearing the Tallit. The *tallit* is worn by males during the morning prayers (except on the Ninth of Av when, as a sign of mourning, it is not worn until the afternoon service), as well as during all the services of the Day of Atonement. In some rites, the *ḥazzan* wears the *tallit* during the afternoon and evening services as well, as does the Torah reader during the *Minḥah* prayer on fast days. The age of first donning the *tallit* differs in the various communities. In the Ashkenazi ritual, small children under bar mitzvah age dress in *tallitot* made according to their size, in the Polish-Sephardi ritual only married men wear them, while in most Oriental rites unmarried men also wear *tallitot*. In some communities it is usual for the bridegroom to wear a *tallit* during the *ḥuppah* ceremony.

It is customary to bury male Jews in the *tallit* which they wore in their lifetime. However, as an act of reverence for the dead, who are no longer able to perform the *mitzvot*, the fringes are removed or torn before the burial.

In Reform synagogues, the *tallit* is part of the synagogue vestments of the rabbi and the cantor. For male congregants, the wearing of a small prayer shawl, resembling a scarf and worn around the neck, is optional. Those called to the reading from the Torah, however, always don a *tallit*.

Before putting on the prayer shawl the following benediction is said: "Blessed art Thou, O Lord, our God, King of the Universe, Who hast sanctified us by Thy commandments, and hast commanded us to wrap ourselves in the fringed garment." The head is first covered with it and the four corners of the *tallit* are thrown over the left shoulder (a movement called *atifat Yishme'elim*, "after the manner of the Arabs"). After a short pause, the four corners are allowed to fall back into their original position: two are suspended on each side. On weekdays the *tallit* is donned before the *tefillin* (which are not worn on certain days), taking precedence because of its greater regularity. Among strictly observant Jews, it is the custom in certain countries to put on *tallit* and *tefillin* at home and then to walk to the synagogue, "enveloped by the *tallit* and crowned by the *tefillin*." They also pray with the *tallit* covering the head; to be enfolded by the *tallit* is as if to be encompassed by the sanctity of the commandments of the Torah, denoting a symbolic subjection to the Divine Will. Generally, though, people pray with the upper portion of the *tallit* resting on their shoulders only, the remainder hanging loose over the

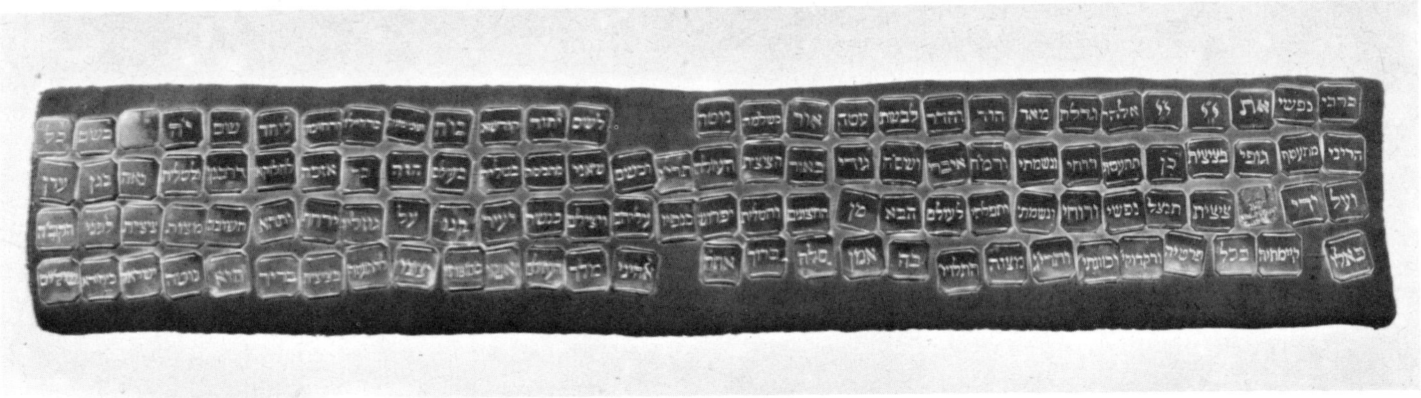

back. The *kohanim,* however, completely cover their heads with the *tallit* during their recital in the synagogue of the Priestly Blessing. In most rites it is customary in the morning service to touch the eyes with the fringes and to kiss them three times during the recital of the last paragraph of the *Shema* which speaks of the commandment of *ẓiẓit.*

Since the ordinary *tallit* is worn only at prayer services, strictly observant Jews wear a *tallit katan,* or small *tallit,* under their upper garment the whole day, so as constantly to fulfill the biblical commandment of *ẓiẓit.* A benediction is recited when putting on the *tallit katan.*

TEFILLIN

The most distinguishing feature of the weekday morning service is the wearing of the *tefillin.* These are two small black leather boxes containing tiny parchment scrolls inscribed with certain scriptural passages, and bound by black leather straps on the left arm and on the head. The *tefillin* are worn in observance of the biblical injunction that the Jew bind "these words"—that is, the words of the Torah—"for a sign upon thy hand and a frontlet between thine eyes." This commandment appears in four almost identical passages in the Torah, none of which mentions the actual term *tefillin.* Interestingly, though, the singular form of the word, *tefillah,* not only refers to either of the two boxes, but also means prayer.

Sources. Of all the commentators on the Bible only the 12th-century exegete Samuel ben Meir takes this command as a figurative one. In his commentary on Exodus 13:9 he says: "According to the essence of its literal meaning it means that it shall ever be as a memorial as though it were written upon thy hand, as in the verse: 'Set me as a seal upon thy heart, as a seal upon thine arm.'" Abraham ibn Ezra considers the same explanation, only to reject it. Apart from this it was accepted that the verse was to be taken literally, and that the words of the Scripture had to be bound on the hand and placed between the eyes, which in practice meant directly above the middle of the forehead. The portions selected for the fulfillment of this commandment were the four passages mentioned above.

The rabbis of the Talmud observed that apart from these verses there is no explicit biblical reference to this ceremony, nor to the manner in which it was to be practiced. Indeed, they regarded it as the classic example of a biblical law, the method of whose observance is wholly derived from the traditions of the Scribes—the rabbinic scholars of antiquity—and immutable. The commandment, that is, promulgated in seminal form in the Written Law, comes to maturation and viability only after undergoing gestation in the womb of the Oral Law.

Beyond the biblical period, the *tefillin* are first mentioned in the Letter of Aristeas, an anonymous literary composition from Jewish Alexandria, dating from about the second century B.C.E.: "and upon our hands, too, He expressly orders the symbols to be fastened." In the first century C.E. Josephus mentions the *tefillin* both of the head and of the hand. The rabbis regarded them as having been instituted at the earliest times, as may be seen from a discussion that has been preserved in the Talmud as to whether the incident of Ezekiel in the Valley of Dry Bones—a passage referring to the sixth century B.C.E.—was a vision or a fact. In the course of its report, the Talmud records the following rejoinder: "Judah ben Bathyra stood up and said, 'I am one of their descendants, and these are the *tefillin* which my grandfather handed down to me from those men.'"

The Name. *Tefillin* are mentioned once in the New Testament under the peculiarly inappropriate name of "phylacteries" (Greek for amulet) and this name has been universally adopted as the English equivalent of the Hebrew word. As has been mentioned, its singular form, *tefillah,* is identical with the word for prayer, but it may be a homonym. Some have interpreted it as derived not from the root of this word, meaning to intercede, but from another root which means to separate or distinguish, indicating that the Jew is thereby distinguished from the non-Jew. Be that as it may, phylacteries—the word of Greek origin suggesting an amulet offering protection against demons—is certainly a misnomer. In its New Testament context it appears as part of a diatribe against the Pharisees: "But all their works they do to be seen of men; they make broad their phylacteries." This charge of the demonstrative nature of the commandment is, in fact, confirmed by the rabbis, who see a reference to the *tefillin* of the head in the verse: "And all the peoples of the earth shall see that the name of the Lord is called upon thee." This verse goes on to say, "and will fear thee;" hence the kabbalists' statement that the fulfillment of the *mitzvah* of *tefillin* affords Israel protection against her enemies.

In History. In ancient times, the *tefillin* were worn only by day. It is even stated that "he who wears *tefillin* at night transgresses a positive commandment," but it is doubtful whether they were generally worn all day. Of Rabban Johanan ben Zakkai and his disciple Eliezer ben Hyrcanus in Ereẓ Israel, as well as of Ada ben Ahavah in Babylon, it is stated that they "never walked four cubits without wearing phylacteries," suggesting that theirs was a practice of special piety. They were worn only by men, though according to one talmudic source, Michal the daughter of Saul wore *tefillin* "and the sages did not protest."

There is evidence of a certain laxity in the fulfillment of this commandment during the talmudic period. The Talmud states that, because the Jews did not risk martyrdom for it during the Hadrianic persecution of the second century C.E., "the precept is still weak with them" and it is certain from the contemporary evidence of the tosafists that the injunction was largely disregarded both in France and in Spain in the 12th and 13th centuries. One tosafist, Jacob Tam, actually quotes the above talmudic passage in extenuation of this laxity, contending that the statement that "a head which does not wear *tefillin* is of a willful sinner of Israel" refers only to one who refuses to wear them out of defiance or contempt. Little more than half a century later Moses of Coucy, who was a French itinerant preacher and likewise a tosafist, states: "In the year 1236 I was in Spain to reprove them . . . and there was a mass repentance; thousands and tens of thousands accepted the duty of donning *tefillin*. . . And so it was in other lands, and afterward my admonitions were accepted in all these places."

The Scriptural Passages. As is stated above, both the *tefillin* of the hand and of the head contain four biblical paragraphs—Exodus 13:1–10 and 11–16; Deuteronomy 6:4–9, and 11:13–

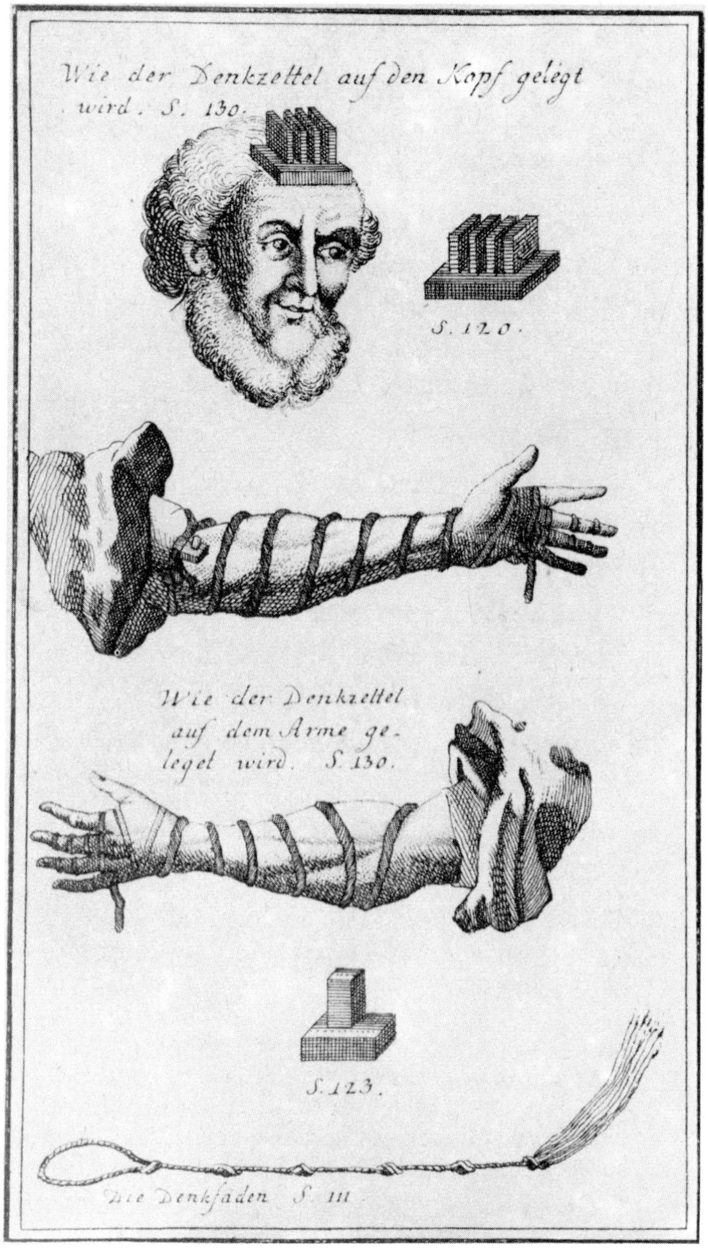

The photographer caught this Jerusalemite putting on the *tefillah shel rosh*. The two engraved silver boxes were used to protect the *tefillin*, particularly in order to prevent the corners becoming rounded. The owner, from 18th-century Poland, used silver boxes to express his love of this commandment. The page illustrating the correct way to put on the *tefillin* is from the first issue of *Der Jude* (Leipzig, 1768), a periodical published by an apostate, Gottfried Selig, with the intention of making the Christian world aware of Jewish rituals and customs. The item at the bottom of the page is the *ẓiẓit*.

21. (The third-listed paragraph is the *Shema*.) In the *tefillah* of the hand they are written on one piece of parchment, which is inserted in the single hollowed cube provided. The *tefillah* of the head, however, is divided into four compartments, and the four paragraphs, each written on a separate slip of parchment and tied, are inserted in them. According to the classical exegete Rashi, they appear in both cases in the order of their occurrence in the Bible; according to his grandson, the above-mentioned tosafist Jacob Tam, the passage from Deuteronomy 11:13–21 in both cases precedes that of Deuteronomy 6:4–9. Rashi's order has been universally accepted, although a small number of individuals of especial piety, in view of possible doubt, substitute "Rabbenu Tam's *tefillin*" for those "of Rashi" for the concluding part of the morning service. In certain isolated Oriental communities, the accepted custom (foreshadowed in the Talmud) is to wear both pairs of *tefillin* simultaneously. The capsules are placed next to each other on the bicep, and in front of one another above the forehead, and the straps are bound around the forearm one over the other.

That the difference of opinion between Rashi and Rabbenu Tam is not a medieval innovation, as had been erroneously thought by some, but the perpetuation of two schools of thought which were followed simultaneously at least as early as the second century C.E., was finally proved in the last decade by a sensational discovery in the Dead Sea Caves. The *tefillin* of both kinds that were there uncovered not only settled this centuries-long argument, but also confirmed dozens of detailed regulations given in the Talmud on the content, form and materials of the *tefillin*. Moreover, they threw new light on numerous passages which, because of the lack of concrete evidence, had for centuries—in fact until 1968—remained obscure.

Apart from the above difference of opinion (which is accompanied by another two or three minute differences) between Rashi and Rabbenu Tam, there is a remarkable uniformity of law, custom and procedure which applies to all rites and communities, and, with a few differences which are noted below, the details which follow are of universal application.

The Capsules. Both the *tefillin* are cubical boxes of leather painted black, and averaging between one and two inches across. The parchment must be made from the skins of ritually clean animals, preferably of a calf, and the scriptural passages written on them by a duly qualified scribe in square ("Assyrian") script, like that of the *Sefer Torah*. The container into which the parchment is inserted is closed with a base of thick leather (*titora*) and stitched to it with 12 stitches of sinew prepared from a kosher animal. Protruding from the back of the *tefillin* base is a hollow extension (*ma'barta*) through which the straps are passed. These straps must also be made from the hide of clean animals and be black on the tanned side, which faces outwards. The arrangement of the straps is determined by the

The discoveries at the Dead Sea site of Qumran included *tefillin* which are thought to date from the first half of the first century c.e. Parchment number two is shown here; it contains Deuteronomy 5:22–33 and 6:1–9 and is 1 x 1$\frac{1}{2}$ inches in size. Shelomo Goren, the Chief Rabbi of Israel, examined these finds from a halakhic point of view and came to the conclusion that the *tefillin* from Qumran were sectarian in nature.

purpose to which they are put. That of the hand *tefillah* ends in the form of a noose to enable it to be tightened on the arm; that of the head has a circlet, tied with a knot, its size adjusted to the circumference of the head, the two ends hanging loosely.

Under the influence of the Kabbalah, the three letters of the Hebrew word *Shaddai* (meaning the Almighty) are represented on both *tefillin*. In the case of the *tefillin* of the head, the letter *shin* appears on the box in bas-relief on both sides, that on the right having its normal form with three strokes, that on the left having four. The knot is made in the shape of a *dalet*, while the *yod* is represented by the end of the strap, which is cut diagonally. In the case of the *tefillah* of the hand, the strap is wrapped around the hand in the shape of the *shin* and the *dalet*, and the knot at the end of the noose is tied in the shape of the *yod*.

Mode of Wearing. The order of donning the *tefillin*, which takes place after the *tallit* is put on, is meticulously laid down. The *tefillah* of the hand is put on first, placed on the upper arm (because of the scriptural phrase "opposite the heart") and the noose is tightened. Through a play on words, the plene spelling of the Hebrew word for "thy hand" in Exodus 13:16 was interpreted homiletically to mean "the weak hand." A left-handed person therefore places it on his right hand, even though it is not "opposite the heart." In any case, the strap is wound seven times around the arm between the elbow and the wrist, and the blessing "to put on the *tefillin*" is recited. The Ashkenazim wind the strap anti-clockwise, the Sephardim (followed by the Ḥasidim) clockwise.

The *tefillah* of the head is then put on, care being taken that its front edge comes only as far forward as the hairline. It is held in place by the narrow black strap that encircles the head, the knot resting on the nape of the neck. The two loose ends are passed over the shoulders and are left to hang down in front. Some are accustomed to pronounce a second benediction—"on the precept of the *tefillin*"—while tightening the strap around the head. However, in deference to the opinion that this second benediction is superfluous, the rabbis ordained that its supernumerary status be indicated by the addition of the words: "Blessed be the name of His glorious kingdom for ever."

The remaining part of the strap of the hand *tefillah* is then wrapped in a prescribed manner around the hand and the middle finger to form the above-mentioned letters *shin* and *dalet*. While making the rings around the middle finger, symbolically representing one's betrothal with the Creator, many worshipers are accustomed to recite the following verses from Hosea, in which God reassures a penitent Israel of His long-suffering patience: "And I will betroth thee unto Me forever. Yea, I will betroth thee unto Me in righteousness and in justice, in lovingkindness, and in compassion. And I will betroth thee unto Me in faithfulness, and thou shalt know the Lord."

In order to express one's reluctance to part with the *mitzvah*, it is customary to remove the *tefillah* of the head with the left hand. Palestinian scholars in the talmudic period were accustomed to recite a benediction (*lishmor ḥukkav*—"to observe His commandments") when they took off the *tefillin*. In explanation of the lapse of this practice, the medieval tosafists point out that some scholars in ancient times used to wear *tefillin* all day, and recite the benediction at night.

Time of Wearing. *Tefillin* are worn on all weekdays, but not on Sabbaths and scripturally-ordained festivals. The reason given in the Talmud is that the Bible refers to them as "a sign"—but the Sabbath itself is likewise so called, and no-one requires more than one sign of the covenant at any one time. The same rule was applied to festivals. In the Diaspora, Ḥasidim do not don *tefillin* during the intermediate days of Passover and Sukkot, while *Mitnaggedim* do; in Israel it is the universal custom not to wear them on the intermediate days. Since the *tefillin* are referred to as *pe'er* ("a diadem of glory") they are not worn on the morning of Tishah be-Av, the anniversary of the destruction of the Temple, their donning being postponed to the *Minḥah* service. In some German congregations this applies to other fast days as well. Nor are they worn by a bereaved person before the burial. Various other persons are

The breastplate, a shield usually made from precious metals placed on the mantle of the Torah scroll, was used in Ashkenazi communities only. Sephardi Torah scrolls were kept in a case (*tik*) which did not lend itself to such additional decoration.
Left: Silver gilt breastplate decorated with a crown, bells, and lions, from Munich, Germany, 1826. The words *Yom Kippur* are engraved on a removable plaque below the Tablets of the Law, signifying that this Torah was rolled to the section read on the Day of Atonement.
Below: Silver, partly gilt, breastplate inlaid with semi-precious stones, Hamburg, Germany, 17th century. The ornate decorations include crowns, columns, and floral designs, and the engraved words signify that this Torah was read on Rosh Ha-Shanah. Jerusalem, Israel Museum.

Left: A set of Torah ornaments from Italy, comprising mantle, finials, crown, and a small breastplate. Mantle: silk embroidered with gold thread, 17th century. Finials: silver, Padua, 18th century. Crown: silver, partly gilt, 1742. Breastplate: silver, 1776. In the background is a *parokhet* (ark curtain) of embroidered Italian silk, Turkey, 18th century. Below: North African ornaments, comprising mantle and finials. Mantle: velvet embroidered with silver and gold thread, backed with leather, Morocco, 19th century. Finials: silver, partly gilt and enamel, 19th century. Jerusalem, Israel Museum.

Outstanding among the lavish decorations with which Jews have embellished the Torah scrolls throughout the ages are the finials (*rimmonim*).
Right: Silver finials with bells and lions, Central Europe, late 18th century. Mishkan le-Omanut, Kibbutz Ein Harod.
Bottom left: Carved and gilded wood finials in the form of towers with painted windows, Morocco, 18th century. Jerusalem, Sir Isaac and Lady Wolfson Museum, Hechal Shlomo.
Bottom right: Silver gilt finials in a triple-tiered architectural structure, Holland, 18th century. Cleveland, Ohio, Olyn and Joseph B. Horwitz Judaica Collection.

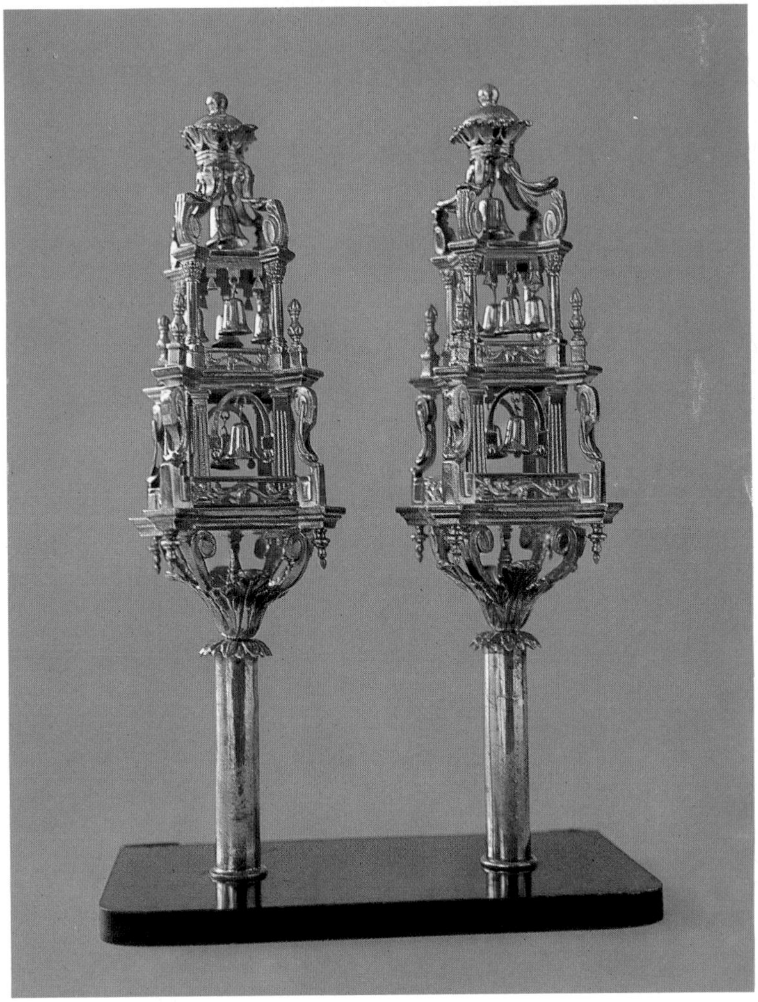

Right: A silver Torah crown ornamented with bells, foliage, and with a second, smaller, crown on top, from Central Europe, 19th century. Mishkan le-Omanut, Kibbutz Ein Harod.
Below: The Lubavitcher *Rebbe*, Menaḥem Mendel Schneerson, holds the Torah crown aloft before it is placed on the handles of the Torah scroll. Jerusalem, Shmuel Gorr Collection.

At the Western Wall in Jerusalem a group of Ḥasidim have set up a stand, manned by volunteers, to encourage visitors there to "lay" *tefillin*. A. Bender, in his "Bar Mitzvah," shows a grandfather instructing his grandson in the performance of the *mitzvah* prior to the ceremony which will mark the boy's attaining the rights and obligations of an adult Jew.

also temporarily exempt, either because of their inability to concentrate or because the body is unclean. Similarly they must not be worn in a cemetery, in an unclean place, or while asleep.

The duty of putting on *tefillin* begins when a boy reaches his religious majority, that is, at the age of 13 years and a day, and is unquestionably the high point of becoming *bar mitzvah*. It is usual to begin to put them on a few weeks earlier for practice, and indeed among Oriental and certain other communities a special ceremony is held to celebrate the event.

Rabbinic Appraisal. The Talmud stresses the supreme importance of the *tefillin* in a variety of ways. In a celebrated aggadic passage even God is represented as donning them. Whereas Israel's *tefillin*, by containing the *Shema*, proclaim their loyalty to the One God, the Almighty's *tefillin* reciprocally contain the verse: "Who is like Thy people Israel, a unique people on earth!" One passage states that a person who does not put them on is a willful transgressor. Another passage teaches that God surrounded Israel with seven precepts, including "*tefillin* on their heads, and *tefillin* on their arms," and "whoever has the *tefillin* on his head, the *tefillin* on his arm, *ẓiẓit* on his garment and a *mezuzah* on his doorpost is buttressed against sinning." In the words of the rabbis, the wearing of *tefillin* induces a serious frame of mind, preventing levity. And their sanctity is seen in the provision that if they are accidentally dropped, the person responsible is obliged to fast for that day. Moreover, in order to guarantee that they are always in a due state of ritual fitness, *tefillin* must be examined once—or, according to another opinion, twice—every seven years.

The kabbalists instituted a meditation before putting on the *tefillin*, which is a perfect example of the seeking of spiritual insights within a ceremonial precept. This meditation, which is basically the amplification of an idea expressed by Maimonides, includes the statement: "He hath commanded us to lay the *tefillin* upon the hand as a memorial of His outstretched arm; opposite the heart to indicate the duty of subjecting the longings and designs of our heart to His service; and upon the head, over against the brain, thereby teaching that the mind, whose seat is in the brain, together with all our senses and faculties, is to be subjected to His service."

The most sacred item in Judaism is the Torah Scroll; great respect is shown to it and love and devotion in adorning it. When they dedicated a new synagogue in the Israel village of Kiryat Malakhi, the Torah was carried to it in procession. The Jews of the island of Rhodes created the beautiful silver piece to "dress" the Torah. Its date is unknown and it may have been used as a girdle around the center, although it has been described as a Torah crown.

In Modern Times. The years since 1967 have seen a worldwide resurgence in the fulfillment of the *mitzvah* of *tefillin*. Since that date, many a Jew going about his daily business—whether in a Diaspora metropolis or in Israel, whether on a university campus or at a busy bus station—has found himself confronted by a bearded young stranger offering him the *mitzvah* of putting on *tefillin*. At the Western Wall alone, scores of thousands from all walks of life have carried out the precept, many of them for the first time.

THE SEFER TORAH

"The *Siddur*," in the words of a modern writer, "is unique in this respect, that it contains not only the words man addresses to his Maker in prayer, praise and supplication, but also the word of God to man. Torah occupies a central position in the *Siddur*. . .This is why the *Tefillah* [i.e. the *Amidah*] is recited quietly; man turns to God Who hears his voice. *Shema*, however, [being a Scriptural passage] is read aloud, since the human ear must hear the word of God addressed to it." The foregoing is basically the explanation offered by the 15th-century Spanish philosopher Isaac Arama.

Its Sanctity. And, indeed, the scroll from which the Torah is publicly read—in the manner described in the next chapter—is the most sacred object in the synagogue. Thus it is obligatory to stand in the presence of a *Sefer Torah*, or Torah scroll, both when the ark is opened and when it is being carried, and it is customary to bow reverently or kiss it when it passes. The bare parchment must not be touched with the hand. So insistent were the rabbis on this that they declared that "he who touches

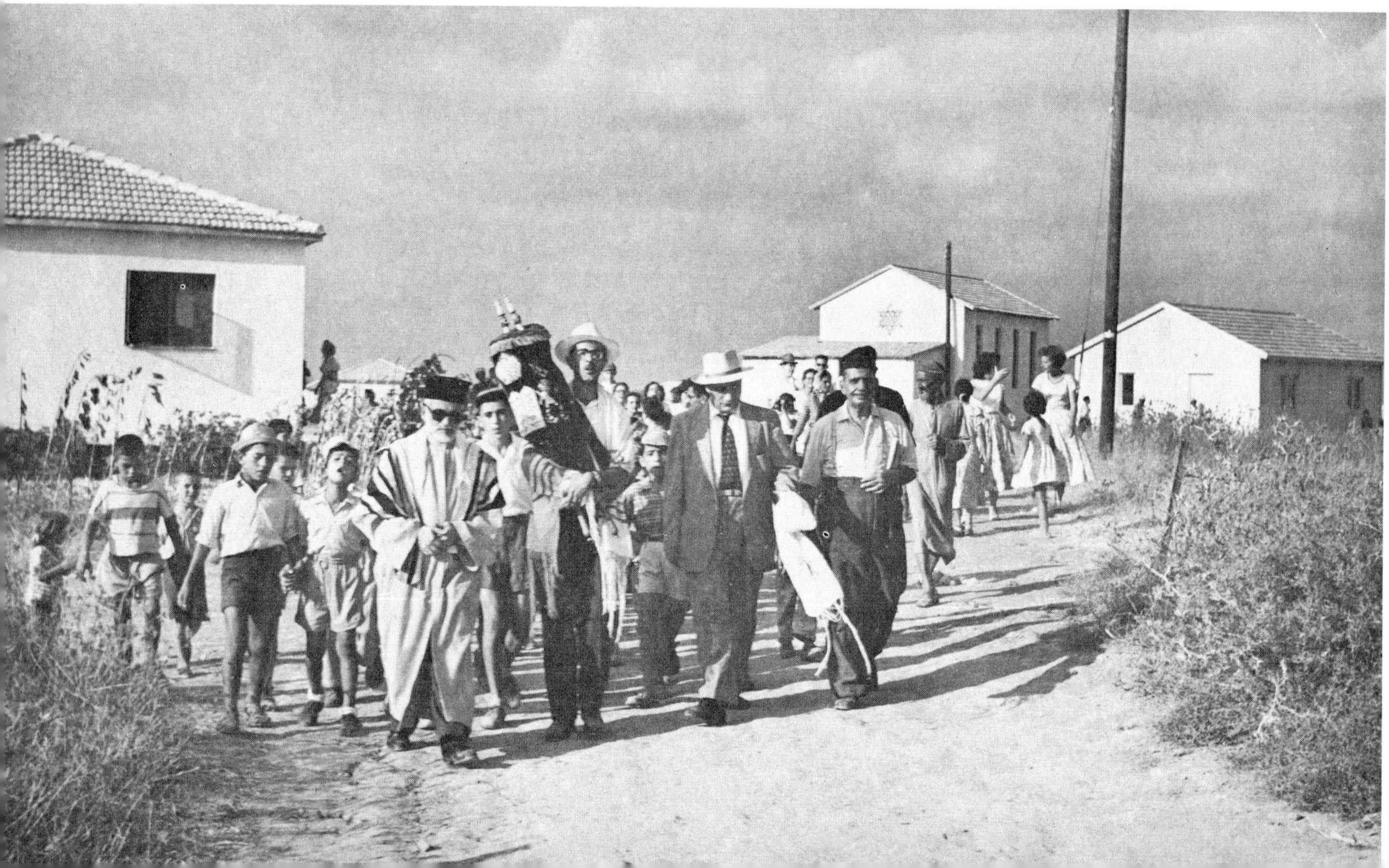

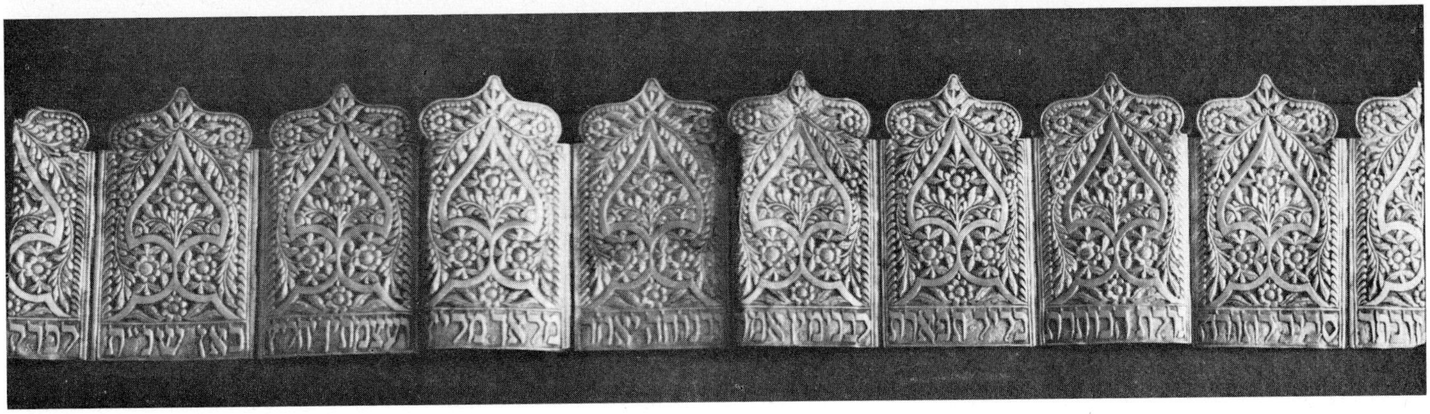

a naked *Sefer Torah* will be buried naked," although the statement was modified to mean either "naked of good deeds" or "naked of the reward for good deeds" which would otherwise have been his due, since he was reading it. For this reason the *yad* or pointer is used for reading, and the Sephardim cover the outside of the parchment with silk for the same reason.

Moreover, it is forbidden to sell a *Sefer Torah* except to provide the means for marrying, for studying, or for the ransom of captives. Should a *Sefer Torah* accidentally fall to the ground, the whole congregation is obliged to fast for that day. It is permitted and even enjoined to disregard the Sabbath in order to save not only the *Sefer Torah* but even its case from destruction, and should it be burnt, one has to rend one's garment in token of mourning; if one saw it torn one has to rend the garment twice, "once for the writing and once for the parchment." The *Sefer Torah* must not be carried about needlessly. Even when it is required for services held at a temporary place of worship, such as at the house of a mourner, it may not be taken unless it is to be read on at least three occasions. An exception is made in the case of a venerable scholar to enable him to hear the public reading. When a scroll is transferred to a permanent site, this is usually done with joyful ceremonial. The *Sefer Torah* is borne through the streets under a canopy, and the procession is accompanied by songs and dances.

Among the Sephardim before the public reading of the Torah, and among the Ashkenazim at its conclusion, the *Sefer Torah* is ceremoniously raised aloft, with a few of its columns exposed to the congregation, who recite the verse: "This is the Torah which Moses set before the children of Israel, according to the commandment of the Lord by the hand of Moses."

The Mishnah describes how in ancient times a *Sefer Torah* accompanied the king in battle, and on the occasion of public fasts during drought, the portable ark with its *Sifrei Torah* was taken out into the public square and the supplications and exhortations were recited in front of it. The Torah scroll also played a central role in the ceremony of *Hak'hel,* the public convocation held every seven years, at which the king could read from it to the assembled pilgrims.

During the Middle Ages, a person taking an oath was reminded of its solemnity by the *Sefer Torah* which he held. For the same reason three leading members of the congregation stand round the *ḥazzan* while he is reciting *Kol Nidrei* on the eve of the Day of Atonement.

The Scribal Craft. Each *Sefer Torah,* in every handwritten letter of each of its 248 columns, is the product of an arduous and exacting labor of love. Its making and writing must accord meticulously with a host of minutely detailed regulations, many of which apply likewise to the *tefillin* and to the *mezuzah.* These directives concern the provenance and preparation of the parchment, quill and ink; the ruling of the columns and the sewing of the sheets; the shape and disposition of the several letters; the repair of errata and the burial of scrolls damaged beyond repair; and the technical and spiritual preparation of the scribe.

The pride of place in the synagogue service which the *Sefer Torah* enjoys is reflected in the ornateness of its decoration. This, however, applies only to its exterior. The beauty of the text itself is sober, correct and classical. According to the Letter of Aristeas, mentioned above in another context, the *Sefer Torah* presented by Eleazar the High Priest to Ptolemy Philadelphus in the third century B.C.E. was written in letters of gold. Such ostentation was subsequently forbidden. "It happened," records the Talmud some centuries later, "that in a *Sefer Torah* in Alexandria all the divine names were written in gold, and when this was brought to the notice of the sages they ordered it to be hidden away."

Ornaments. Once written, though, the scroll is dressed and decorated with a colorful range of resplendent ornaments. Covering the scroll in an Ashkenazi synagogue is a mantle, usually of velvet or silk, and embroidered with traditional symbols. The front of the mantle, in turn, is sometimes covered by a decorative metal breastplate with conventional stylized symbols in bas-relief. From the top of this mantle protrude two carved wooden staves, called *aẓei ḥayyim,* or trees of life. On these the long parchment scroll is rolled. When it is closed and held upright, these staves are sometimes surmounted by finials, ornaments of chased silver or other decorative material.

These are known in Hebrew as *rimmonim,* which literally means pomegranates, perhaps an allusion to their once conventional form.

The ancient metaphor *keter Torah,* the crown of the Torah, referring to the majesty of the divine Law, finds tangible expression in the use of an actual crown which rests on the staves, with or without their decorative finials. The earliest mention of an actual crown appears in the year 1000, in the responsum of a Spanish rabbi in answer to a question about the use of women's jewelry in making a Torah crown. A second reference occurs in the records of the province of Arles, France, where a contract dated 1439 is recorded in which the Jewish community ordered a crown from a Christian goldsmith and also provided for the further embellishment of one they had.

During the reading of the Torah it is forbidden to touch the parchment. The pointer, or *yad* (meaning hand) which is therefore used is frequently quite literally a hand with a pointing finger, and is sometimes even encrusted with semi-precious stones, bracelets, and rings. The moden pointer is more austere.

After the Torah reading, the scroll is rolled together on its *aẓei ḥayyim* and kept tight, in antiquity and today in the East by kerchiefs (or *mitpaḥot*), but in Europe by a wrapper which is usually a simple, long, wide ribbon. However, in some East European communities, the wrapper was made of a baby boy's swaddling cloth cut into strips, which were joined to form a long runner. This was embroidered or stencil-painted with the child's name and date of birth, together with the traditional blessing that he grow up to study the Torah, to marry in due course, and to perform good deeds. These themes were favorite subjects in folk art, and embroidered representations of them were interspersed with pictures of animals or birds. When the little boy (at four or five) first visited the synagogue, he brought this wrapper as his gift to the Torah; at his bar mitzvah the Torah which he read from was clothed in his wrapper.

The Sephardi Scroll. The Sephardi Torah case of the Oriental communities is made of wood decorated in embossed leather or chased metal. The two halves of the cylindrical box are hinged vertically so that they may be opened like a book to

reveal the Torah, which is read standing up-right without being removed. The scroll is rolled to the required column by manipulation of the staves which protrude from the top of the box and are surmounted by fixed *rimmonim* which are carved and brightly colored.

In these ways—each community after its taste, each century after its style—long-forgotten scribes, silversmiths and seamstresses have fulfilled the rabbinic injunction: "Have a beautiful *Sefer Torah* prepared, copied by an able scribe, with fine ink and fine calamus, and wrapped in beautiful silk."

THE ARK

In housing the scrolls, the ark enjoys a degree of vicarious sanctity. Placed in the eastern wall of the synagogue—or in whichever wall faces Jerusalem—it serves the congregation as a focus of attention, particularly when it is opened for prayers of special solemnity. This occurs predominantly in Ashkenazi usage and especially during the High Holidays.

Opening the Ark. The practice may well be an echo of a ritual described in the Mishnah, and mentioned above. On the public fast days declared in times of danger and need, for example in times of drought and pestilence, the ark was carried into the town square, where penitential prayers were recited. It was covered with ashes, symbolic of the unworthiness of the congregation, or perhaps of the fact that God suffers with His people. A further explanation of the practice of *petiḥah*—the opening of the ark at specified points in the liturgy—is offered by Rabbi Mordecai Jaffe, a Bohemian scholar of the 16th century: "The high priest entered the Holy of Holies in the

The ark in which the Torah scrolls are housed has been created in different styles throughout the ages. The modern, unassuming ark of the synagogue in Fribourg, Switzerland, is in sharp contrast to the elaborate structure in the Nuremberg Reform synagogue (consecrated in 1874 and demolished on August 10, 1938). The curtain on the ark also became an art medium. It was customary to have some sort of valance in order to conceal the curtain rod. The valance, like the *parokhet* itself, is often inscribed with the name of the donor and/or the name of the deceased person in whose honor it was donated. The valance shown here is from 19th-century Tunis.

Temple once a year, on the Day of Atonement, in token of the special sanctity of the day; so too today the most significant prayers are recited before the open ark to stress their special importance." And, indeed, the congregation rises for all prayers which are recited when the ark is open. In individual prayer, too, it is not uncommon for men or women to open the ark in times of tribulation to offer private prayers for a relative in illness or distress.

Its Sanctity. As well as serving as a focus of worship, the ark is also a reminder of the biblical Ark of the Covenant in which the Tables of the Law were kept. Accordingly, among Ashkenazim it is generally called the *aron* or *aron kodesh* ("Holy Ark"); among Sephardi communities, it is known as the *heikhal* or sanctuary; and it is similarly called the *ehal* by the Spanish and Portuguese congregations of London and Amsterdam. In the Mishnah, however, it is known as the *tevah* ("chest" or "box"). Thus the mishnaic term *yored lifnei ha-tevah* ("go down before the ark") means to lead the congregation in prayer, as the ark was generally raised above the floor level on which the reader's lectern was set.

Since the ark is the holiest part of the synagogue after the Torah scrolls themselves, it is permissible to sell the pews or the reading desk and apply the proceeds to the purchase of an ark, because they are of a lesser degree of sanctity, but it is forbidden to sell an ark even in order to build a synagogue, because "one may not descend in matters of holiness." For the same reason, it is forbidden to make any secular use of the ark, and when it is no longer usable it must be stored away. One may not sleep in the vicinity of the ark, nor sit with one's back to it. It is related that Rabbi Jacob Segal Moellin (the Maharil) used to bow three times in the direction of the ark when he passed it on departing from the synagogue, "like a disciple taking leave of his master." And there is even a rabbinic statement that the ignorant die because they refer to the ark as *arana* (Aramaic for box), without the adjective "holy."

As a mark of deference, it is the accepted practice not to leave the ark empty. Hence, when all the Torah scrolls are taken out on the festivals of Hoshana Rabbah and Simḥat Torah, a lighted candle, symbolic of the light of the Torah, is often placed there; however, halakhic objections have been raised to this custom.

Its Shape and Form. The scrolls were originally kept in a movable receptacle which served both as their repository and as a pulpit. In the synagogue of Dura-Europos (c. 245 C.E.) a niche in the wall facing Jerusalem was fitted to receive the scrolls which are thought to have been placed in a low, wooden cabinet. Such cabinets in ordinary use are pictured in Pompeian frescoes. Representations of contemporary arks are found in paintings and graffiti in the ancient Jewish catacombs in Rome, as well as on the third- and fourth-century specimens of gold glass from Jewish catacombs in that city. The scrolls are depicted lying on shelves in the open cabinets.

In the Middle Ages, however, the ark took the form of a taller niche or cabinet in which the scrolls stood upright, mounted, wrapped in cloth and sometimes topped with finials. This is the type represented in 14th- and 15th-century illuminated Hebrew manuscripts of Spanish and German origin. In 15th-century Italian Hebrew manuscripts, a new type appears: the freestanding, tall, double-tiered cupboard, the upper tier fitted to take the scrolls and the lower one to contain ceremonial objects. A Gothic ark from Modena from the year 1505, decorated with carved panels, is in the Musée Cluny, Paris. A more elaborate Renaissance ark from Urbino with painted decorations (1550) is in the Jewish Museum in New York. The Sephardi synagogue in Amsterdam (1675) has a baroque ark, occupying the whole width of the nave. Here a new feature is the twin tablets of the Ten Commandments set on top of the structure. This feature, taken over by the Sephardi synagogue in London in 1701, was later adopted generally.

A baroque structure, adorned with columns, pilasters, broken cornices, pediments, and vases became standard in German synagogues in the early 18th century. The style quickly spread to Eastern Europe, where it inspired Jewish wood and stone carvers to create their masterpieces of folk art. Lions, birds, dolphins, stags and eagles intertwined with open-work scrolls covered the double-tiered ark, with the door set into the lower story and the Decalogue into the upper level. The built-in ark, such as the one of 1763 in the Touro synagogue

Another art medium in the synagogue is the *ner tamid*, the eternal light. The 19th-century silver filigree example is from Morocco; Ibram Lassaw's modernistic example, which presumably worked by light reflected from a projector, is in Temple Beth El, Springfield, Massachusetts. One of the focuses of the synagogue is the *bimah* which has also been constructed in innumerable styles, as is clear from that of the Grodno wooden synagogue in the latter half of the 18th century and that of the Italian 18th-century Siena synagogue.

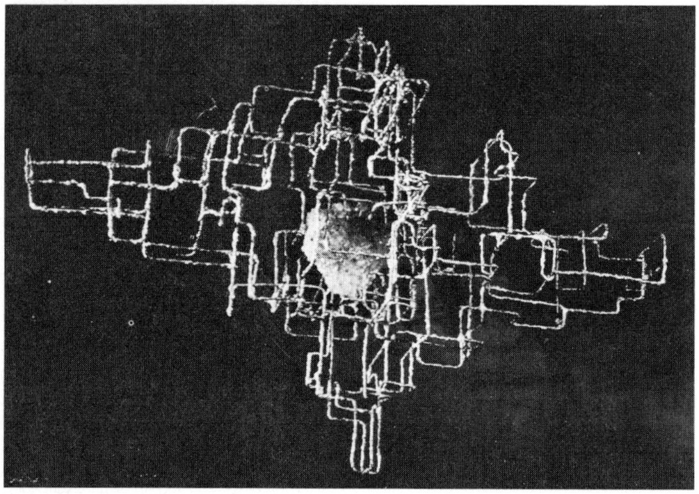

in Newport, Rhode Island, appeared in the late 18th century, as a product of the then dominant classicism. The cabinet is built into the wall and projects slightly. However, the most common type of ark in the U.S.A. until the 1840s was a neoclassical structure with a curved, convex front and sliding doors. From the 1850s and 1860s the arks of the Moorish-style synagogues in Europe and America were designed to match the buildings of which they were the architectural climax. They featured bulbous domes and horseshoe arches, and were covered with geometrical polychrome decorations.

In 1925 an attempt was made to revive the original portable style of the Ark of the Tabernacle, in Temple Emanu-el in San Francisco, California. Here the ark, a house-like structure in cloisonné enamel with a double-pitched roof, resembles a Gothic jewel case or reliquary. It is placed sideways so that the *ḥazzan* taking out the scroll does not turn his back to the worshipers. After World War II, the creation of arks became an art form; artists began to experiment with new and daring forms, and with the use of unconventional materials, such as concrete and glass.

In recent years, ornately carved and opulently gilt Renaissance arks from the deserted synagogues of extinct Italian communities have been transferred to Israel where, transmigrated and refurbished, they are once again able to enhance the respective synagogues of their new incarnation.

The Parokhet. Concealing the doors of the Ashkenazi ark there is traditionally a curtain. It takes its name from its counterpart in the Temple—the *parokhet* which hung in front of the Holy of Holies. It is commonly embroidered with the names of the donors or those in whose memory it may have been dedicated, as well as with appropriate scriptural quotations. Certain stylized motifs have become conventional. Frequently the *parokhet* has a valance hanging in front of its upper part, this being reminiscent of the cover of the Ark of the Covenant which stood in the Temple.

In Eastern Europe in the Baroque period, the *parokhet* was sewn by ladies of the congregation, often from bits of clothing worn on important occasions, a custom which now seems to be returning in some American communities.

The Eternal Light. Since the 18th century a lamp is usually suspended in front of the ark. This is known as the *ner tamid* (Hebrew for eternal light). In centuries past it consisted of a wick burning in olive oil, and it was considered a meritorious deed and an honor to give donations for its upkeep. Indeed, people who did so are specially mentioned in the *Mi she-Berakh* prayer recited after the Torah reading in the synagogue on Sabbath mornings. In modern times, however, the *ner tamid* is an electrical bulb. The lamp and its chains are usually made of precious metal and it has now become a vehicle for artistic expression.

The institution of the *ner tamid* in the synagogue is a symbolic reminder of the *menorah* which burned continually in the Temple, as the synagogue is considered a spiritual replica of the Temple or, in the words of the Talmud, "a miniature sanctuary." Originally, therefore, the *ner tamid* was placed in a niche in the western wall of the synagogue in remembrance of the position of the *menorah* in the Temple. Later, however, it was suspended in front of the ark. In many East European synagogues which were built of wood, the *ner tamid* was placed in a special vaulted stone niche because of the danger of fire. The *ner tamid* has also been interpreted as being symbolic of

God's presence amid Israel, or as the spiritual light which emanated from the Temple.

THE BIMAH

Besides the ark, there is another focal point in the synagogue—the *bimah*. This is the platform which accommodates the desk from which the Torah is read. Occasionally the rabbi delivers his sermon from the *bimah*, and on Rosh Ha-Shanah the *shofar* is blown there. In addition, in Sephardi synagogues the *ḥazzan* conducts most of the service from the *bimah*. In some Ashkenazi synagogues, on the other hand, the *ḥazzan* has a separate reading stand to the right of the ark and facing it, and it is from there that he leads the service. This lectern is called the *ammud*. Alternative names for the *bimah* are *almemar* (from the Arabic *al-minbar*, meaning platform) or, among Sephardi Jews, *tevah* (or box). The use of the *bimah* as a lectern for reading the Torah in public was known as early as the times of Nehemiah, in the fifth century B.C.E. Raised platforms were also known in Second Temple times, and the Talmud mentions a wooden pulpit in the center of the synagogue of Alexandria in Egypt.

In Orthodox synagogues of the Ashkenazi rite the *bimah* is often in the center, with some seats intervening between it and the ark. In Sephardi and Oriental synagogues the *bimah* is placed in the middle of the room opposite the ark and without intervening seats. From the 16th century certain Italian architects devised an imaginative synagogue design which poised the two foci—the ark and the *bimah*—at opposite ends of the synagogue. The congregants, ranged in two banks of pews facing each other on either side of the central aisle, were thus able with equal convenience to face both foci.

With the inception of the Reform movement, the placing of the *bimah* directly in front of the ark—or, frequently, its incorporation in the platform on which stood the ark—became the shibboleth of synagogal and liturgical change, and the subject of a prolonged and heated dispute.

The *bimah* in the various communities of the world has assumed an unimaginably wide range of shapes and forms. For example, in medieval Spain it was wooden, raised on columns, and reached by a stairway; in Eastern Europe from the 16th century it was often enclosed by a wrought-iron cage; while in parts of Central and Eastern Europe its four arching pillars supported the vaulted ceiling, so that the *bimah* became a roofed structure.

With this extreme variety of style, the *bimah* typifies many of the synagogal accessories of prayer, since the beauty of ritual objects is very much in the eye of the worshiper.

V Standard Prayers

The Shema
Amidah
The Reading of the Torah
Amen
Ashrei
Barekhu
Ya'aleh ve-Yavo
Taḥanun
Hallel
Aleinu
Adon Olam
Yigdal
Kaddish

אור בקר
והוא ספר כולל תפלות ערב ראש
חדש וראש השנה ויום הכפורים
ולמנחת שובבים ·

לקיטו׳ מספרי קדמונינו ועוד נוספו עליהן תחנו׳
ובקשות ושירות ותשבחות מחודשות לצורך הזמן
מהרב המופלא לא יסולא , כמה״רר יוסף
פיאמיטא נר״ו , והובא ע׳ הדפוס לתשוקת
הנגיד היקר ונעלה כמ״ר מיכאל מורגיו
יצ״ו ·

בויניציאה

Nella Stamparia Vendramina
Con Licenza de Superiori

בשנת · אש״ר
לאיבשוקוי׳ לפ״ק

The title page of *Or Boker*, a compilation of prayers for the eve of Rosh Ḥodesh, Rosh Ha-Shanah, the Day of Atonement and other occasions. The book, which was printed in Venice in 1741, was compiled by Rabbi Joseph Fiammetta who was rabbi in Ancona. The book was published with "the licence of the Superiors" which, in fact, constituted a copyright protecting the printer.

An abbreviated form of the *Shema* from a Reform prayerbook, 1889. The *Copenhagen Seder Birkat ha-Mazon* (1728, originating from Movaria) is the text of the Grace after Meals with benedictions and prayers for sundry occasions. The page shown contains *Keri'at Shema al ha-Mittah*, the recitation of the *Shema* before retiring.

Taken collectively, the prayer services which comprise the *Siddur* may be said to resemble a symphony, whose movements bear a family likeness to each other, even though the themes and motifs which occur and recur at various intervals are subjected to all manner of variations and modulations, here articulated by the wind instruments, there sung by the strings.

The *Shema*, for example, is the core of more than one prayer service, but its setting in the Morning Service is not identical with its context in the Evening Service, nor is the degree of its emphasis at one season of the year identical with its meaningfulness on some other liturgical occasion. The *Amidah*, too, has a standard basic structure, which varies from service to service according to the dictates of the time of day, the season of the year, and even the changing circumstances of the individual worshiper. The reading of the Torah is another classic case of a standard component of the prayer services, which finds its way—in various forms—into the liturgy of a great many occasions.

So, too, all the other items treated in this chapter—such as *Aleinu* and *Kaddish*—are self-contained motifs which appear in a variety of contexts according to the needs of the various prayer services.

THE SHEMA

The core of both the morning and evening daily services is the Jew's confession of faith, which bears witness that God is One, and expresses the duty of loving and serving Him with one's whole being. Taking its name from the first word of the doxology found in Deuteronomy 6:4, it is called the *Shema*, or *Keriat Shema* ("the reading of the *Shema*"). As it had developed by at least as early as the second century C.E. the *Shema* consisted of three portions of the Pentateuch–Deuteronomy 6:4–9, Deuteronomy 11:13–21, and Numbers 15:37–41—in this order, together with certain benedictions to be recited before and after it.

It is difficult to determine the stages through which this tripartite recitation came into being. The Nash Papyrus, a valuable biblical text dating from the Hasmonean period (the second century B.C.E.), contains the Ten Commandments and the first portion of the *Shema*. This combination corresponds to the Torah readings included in the daily morning liturgy of Second Temple times, as recorded in the Mishnah. There it is stated that in the Temple all three portions of the *Shema* were recited together with the Ten Commandments, and explicit reference is made to the benediction after the *Shema*, which opens with the words *Emet ve-Yaẓiv* and to another benediction before the *Shema*, which is identified at a later period with *Ahavah Rabbah*. At a later period, too, there are indications that special significance was attached to the first verse of the *Shema*. It is not implausible, therefore, to see the successive stages in the development of the *Shema* prayers as follows: the reading of the first verse; the reading of the first portion; later the reading of all three portions, together with *Emet ve-Yaẓiv*, and *Ahavah Rabbah*; and ultimately the addition of the other benedictions.

It was a long-established practice at the beginning of the present era to recite the *Shema* in the evening and in the morning, as can be seen from the fact that the schools of Hillel and Shammai of the first century C.E. debated how it should be read. The school of Shammai took the words "when you lie down and when you get up" literally, and ruled that the evening *Shema* should be recited while reclining and the morning *Shema* while standing upright. The school of Hillel ruled that "when you lie down . . ." refers to the times of reading, that is, in the evening and in the morning, but that no special posture is required. The ruling followed, as is most often the case, is that of the school of Hillel. There was considerable discussion in this period as to these prescribed times for the statutory recitation of the *Shema*. The eventual ruling is that the evening *Shema* may be recited from nightfall until dawn, though ideally it should be recited before midnight; the morning *Shema* may be recited from the first sign of dawn until a quarter of the daylight hours have passed.

In Jewish Thought. The *Shema* is, in Jewish thought, the supreme affirmation of the unity of God, and is frequently called "the acceptance of the yoke of the Kingdom of Heaven." The original meaning of the first verse, "Hear O Israel, the Lord is

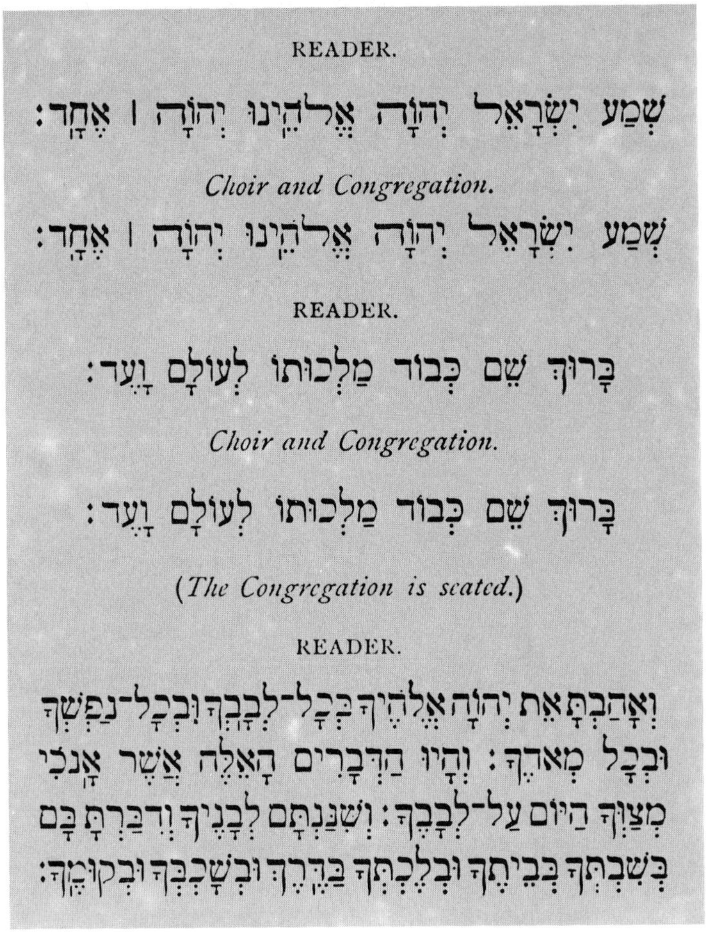

READER.

שְׁמַע יִשְׂרָאֵל יְהוָה אֱלֹהֵינוּ יְהוָה ׀ אֶחָד׃

Choir and Congregation.

שְׁמַע יִשְׂרָאֵל יְהוָה אֱלֹהֵינוּ יְהוָה ׀ אֶחָד׃

READER.

בָּרוּךְ שֵׁם כְּבוֹד מַלְכוּתוֹ לְעוֹלָם וָעֶד׃

Choir and Congregation.

בָּרוּךְ שֵׁם כְּבוֹד מַלְכוּתוֹ לְעוֹלָם וָעֶד׃

(*The Congregation is seated.*)

READER.

וְאָהַבְתָּ אֵת יְהוָה אֱלֹהֶיךָ בְּכָל־לְבָבְךָ וּבְכָל־נַפְשְׁךָ
וּבְכָל־מְאֹדֶךָ׃ וְהָיוּ הַדְּבָרִים הָאֵלֶּה אֲשֶׁר אָנֹכִי
מְצַוְּךָ הַיּוֹם עַל־לְבָבֶךָ׃ וְשִׁנַּנְתָּם לְבָנֶיךָ וְדִבַּרְתָּ בָּם
בְּשִׁבְתְּךָ בְּבֵיתֶךָ וּבְלֶכְתְּךָ בַדֶּרֶךְ וּבְשָׁכְבְּךָ וּבְקוּמֶךָ׃

our God, the Lord is One,'' may have been that, unlike the pagan gods who have different guises and localities, God is one. At first the main emphasis in the *Shema* was seen to be in opposition to polytheism; there is only one God, not many gods. Rabbi Akiva in the second century recited the first verse of the *Shema* just before his execution by the Romans and, following him, Jewish martyrs of later generations recited it as they went to their death. From earliest times, the word *eḥad* (''one'') was understood also to mean ''unique.'' God is not only one and not many; He is totally other than what paganism means by gods. Seen in this light, the *Shema* is not only an affirmation that there are no other gods, but also that God is the Supreme Being. God is different from anything in the universe He has created. This was the general view of the medieval Jewish philosophers and kabbalists. In ḥasidic thought, the further idea is read into the *Shema* that there is only God, the whole universe existing in Him, as it were, and only enjoying an independent existence from the human standpoint.

The First Verse. Christian exegesis in the Middle Ages taught that there are three divine names in the first verse of the *Shema* and suggested that they refer to the Trinity. Jewish commentators were naturally at pains to contradict this, and a current interpretation was that, in fact, the *Shema* asserts the opposite, that there is only one God, and no three persons in the Godhead. Thus, for example, the *Zohar* which is strongly anti-Christian in intent, repeatedly stresses that the ten diverse manifestations of divine power described in the Kabbalah jointly constitute a unity with the Infinite.

The usual translation of the first verse of the *Shema* is, ''Hear, O Israel: the Lord our God, the Lord is One.'' Other translations are: ''The Lord our God is one Lord,'' and ''The Eternal, the Eternal alone, is our God.'' The word ''Israel'' in this first verse is understood by the Midrash as referring to the patriarch Jacob whose alternative name it was. The devout Jew addresses himself to his ancestor to declare that he has remained faithful to the credo. Abudraham, a liturgical commentator of the 14th century, understands it to mean that each Jew addresses the ''Israel'' part of his soul, speaking to the highest within him. Abudraham also remarks that the letter *ayin* of the word *Shema* and the letter *dalet* of the word *eḥad* are traditionally written larger than the other letters in the Torah scroll so as to form the word *ed* which is Hebrew for witness. The text itself thus gives a mystical hint that the Jew testifies to God's unity when he recites the *Shema*.

Barukh Shem Kevod. After the first verse of the *Shema* it has been customary, since rabbinic times, to recite quietly the doxology uttered as a response in the Temple: *Barukh shem kevod malkhuto le-olam va-ed* ("Blessed be His name, whose glorious kingdom is forever and ever," or "Blessed be His glorious Kingdom forever and ever"). This formula of ancient origin is based upon a verse in Nehemiah, dating from the fifth century B.C.E.: "Stand up and bless the Lord your God from everlasting to everlasting; and let them say: Blessed be Thy glorious Name, that is exalted above all blessing and praise." Talmudic sources a few centuries later record that it was not customary in the Temple to respond "Amen" after blessings pronounced by the priests, but rather the above-mentioned doxology. This was also the custom after the high priest pronounced the Holy Name (the Tetragrammaton) in his public confessions on the Day of Atonement. This is the same formula which is pronounced in the daily prayers after the first verse of the *Shema*.

In the Orthodox ritual this sentence is pronounced in a whisper, either because it is not biblical as is the rest of the *Shema*, or because it is recited by the angels in heaven, their song of praise corresponding to the people of Israel's recitation of the *Shema*. The Midrash explains that these words were uttered by the patriarch Jacob on his deathbed when his sons declared their loyalty by reciting the *Shema*. Since Jacob said it, we too repeat it, but since Moses did not say it we recite it in a whisper. Another midrashic explanation is that when Moses went up on high he heard the ministering angels saying *Barukh Shem*, and he brought it down for Israel to emulate. Since it was borrowed from the angels, only when Israel is as pure as the angels may it be recited in a loud voice. Thus, it is said aloud in Orthodox synagogues only on the Day of Atonement, for on this day "Israel is as pure as the angels." It has also been suggested that precisely because the phrase was recited aloud when the Temple stood in all its glory, after the Destruction it should be said in an undertone. Another explanation of this practice is that martyrs used to pronounce the *Shema* as they met their death, while their relatives, out of fear, responded quietly; on the Day of Atonement, however, when all are ready for martyrdom, it is pronounced aloud. In the Ashkenazi rite, at the close of the *Ne'ilah* service on the Day of Atonement, this formula is pronounced aloud three times as a solemn affirmation of the faith of the Jew in the unity of the Creator, and in anticipation of the day when this belief will be realized by all mankind.

Various suggestions have been made to account historically for the insertion of *Barukh Shem*. It may have been introduced by the Pharisaic opponents of Herod and the Sadducean priesthood in order to emphasize the belief in the sole sovereignty of God as against the aristocratic tendency to admit the sovereignty of the caesars; or as a response at a time when the *Shema* was read verse by verse, led by the reader.

Manner of Recitation. So central is the *Shema* to the Jew's daily devotions that the sages surrounded its recitation by detailed regulations. Ideally the *Shema* should be recited throughout with *kavannah*, that is, with undivided and devout concentration on the meaning of the words; if, however, this was not done, it is unnecessary to repeat it, provided the first verse was recited with due concentration. If the *Shema* is recited while walking, one is obliged to stand still for the recitation of the first verse. It is customary too to place the right hand over the eyes while reciting the first verse as an aid to concentration and, for the same reason, the first verse should be recited aloud. One should not gesticulate while reading the *Shema* but should recite it in awe and trembling. The *Shema* should be recited loudly enough for it to be heard by the ear, since it is said: "Hear, O Israel." Care must be taken to enunciate the words clearly, and this applies especially to any two consecutive words, the first of which ends and the second of which begins with the same letter. Though ideally to be read in Hebrew, the *Shema* may be recited in any language, but with the same clarity of enunciation one is expected to use for the

Hebrew. If one is in doubt as to whether he has recited the *Shema,* it is necessary to recite it again.

In considering the case of the worshiper who was otherwise occupied when the time came for the reading of the *Shema,* the rabbis ruled that a person engaged in public affairs falls in the same category as one studying the Torah. Moreover, "if a man be engaged in studying the Torah and the time comes for recital of the *Shema,* he shall leave off studying and recite the *Shema;* . . . if he be engaged in the affairs of the public, he shall not leave off but complete this work, and then recite the *Shema* if there remain time to do so."

It is forbidden to interrupt the recitation of the *Shema,* as it is to recite it in a place that is not scrupulously clean, or in front of the naked body. Women (who are exempt from carrying out certain positive precepts dependent on a given time) and small children have no obligation to recite the *Shema.* Many women, nonetheless, do recite it.

Devout Preparation. Old devotional manuals sometimes advise the worshiper to recite the *Shema* bearing in mind that if he is called upon to suffer martyrdom for the sanctification of God's name he will do so willingly and with joy. One author also advises the worshiper to prepare himself for reading the *Shema* with the following meditation: "I believe with perfect faith that Thou art one and unique and that Thou hast created all worlds, upper and lower, without end; Thou art in past, present and future. I make Thee King over each of my limbs that it might perform the precepts of Thy holy Torah, and I make Thee King over my children and children's children to the end of time. I will, therefore, command my children and grandchildren to accept the yoke of Thy Kingdom, Divinity, and Lordship upon themselves, and I will command them to command their children in turn, all of them, up to the last generation, to accept the yoke of Thy Kingdom, Divinity, and Lordship."

El Melekh Ne'eman. The total number of the words of the *Shema* together with the *Barukh Shem* is 245. It is customary for the *ḥazzan* to repeat the last two words of the *Shema* and the first word of the passage which follows, thus bringing the total up to 248, corresponding to the traditional number of organs of the body and the number of the positive commandments in the Bible. A midrashic teaching derives this custom from the Psalmist's call: "All my bones shall say: Lord, who is like unto Thee!" When the *Shema* is recited in private prayer, the number is made up by reciting the three words *El Melekh ne'eman* (meaning "God, faithful King") before the recital of the *Shema.* The rabbis interpreted the word Amen as being composed of the initial Hebrew letters of these three words. The phrase, however, is pronounced only in private prayer and not at public services where any inter-polation, even Amen, between the preceding benediction and *Shema* is omitted (according to some opinions) as an unwarranted interruption.

The Benedictions. The statutory recitation of the *Shema* is preceded in the Morning Service by two benedictions and followed by one, while in the Evening Service (which is discussed in Chapter VI) it is preceded by two benedictions and followed by two. This provision is laid down in the Mishnah, on the basis of texts which had been current in the centuries before the Common Era. In both services, the *Shema* with its framework of benedictions is introduced by *Barekhu,* the invitation to congregational worship, and followed by the *Amidah.* These elements of the services are discussed later in the present chapter.

The first of the benedictions preceding the *Shema* in the Morning Service is the *Yoẓer* prayer, an expression of thanksgiving for the creation of light and for the daily renewal of the whole of Creation. Its opening words are almost a paraphrase of a verse in Isaiah: "I am the Lord, and there is none else; I form light and create darkness, I make peace and create evil." It has been suggested that this unequivocal declaration of monotheism was introduced into the daily liturgy as an explicit denial of the ancient belief of Persian Zoroastrianism, that there were two gods—one the source of light and goodness, the other responsible for darkness and evil. The change in the last word of the benediction—which reads "Who creates all things" instead of speaking of the creation of evil—is evidently intended to teach that nothing, ultimately, is evil that comes from the hand of God.

This page from the *Jerusalem Mishneh Torah* (written in Spain and illuminated in Italy, c. 1400) is the opening page of the "Laws of the Recitation of the *Shema*" which begins the section of the work known as *Sefer Ahavah*, "The Book of Love." The upper illustration shows a man, enveloped in a *tallit*, holding a Torah scroll, while at the foot of the page a man recites the *Shema* at his bedside.

The eighth-century mystic who wrote this opening paragraph proceeded from the praise of the Creator for the marvels of the universe, to a poetic description of the adoration of the Creator by the hosts of heaven. This description centers around the same verses from the visions of Ezekiel and Isaiah which constitute the core of the *Kedushah*. This is discussed below in the context of the *Amidah*. The various classes of angels are described as praising God for the many wonders of His universe, including His constant and continuous renewal of the act of creation. Since, however, every compound benediction is so constructed that its statutory closing formula is foreshadowed by the preceding few words, this first benediction—which ends by blessing the Creator of the heavenly luminaries—is preceded by a repeated mention of the creation of light, the theme with which the *Yoẓer* prayer opened. In some rites, this mention takes the form of a quotation from Psalms which thanks "Him that makes great lights, for his lovingkindness endures for ever." In other rites, a petition is added, in which the idea of light is used metaphorically to signify the Messianic age: "Cause Thou a new light to shine upon Zion, and may we all be worthy soon to enjoy its brightness." On this note the first of the complex benedictions preceding the morning recitation of *Shema* comes to a close.

The second benediction, which immediately precedes the *Shema* in both the *Shaḥarit* and *Ma'ariv* services, is a fervent expression of thanksgiving for the divine gift of the Torah. *Ahavah Rabbah* (meaning "with great love") and *Ahavat Olam* ("with everlasting love") are two versions of the opening words of this benediction. In the Talmud there is a difference of opinion as to which is the correct version; this controversy continued even into medieval times. As a compromise decision, *Ahavah Rabbah* was adopted for the morning service and the other for the evening. The Sephardi and Italian rites, however, include only *Ahavat Olam*. It is not clear whether the difference between the two versions was limited to the opening formula or whether it extended to the content. From Saadiah Gaon's prayer book it would appear that the former is the case. In their present form the two prayers have the same basic theme, but they differ considerably in presentation, *Ahavah Rabbah* being the longer and the more complex of the two. Both benedictions give God's love as the explanation for Israel's receiving the Torah. The prayer introduces the *Shema*—which is, of course, a Torah reading—and the worshiper undertakes constant preoccupation with its study and observance. In both versions God is besought to continue bestowing His love on His People, but in *Ahavah Rabbah* the idea of the election of Israel is stressed. *Ahavat Olam* ends: "Blessed art Thou, O Lord, Who loves His people Israel, "whereas *Ahavah Rabbah* closes with: "Who has chosen His people Israel in love." The Mishnah, as interpreted in the *Gemara*, records that *Ahavah Rabbah* was the benediction with which the priestly prayer service in the Temple commenced. According to the *halakhah* either of the two can serve as a substitute for the *Birkat ha-Torah*, the blessing to be recited before study. And in the Middle Ages various *piyyutim* were composed for insertion on festivals into both *Ahavah Rabbah* and *Ahavat Olam*.

Synagogues are often housed in various communal institutions. The old people's home in the Polish city of Radom, for example, had its own synagogue, which is illustrated below. The Jewish community was founded there in the 17th century, and by the eve of World War II numbered 30,000 souls. In 1965 Radom had only seven Jews.

The Reform ritual has retained the traditional text of the former prayer but has abbreviated the latter considerably, omitting the messianic references. *Ahavat Olam* has been set to music by Mombach and others, and forms part of the repertoire of most synagogue choirs.

Recitation before Retiring. In addition to the twice daily reading of the *Shema* as part of the morning and evening prayers, the practice was introduced in the amoraic period—between the third and fifth centuries—of reciting the first section before retiring at night. This is known in Hebrew as *Keri'at Shema al-ha-Mittah*. The source in the Talmud is the statement of Rabbi Joshua ben Levi: "Though a man has recited the *Shema* in the synagogue, it is meritorious to recite it again on his bed." The biblical proof text given was the Psalmist's counsel: "Tremble and sin not; commune with your own heart upon your bed, and be still." Later on in the same talmudic passage the practice is connected with the fear of demons, but it is uncertain whether this was the true origin of the custom. Maimonides, as usual in such circumstances, makes no mention of the demon motif but simply records the duty of reciting the first paragraph of the *Shema*, and he takes "upon the bed" not as an indication of time, but literally. The night prayer as such is discussed in Chapter XI.

At Other Times. The first verse of the *Shema* is also recited in the early morning; when the Torah scroll is taken from the ark for public reading on Sabbath and festivals; during the *Kedushah* of the *Musaf* service on the same occasions; and it is the last sentence uttered by the believer on his deathbed. The first verse of the *Shema* is recited once, and *Barukh Shem* three times, at the concluding *Ne'ilah* service on the Day of Atonement. And the first two paragraphs of the *Shema*, as has been explained in the previous chapter, are inscribed on the parchment scrolls of both the *mezuzah* and the *tefillin*.

Hak'hel. The Bible enjoins that "at the end of every seven years, at the time of the year of release, at the Feast of Tabernacles," there is to take place an assembly of the whole people, "men, women, children, and the stranger that is within your gates." The purpose of this assembly—called *Hak'hel*, meaning to congregate—is "that they may hear and so learn to revere the

Lord your God and to observe faithfully every word of this Teaching."

The Mishnah describes the details of this ceremony, for which a wooden platform was set up in the Temple court. "The *ḥazzan* (that is, the officiant) of the synagogue would take a *Sefer Torah* and hand it to the chief of the synagogue, who gave it to the deputy high priest, who in turn handed it to the high priest. The high priest handed it to the king, who received it standing and read it while seated." The passages read were not "all the words of the Torah"—a phrase which occurs in connection with this ceremony—but selected passages from Deuteronomy, which include the first two paragraphs of *Shema*. The reading was concluded with eight benedictions, seven of which are identical with those pronounced by the high priest on the Day of Atonement.

In Samaritan Marriage. The *Shema* comprises one of the stages in Samaritan marriage. The *Kiddushin,* a kind of betrothal, takes place in the bride's home, and even a minor priest can perform the ceremony simply by reciting the *Shema* and various other verses from the Pentateuch.

AMIDAH

Next to the *Shema,* the most essential part of the prayer services is the *Amidah,* a series of benedictions expressing praise, thanksgiving, confession and petition. Recited silently three times daily, this prayer is named after the position in which it is recited (since the word *Amidah* means standing). However, it is perhaps more popularly known among Ashkenazim as the *Shemoneh Esreh* (Eighteen) because of the 18 benedictions it originally comprised. So basic is its position in each of the prescribed daily services that in talmudic sources it is also known simply as *Ha-Tefillah,* that is, "the prayer" par excellence.

Mode of Recital. The requirement that the worshiper face Jerusalem applies in particular to the *Amidah.* It is said in an undertone; no interruptions of any kind are permitted. At the beginning and end of the first and of the penultimate benediction, the worshiper bends his knees and bows. The prayer is recited by each individual during each of the three daily services: *Shaḥarit* (the Morning Service), *Minḥah* (the Afternoon Service) and *Ma'ariv* or *Arvit* (the Evening Service). On Sabbaths, New Moons and the scriptural festivals, furthermore, it constitutes the main element of *Musaf* (the Additional Service); and on the Day of Atonement alone it is recited a fifth time, for the *Ne'ilah* (the solemn Concluding Prayer).

In congregational worship—that is, when there is a *minyan*—the *sheliaḥ ẓibbur* or reader repeats the *Amidah* aloud and a number of additions are made. The original purpose of the repetition was to enable uneducated persons who did not know the prayers to fulfill their duty by listening to the recital and responding "Amen" after each benediction. In fact, though, it has long been the custom for the reader to repeat the *Amidah* even if all the congregants are able to pray themselves. The *halakhah* originally considered the *Amidah* of the Evening Service to be optional (though it has long become the invariable practice to recite it), and it is therefore not repeated aloud. An exception is the repetition on Sabbath eve of an abbreviated version, in which seven benedictions are telescoped into one single benediction. This was originally seen as a kind of *Kiddush.*

Structure and Style. There are various forms of *Amidah* for different occasions. On weekdays, the *Amidah* originally comprised 18 benedictions which later became 19; on fast days one further benediction is added in the repetition by the reader, and in ancient times, on some public fasts, six were added to the regular 19. On Sabbaths and festivals there are only seven benedictions, except in the *Musaf* of Rosh Ha-Shanah, which has nine. In cases of emergency or illness, the intermediate blessings of the weekday *Amidah* may be combined into one. This condensation, known as *Havinenu,* is discussed later in this chapter. All the various forms have in common the first three and the last three benedictions; the former are devoted to the praise of God, the latter, among other themes, to thanksgiving. On weekdays, the intermediate benedictions are petitions, and the *Amidah* is, therefore, predominantly a prayer of supplication. Its structure follows the scheme: praise, petition, thanksgiving. The Talmud states that this style is that appropriate to "a servant making requests of his master"; for "a man should always praise God first, and pray (i.e. petition for his needs) afterward."

Throughout the *Amidah,* with the exception of the first section and some of the concluding formulae, the worshiper addresses God directly, as "Thou"—for the *Amidah* is the means through which the individual communes directly with God. In the words of the sages, "the worshiper must turn his heart to Heaven" and "must see himself as if he were in God's presence." Some rabbis even forbid the recital of the *Amidah* if the worshiper's mind is not tranquil and if he is not certain of his ability to recite the entire prayer with *kavvanah,* that is, with sustained concentration. Both in praise and in petition, the plural pronoun "we" is used throughout the *Amidah* even when it is recited silently by the individual, indicating that it was always conceived as a communal prayer. Even when the individual worshiper recites it, he prays not on his own behalf but as a member of the congregation.

Evolution and Redaction. Fixed community prayers gradually came into being during the Second Temple period. People would meet for joint prayers and, in the course of time, orders of prayer developed, along the lines referred to in Chapters II and XII. At first, these differed widely from group to group and there is no reason to assume that the orders of prayer were instituted at any given time by a central authority. It is, however, almost certain that by the end of the Temple period the recitation of the 18 benedictions of the weekday *Amidah* had become the general custom. Their exact sequence and the content of the individual benedictions were probably still uncrystallized. In the original Hebrew version of Ben Sira, a book of the Apocrypha also known as Ecclesiasticus, which dates from the second century B.C.E., there is a hymn which some scholars have identified as a quasi-*Amidah*. However, the absence of anything resembling the *Amidah* in the liturgical fragments of the Dead Sea Scrolls found so far may be significant. There is explicit evidence that the seven benedictions for Sabbaths and the festivals and the nine for Rosh Ha-Shanah were accepted as the norm by the schools of Hillel and Shammai. A few decades later on in the first century C.E., soon after the destruction of the Temple, the *Amidah* was edited finally in Jabneh, by Rabban Gamaliel II and his colleagues. Even then, only the order and general content and the formulae of the actual benedictions were standardized; the wording in the body of the paragraphs was left to be formulated by the individual worshiper or reader.

Attempts to reconstruct the "original" text of the *Amidah* or to ascertain the date when each section was "composed" are therefore pointless, especially in view of the ancient rabbinic ruling that benedictions were not to be written down. It was probably in the early geonic period, after the seventh century, that definite versions of the *Amidah* were established and committed to writing; even then, those current in Ereẓ Israel and Babylonia differed widely in their texts, though not, on the whole, in their contents. The former, that of Ereẓ Israel, is known principally through the Cairo *Genizah,* the ancient storehouse for discarded manuscripts which was referred to in an earlier chapter. The latter version, the Babylonian, is basic to all the current recensions. Today, the texts in the traditional rites vary only slightly, and entirely different versions of a benediction are preserved only in rare cases, such as the respective wordings of the last benediction, the prayer for peace: *Sim Shalom* and *Shalom Rav* in the Ashkenazi rite, while in the Sephardi and Yemenite rites only *Sim Shalom* appears. This is true, however, only of the prescribed standard text of the different forms of the *Amidah;* there is great variety as regards the optional *piyyutim* that were inserted for special Sabbaths and for the festivals, in the manner discussed in Chapter II. In most congregations such insertions are made only on Rosh Ha-Shanah, the Day of Atonement, and a few other occasions, such as the prayer for dew on the first day of Passover and for rain on Shemini Aẓeret.

The Weekday Amidah. This *Amidah* falls naturally into three groups of benedictions—introductory, intermediate and concluding—whose contents and sequence are given below.

THE INTRODUCTORY BENEDICTIONS—PRAISE.

1. The Mishnah calls the first blessing *Avot,* "fathers," as God is addressed as the "God of Abraham, God of Isaac, and God of Jacob." This reference to the nation's remote ancestry is an expression of *zekhut avot,* the suppliant's reliance upon the merit of the patriarchs, and thus stresses the continuity of the

Morning prayers at Kibbutz Sa'ad, located near the Gaza strip. The daily work schedule of the kibbutzniks does not permit them to pray together, so they join together in small groups.

Jewish people. It extols God as great, mighty, and awesome, and concludes with *Barukh . . . magen Avraham* ("Blessed be . . . the Shield of Abraham").

2. The second benediction praises God for His deeds of *gevurot* ("power"). Among the manifestations of God's power are His provision of sustenance for all living creatures, His healing the sick, and His causing the rain to fall. In addition, there is repeated reference to the resurrection of the dead—an emphasis which points to the controversy on the subject between the Pharisees and the Sadducees in the latter part of the Second Temple period. The benediction, which concludes with *Barukh . . . meḥayyeh ha-metim* ("Blessed be . . . He Who revives the dead") is therefore also known as *Teḥiyyat ha-Metim* ("Resurrection of the Dead").

3. The third benediction speaks of God's holiness, which gives it its Hebrew name, *Kedushat ha-Shem*. When the *Amidah* is repeated at public services, it is amplified into the *Kedushah* described later in this chapter. The benediction concludes with *Barukh . . . ha-El ha-Kadosh* ("Blessed be . . . the Holy God").

The Intermediate Benedictions—Petition. The 13 petitions (4 to 16) may be subdivided into two distinct groups: benedictions 4 to 9 are concerned with general human, everyday needs, both spiritual and material, while benedictions 10 to 15 give expression to specifically Jewish-national aspirations, all concerned with various aspects of messianic redemption.

4. The fourth benediction is for the gift of wisdom and understanding. It concludes with *Barukh . . . ḥonen ha-da'at* ("Blessed be . . . the gracious giver of knowledge").

5. The need for God's help in the human striving for a conciliation with Him through Torah and worship is the theme of the fifth benediction. It concludes with *Barukh . . . ha-rozeh biteshuvah* ("Blessed be . . . He Who delights in repentance").

6. The sixth paragraph is a request for forgiveness. It concludes with *Barukh . . . ḥannun ha-marbeh lislo'aḥ* ("Blessed be . . . He Who is gracious and abundantly forgiving").

7. The seventh benediction is a plea for deliverance from affliction. Appearing in a context of requests for private and everyday needs, this benediction would appear here to be out of place. It is, however, concerned (at least in its original intent) with the saving of individuals or of the community from troubles and afflictions of a transient nature, and not with eschatological salvation. The benediction concludes with *Barukh . . . go'el Yisrael* ("Blessed be . . . the redeemer of Israel").

8. The eighth benediction is a plea for the healing of the sick. It concludes with *Barukh . . . rofe ḥolei ammo Yisrael* ("Blessed be . . . He Who heals the sick of His people Israel").

9. In the ninth benediction God is petitioned to bless the produce of the earth and grant a fertile year. It is, therefore, called *Birkat ha-Shanim* ("Blessing of the Years") and concludes with *Barukh . . . mevarekh ha-shanim* ("Blessed be . . . He Who blesses the years").

The following paragraphs, benedictions 10 to 15, deal with national petitions.

10. The tenth blessing is a request for the ingathering of the exiles, or *Kibbutz Galuyyot*, to the land of Israel. It concludes with *Barukh . . . mekabbez niddeḥei ammo Yisrael* ("Blessed be . . . He Who gathers the banished ones of His people Israel").

11. The eleventh benediction appeals to God to restore righteous judges and sovereign courts, and reign Himself over Israel. There are indications, however, that this was originally concerned with the messianic "Day of Judgment," when all evildoers would be punished; the phrase "and to justify us in judgment" (still found in certain rites) conforms to this notion. The benediction concludes with *Barukh . . . melekh ohev zedakah u-mishpat* ("Blessed be . . . the King Who loves justice and judgment").

12. The twelfth benediction asks God to destroy the *malshinim* ("slanderers" or "informers"), all His enemies, and to shatter the "kingdom of arrogance." These terms are discussed below. The text of this benediction, known as *Birkat ha-Minim* ("Benediction concerning Heretics"), has undergone many changes. It concludes with *Barukh . . . shover oyevim u-makhni'a zedim* ("Blessed be . . . He Who breaks the enemies and humbles the arrogant").

13. The thirteenth benediction supplicates God to have mercy upon the righteous, the pious, the elders of the people, the true proselytes, and all those who trust in Him. It concludes with

Barukh . . . mish'an u-mivtaḥ la-ẓaddikim ("Blessed be . . . the support and trust of the righteous").

14. The next benediction entreats God to rebuild Jerusalem, to dwell there, and to restore the dynasty of King David to Israel. It concludes with *Barukh . . . boneh Yerushalayim* ("Blessed be . . . He Who rebuilds Jerusalem").

15. The fifteenth benediction seeks the re-establishment of the kingdom of David as part of the national yearning for salvation. It concludes with *Barukh . . . maẓmi'aḥ keren yeshu'ah* ("Blessed be . . . He Who causes the horn of salvation to flourish").

16. The sixteenth blessing closes the intermediate section of the *Amidah* with a plea for the favorable acceptance of prayer. It concludes with *Barukh . . . shome'a tefillah* ("Blessed be . . . He Who hearkens unto prayer").

THE CONCLUDING BENEDICTIONS—RESTORATION OF ZION, THANKSGIVING, PEACE.

17. The seventeenth benediction begs God to reinstate the *avodah* ("the Temple service"), and to return the Divine Presence to Zion. It concludes with *Barukh . . . ha-maḥazir Shekhinato le-Ziyyon* ("Blessed be . . . He Who returns the Divine Presence unto Zion"). The 14th and the 17th benedictions could not have been in their present form before the Destruction of the Temple. This is not to say that they did not exist before that date. The versions preserved in the Cairo *Genizah* might have been used in the days when the Temple still stood, when benediction 17 was evidently a petition that the sacrifices offered in the Temple be favorably accepted.

18. The eighteenth benediction is given in two forms, one to be said silently by the individual when he recites the *Amidah* by himself, the other to be said by the congregation during the *ḥazzan*'s public repetition. In both forms it is an expression of gratitude to God for all His mercies. The benediction is called *Hodayah* ("Thanksgiving") and concludes with *Barukh . . . ha-tov shimkha u-lekha na'eh lehodot* ("Blessed be . . . He Whose name is good and to whom it is fitting to give thanks").

19. The last benediction is a petition for peace. It is called *Birkat ha-Shalom* ("Benediction concerning Peace") and on some occasions is preceded by the Priestly Blessing, recited by the worshipers of priestly descent. The latter concludes with the word *Shalom* ("peace") so that the benediction comes as a kind of response to the blessing. It is, therefore, also called *Birkat Kohanim* ("Priestly Blessing"), and concludes with *Barukh . . . ha-mevarekh et ammo Yisrael ba-shalom* ("Blessed be . . . He Who blesses His people Israel with peace").

THE ADDITIONAL BENEDICTION. The 15th benediction is the later addition to the original 18. In the old Palestinian ritual, no separate benediction was devoted to the re-establishment of the Davidic kingdom, and the petition was included in the 14th benediction, the request for the rebuilding of Jerusalem. (In most present-day rites, it is still mentioned there.) The weekday *Amidah*, as found in the Cairo *Genizah*, does not have this benediction; nor did the Palestinian *paytanim* mention it in their poetic compositions, or *kerovot*, based on the *Amidah*. In talmudic times its recital as a separate benediction became the general custom in Babylonia and from this the present custom developed. Even though it is of Palestinian origin, it was not accepted there as standard practice.

The 12th benediction, *Birkat ha-Minim*, was introduced in the first century in Jabneh by Samuel ha-Katan at the request of Rabban Gamaliel II. The view, voiced already in some late talmudic sources, that this was the added benediction has been questioned on the basis of the above observations. Nor is there sufficient foundation for the theory that prior to the introduction of this latter benediction the total number was only 17. The sources clearly indicate that Samuel did not add a new benediction, but added either a new point or enlarged on the meaning of an existing benediction previously known as *Shel Paroshin* ("concerning the dissidents") or *Shel Resha'im* ("concerning the wicked"). This he did by applying it specifically

An Italian prayerbook for the whole year, copied in the 14th–15th century. The highly decorated pages show the beginning of the *Musaf Amidah* for Passover. Only the central benediction celebrating the special holiness of the day is printed and not the standard opening and closing benedictions. For these, the user had to turn to the page where they first appear in the *maḥzor*.

to Jewish heretics and informers. In his age, the generation following the Destruction of the Second Temple, the subjugated people were frequently martyred through the activities of Jewish sectarians and dissidents who acted as informers for the Roman authorities. Granted this historical context, it is generally assumed that the new foundation was meant to force the Judeo-Christians of that period out of the Jewish community. Indeed, in the version recovered in the Cairo *Genizah,* the word that recurs is *Noẓerim,* literally "Nazarenes," that is, Christians.

Medieval Christian censorship viewed this paragraph as a malediction directed against Christians in general. This view, however, is rendered absurd by a study of the many metamorphoses which the benediction underwent, both before and after the advent of Christianity. In point of fact, the changing historical situations which produced these varying forms are reflected in the variant readings still extant. To begin with, scholars have traced the origins of this prayer to the period of the Syrian-Hellenistic oppression in the time of the Second Temple, more specifically to the second century B.C.E. It was then directed against the Jews who collaborated with the foreign invader of that time. A century later it was directed against the Sadducees, and was in fact known as "the Benediction concerning Sadducees." Then comes the stage referred to above, when—in the first century C.E.—the prayer was invoked against the Judeo-Christian and Gnostic sects and other heretics, who were collectively known as *minim,* as well as against gentile oppressors. (The phrase "the kingdom of arrogance" in this period was clearly intended to designate Rome.) In fact, to avoid any suspicion of heresy, the *ḥazzan* leading the public worship had to be certain to recite this prayer. So important was this, that if he omitted it by error, he had to retrace his steps and recite it—a requirement that does not apply to any other benediction. Later national crises and persecutions, in the Dark Ages and in the medieval period, produced new textual variants which in each case likewise reflect the time and the place.

Irrespective of whether their rationale was legitimate or not, however, Christian censors repeatedly tampered with this text so that it could not be construed as referring, however obliquely, to Christianity. In consequence of their misreading, which defies all the historical evidence, certain hypersensitive Jewish editors in recent years have substituted the impersonal terms "slander" and "evil" for "slanderers" and "evildoers." In several Reform rites, the prayer has been further modified, or omitted.

Havinenu—the Amidah Condensed. Many briefer forms of the *Amidah* have been known throughout the ages. One of Ben Sira's hymns is understood by some to be such an abbreviation, and the leading rabbis of the Mishnah and Talmud favored the use of shortened forms of the *Amidah*. The one that achieved general recognition in the liturgy takes its name from its initial word, *Havinenu,* which is Hebrew for "Give us understanding." This passage may be recited instead of the *Amidah* in cases of emergency, such as when a person is pressed for time because of extraordinary circumstances, or is ill and unable to concentrate for any length of time. The *Havinenu* prayer consists of a shortened version of the 13 intermediary benedictions of the *Amidah* and concludes with the words "Blessed art Thou, O Lord, Who hearkens unto prayer." It is preceded by the three introductory benedictions of the *Amidah* and ends with the usual three concluding blessings.

There are several versions of the *Havinenu*. The text known from the Babylonian Talmud is ascribed to Mar Samuel, who lived in the second-third centuries, and is the commonly accepted version. A century later Abbaye, also a renowned talmudic scholar, scorned those who substituted the shortened *Havinenu* formula for the full *Amidah*. The law, as finally crystallized, however, permits such a substitution, except during the evening service at the termination of the Sabbath, when the fourth benediction (*Attah ḥonen*) is supplemented by the *Havdalah,* the pronouncement of the separation between Sabbath and weekday, and during the winter season when the petition for rain (*ve-ten tal u-matar*) must be said in the ninth benediction of the *Amidah*.

Insertions. The prayers described above are the regular weekday *Amidah* and its abbreviated form, *Havinenu,* as they figure in private devotions. In congregational worship, however, certain

additions are made during the *ḥazzan's* repetition of the *Amidah*. In one instance—on fast days—this addition consists of a twentieth benediction, *Aneinu*. This passage finds its place after the seventh paragraph with which, being likewise a petition for salvation in troubled times, it is thematically connected. All other additions take the form of interpolations within the standard framework of 19 benedictions. One such example—the alternative form of *Modim* which is recited by the congregation during the *ḥazzan*'s repetition of the *Amidah*—is described above in the context of the 18th benediction. Two other major examples—the doxology known as *Kedushah* and the Priestly Blessing—are discussed hereunder.

THE KEDUSHAH. The third blessing of the *Amidah* is known as the *Kedushah* (which means holiness). The blessing's full name is *Kedushat ha-Shem* ("Sanctification of the Name") to distinguish it from *Kedushat ha-Yom* ("Sanctification of the Day"). The central blessing of the *Amidah* of the Sabbath and festivals. Popularly, however, the term *Kedushah* refers to the additions and responses recited by the *ḥazzan* and congregation as part of the third benediction during the repetition of the *Amidah*. The word *kadosh* (meaning holy) represents the main theme of this doxology, hence the name *Kedushah*.

The *Kedushah,* which is inserted at the beginning of the third benediction, is recited only by a quorum of ten men (a *minyan*), since it is written: "I will be hallowed among the children of Israel"; in consideration of its context, this verse is interpreted to imply that at least ten Jews must be present. The nucleus of the different forms of the *Kedushah* consists of the following three biblical passages: "Holy, holy, holy, is the Lord of hosts; the whole earth is full of His glory"; "Blessed be the glory of the Lord from His place"; "The Lord will reign for ever, Thy God, O Zion, unto all generations; praise the Lord."

To these verses various additions were made during the first millennium of this era. Some of the changes were adopted in all liturgies, while others remained part of only one or two local rites. The actual text of the basic *Kedushah* is not cited in the Talmud, although the prayer is mentioned. It may be that the essential *Kedushah* text was already standardized during the tannaitic period, in the first centuries of this era, if not earlier. Natronai Gaon, who lived in the second half of the ninth century, opposed any change in the *Kedushah* text, because "we do not change our usage from that which the scholars of the Talmud taught." Additions, however, have been made to the texts of the various daily, Sabbath, and festival *Kedushot*. The most important of these insertions is the *Shema*—"Hear, O Israel"—in the *Kedushah* of *Musaf,* an addition which dates from the sixth century C.E., when the Jewish communities of the Byzantine Empire attempted to circumvent a prohibition against its recitation in the synagogue. The Jews thought that its insertion in such an unlikely position as the *Kedushah* of the *Musaf* service would not be suspected by the authorities. Saadiah Gaon, in the tenth century, and Maimonides, in the twelfth, later abrogated the recitation of the *Shema* during the *Musaf* service, and as a result the Yemenite and Persian rituals do not retain the insertion. All other rituals, however, preserve this vestige of an ancient community of desperate believers.

Bernard Picart (1673–1733) was a Protestant French artist and engraver who fled religious persecution in his homeland and and settled in Amsterdam. There he made many engravings of synagogue scenes and even included himself (hatless) in one. The scene here shows the Priestly Blessing. Because of the position of the priests' hands in that ceremony, outspread hands have become the symbol of the *kohanim*. The silver belt buckle (Austria, 1825) also has a crown with the words *keter kehunah*, the "Crown of the Priesthood."

There are occasions when unusual pressure of time precludes the repetition of the *Amidah*. For example, nine men may have been kept waiting for a tenth, so that they can pray the *Minḥah* service together, and they are finally able to start the Afternoon Service perilously close to sunset. In these circumstances, they may decide that if they will not be able to repeat the *Amidah* in full, they might at least be able to salvage the recitation of the *Kedushah*. In such a case, the reader begins the three introductory benedictions of the *Amidah* aloud, and the congregation joins him for the responsive reading of the *Kedushah*. At its conclusion, the whole *minyan* (including the *sheliaḥ ẓibbur*) simply completes the *Amidah* in silence, and proceeds with the remainder of the service. This emergency arrangement is commonly known by its Yiddish name—a *hoykhe Kedushah*—literally, a *Kedushah* pronounced aloud.

There are three alternative introductions to the *Kedushah* which are favored by the various rituals and recited on different occasions. Though the wording is different in each case, they all introduce the above-quoted verses by alluding to the mystical harmony of all created beings, both human and angelic, who in unison proclaim the majesty of their Creator.

The form of the *Kedushah* hitherto discussed, namely, that recited during the repetition of the *Amidah*, is called *Kedushah da-Amidah* ("Standing *Kedushah*"), since it may be recited only when standing. An abridged form, called *Kedushah di-Yeshivah* ("Seated *Kedushah*"), is recited after *Barekhu* during

the Morning Service. It is permissible to recite this passage when seated, since it is not so much a statement made by the worshiper on his own behalf, as a description of the angels' acknowledgment of God's sovereignty, as related in both Isaiah and Ezekiel. A third form, *Kedushah de-Sidra* (i.e. that recited at the conclusion of study), appears toward the end of the daily morning service for the benefit of those who missed the *Kedushah* previously recited during the repetition of the *Amidah*. The series of verses composing this *Kedushah* begins with the words: "And a redeemer shall come to Zion," and is therefore usually referred to by its opening Hebrew phrase, as *U-va le-Ẓiyyon*. It also includes two of the basic three passages, from Isaiah and Ezekiel, with their Aramaic translations. The *Kedushah de-Sidra* probably derives its name from the Babylonian custom of holding rabbinical discourses after the morning service. Together with a prayer for the observance of the Torah, this *Kedushah* would be recited upon the conclusion of the lecture. It is also recited before the reading of the Torah during the Afternoon Service on Sabbath and festivals, and after reading Psalm 91 at the conclusion of the Sabbath. It was with this *Kedushah* in mind, with its joint emphasis on the majesty of the Creator and on the eternity of the Law, that the talmudic sages said: "The world is maintained by virtue of the recitation of the *Kedushah*."

Among *ḥazzanim* the *Kedushah* has always been a favorite showpiece—perhaps because during its rendition the congregation is obliged to stand in silence. One cantorial manual, the so-called "Hanoverian Compendium" of 1744, records over 40 ornate settings. Because of the mystical connotations of the *Kedushah*, controversies had already arisen in the 17th century about cantorial repetitions of the Divine Name and of the word *keter* (meaning "crown") in such artistic compositions, since these were thought to contain the unsavory implication of dual divinity (in Hebrew, *shetei rashuyyot*), which would imply a negation of the unity of God.

THE PRIESTLY BLESSING. The other major interpolation in the *Amidah* when it is repeated in congregational worship is the benediction of the priests. Recited daily by the *kohanim* in the Temple, this is the formula in the Book of Numbers with which the priests are to bless Israel. The verse which follows—"They shall invoke My name on behalf of the Israelites and I will bless them"—makes explicit the intent of the ordained formula: to invoke the power of Him Who alone dispenses blessing. The benediction has been customarily translated as follows: "May the Lord bless you and keep you; may the Lord make His face to shine upon you and be gracious to you; may the Lord lift up His countenance upon you and grant you peace."

Every morning and evening, at the time of the daily offering, the priests ascended a special platform in the Temple called the *dukhan*. (The Yiddish verb *dukhenen*, meaning to deliver the Priestly Blessing, is derived from this Hebrew noun.) The *kohanim* pronounced the Blessing with their hands uplifted; hence in rabbinic literature the alternative name for the Priestly Blessing (*birkat kohanim*) is "the raising of the hands" (*nesi'at kappayim*). On Sabbaths and festivals the Priestly Blessing was also pronounced at the *Musaf* service, and on certain public fast days during the *Minḥah* service as well. In the Temple the priests uttered the Tetragrammaton, the Ineffable Name, whereas in the synagogues the lesser alternative divine name *Adonai* was substituted. The congregation then responded: "Blessed be the Lord God, the God of Israel, to all eternity."

After the destruction of the Temple and the cessation of the sacrifical cult, this blessing as practiced in the synagogues became the main remnant of priestly ritual. It was inserted into the last benediction of the *Amidah* and still today every adult *kohen* is enjoined to perform this function, unless disqualified by certain physical and other defects. Thus a *kohen* may not participate in the ritual if he has committed murder or idolatry, married a woman forbidden to him, or is intoxicated. He is also disqualified if he suffers from certain physical deformities or is unable to articulate the words properly. It has been argued, in explanation of these last-mentioned restrictions, that physical defects might distract the attention of the congregants, or that bodily perfection serves as a symbol for a perfect soul.

If all worshipers are priests, some of them ascend to say the blessing while the rest listen to it as congregants. Those in mourning are exempted from participating in the ritual; they

leave the synagogue momentarily before the *ḥazzan* invites the priests to ascend the platform. Originally the Priestly Blessing was part of the morning service each weekday, but as the daily business of the people did not allow them to concentrate with the desired sense of joyful devotion it was reserved, in the Diaspora, for holidays. The general Ashkenazi custom is to recite it only on the High Holidays and the three pilgrim festivals at the *Musaf* service. In Ereẓ Israel, it is customary to recite it every time *Musaf* is said, as well as on Sabbath, both at *Shaḥarit* and *Musaf;* in Jerusalem, and in certain other parts of the country, every day. If the Priestly Blessing is not pronounced for some reason by the *kohanim,* its text is recited by the *ḥazzan* toward the end of his repetition of the *Amidah,* before the 19th benediction.

A curious historical sidelight on the question of when the Priestly Blessing should be recited can be found in the aftermath of the messianic movement of Shabbetai Ẓevi in the 17th century. The community of Portuguese Jews in Amsterdam had always followed the Diaspora custom of pronouncing the Priestly Blessing only on the major festivals. In their messianic enthusiasm at what they believed to be the beginning of the Redemption, they had the Blessing recited every Sabbath. After the tragic disappointment of the false messiah's conversion to Islam they inquired of Rabbi Jacob Sasportas, an opponent of the movement whether, since it was a good custom, they should continue it notwithstanding the fact that it had been inspired by a mistaken belief and conceived, as it were, in sin. Rabbi Sasportas, in a long and detailed responsum, ruled that the custom should be discontinued temporarily as a demonstration of their return to the true faith, but that after a suitable pause the recitation of the Priestly Blessing should be instituted every day of the week, and not only on the Sabbath.

The general procedure of the Priestly Blessing is as follows. After joining the rest of the congregation in the responses of *Kedushah,* the priests leave their places to prepare themselves, removing their shoes, and washing their hands with the assistance of the Levites, after which they ascend the platform or the steps before the Ark. The *ḥazzan* then recites the prayer: "Our God and God of our fathers, bless us with the threefold blessing of the Law, written by the hand of Moses Thy servant, which was spoken by Aaron and his sons, the priests . . . " At this last word, "*kohanim,*" the priests pronounce the benediction for the *mitzvah* of the Priestly Blessing, in the meantime turning from the Ark to face the congregation. In Israel, however, it is customary for a member of the congregation to call out "*kohanim*" immediately after the 18th blessing of the *Amidah,* at which the priests begin their benediction. The *ḥazzan* then says each word of the Priestly Blessing, which is repeated aloud by the priests.

The *kohanim* recite the blessing with their *tallitot* drawn forward to cover their heads and their hands which are stretched out at shoulder height with the palms facing forward. The hands are held touching at the thumbs, with the first two fingers of each hand separated from the other two, thus forming a sort of fan. This figure became the heraldic device, so to speak, of the *kohanim,* and is often inscribed on their tombstones. It has become the custom not to look at the *kohanim* while they are pronouncing the Priestly Blessing. The reason for this is the mystical imagery, building on a verse in the Song of Songs, which pictures the Divine Presence as looking through the gaps formed by the priests' fingers. It would, of course, be presumptuous for a mortal to venture to look the Divine Presence in the face, so to speak. This explains why the *kohanim* cover themselves with their *tallitot.* In many communities the other congregants do the same, and fathers listening to the benediction draw their children to themselves and cover them too with the *tallit.*

Originally the congregants listened silently to the Priestly Blessing, but in the course of time they began to accompany it with the hushed recital of appropriate biblical quotations. There is a widespread custom to respond "Amen" after each of the three sections of the Priestly Blessing when it is said by the *kohanim,* and "So may it be Thy will," when the *ḥazzan* recites it. In the course of time considerable mystical power came to be ascribed to the Priestly Blessing, especially the power to neutralize bad dreams, which were considered to be evil omens for the future. Thus, a special prayer that the Almighty turn bad dreams into blessings was inserted in some rites, and said by

The equipment used by the Levites to wash the hands of the *kohanim* for Priestly Blessing has become an art medium. The jug and basin set was designed and executed by Ludwig Y. Wolpert in 1938, while the silver pitcher is from 18th-century Moravia. According to the inscription, it belonged to Gershon Politz, provincial rabbi in Moravia. A festival attraction in Jerusalem is the mass Priestly Blessing that takes place at the Western Wall on Ḥol ha-Mo'ed. Priests from all over the country go there to participate. The scene was photographed on an intermediate day of Passover, 1972.

the congregants at certain points in the text. Later, other prayers of kabbalistic origin were added to those recited by the congregation. These necessitated the prolonging of the Priestly Blessing, which was accomplished by the insertion of a chant before the final word of each section. Some rabbis opposed this custom, maintaining that it marred the solemn character of the Priestly Blessing, but it became widely accepted.

In Conservative Judaism the recital of the Priestly Blessing by the *kohanim* is optional. Reform Judaism has discarded the notion of special priestly privileges or duties in modern times; the Priestly Blessing is read by the rabbi as a closing benediction at the end of the service.

The threefold Priestly Blessing is also used as a formula of benediction at other ceremonies such as circumcisions or weddings, where it is recited by the officiating rabbi, and in the blessing of children.

In Private Worship. On specific occasions, other additions to the *Amidah* are made in the individual's recitation as well. These are mentioned here, and explained more fully in those chapters which deal with the respective occasions of their inclusion. In the rainy season, for example, mention is made in the second benediction of God's power which causes the rain to fall; in the ninth, a petition is made for rain. On the New Moon and on the intermediate days of Passover and Sukkot, the significance of the occasion is mentioned in the *Ya'aleh ve-Yavo* prayer, inserted into the 17th benediction. The miracles wrought in ancient times on Ḥanukkah and Purim are briefly described in the *Al ha-Nissim* prayer which is added to the 18th benediction. On public fast days a special supplication, *Aneinu*, is interpolated in the 16th benediction in the silent recitation; it has already been mentioned that during his repetition of the *Amidah* the reader recites this as a separate benediction between the seventh and eighth benedictions. In the Afternoon Service on the fact of the Ninth of Av, the 14th benediction is elaborated with a lamentation on the destruction of the Temple. During the Ten Days of Penitence in the New Year season, petitions requesting God to remember His creatures charitably and to inscribe them in the Book of Life are introduced into the first two and the last two benedictions. During the same period, the third benediction concludes with *ha-melekh ha-kadosh* ("the holy King") instead of *ha-El ha-kadosh* ("the holy God"), and the 11th with *ha-melekh ha-mishpat* ("the King of Judgment"). In the Evening Service at the conclusion of the Sabbath, a paragraph of *Havdalah*, or separation, is inserted into the fourth benediction.

Additions by an individual worshiper are also in order, provided they are appropriate to the theme of the particular benediction to which they are appended. Thus it is customary in some rites to add to the eighth benediction a prayer for a sick member of the family, whose name is mentioned; and a request for forgiveness for some particular sin may be added to the sixth (or 16th) benediction. The conclusion of the *Amidah* was held to be particularly appropriate for the addition of spontaneous individual prayers. In fact, some of the tenderest of all recorded prayers are the private meditations which the sages of the Talmud used to append to the *Amidah*, each man praying as the spirit moved him. This explains why these

concluding meditations, alone in the whole *Amidah,* are expressed in the singular.

Rabbi Eleazar, for example, used to add the following petition: "May it be Your will, O Lord our God, to cause to dwell in our lot, love, brotherliness, peace, and friendship; to widen our boundaries through disciples, to prosper our goal with hope and with future, to appoint us a share in the Garden of Eden, to direct us in your world through good companions and good impulse; that we may rise in the morning and find our heart await to fear your name." Rabbi Zeira was accustomed to add the following prayer: "May it be Your will, O Lord our God, that we do not sin, so that we fall not into dishonor nor be disgraced before our fathers." Rabbi Ḥiyya, when he had ended his prayer, spoke thus: "May it be your will, O Lord our God, that your Torah be our craft, that our hearts be not overcast, nor our eyes somber."

Rav Hamnuna used to add these words to his prayer: "May it be your will, O Lord our God, to place us in a corner where there is light, and not in a corner where there is darkness, so that our hearts may not be overcast, nor our eyes somber." These are the words of Rabbi Alexander, when he had ended his prayer: "Master of worlds, it is known and apparent before you that it is our will to do your will. But what is hindering us? The ferment in the dough [i.e., the evil inclination], and servitude to the kingdoms. May it be your will to wrest us out of their hands, so that we may again do the commandments you have willed, with a whole heart." Rava spoke thus, after he had made his prayer, and his words are repeated in the *Amidah* of the Day of Atonement: "My God, before I was formed I was worth nothing, and now that I am formed, it is as though I had not been formed. Dust I am in life, and how much more in death! Here am I, in your presence, like a vessel filled with shame and disgrace. May it be your will, O Lord my God, that I sin no more. And the sins I have committed, wipe them away in your great mercy, but not with suffering and grave sickness."

And Mar, the son of Ravina, when he had ended his prayer, spoke thus: "My God, keep my tongue from evil, and my lips from speaking guile. To those who curse me, let my soul be silent, my soul shall be to all as dust. Open my heart to your Torah, let my soul hasten to do your commandments. And succor me from evil schemes, from evil impulses, and from evil women, from all evil that rushes to come into the world. But as for those who think evil against me, break their plots and destroy their thoughts. Let the words of my mouth and the meditation of my heart be acceptable in your presence, O Lord, my rock, my redeemer." It is the prayer of Mar, the son of Ravina, that found its way into the *Siddur,* and which thus (with minor changes) became the private meditation that concludes every *Amidah.*

There is perhaps a meaning in the fact that the *Amidah* opens with a verse in the singular ("Open Thou my lips . . . "), continues throughout the 19 benedictions in the plural, adds the above-mentioned paragraph in the singular, but—as the last word—adds a request for peace, in the plural. This may be said to reflect the delicate tension between private and communal prayer that characterizes Ashkenazi worship. (Sephardi worship, by contrast, is more strictly a group activity, in which all the individual voices merge, typically, in a loudly articulated rhythmic chant recited in unison.) In fact, the Yiddish term *davenen*—a word of disputed etymology signifying the act of worship—suggests the way in which the individual, in the course of his effort at finding a meaningful individual interpretation of the statutory text, weaves his way in and out of the devotions of the congregation of which he is a part.

The ultimate in this direction is reached in some rites when a biblical verse is added just before the end of the last paragraph, which ends the *Amidah* on a note which is at once personal and mystical. For in the teachings of the Kabbalah, it is through the letters of a man's personal name that the divine life-giving force flows to nourish his soul. Accordingly, the first and last letters of the verse chosen are identical with the first and last letters respectively of the Hebrew name of the worshiper. This allows him an individual, personal identification—through "his" verse—with the Torah (the Tree of Life from which it is culled) and with the *Amidah* (the prayer par excellence) which it brings to its conclusion.

Two American military chaplains reading the Torah in Luxembourg in 1945. The army chaplains played an important role in maintaining the morale of the Jewish troops and conducting prayer services was a central duty.

THE READING OF THE TORAH

History. "And when the seventh month was come, and the children of Israel were in their cities, all the people gathered themselves together as one man into the broad place that was before the water gate; and they spoke unto Ezra the scribe to bring the book of the Law of Moses, which the Lord had commanded to Israel . . . And he read therein before the broad place that was before the water gate from early morning until midday, in the presence of the men and the women, and of those that could understand; and the ears of all the people were attentive unto the book of the Law. And Ezra the scribe stood upon a pulpit of wood, which they had made for the purpose . . . "

This event was a catalyst in the ferment of national regeneration which took place in the fifth century B.C.E. among the returned Babylonian exiles. A similar function had been served in the time of Josiah, king of Judah, in the seventh century B.C.E., by the public reading of a newly-discovered scroll of the Torah. These readings both bring to mind the *Hak'hel* ceremony referred to earlier in this chapter, in which the people were commanded to assemble once every seven years in order that the Torah be read "in their hearing." This *mitzvah* traditionally devolved upon the king. And, indeed, two centuries before Josiah, King Jehoshaphat had sent out high officials, priests and Levites to teach the Torah on his behalf: "And they taught in Judah, having a book of the Law of the Lord with them; and they went about throughout all the cities of Judah, and taught among the people."

Strangely, these few passages are virtually the only biblical references to a public Torah reading. Furthermore, referring as they do to isolated cases, they do not help establish when the custom of regular Torah readings started.

The practice is undoubtedly ancient. The Talmud ascribes to Moses the rule that the Torah should be publicly read on the Sabbath, on festivals, and on the New Moon, and to Ezra the inauguration of the reading on Mondays, Thursdays, and Sabbath afternoons. Those who regard this ascription as hyperbolic still regard it as an indication of the high antiquity of the tradition of regular public readings. Some of these scholars assume that it dates from early in the third century B.C.E., since the Septuagint was apparently compiled for the purpose of public reading in the synagogue. Philo and Josephus refer to public Torah readings as an ancient practice. This contention is supported by evidence in the New Testament: "For Moses of old time hath in every city them that preach him, being read in the synagogue every Sabbath day." Some scholars are of the opinion that originally the Torah was read only on the festivals and on certain Sabbath days before the festivals; the reading was to instruct the people as to the significance of these days.

At any rate, it is clear from the Mishnah that by the end of the second century C.E. there were regular Torah readings on Mondays, on Thursdays, and on Sabbaths; special readings for a number of Sabbaths before Passover; and special readings for the festivals, including the post-scriptural festivals of Ḥanukkah and Purim, as well as for the fast days. The length of the reading, however, seems not to have been fixed by that time (though at some point the reading of uncontinuous selections was prohibited). Rabbi Meir states, for instance, that the practice was to read a short portion on Sabbath mornings, the portion that followed on Sabbath afternoon, and further portions on Monday and Thursday. According to Rabbi Judah, the procedure was to begin the reading each Sabbath morning, not from the end of the Thursday portion, but from that of the previous Sabbath morning.

THE TRIENNIAL CYCLE. The earliest reference to a fixed cycle of consecutive readings is found in the Babylonian Talmud, where it is stated that "in the West" (that is, in Ereẓ Israel) the reading of the Torah was completed in three years. The old division of the Pentateuch into 153, 155, or 167 *sedarim,* or divisions, is based on this triennial cycle. (The singular form

This photograph was taken in Templo Maghen David, the community of Sephardi Jews in Santiago, Chile. Although the synagogue is Sephardi, the Torah scrolls used are in the traditional Ashkenazi style. One is marked *rishon* (first), and the other *sheni* (second) to indicate to the Torah reader with which scroll to start. On this particular occasion there was a *musaf* reading from the Torah.

of this word is *sidrah;* an alternative term is *parashah*.) Late in the 19th century the scholar Adolf Buechler attempted with great ingenuity to reconstruct the weekly portions of the triennial cycle, assuming the cycle to have begun on the first day of Nisan. On the basis of his reconstruction, he proceeded to explain various traditions regarding events of the past (for example, that Moses died on the seventh day of Adar, and that Sarah was "remembered" and rendered fertile on the first day of Tishrei). Buechler contended that since the portions describing these events were read once every three years at these times, the tradition grew that the events themselves had taken place then.

In Babylon and other communities outside Palestine, an annual cycle was followed according to which the Pentateuch was divided into 54 *sedarim*. This became the universal Jewish practice, except for certain isolated instances. In Palestine, too, the triennial cycle was superseded by the annual, possibly under the influence of Babylonian immigrants. However, the eminent 12th-century traveler Benjamin of Tudela writes of Cairo: "There are two large synagogues there, one belonging to the land of Israel and one belonging to the men of the land of Babylon . . . Their usage with regard to the portions and sections of the Torah is not alike; for the men of Babylon are accustomed to read a portion every week, as is done in Spain, and is our custom, and to complete the Torah each year; while the men of Palestine do not do so, but divide each portion into three sections and complete the Torah at the end of three years. The two communities, however, have an established custom to unite and pray together on the day of the Rejoicing of the Torah, and on the day of the Giving of the Torah." Also in the 12th century, Maimonides writes that the general custom was to follow the annual cycle, though the triennial cycle was nevertheless followed in some places.

Since the early part of the 19th century, various attempts have been made to reintroduce the triennial cycle. A query on this subject was addressed by an Anglo-Jewish congregation to Buechler, who replied: "If you ask me about the law, I have to answer that it is against our codified law from the 12th century onward, and even much earlier in Babylon, whence our law proceeded. If you introduce the triennial cycle, you separate yourself from the main body of Judaism."

READING AND TRANSLATION. The Mishnah rules that three persons take turns at reading the Torah on Sabbath afternoons, on Mondays, and on Thursdays; four on *ḥol ha-mo'ed* (the intermediate days of the festivals) and on the New Moon; five on a festival; six on the Day of Atonement; and seven on a Sabbath morning. The privilege of reading the first portion of the day was given to a priest (*kohen*), the second to a Levite, and the others to Israelites of lay descent. Originally, each person read his own portion. In time, with the deterioration of Torah learning among the lay people, a special official of the synagogue read the portion for the person honored. The original practice was that the person called first recited the benediction before the Torah and the person called last, that after the Torah; later the custom developed for each person to recite the benedictions before and after the particular passage to which he was called.

According to talmudic law, a woman can be called up to the reading of the Torah scroll in the synagogue; however, because of the "honor of the congregation," they were not. One possible explanation of the term "honor of the congregation" is the fact that in talmudic times and before, each individual read the portion to which he was called. Thus, in order not to embarrass the men who could not do so—the reading according to certain melodic and linguistic traditions requiring a special skill—women were not called. The Reconstructionist and Reform movements have instituted the practice of calling women to the Torah. In recent years the central body of the Conservative movement has likewise given its sanction to this practice, through the decision as to whether to implement it is left to congregational rabbis.

In the ancient period, it was customary to translate the Hebrew text into the vernacular at the time of the reading; in Palestine and Babylon the translation was made into Aramaic. This *targum,* or translation, was carried out by a specially appointed congregational official called the *meturgeman.* In the course of time, the practice of translating into the vernacular was discontinued.

The memory of this tradition has been clearly preserved, however, since it provides the historical basis for the rabbinic interpretation of a verse describing Ezra's public reading: "And they read in the book, in the Law of God, distinctly; and they gave the sense, and caused them to understand the reading." This the Talmud expounds as follows: "'And they read in the book, in the Law of God'—this refers to the Hebrew text; 'distinctly'—refers to the Aramaic *targum;* 'and they gave the sense'—indicates the division into verses; 'and caused them to understand the reading'—by chanting it according to the traditional melodic accents."

The Reading Today.

The Division of Passages. The Pentateuch is divided into 54 portions; one is to be read each Sabbath, starting with the opening chapters of Genesis on the Sabbath following Sukkot. Two such portions are sometimes read on a single Sabbath in order that the cycle be completed by the festival of *Simḥat Torah,* which immediately follows Sukkot, one year later. This elasticity is required for two further reasons. Firstly, the cycle always needs to be completed on time, whether in the case of a regular year of twelve lunar months, or in the case of a leap year, when an additional month—Adar II—is intercalated before the month of Nisan. Secondly, when a festival falls on a Sabbath, that week's regular portion is deferred to the following week. Instead, a passage dealing with the history or theme of that festival is read from one scroll, and the relevant portion from the Book of Numbers describing the sacrifice offered in honor of that festival is read from a second scroll.

This deferment of a regular Sabbath portion has a curious corollary. In the Diaspora, due to early calendrical considerations, an additional day is observed on various Scriptural festivals, so that Shavuot, for example, lasts for two days instead of one. It follows that additional days thus displace regular Sabbath portions, and congregations in Israel and in the Diaspora do not read the same passages on any given Sabbath. A visitor from Israel can thus be surprised to find a Diaspora synagogue repeating the portion he had heard on the previous Sabbath. Having become accustomed to the new situation, he returns home, only to find that he has missed one week's portion altogether. To cope with a related predicament, tourists visiting Israel for one of the festivals, and continuing to observe the extra day in accordance with their accustomed practice, frequently band together to form a *minyan* in some pre-arranged hotel. There, in that enclave of the Diaspora, they alone in all the country read the Scriptural passages appropriate to their festive day.

Synagogal Procedure. Toward the end of the Morning Service on Sabbaths and festivals, the ark is opened in readiness for the reading, to the accompaniment of verses which speak in exaltation of the Law and of its Author. Those verses are either said or chanted by the entire congregation; in synagogues that employ a *ḥazzan* and a choir, their rendition makes this moment one of the high points of the service, not only emotionally and conceptually, but musically as well. The majesty of the moment is reflected in a cantorial tradition that marks the advent of the Reading of the Law by a bold transition—from the muted strains of the minor key to the regal cadences of a processional in a major key.

It is significant that one of these verses is the prayer uttered by the Children of Israel in the wilderness, invoking divine

protection whenever the Ark of the Covenant was to be borne aloft to lead them in their wanderings. It thus highlights the parallelism between the ancient Sanctuary and today's miniature sanctuary, the synagogue, and between the Ark of the Covenant which in ancient times housed the Tablets of the Law and the ark which today houses the scrolls of the Torah.

BERIKH SHEMEIH. As the ark is opened, it has become the custom in many congregations over the last few centuries to read a certain excerpt from the *Zohar,* the classic work of Jewish mysticism. This passage is introduced in the *Zohar* in the following manner: "When the Scroll is taken out in the congregation for the public reading, the gates of the Heavens of Mercy open, and celestial love is aroused. It is then fitting for a man to recite this prayer." The *Berikh Shemeih*—for so it is known by its opening words—is a powerful and simplistic personal prayer, in which the individual affirms his loyalty to the divine command, and seeks to be assured of God's nearness.

THE THIRTEEN ATTRIBUTES. Another custom whose origins lie in Jewish mysticism is the recital on festivals of the Pentateuchal passage which enumerates the Thirteen Attributes of Divine Mercy. This statement of God's love and justice is pronounced only in congregational worship when the Sefer Torah is read, or on fast days.

RIBBON HA-OLAM. The last supplication to be said while the ark is open but before the scrolls are removed is *Ribon ha-Olam,* a relatively recent prayer for personal welfare. It was composed by Nathan Nata Hanover, who is better known as the chronicler of the Cossack massacres of Polish Jewry which began in 1648. It is recited only on festivals; however, being (like the Thirteen Attributes) a supplicatory prayer, it is likewise not recited when a festival falls on the Sabbath.

SHEMA YISRAEL. At this point the *ḥazzan* takes the *Sefer Torah* from the congregant who had been honored with the opening of the Ark. and solemnly pronounces the *Shema,* which the congregation repeats in unison. This communal profession of faith was understood by the Emperor Justinian to be of such power that in the year 533, on the advice of his court clerics, he outlawed its practice throughout the Byzantine Empire. The next sentence to be so chanted is likewise a statement of God's unity. Thereafter, the *ḥazzan* invites the congregation to join him in words of praise. As they do this, frequently in song, the *ḥazzan* bears the scroll in procession around the synagogue, starting at the ark, and ending at the *bimah,* the platform at which it is to be read.

During this circuit the congregation stands, in accordance with the rabbinic interpretation of a well-known biblical verse: "Thou shall rise up before the hoary head and honor the face of an old man, and thou shalt fear thy God: I am the Lord." The rabbis taught that one is obliged to stand not only when a man of mature years passes by, but also when a man mature in Torah learning passes by. Furthermore—for so the argument developed—if one must rise before those who study the Torah, how much more should this obligation apply in the presence of the Torah itself. Moreover, in token of affection, it has become customary for the congregation to kiss the scroll as it is borne around on its way to the reading desk.

When the Torah is read on less leisurely occasions—such as on Monday and Thursday mornings, when congregants are understandably in a hurry—the opening of the ark and indeed the whole procedure of the Reading of the Torah is stripped of much of its accompanying text, music, and pomp.

THE ALIYAH. On Sabbath, as has been stated above, seven people are called up to the *bimah* for the reading. This honor is called an *aliyah,* which means ascent, for more than one reason. In the first instance, being "called up" involves ascending the steps of the platform from which the Torah is read. Moreover, in ḥasidic thought, the *aliyah*—to the man who by devout intent utilizes that propitious moment—is a time of spiritual ascent. For the kabbalists taught that the reading of the Torah is a dramatic re-enactment of the Revelation at Sinai. The reader who utters the words stands in place of the Almighty, the person called to hear the reading represents the people who assembled to receive the Torah, while the role of Moses is filled by the *gabbai,* the official who stands at the side of the reader and apportions the *aliyot.*

Being called to the first *aliyah* is the prerogative of a *kohen,* and the second is that of a Levite. If no *kohen* is present, a Levite is usually called to the first portion. If no Levite is present,

The Torah scroll is so sacred that one should not touch the actual parchment with one's bare hand. In order that the reader keeps his place in the text, a pointer is used which is generally known by the name *yad* (hand). The filigree silver *yad* shown here is from 19th-century Poland, and the inscription reads: "In the year 5648 (1889)." The Torah scroll in the other illustration was written in Persia in 1799. The case is in the traditional Sephardi fashion, and the reader is using a *yad*.

the *kohen* is called again to the second portion. Neither a *kohen* nor a Levite may be called to any of the remaining five portions. However, since most authorities permit the calling up of more than the standard number of people (on Sabbath alone), a *kohen* or a Levite may be called to the last of the additional portions. In cases of such further subdivision, no portion contains fewer than three verses, nor ends on an inauspicious note, such as the account of a national misfortune.

A congregant is called to the reading by his Hebrew name and that of his father; if he is a *kohen* (or a Levite, or a rabbi) then that is mentioned too, thus: "Arise, Aharon ben Yaakov *ha-kohen*." The surname, being a relatively recent innovation, is ignored. A father and son, or two brothers, are not called consecutively to the reading. One explanation advanced for this is that it serves to prevent any misunderstanding of the rule which prohibits near relatives from testifying together.

Upon hearing his name announced, a congregant approaches the *bimah* by the shortest route and, when returning to his seat, does so by the longest route, thus giving symbolic expression to his eagerness to be called and his reluctance to leave. This sentiment also lies behind the custom whereby at the completion of his own portion, he tarries at the side of the next person to be called, until that portion is also completed, before returning to his seat. (When the routes are equidistant, the congregant ascends by the right and descends by the left.)

Since the number of *aliyot* is limited, certain persons take precedence. First among these is a bridegroom on the Sabbath preceding his marriage. Since he is about to hallow unto himself a wife "according to the law of Moses and Israel," it is fitting that on this occasion he should be formally confronted with that Law and reminded of the obligations which it entails. Traditionally, the bridegroom is also called up on the Sabbath after the wedding, taking precedence even over a bar mitzvah boy, who is second in the line of priorities.

The latter is followed by a man whose wife has just given birth; if the baby is a girl, this is the occasion for the name-giving. The next two places are occupied in turn by a person on the *yahrzeit* day which marks the anniversary of a parent's death, and by a man rising from *Shiv'ah*, the seven days of mourning.

The order described above is the formally recognized hierarchy. Theoretically, the remaining *aliyot* should be of equal value, particularly since the ancient appointment of one reader for all portions democratized the service so that the humblest illiterate could now take his turn next to the most illustrious scholar. In practice, however, the above hierarchy is supplemented by a parallel, uninstitutionalized evaluation system. Thus, for example, being called up on the Sabbath to the third or the sixth *aliyah* has become a coveted honor. The reason in the former case may be that it is the first *aliyah* which is open to any congregant who is neither a *kohen* nor a Levite. The de facto aristocracy of the sixth *aliyah* remains a riddle. Nonetheless, cases have even been known of a congregant taking offense because he was called up for the fifth portion, "one before the sixth." However irrational his complaint, the fact

remains that for certain *aliyot* there is a tacit understanding in many congregations that they should be alloted to individuals of especial piety, scholarship, or repute.

The same applies in certain circles to the last *aliyah,* particularly when this reading concludes one of the five books of the Pentateuch. In such a case this *aliyah* is called *ḥazak* (which in Hebrew means "Be strong!"). As the last verse is read, the congregation rises and intones together: "Be strong, be strong, and let us strengthen ourselves"—that is, in the study and practice of the Torah. Other valued *aliyot*—for which the congregation also rises—are the portions which include the Song of the Sea and the Ten Commandments.

At the opposite end of the prestige scale are the passages which deal with the retribution awaiting Israel in the event of her future backsliding. In many congregations it is the custom for the reader to take this portion himself; few congregants vie with him for the privilege.

In order to remove allegations of arbitrariness in the apportionment of *aliyot*—and in order to help at the same time to replenish synagogal funds—some congregations are accustomed to auctioning *aliyot,* especially on the High Holy Days. In many places this practice has been discontinued on grounds of both principle and decorum.

The reader (or *ba'al koreh*) prepares himself by conscientiously rehearsing the portion he is to read. Since the scroll may contain only the Hebrew words made up of consonants—supplemented by neither vocalization symbols for the vowels, nor punctuation signs, nor musical notations—a perfect reading indicates a considerable effort of memorization. If however, a word is misread so that its meaning is changed, it must be repeated. On occasion, a whole verse has to be repeated, and few traditional congregations are without half a dozen conscientious listeners who zealously make themselves heard whenever they suspect the slightest slip.

The reading is valid only if the scroll is fit for use (*kasher*). It is rendered unfit (*pasul*) if a single letter has been omitted or even, in certain cases, partially obliterated. Should such a blemish be discovered in the course of the reading, the scroll is returned to the ark, but its wrapper is bound around the mantle instead of inside it, as an indication that the scroll is not to be used again until corrected. On a Sabbath, even if several congregants have already been called up, seven persons are called up to the reading which is resumed from another scroll.

THE BENEDICTIONS. When a congregant is called to an *aliyah,* he first invites his fellow worshipers to join him in a benediction: "Bless ye the Lord, Who is to be blessed." To this they respond: "Blessed be the Lord Who is to be blessed for ever." He repeats this, and continues: "Blessed art Thou, Lord our God, King of the Universe, Who has chosen us from all peoples, and has given us His Torah. Blessed art Thou, O Lord, Giver of the Torah."

As he intones the text according to the intricate traditions of cantillation, the reader customarily points to the place with an ornate *yad.* This enables the worshiper to follow the reading of the passage to which he was called. At its conclusion, he recites one further benediction: "Blessed art Thou, Lord our God, King of the Universe, Who has given us the Torah of truth and has planted everlasting life in our midst. Blessed art Thou, O Lord, Giver of the Torah."

The passage over which these benedictions are being made is, of course, part of the Written Law—Scripture. Yet Jacob ben Asher, a medieval luminary who was an authority on Scripture and Jewish law, interpreted the above-quoted concluding benediction as follows: "Torah of truth" refers to the Written Law, while "everlasting life" refers to the oral tradition. In this way he highlighted the intrinsic continuity that binds the Oral Law to its parent, the Written Law. In a nexus of reciprocal nourishment, the Oral Law draws its sanction from the Written Law, whose perpetuation it meanwhile ensures through its own growth.

The Reconstructionist trend in Judaism, which repudiates the notion of the election of Israel, has changed the wording of the first benediction to read: "Who has brought us close to His service," instead of "Who has chosen us."

Among certain North African Jewish communities each individual being honored with an *aliyah* first shares the privilege with his fellow-congregants by invoking upon them the blessing with which Boaz greeted the reapers of Bethlehem: "The

The case of the Torah scroll being read in the Afghanistan synagogue is far less elaborate than the Persian. The reader is also using a silver *yad*. The depiction of the reading of the Torah in Kai-Feng-Fu in China was the work of an 18th-century Jesuit missionary. For some reason he called the stand on which the Torah was being read the "Chair of Moses." Perhaps the local Jews of the time used to refer to it as such.

Juif de Caifum lisant la Bible à la
chaire de Moyse, avec deux Souffleurs.

Lord be with you!" To which the congregation responds: "The Lord bless thee!"

THE GOMEL BLESSING. There is another situation in which one worshiper is blessed by his fellows in unison. Being called up to the Torah is the occasion for a benediction of thanksgiving which is recited by a person who has been saved from danger. It takes its name from its key word, *ha-gomel,* which means "He Who bestows."

The Talmud lists four categories of people, all mentioned in Psalm 107, who are obligated to recite this benediction: those who have voyaged across the sea or who have crossed a wilderness, those who have recovered from a serious illness, and those released from prison. The rabbis of the Talmud derive this duty from two verses of the above Psalm: "Let them give thanks unto the Lord for His mercy, and for His wonderful works to the children of men. Let them exalt Him also in the assembly of people, and praise Him in the seat of elders." Accordingly, the blessing should preferably be said in the presence of ten men ("an assembly of people"), two of whom should be scholars ("in the seat of the elders"). It is to be pronounced within three days after the person has been delivered from danger. These conditions are satisfied by the custom of saying the benediction after one has been called to the Torah on a Monday, Thursday, or Sabbath.

The wording that appears in the Talmud is: "Blessed be He Who bestows lovingkindness." In practice, the accepted text amplifies this as follows: "Blessed art Thou . . . —He Who does good unto the undeserving, and Who has dealt kindly with me." To which the congregation responds: "He Who has shown thee kindness, may He always deal kindly with thee."

In addition to the four classical categories of people obliged to recite the benediction it is customary in some communities for women after childbirth to recite it in front of the ark after the service. The *Gomel* blessing may also be recited by an entire community. Today, in the spirit of the rule laid down in the Talmud, it is customary for it to be pronounced after an international flight, and in Israel it is recited by military reservists after a stretch of active service.

MI SHE-BERAKH. As each person completes his *aliyah* by reciting the benediction that follows the reading of his portion, the *gabbai* who stands at the side of the *bimah* customarily invokes divine blessings upon him in a short prayer which opens with the words *Mi she-Berakh*: "May He Who blessed our forefathers Abraham, Isaac and Jacob, bless [the congregant who is named] and prosper all the work of his hands . . " The formula employed sometimes makes reference to the amount of charity being pledged by the congregant in question; in the interests of decorum, this element is often dispensed with. The operative Hebrew words which immediately precede the sum announced are—as generally pronounced—*ba'avur she-nodar*. In many Anglo-Jewish congregations, a popular corruption of this term has produced the etymological mongrel, *shnodder,* a noun which means "the amount pledged in synagogue."

On a joyous occasion—a bar mitzvah, a forthcoming marriage, or the birth of a child—the prayer is worded so as to make reference to the event, and the father of a newborn girl

Bernard Picart's copper engraving of this synagogue scene shows the *Hagbahah* ceremony in the synagogue. The person lifting up the Torah scroll has opened it as wide as he can so that the congregation should be able to see as much text as possible. The page with the *Mi she-Berakh* prayer which is made at the Torah reading dates from the 18th century and is an invocation for the welfare of all those members of the congregation who have undertaken to fast Monday, Thursday and Monday. This reference is to the *Behab* fasts which the pious observe after the major festivals. The music is the intonation of the prophets according to the Yemenite tradition.

usually gives his daughter her name on this occasion. Since the Middle Ages it has been likewise customary to invoke a blessing for the sick at the time of an *aliyah*. In such cases, the formula includes the name of the friend or relative concerned. In the case of a woman, the introductory words substitute the names of the matriarchs for those of the patriarchs.

RAISING THE SCROLL. Either before or after the reading, the *Sefer Torah* is opened and raised aloft, a ceremony known in Hebrew as *hagbahah*. This is done in such a way as to enable the congregants to see three of the written columns, whereupon they testify aloud: "This is the Law which Moses set before the children of Israel, according to the word of the Lord, by the hand of Moses." In various rituals, additional verses are recited, all dealing with the place of the Torah in the scheme of things. For example: "It is a tree of life for those who hold fast to it; and all of those who uphold it are rendered happy."

In the Ashkenazi ritual, the *hagbahah* is performed after the reading from the Pentateuch and before the reading from the Prophets. In many ḥasidic synagogues it is done with an open scroll before the reading, and again—with a closed scroll—

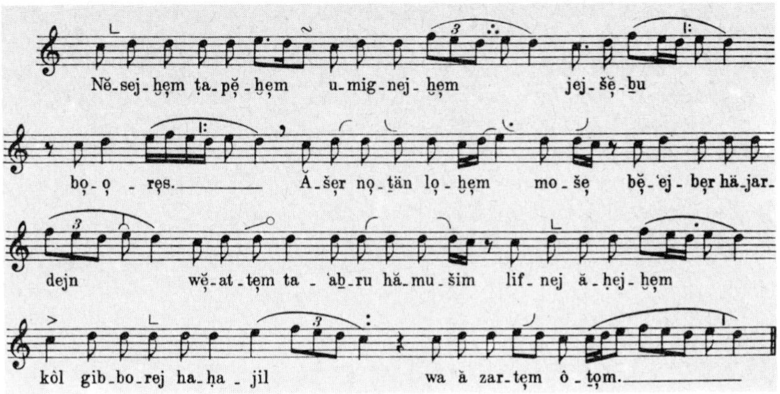

after the reading. In the Sephardi ritual, *hagbahah* is done before the reading, as follows: The person who takes the *Sefer Torah* from the ark opens its cylindrical case and carries it open to the *bimah,* displaying a few columns of text. The rationale behind this custom is obvious: the scroll is thus shown to be a true *Sefer Torah* before it is actually read.

After the reading, the person who removes the scroll from the *bimah* (with or without *hagbahah,* according to local custom) sits down. Another congregant (in the case of an Ashkenazi scroll) binds it with its wrapper, dresses it with its mantle, and replaces the various ornaments described in Chapter IV. This task is called *gelilah,* which is Hebrew for "rolling together." According to the Talmud, this is a greater honor than to be called to the reading. Notwithstanding, it is customary in certain countries for the ceremony to be performed by minors who, because they have not yet reached the age of bar mitzvah, are not qualified to be called to the reading. Not so the ceremony of *hagbahah*. Indeed, in the Western Sephardi ritual, this privilege is reserved for an honorary official, or for members of an honorary brotherhood whose name—*levantadores*—indicates their coveted prerogative.

The Haftarah. The practice of rounding off the Torah reading with a passage from one of the prophetic books is mentioned in the Mishnah. The passage chosen is known as the *haftarah,* which means "completion," or taking one's leave. Typically, the *haftarah* accords in theme with the day's Pentateuchal reading. There is evidence that in some ancient communities selections from the Hagiographa were also read. This would explain the frequent quotations from this third part of the Bible found in the midrashic passages which comment on Pentateuchal themes. The dictum of Rabbi Akiva that one who reads the "external books" has no share in the world to come refers, in all probability, to the public reading of books outside the canon of the Bible, such as those of the Apocrypha.

The portion from the Prophets is read on Sabbaths and festivals during the Morning Service and on fast days at the *Minḥah* service only. Exceptions are the Day of Atonement and the Ninth of Av, when there is a *haftarah* after the Torah reading both in the Morning and the Afternoon Services. There is, however, evidence that during the talmudic period a *haftarah* was read at *Minḥah* on Sabbaths, and in some places the custom continued until the end of the geonic period.

Unlike the Sabbath readings from the Pentateuch which together constitute a consecutive reading, the *haftarah* is a portion from a book of the Former or Latter Prophets. Only two prophetic books are read completely as *haftarot*: the Book of Obadiah, which consists of only 21 verses, and the Book of Jonah, which is the *haftarah* for the *Minḥah* service of the Day of Atonement. There were two criteria which determined the selection of a particular *haftarah.* When no other considerations prevailed, the choice was determined by the similarity of the contents of the prophetic portion to those of the portion of the Pentateuch read. Thus, for example, the *haftarah* to the portion *Be-Shallaḥ,* in which the Song of Moses appears, includes the Song of Deborah. Likewise, for the portion *Shelaḥ,* which describes the incident of the twelve spies sent by Moses, the *haftarah* chosen concerns the spies sent some decades later by Joshua.

For about one third of the *haftarot,* however, this criterion is abandoned, and the choice for the Sabbaths in question is determined either by the calendar or by historical considerations. For ten successive weeks, from the Sabbath before the fast of the 17th of Tammuz until the Sabbath before Rosh Ha-Shanah, the *haftarot* consist of three passages of tribulation (*pur'anuta*) and seven of consolation (*neḥemta*). Special *haftarot* are also read on a Sabbath on which Rosh Ḥodesh falls, as is the case too on the Sabbath which falls on the day before Rosh Ḥodesh, on the Sabbath before Passover, on the Sabbath of the Ten Days of Penitence, and on the Sabbath (or Sabbaths) of Ḥanukkah. The choice of the *haftarot* for the Four Special Sabbaths, which are discussed in Chapter VII, depends on the additional portion read on these days, and not on the ordinary Sabbath portion. On festivals and fast days the *haftarah,* like the Torah reading, consists of a portion appropriate to those days. In a few cases the *haftarah* is not a continuous portion.

HISTORY. The origin of the custom of reading a portion of the Prophets after the Torah reading is unknown. The most

A section of A. Z. Idelsohn's *Comparative Table of Torah Cantillation Motifs.* Idelsohn (1882–1938) was one of the most famous Jewish musicologists of his time. In 1905 he settled in Jerusalem and worked as a cantor and music teacher. His confrontation with the various Jewish communities in Jerusalem stimulated him to collect and study their musical heritage. Idelsohn is considered to be the founder of modern Jewish musicology and one of the pioneers of ethno-musicology.

plausible suggestion (dating from not earlier than the 14th century) is that the custom was instituted during the persecutions by Antiochus Epiphanes which preceded the Hasmonean revolt in the second century B.C.E. According to this theory, when the reading of the Torah was outlawed, a substitute was found by reading a corresponding portion from the Prophets; and the custom was retained after the decree was repealed. One scholar is of the opinion that it was instituted to express defiance against the Samaritans, who denied the canonicity of the Prophets (except for the Book of Joshua) and later—also for demonstrative, theological reasons—against the Sadducees.

The earliest actual reference to the reading of a *haftarah* is found, interestingly enough, in the New Testament, where it is stated that "after the reading of the law and the prophets" Paul was invited to deliver an exhortation. Another reference mentions that during a Sabbath service in Nazareth, the Book of Isaiah was handed to Jesus, "and when he had opened the book, he found the place where it was written," the passage being Isaiah 61:1–2. Unfortunately, the Greek word in question does not make it clear whether the passage read was fixed beforehand or whether it was chosen at random.

Whatever references there are in talmudic literature to the specific selection of a *haftarah* have to do with special occasions, such as festivals, and red-letter Sabbaths. However, nowhere in the Talmud are the *haftarot* given for ordinary Sabbaths, these not being fixed until after the talmudic period. The only other mention of the matter in tannaitic literature is the prohibition against reading certain prophetic passages—such as the account of the vision of the heavenly chariot in Ezekiel or the story of Amnon and Tamar—for reasons of possible theological misunderstanding, or of delicacy. These mishnaic passages would seem to indicate that in mishnaic times the choice of the *haftarah* was not fixed, and as late as geonic times different *haftarot* were in vogue in different localities. Even some of the *haftarot* mentioned in the Talmud are not those established at the present time, and to this day there are certain variations of choice, mostly between Sephardim and Ashkenazim, but also between different Ashkenazi rites. When the triennial cycle of Torah reading was in vogue in Ereẓ Israel, there was naturally a *haftarah* to each portion, and their number must therefore have been about 150. Another source of variation is the fact that there are *haftarot* for the additional day of certain festivals in the Diaspora which are never read in Ereẓ Israel, where the second day is not observed.

PROCEDURE. The person honored with the reading of the *haftarah* is known as the *maftir*, or leave-taker, since before he reads the passage from the prophets, the last few verses of the week's Pentateuchal portion are repeated for him. The purpose of this repetition is to affirm the authoritative status of the passage from the Prophets by coupling it with the week's portion from the Five Books of Moses. The repeated reading takes the form of a regular *aliyah*, complete with the benedictions, except for its brevity, though it is never shorter than three verses. As the *maftir* is not included in the minimum obligatory number of seven persons for a Sabbath reading, he may be a *kohen*, a Levite, or even—in certain congregations—a minor from the age of ten.

On festivals, New Moon, and the Four Special Sabbaths, however, there is no repetition. Instead, the *maftir* is called to the special additional portion for those days which is read from a second scroll. With the completion of that reading, the Sefer Torah is raised and rolled up, and only then does the *maftir* read the *haftarah,* preceding it with two blessings and concluding the reading with three blessings. On Sabbaths and festivals, a fourth blessing is added to these, its formula being changed according to the nature of the day. The text is given in Tractate *Soferim,* with slight variations from the text as established today. The *haftarah* is sung according to a special cantillation, and the custom has developed for the two introductory blessings to be chanted to the same melody. The Sabbath *haftarah* consists of a minimum of 21 verses, but for the festivals 15 suffice.

Unlike the Pentateuchal reading, it is not obligatory for the *haftarah* to be read from a manuscript scroll; it may be read from a printed book. This means, incidentally, that being fully punctuated and vocalized, it demands less expertise so that almost any layman can read it when called up. In some congregations, however, especially in Israel, the *haftarah* is read from a scroll of the Prophets, which is handwritten on parchment, unvocalized like a Torah scroll. Despite the general prohibition against committing to a scroll only sections of the Prophets, as opposed to complete Books of the Prophets, an exception was made in the case of a scroll containing only the *haftarot;* such a scroll is, in fact, mentioned in the Talmud. The more common practice in Israeli synagogues is to read the *haftarah* from a complete volume of the Bible, as is done in the Diaspora.

The custom has become almost universal to reserve the reading of the *haftarah* for a bar mitzvah boy, but this is largely in order to provide him with the opportunity to display his prowess. Some *haftarot,* however, are regarded as being of such importance that a minor, and in some places even a bar mitzvah, is precluded from reading them. They include the *Merkavah* which is read on Shavuot—the first chapter of Ezekiel which relates his vision of the celestial chariot; the jubilant Song of David which is read on the seventh day of Passover; and the *haftarah* on the Sabbath of the Ten Days of Penitence, which serves as a reminder to the congregation of the awe of that season. The same rule applies to the *haftarah* of *Shabbat Zakhor,* one of the Special Sabbaths, because in this case the separate Torah reading of the *maftir*—on the remembrance of Amalek—is considered to be an obligation of explicit biblical authority. For this reason, each word of this brief passage is enunciated with special punctiliousness and listened to even more carefully than is a regular reading.

During the talmudic period, when the biblical reading was accompanied by its translation into Aramaic, the Torah reading was translated verse by verse, while the Aramaic version of the *haftarah* was given after every three verses, unless each verse constituted a separate paragraph. The person who read the *haftarah* was traditionally invited to be *pores al shema,* a phrase to which different interpretations are given; in the context it appears to mean that he was asked to continue as the reader of the *Musaf* service which followed.

Cantillation. Mention has been made of the fact that the Torah is read to a particular series of melodic phrases, which together constitute a specialized musical style known in English as cantillation. This style has a long history, and its contemporary rendition shows marked variations not only as from one group of biblical texts to another, but also as between the heritage of different regions and communities. These variations are further colored by liturgical circumstances involving both the content and the context of any particular passage, and the season in which it is read.

Historical Development. The musical intonation is closely linked with the accents which accompany the traditional masoretic text, and is governed by fixed rules and practices. However, public reading from the Bible is attested much earlier than the establishment of the written systems of accentuation. In the Bible itself cantillated readings are mentioned only in connection with special occasions. Although, as far as the musical element is concerned, talmudic sources merely say that the Bible was to be read and studied only by melodic recitation, it is inconceivable (in view of the strict regulation of every other element of the scriptural reading) that the melodic rendition could have been left to the ad hoc invention or choice of the reader. The system developed by Tiberian scholars in the seventh century of indicating the signs and functions of the accents and vowels was based on existing practices. This applied not only to the pronunciation and grammatical basis and syntactical structure of the text, but also to its musical rendition. Indeed, the earliest surviving treatise on this system, Ben-Asher's *Dikdukei ha-Te'amim* (written before the tenth century) mentions a melodic element (*ne'imah*) in the characterization of several of the accents. But neither this system nor the preceding Palestinian and Babylonian systems seem to show the intention of establishing a complete correspondence between each accent sign and a specific melodic motif. This implies that no such correspondence existed in practice at that time, and there was no intention to create it artificially, on the part of the masoretes, as the scholarly guardians of the traditional (or masoretic) text are known.

Comparative studies of the living traditions of the present, and the evidence gleaned from the medieval and later masoretic treatises, reveal that only in the Ashkenazi Diaspora was the system developed and augmented with the aim of having each accent sign expressed by a distinct melodic formation. The farthest point along this path is reached by the Ashkenazi cantillation of the Torah. Even there, however, one finds different accent signs expressed by identical melodic formations, and identical accent signs expressed by different melodic formations. Other traditions are still more limited in their repertoire of distinct melodic motifs and content themselves with the expression of the divisive accents within the sentences, or even of the major divisive accents only. This style is probably not the result of any erosion or loss of knowledge, but may well be the surviving evidence of the earliest stages of the system.

Rendition. The musical rendition of the text in conformity with the accent signs is based on the convention that each sign or group of signs represents a certain melodic motif. The graphic symbol, however, does not stand for an absolutely predetermined sequence of tones. As in all music cultivated by oral tradition, the motifs exist as ideals to be realized in performance, within certain margins of flexibility. Preservation of the ideals, that is, the style, is assured by several factors: the well-defined grammatical and syntactical functions of the accents; the deliberate teaching by which the tradition is handed on from generation to generation; and the constant public practice of the system in the synagogue, where not only the layman's rendition (when called up to read) but even that of the specialized reader, is always subject to the critical ear of the more knowledgeable members of the community. The margin of flexibility, on the other hand, makes it possible to link, or rather blend, the motifs as they are recalled and enunciated successively by the reader so as to create a melodic organism. The style itself remains constant, but each reader may interpret it with a certain individuality. In fact, he will never repeat his previous performance precisely when he reads the same passage on another occasion.

Theoretically, the accent signs are divided into only two categories: the accents of the Books of Psalms, Proverbs and Job, and the accents of the remaining twenty-one books of the canon of the Bible. In practice, the musical renditions show a much greater diversity of styles.

Separate melodic conventions exist for the Pentateuch, the prophetic books (as read in the *haftarah*), and for several of the books of the Hagiographa (specifically, the Five Scrolls). These may not be interchanged, and indeed explicit prohibitions are found in several rabbinic sources. Nevertheless there exists a kind of infiltration of motifs from one book to the other, as evinced by the appearance of motifs from the cantillation of the Torah in that of the *haftarah*. Some motifs may also be common to more than one book, such as certain elements in the cantillation of the Books of Esther and Lamentations in the Ashkenazi tradition. In principle, however, each book has its distinct and characteristic melodic style.

Most regional traditions have special festive styles for the reading of certain passages—especially the Song of the Sea and the Decalogue—and often also for the Blessing of Moses and the Priestly Blessing. The Ashkenazi tradition is particularly rich in special intonations which vary according to the mood of the text. Thus, the warnings and rebukes which are listed at length in Deuteronomy have their own appropriate tone. Sometimes intonations emphasize the importance of certain single verses in the Torah. For example, the voice is dramatically raised for the ominous turning points in the plot of the Book of Esther. Chapters and verses referring to calamities, such as several verses in the Book of Esther, are read in the style of the Book of Lamentations. And again, verses or parts thereof which denote supplication and the request for pardon are intoned in the style in which the Torah is read on the High Holy Days. In fact, in the reading of the Book of Esther in certain branches of Ashkenazi tradition there is even one melodic quotation from the prayer mode of the High Holy Days, and another from that of the *seliḥot*.

During the three Pilgrim Festivals the reading of the Torah is more festive than usual, with more ornamentations and prolongations. The melancholy atmosphere of the Ninth of Av influences the reading of the *haftarah* on the preceding Sabbath, the reading of the Torah on the Ninth of Av itself—which is done softly and is sometimes rendered almost without the accents—and its *haftarah* as well. As an example of reciprocal influence between regional styles, it may be noted that the Ashkenazim of Holland read the Torah on the Ninth of Av in a style related to the *haftarah* style of the Polish-Lithuanian region. On the High Holy Days and Hoshana Rabba, the Ashkenazi tradition has a somber style for the reading of the Torah—"in a low melody, as if plaintive," as noted in a *maḥzor* published in 1557. On the Sabbath nearest the wedding day, among some Near Eastern communities, the section from Genesis beginning "And Abraham was old" is read in the presence of the bridegroom in a festive style, doubtless as an omen of blessing.

Regional Traditions. The living traditions of the present may be classified according to five major regional styles: Yemenite, Ashkenazi, Middle Eastern and North Africa, Jerusalem Sephardi, and the diverse local styles of the northern Mediterranean lands.

The Yemenite style is particularly rich in distinct sub-styles for the biblical books and for particular chapters, and in various divisions among single and group readers. The Ashkenazi style is the earliest to be documented in musical notation. Curiously, this was first done by a Christian Hebraist, Johannes Reuchlin, in 1518. Its melodic elements have been preserved most tenaciously among the Western Ashkenazi communities, including those of southern Germany. The Eastern Ashkenazi Torah style (known as Polish-Lithuanian) is somewhat different from the Western one. The *haftarah* style is particularly well developed in Eastern Europe, and is nowadays common to both the Eastern and Western Ashkenazi communities. The Middle Eastern and North African style is current from Cochin to Algeria, through Persia, Bukhara, Iraq, Syria, Kurdistan, the Caucasus, and North Africa. There is a close connection between this style, and the styles of the European Sephardi communities in Italy, France, Holland, England, and America. It can also be traced in some Balkan communities, notably those of the Romaniot rite, and its influence is also noticeable in the intonation of the Song of Songs of the Polish-Lithuanian tradition. The earliest notation of this style was published in 1699 in the Hebrew Bible edited by Daniel Jablonski, for whom it was furnished by David de Pinna, one of the *parnasim*, or wardens, of the Portuguese community of Amsterdam.

The Jerusalem Sephardi style is found around the eastern shores of the Mediterranean, from Turkey and the Balkan communities to North Africa, and centered in Ereẓ Israel. Due to the prestige of its association with Jerusalem and Ereẓ Israel, it overlaid and frequently even ousted many local traditions throughout the Mediterranean countries. The Torah style in this tradition cannot represent the pre-expulsion Spanish tradition, since it is found neither in North Africa nor among the European Sephardim; it seems in fact to be a relatively recent development. Finally, the North Mediterranean styles are typically restricted to the few communities in this area, such as Rome and Carpentras (in Provence) which have distinct local styles of their own. The Carpentras tradition survives only in notation, since the community itself no longer exists.

In Israel, the ingathering of the exiles has caused a major deterioration in many of the local and regional traditions brought into the country, since the immigrants often could not keep up their homogenous associations centered around the synagogue. The breakdown of the traditional education system

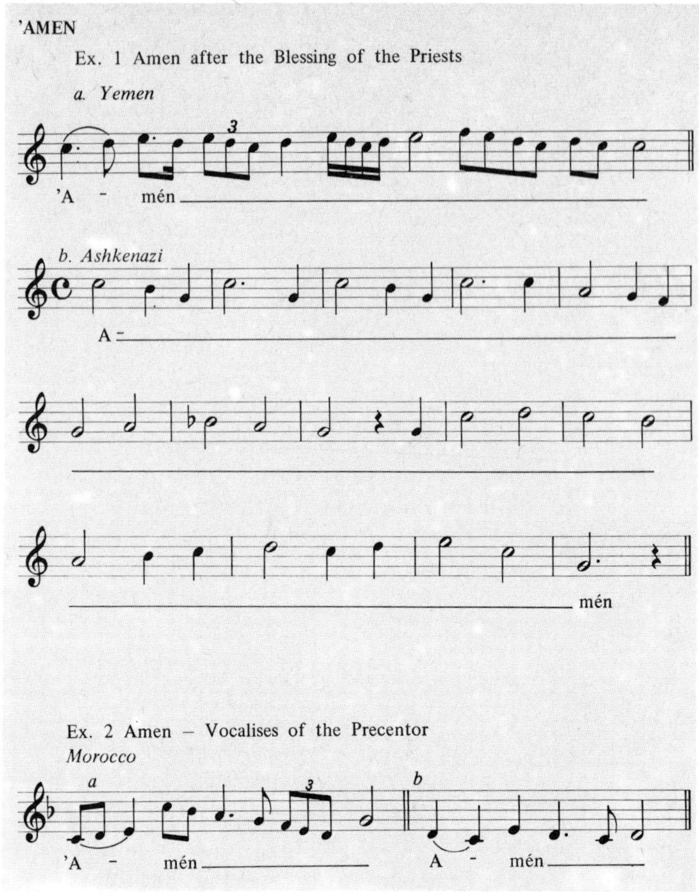

According to the Talmud, the word "Amen" should be drawn-out in pronunciation, an act which is said to prolong life. Thus Amen has been given distinctive melodies for the various places in which it is found in the liturgy. The music shown is for Amen after the Priestly Blessing according to the Yemenite and Ashkenazi tradition, and a Moroccan Amen for the *ḥazzan*.

(there is no organized *ḥeder* of any community except the East Ashkenazi) has also broken the chain of tradition. The regional styles thus tend to disappear in the pressure of the melting pot, yielding to two diminant styles: the East Ashkenazi style is gradually adopted in most Ashkenazi synagogues, and the Jerusalem Sephardi style prevails (especially for the reading of the Torah) in most of the synagogues of the Near Eastern and North African communities. In the latter, the virtuoso status and pretensions of the *ḥazzan* or *ba'al kore,* and the influence of the traditions of Arabic art music, at present come near to completely eroding the traditional base of masoretic cantillation proper.

AMEN

Originally an adjective meaning "true," this word came to be an expression of endorsement or agreement with a blessing, oath, or the like. In this sense, it is variously translated "it is true," "so be it," and "may it become true." More usually it is simply transliterated, and has thus been borrowed intact by all the languages of the world. It appears 30 times in the Bible, and usually stands alone, though in one or two places it is followed by a more explicit prayer formula. In the service of the Second Temple, Amen was the response to all prayers and blessings. In the vast synagogue of classical Alexandria one of the synagogue officials signaled with a flag from the central reading platform in order to let the congregation know when to respond Amen after blessings. It may be assumed that in Temple and talmudic times responding Amen was the main form of participation in the service, not only because congregations were unfamiliar with the prayer texts but also because public worship mainly took the form of responsive reading. The saying of Amen is held by the rabbis to be equivalent to reciting the blessing itself, and such religious value has been attached to it, that it has been said to be superior to the benediction that occasions the response. The rabbis further taught that a person should not usually respond with Amen to a blessing he himself has recited, the only exception now being the third blessing of the Grace after Meals. (In this case, too, it does not have its usual meaning; rather, it serves to mark off the three benedictions of biblical provenance from the following one, which is a later addition of rabbinic origin.) This prohibition may be a reaction to the Christian custom of concluding every prayer with Amen. Indeed, the early church borrowed the use of Amen together with much of the liturgy, and it is found in the New Testament 119 times.

Amen is used as a response to blessings recited both privately and in the synagogue liturgy. As has been mentioned, the congregation also responds Amen after each of the three verses of the Priestly Blessing. In some rites the response after each verse is *ken yehi raẓon* ("May this be His will"). To this day, the traditional response to any good wish is *Amen, ken yehi raẓon*. After each paragraph of the *Kaddish* and after a number of other prayers, such as the *Mi she-Berakh* formulas in the Sabbath morning service, the reader invites the congregation to respond Amen by saying *ve-imru Amen,* or *ve-nomar Amen* (meaning respectively, "and say Amen" and "let us say Amen"). Numerous rules are given concerning how Amen should be recited; for example, clearly but not too loudly, and neither snatched nor mumbled. An "orphaned" Amen is one which is said prematurely, so that it is left stranded, without the parent blessing which occasioned it. In a number of aggadic

Left: *Kiddush Levanah* ("Sanctification of the Moon"), the prayer of thanksgiving recited while the moon is waxing, is illustrated in "New Moon Prayer," a late 19th-century painting by A. Bender. The prayer, preferably recited in the open air, celebrates the renewal in nature symbolized by the moon, as well as Israel's renewal and redemption. Jerusalem, Israel Museum Reproduction Archives.
Below: "Study" is the title of this painting by Isidor Kaufmann which shows a typical scene in a ḥasidic *shtibl*. Mishkan le-Omanut, Kibbutz Ein Harod.

כה
נדבת
ריזל הירשפעלד ע״ה
בונה בת חיים
הובא אל הקדש פנימה

Opposite: The lavish Altneushul in Prague, one of the oldest synagogues in Europe, dates at least to the 12th century. The Ark of the Law, shown here, was made in the 14th century. Photo State Jewish Museum, Prague.
Right: This unusual *shtender* (prayer lectern) with its silver-plated brass *Shivviti* plaque is from Lithuania, 1853. Mishkan le-Omanut, Kibbutz Ein Harod.
Below: The *hakkafot* in the synagogue during Simḥat Torah are shown in "The Rejoicing of the Law in the Ancient Synagogue of Leghorn," by Solomon Alexander Hart, 1841/42. New York Jewish Museum, Oscar Gruss Collection.

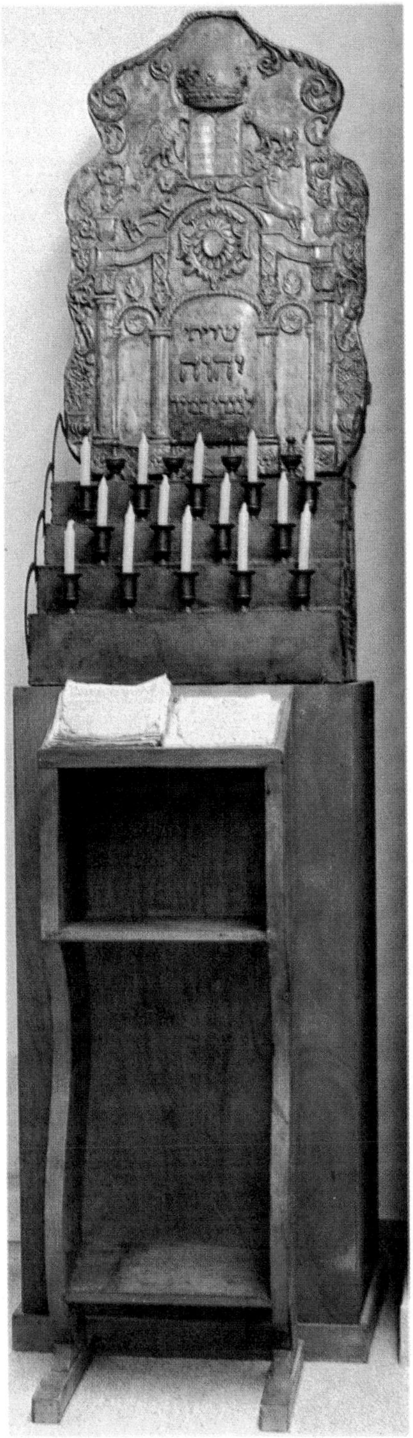

Right: The bar mitzvah, the Jewish boy's initiation into manhood and communal life, is celebrated with great pomp and ceremony and is one of the most important events in the life of the modern Jewish family. The ceremony pictured here was held in the synagogue of the Hadassah Medical Center in Jerusalem, framed by the magnificent stained-glass windows by Marc Chagall. Photo Werner Braun, Jerusalem.
Below: The two reconstructed arks and the foresection of Rabbi Johanan ben Zakkai's "underground" synagogue in the Jewish Quarter of the Old City, Jerusalem. Its style is Late Gothic and above the arks is a fresco depicting "Heavenly Jerusalem," surrounded by biblical quotations. Photo Werner Braun, Jerusalem.

passages the rabbis stressed the great religious value of responding Amen: it prolongs life; the gates of Paradise will be opened to him who responds with all his might; his sins will be forgiven; any evil decree passed on him will be annulled; and he will be spared from punishment after death. The Talmud also offers a homiletical etymology of Amen by explaining it as made up of the initial letters of *El Melekh Ne'eman,* ("God, faithful King")—a phrase by which the reading of the *Shema* is preceded when recited in private worship. Indeed, the rabbis taught that when He hears a benediction, God Himself (as it were) nods Amen to the blessing given to Him by mortal man.

ASHREI

The first reading from Psalms to be memorized by every daily worshiper is probably *Ashrei.* In praise of this reading the Talmud states that whoever recites *Ashrei* three times daily is assured of life in the world to come. Accordingly, it is read twice in the Morning Service—once as part of the *Pesukei de-Zimra* and once toward the end of *Shaḥarit*—and at the opening of the Afternoon Service. In addition, it serves as the opening to the *Seliḥot* services at dawn during the penitential season in the months of Elul and Tishrei. On the Day of Atonement, Sephardim recite it at *Ne'ilah,* the concluding service, as well as *Minḥah,* the afternoon service; Ashkenazim say it at the latter only.

Ashrei consists basically of Psalm 145, which is the only Psalm to bear the title *tehillah* (meaning praise), the word from which the entire Book of Psalms takes its Hebrew name. The initials of its verses are arranged alphabetically, except that the letter *nun* is not represented. A talmudic homily suggests in explanation that this letter also begins a certain verse from Amos prophesying the destruction of Israel. However, in the Psalm Scroll recently discovered among the Dead Sea Scrolls there is a verse beginning with the letter *nun,* reading as follows: *Ne'eman Elohim bi-devarav, ve-ḥasid be-khol ma'asav,* "God is faithful in His words, and pious in all His works." Furthermore, in these ancient scrolls each line ends with the refrain: *Barukh Adonai u-varukh shemo le-olam va-ed*—"Blessed is the Lord, and blessed be His name for evermore." This structure would indicate that the Psalm was spoken antiphonally—an individual reciting and the congregation responding—in a liturgy dating to as early as the Second Temple. In the Psalm the author declares that he will praise God because He is "gracious," "merciful," "slow to anger," and "good"; "He supports the fallen" and gives mankind its "food in due season." God is close to all "who call upon His name in truth" and "preserves all who love Him."

Psalm 145 is introduced by two verses, both from the same Book, both opening with the word *Ashrei,* and reading as follows: "Happy are they that dwell in Thy house: they are ever praising Thee"; and "Happy is the people whose lot is such; yea, happy is the people whose God is the Lord." The Talmud explains these two verses as referring to the pious who arrive at the synagogue early, before the start of the service proper. The reading is rounded off with the addition of one more verse, also from the Psalms.

Ashkenazim customarily touch the *tefillin* at verse 16: "Thou openest Thy hand, and satisfiest all living," whereas the Sephardim open their hands in symbolic gesture. In Reform synagogues *Ashrei* is recited in the vernacular; in many Conservative synagogues it is read responsively in Hebrew.

BAREKHU

The opening word of the call to worship by the *sheli'aḥ ẓibbur* at the formal beginning of the daily morning and evening services is *Barekhu,* meaning "Bless." It comes from the same three-letter root as does the word *barukh,* a term whose varied meanings were discussed in connection with the benediction formulae in Chapter II. In the context of the call to worship the word "bless" is the equivalent of "praise." The full invocation is *Barekhu et Adonai ha-mevorakh* ("Bless ye the Lord who is [to be] blessed"). The congregation responds *Barukh Adonai ha-mevorakh le-olam va-ed* ("Blessed be the Lord who is [to be] blessed for ever and ever"). *Barekhu* is also recited by the person who is called up to the Torah reading (as was explained earlier in the present chapter) and there too is

ראשון של פסח
ברכו
את יהוה המבורך
ברוך אתה יהוה אלהינו מלך העולם אשר בדברו מעריב ערבים
בחכמה פותח שערים ובתבונה משנה עתים ומחליף את
הזמנים ומסדר את הכוכבים במשמרתיהם ברקיע כרצונו
בורא יום ולילה גולל אור מפני חושך וחושך מפני אור
ומעביר יום ומביא לילה ומבדיל בין יום ובין לילה יהוה
צבאות שמו . אל חי וקים תמיד ימלוך עלינו לעולם ועד

followed by the same congregational response. The absence of this invocation before the *Minḥah* service can perhaps be explained by the fact that this service does not include the *Shema,* to which *Barekhu* usually serves as an introduction. *Barekhu* is considered to be one of the *devarim she-bi-kedushah,* the holy texts that may be recited only in the presence of a *minyan* of ten men.

This invocation possibly originated in the time of Ezra, as might have the practice of standing at *Barekhu;* a suggestion based on a verse in Nehemiah: "Then the Levites . . . said: 'Stand up and bless the Lord your God . . .'" A shorter formula, *Barekhu et Adonai,* occurs in the Book of Psalms. In the opinion of Rabbi Akiva the liturgical invocation, in accordance with this scriptural precedent, should consist simply of *Barekhu et Adonai,* whereas the formula *Barekhu et Adonai ha-mevorakh* was advocated by his contemporary, Rabbi Ishmael. The latter formula was preferred by most of the *amoraim*—their views being recorded in the Talmud—and became standard. There is evidence that in the early period *Barukh Adonai ha-mevorakh . . .* was the response to *Barekhu,* only in the Torah reading, while different responses were used for *Barekhu,* when it was recited as the invocation to worship. These responses were *Barukh Shem kevod malkhuto le-olam va-ed* ("Blessed be His Name, whose glorious kingdom is for ever and ever"), the standard response when the Divine Name was mentioned in the Temple; and *Yehei shemeih rabba mevorakh le-alam u-le-almei almayya* ("May His great Name be blessed for ever and to all eternity"). In the course of time, however, *Barukh Shem kevod . . .* became the response to the *Shema* only; *Yehe Shemeih rabba . . .* was reserved for the *Kaddish;* and *Barukh Adonai hamevorakh . . .* became the exclusive response to *Barekhu.*

At one time *Barekhu* was also used as a summons to recite Grace after Meals, but in the amoraic period it was felt that this second-person form of address removed the leader from group participation, and the invitation was standardized to *Nevarekh* ("Let us bless"). This objection, however, did not apply to *Barekhu* in the synagogue. The Reader there employs the second-person form, though only when inviting the congregation to join him in prayer. And even then he repeats the congregational response, thus associating himself with the praise of God.

The Sephardi rite, as well as the rites of some ḥasidic congregations and most congregations in Israel, retained the somewhat paradoxical practice of reciting *Barekhu* at the conclusion of the daily morning and evening services (when there is no Torah reading). The custom accommodates worshipers who arrive too late to hear *Barekhu* at the opening of the services.

YA'ALEH VE-YAVO

Most festive occasions are marked in the liturgy by the addition to the *Amidah* and the Grace after Meals of a short paragraph which is entitled, after two words in its opening line, *Ya'aleh ve-Yavo.* These words mean: "May [our remembrance] arise and come . . . before Thee." This additional prayer is recited during the evening, morning, and afternoon *Amidah* (with the exception of Rosh Ha-Shanah and the Day of Atonement), as well as during the Grace after Meals, on the New Moon and on all Scriptural festivals. First mentioned in the Talmud, its style—of structured, classical lucidity—is similar to that of the

The cantor's invitation to communal prayer, *Barekhu*, is generally considered to be the start of the service proper. The page on the left is from a *maḥzor* (1816) which was donated for synagogue use in Frankfort-on-Main. The book was printed on vellum with some of the first pages handwritten. This *Barekhu* page is one of the latter, and is the beginning of the evening service for the first night of Passover. The other page is from the *Leipzig Maḥzor* (South Germany, 13th/14th century) and is a morning service *Barekhu* for Special Sabbaths. The illustration shows a cantor with two of the community leaders.

early *paytanim*. Specific mention is made of the occasion on which it is said (e.g. "this festival of Passover") in the course of the request for "deliverance, happiness, grace, kindness, mercy, life, and peace."

According to Rashi, the celebrated exegete of the 11th century, it is also a "supplication for Israel and for Jerusalem, and for the reinstitution of the Temple service and of the sacrifices of the day." For this reason the prayer is recited during the 17th benediction in the *Amidah* and the third in the Grace after Meals, which deal with those subjects. The problem as to whether its omission during the recital of either of these benedictions requires that it be repeated is answered differently according to the occasion and the festival.

In communal worship, when in the course of this prayer the reader recites the phrases "remember us O Lord our God [on this festive day] for good," "be mindful of us for blessing," and "save us unto life," it is customary for the congregation to respond to each with "Amen."

TAḤANUN

The Hebrew word for supplication is the name of a prayer which is a confession of sins and a petition for grace. It forms part of the daily morning and afternoon services and is recited after the *ḥazzan's* repetition of the *Amidah*. The *Taḥanun* begins in the Ashkenazi rite with a silent recital of David's utterance after being rebuked by the prophet Gad for his sin of numbering the people: "Let us fall, I pray thee, into the hand of the Lord, for His mercies are many, but let me not fall into the hand of men." It is, therefore, also called *nefilat appayim* ("prostration prayer," literally "falling on the face"). Since prostration during petitions is mentioned in the Bible, it was customary to recite the *Taḥanun* prostrated. In modern times, however, the prayer is recited in a seated position, with lowered head and face buried in the bend of the arm. This position is assumed only where there is a Torah Scroll to designate the sanctity of the place.

In the Sephardi ritual, it is customary to start the *Taḥanun* with a silent confession of sins (*Viddui*), followed by David's above-mentioned supplication (as in the Ashkenazi ritual). The central part of *Taḥanun* is a penitential Psalm, Psalm 25 in the Sephardi, and Psalm 6 in the Ashkenazi ritual. This is supplemented by additional penitential prayers and *piyyutim*. In the Ashkenazi rite there follows part of a *piyyut* (*Shomer Yisrael*) which also occurs in the *Seliḥot* liturgy. The last passage of the *Taḥanun,* starting with a quotation from Chronicles (*Va-anaḥnu lo neda*), is a shortened form of the whole prayer and was instituted so that latecomers to the morning service could attend the reading from the Torah, which follows the *Taḥanun*. The *Taḥanun* prayer is omitted on Sabbaths, festivals, semiholidays, New Moons, as well as from the *Minḥah* service preceding these special days; during the month of Nisan; and on the Ninth of Av. At a circumcision in the synagogue, when a bridegroom attends the service during the first seven days after his wedding, and at prayers held at the homes of mourners, the *Taḥanun* is also omitted.

The origin of the *Taḥanun* dates back to the talmudic period in Babylonia. Although the prayer was known as *nefilat appayim,* the prostration prayer, many rabbis, such as Eleazar ben Hyrcanus, Abbaye, Rava, and especially Rav refused to prostrate at this prayer, either because they considered com-

An illustration from the *Kaufmann Haggadah* (14th-century Spain). At the beginning of the Psalm in the *Hallel* prayer which starts: "When Israel left Egypt. . . " the Israelites led by Moses are passing the gate of a medieval town, from which the Egyptians are looking down. The *Aleinu* prayer from the *Leipzig Maḥzor* is from the *Musaf* service for Rosh Ha-Shanah. The word in the 11-pointed star is *Hu* and begins the sentence "He is our God and there is none other."

plete prostration forbidden outside the Temple in Jerusalem or because they regarded it as not obligatory for a distinguished personage. By the time of the *geonim* the posture had already been modified to sitting (or half-sitting), with the head inclined on the arm. The exact date of the various parts making up the *Taḥanun* cannot be established with certainty. The view that the *Taḥanun* was originally a supplication supplemented by confession of sins recited in private without fixed form is strengthened by the fact that there is considerable variety in the versions given in the various early prayer books, such as those of Saadiah Gaon early in the tenth century, and of Maimonides, late in the twelfth century. In fact its final version evolved only in the 16th century.

HALLEL

The classical expression of joyful thanksgiving for divine redemption is *Hallel.* This word, meaning praise, is the name given to Psalms 113 to 118 when this cycle forms a unit in the liturgy.

Hallel is recited in two forms. The first is the "full" *Hallel* consisting of the above six Psalms. It is chanted in the synagogue on Sukkot, Ḥanukkah, the first day of Passover (the first two days in the Diaspora), Shavuot, and (in many synagogues) on Israel Independence Day. *Hallel* is also recited during the Passover *Seder* service, when it is known as *Hallel ha-Miẓri* ("the Egyptian *Hallel*") because of the Exodus from Egypt which the *Seder* commemorates. On this occasion it is recited in two parts, which are read before and after the *Seder* meal respectively. The second form in which this cycle appears is the "half" *Hallel,* consisting of the "full" *Hallel,* excepting Psalms 115:1–11, and 116:1–11. According to the rite of the Yemenites, the order is slightly different, based on the view of Maimonides. The "half" *Hallel* is recited in the synagogue on the New Moon and on the last six days of Passover.

The term *Hallel ha-Gadol* ("the "Great *Hallel*") refers only to Psalm 136, which is recited during *Pesukei de-Zimra* at the Morning Service on Sabbaths and festivals. It is the daily Psalm on the last day of Passover in those rites where the regular daily Psalm is replaced on the festivals by special readings. It is also added to the *Hallel* when it is recited at the *Seder*. Moreover, according to the Mishnah, this Psalm was sung on joyous communal occasions, such as on the appearance of the long-awaited rain after a period of severe drought.

In the Talmud, various origins are attributed to the custom of reading *Hallel.* Rabbi Eleazar claims that it was Moses and the people of Israel who first recited *Hallel;* Rabbi Judah states that it was the Prophets who instituted its recitation for every occasion that the people of Israel should be redeemed from potential misfortune. The Talmud relates that *Hallel* was recited by the Levites in the Temple, and it was also chanted on Passover eve, during the sacrifice of the paschal lambs. *Hallel* became part of the synagogue service at an early stage, and in talmudic times, communities in Ereẓ Israel added it to the end of the Evening Service for Passover. This practice later spread to the Diaspora, and is still the custom among Oriental Jews and Ḥasidim, and in most synagogues in Israel.

Hallel is recited on all major biblical festivals, with the exception of Rosh Ha-Shanah and the Day of Atonement; the solemnity of those occasions, when each mortal's destiny is being decided, is deemed unsuitable for Psalms of joy. Similar considerations cause these Psalms to be omitted when prayers are conducted in a house of mourning on the New Moon and Ḥanukkah. *Hallel* is not recited on Purim, since the Scroll of Esther is considered the festival's *Hallel.* One rabbinic tradition explains that only the "half" *Hallel* is recited on the last six days of Passover, because the joy of the occasion is mitigated by the calamity that then befell the Egyptian host when pursuing the Israelites. Another reason given is that no different sacrifice was offered each day. On Sukkot the *lulav* is waved during the refrains of certain verses of Psalm 118. *Hallel* may be recited at any time during the day, although in the synagogue it is recited immediately after the morning service. Special benedictions are recited before and after *Hallel,* except at the *Seder* service when no benediction is recited before it.

There is a difference of opinion among the early authorities as to whether the obligation to recite the *Hallel* is to be considered of biblical or of rabbinic authority. The recitation on the

New Moon is considered to be a custom, as distinct from a formal law, and there are some opinions that on that day it is recited only in congregational prayers. Similarly there are authorities who ruled that for the full *Hallel* the benediction should read "Blessed art Thou . . . who hast commanded us finish (*ligmor*) the *Hallel*" instead of the customary "to read (*likro*) the *Hallel.*" According to the *tosafot,* the *Hallel* may be recited in any language. In any case, it should be read standing, except at the *Seder* service.

Various traditions are related to the manner in which the *Hallel* is chanted. In some communities, it was sung antiphonally; in others (as is still the practice among Yemenite Jews) the congregation responded with *Hallelujah*! after each half of a verse. Among Ashkenazi Jews, it is customary to repeat certain of the verses of Psalm 118.

Opinions and customs differ regarding the recital of *Hallel* on Israel Independence Day. Among those who incorporate it as a central feature of the special liturgy of the day, some give the occasion greater festive status by introducing its recitation with a benediction, while others read the *Hallel* without this introduction. The various opinions are discussed in Chapter IX.

ALEINU

This, one of the most sublime of all the prayers in the liturgy, is a passage almost without parallel—in the loftiness of its language, in the intimacy of its association with martyrdom, and in the vigor with which it was censored. *Aleinu le-Shabbe'aḥ* ("It is our duty to praise [the Lord of all things]"), originally introduced the *Malkhuyyot* section of the Additional Service of Rosh Ha-Shanah. This is a passage in which the kingship of God is proclaimed, and in which the *Aleinu* is recited with great solemnity. Its theological importance secured for it, from the 12th century at least, a special place in the daily order of service; first at the conclusion of the morning service, and later at the end of the other two daily services as well. As with some other prayers, the *Aleinu* has been taken over from the New Year liturgy into the additional service of the Day of Atonement. In its style, *Aleinu* resembles the early *piyyut,* being composed of short lines, each comprising about four words, with a marked rhythm and parallelism.

The prayer is referred to in the classical rabbinic sources as *Teki'ata de-vei Rav* ("The *Shofar* Service of Rav") and it has therefore been ascribed to Rav, the third century Babylonian teacher. But the *Aleinu* may be considerably older. According to one popular tradition, it was composed by Joshua; according to another, it was written by the Men of the Great Assembly during the period of the Second Temple. And indeed there are good reasons for placing it within that period, because there is no mention of the Temple restoration in the prayer, while there is reference to the Temple practice of prostration. In the Ashkenazi rite prostration during *Aleinu* is still customary in most communities during the services of Rosh Ha-Shanah and on the Day of Atonement, while in all other services the congregants simply bow when reciting the words "we bend the knee . . . " The description of God as the "King of the king of kings" may be due to Persian influence, since the Persians described their king as "the king of kings." It has been suggested that the prayer has its origin in early Jewish mysticism; a version of *Aleinu* was recently found among hymns used by the early mystics.

The main theme of the prayer is the kingdom of God. In the first part, God is praised for having singled out the people of Israel from other nations, for Israel worships the One God while others worship idols or many gods. The second paragraph expresses the fervent hope for the coming of the kingdom of God, and the universal ideal of a united mankind which will recognize the only true God, and of "a world perfected under the kingship of the Almight." The juxtaposition of the two paragraphs provides a coherent theology connecting the idea of a chosen people (Israel) with a challenge—that this distinctiveness has for its purpose religious union and the perfection of mankind under the kingdom of God.

In the Middle Ages *Aleinu* was censored by Christians as containing an implied insult to Christianity. They claimed that the verse "for they prostrate themselves before vanity and emptiness and pray to a god that saveth not" was a reference to Jesus. Pesah Peter, a 14th-century Bohemian apostate,

This *Aleinu* prayer from a 14th/15th century Italian prayerbook has been censored. The sentence, "For they (the non-Jews) prostrate themselves to the powerless and the empty, and pray to a god that cannot save," has been changed into the past tense; the implication is that that statement does not apply to contemporary non-Jews.

spitefully alleged a connection between the numerical value of the Hebrew word *va-rik* meaning "and emptiness" and *Yeshu,* Hebrew for Jesus. Other celebrated anti-Semites (including the 17th-century polemicist Eisenmenger) repeated the charge, and Jewish apologists including Manasseh Ben Israel and Moses Mendelssohn were at pains to refute it. However, a 13th-century rabbi does mention a tradition that the numerical value of *la-hevel va-rik* ("vanity and emptiness") equals *Yeshu u-Muhammad* (Jesus and Muhammad). Some ecclesiastical censors also deleted the previous passage: "Who did not make our portion like theirs, nor our lot like that of all their multitude." Eisenmenger refers to the custom of spitting at the offending word which he interprets as an additional insult to Christianity. This was, no doubt, a popular gesture suggested by the double meaning of *rik* ("emptiness" and "spittle"). In view of this accusation, rabbis such as Isaiah Horowitz discouraged the indecorous practice. (Incidentally, the popular Yiddish phrase, *er kummt tsum oysshpayen,* meaning "he arrives at the spitting," came to describe someone who arrived at a service as late as the concluding *Aleinu.*) The censors remained adamant even when it was pointed out that the offending phrase is found in Isaiah, many centuries before the Common Era, that the *Aleinu* prayer as a whole is probably pre-Christian, and that if Rav was the author, it was composed in a non-Christian country. The line had nonetheless to be removed from Ashkenazi prayer books. In 1703 its recital was prohibited in Prussia. The edict, which provided for police enforcement, was renewed in 1716 and 1750. Even earlier, some communities omitted or changed the offending lines as an act of self-censorship (e.g. by replacing *she-hem,* "for they [prostrate themselves before vanity]" with *she-hayu,* "for they used to . . ."). The Sephardim—especially in Oriental countries—retained the full text, and it has now been restored to some prayer books of the Ashkenazi rite as well.

It is with good reason that *Aleinu* has come to epitomize the spirit of Jewish martyrology. The contemporary *paytan,* Ephraim of Bonn tells how the Jews of Blois, in France, martyred as the result of a blood libel in 1171, went to their death chanting *Aleinu* to a soul-stirring melody, which "at the outset . . . was subdued, but at the close was mighty." The messianic theme of the second paragraph would have made it especially significant for the Jew in the tragic moments of his history, and it takes its place next to the *Shema* as a declaration of faith. Indeed, its introduction into the daily service may have been an act of defiance when Christian persecution was becoming ever more oppressive, during the centuries of the Crusades.

The solemnity of the *Aleinu* is expressed musically in different ways. In Ashkenazi tradition, its appearance in the *Musaf* service of the High Holy Days is a notable climax, its majestic melody belonging to the class of unchangeable *Mi-Sinai* tunes discussed in Chapter III. This tune consists of seven melodic sentences or themes, always produced in the same order. Three of these are shared with the familiar melody of *Kol Nidrei.* Every Ashkenazi country has produced a cantorial tradition which has interpreted the *Aleinu* melody with its own elaborations and variants, including extended flourishes and ad-libbed fantasias. Some of these even attempt to give musical expression to the mystical intentions or *kavvanot* connected with the prayer.

שחרית

אדון

ברוך

ברוך

ברוך

והערב

The prayer *Adon Olam* from a 17th-century Frankfort-on-Main prayerbook. Here *Adon Olam* is situated at the very beginning of the service before the daily benedictions.

In striking contrast, the Sephardi and eastern communities sing the *Aleinu* to one of their regular prayer modes.

ADON OLAM

This rhymed hymn enjoys the unusual distinction of being recited in some communities as a wedding song (as in Morocco) while in many others it is recited by those present at a deathbed. The paradox is explained by its contents: it suits both occasions, in that it expresses man's absolute trust in God's providence. At the same time it extols His eternity and unity, its title meaning "Lord of the Universe."

In the Ashkenazi rite it comprises 12 verses; the Sephardi version has 16. The author is unknown, though its composition has been attributed to Solomon ibn Gabirol, who lived in Spain in the 11th century. The hymn may, however, be much older and stem from Babylonia. It has appeared as part of the liturgy since the 14th century in the German rite, and has since been incorporated into the rite of almost every community, usually as part of the *Shaḥarit* service. Its main place now is at the conclusion of the Sabbath and festival *Musaf* service (among Sephardim on the Day of Atonement as well) and of the *Kol Nidrei* service. It also appears as the conclusion of the Night Prayers. Indeed, it has been suggested that this was its original place, in view of the concluding lines, which are here given in Israel Zangwill's translation:

I place my soul within His palm
Before I sleep as when I wake,
And though my body I forsake,
Rest in the Lord in fearless calm.

Other English verse translations include the version incorporated by George Borrow in his novel *Lavengro;* the hymn has been translated into many European languages as well.

Adon Olam is generally sung by the congregation. In the Ashkenazi tradition it is also sometimes rendered by the cantor on certain festive occasions, its melody then being adapted to the *nusaḥ* of the service into which it is incorporated. The great number of melodies for *Adon Olam* includes both original settings, and borrowings from Jewish and gentile sources, whether folk tunes from Germany or romances from Tangiers. This is a continuing process, in Israel as in the Diaspora. One of the more ambitious settings for the hymn is the composition for eight voices published by Solomon de Rossi in Venice in 1622. In one of its less sophisticated settings, *Adon Olam* is sung in many schools in Israel at the end of morning prayers.

YIGDAL

The Thirteen Articles of Faith as formulated by Maimonides have been paraphrased in a hymn known by its opening word as *Yigdal* (which in Hebrew means "May He be magnified"). The authorship of the *Yigdal* prayer is attributed by some to Daniel ben Judah, a judge in a rabbinical court in Rome in the first half of the 14th century. It has also been ascribed to the versatile poet Immanuel ben Solomon of Rome, a contemporary of Daniel. *Yigdal* is metrically constructed and has

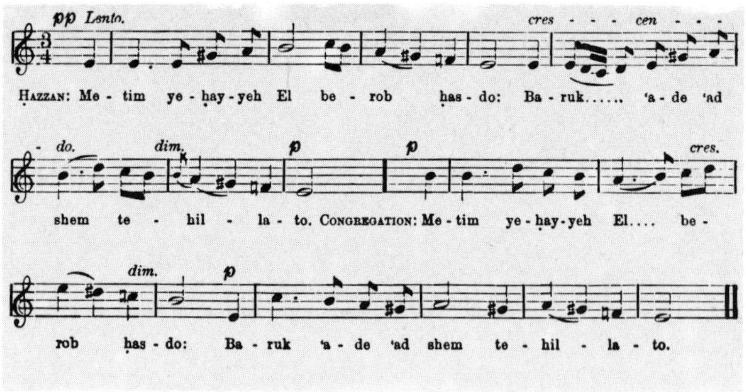

a single rhyme throughout. Although other poetical renditions of these principles of faith were composed during the medieval period, *Yigdal* alone became incorporated into the daily liturgy. In the Ashkenazi ritual, it is usually printed at the opening of the daily *Shaḥarit* service, but recited (as in the Sephardi, Italian, and Yemenite rituals) only at the conclusion of the Friday and festival evening services. Ḥasidim do not recite this hymn at all. The Ashkenazi hymn consists of 13 lines, one for each creed. The Sephardi version contains an additional line: "These are the 13 bases of the Jewish faith and the tenets of God's law."

Various rhymed English translations of *Yigdal* have been composed, such as that of Alice Lucas (1852–1935). Her rendition includes the following two couplets, each of which deals with one principle of Maimonides' formulation—the immutability of the Torah of Moses, and the omniscience of the Creator, respectively:

This Law God will not alter, will not change
For any other through time's utmost range.
He knows and heeds the secret thoughts of man:
He saw the end of all ere aught began.

The many melodies for *Yigdal* seem to have been composed, evolved, or adapted more or less independently in each local community. Where the Ashkenazi custom prevails, and also in Yemen, the melodies of *Yigdal* are generally based on the music of the usual prayer mode and, in this sense, tend toward standardization and a lack of individuality. In the Sephardi Diaspora, however, *Yigdal* has a great number of distinct tunes; none of them seems to be particularly old and all of them draw strongly upon the reservoir of para-liturgical and secular tunes available within the community and from the surrounding population, such as folk songs and military marches. The only element common to most of these is the character of the melodies which, together with the way in which they are sung by the congregation, combines the moods of pride and cheerfulness.

One *Yigdal* melody has achieved particular fame—the so-called "Leoni *Yigdal*." It is attributed to Meyer Leon, known as Leoni, who was *ḥazzan* at the Duke's Place Ashkenazi synagogue in London. Thomas Olivers, a Welseyan minister, once heard Leoni sing this *Yigdal* there, whereupon he decided to render the hymn into English and to introduce it into Christian worship together with its melody. (In another version of the story Olivers first translated the text and then went to Leoni to ask for "a synagogue melody to suit it.") Olivers' translation, *The God of Abraham Praise,* first published in 1770, became popular immediately, and is sung to this day in the Anglican service as a processional or as a hymn for other occasions. It has also been adopted by the hymnals of several other English-speaking Protestant denominations. The liturgical musicologist A. Z. Idelsohn attempted to relate the Leoni *Yigdal* in a large comparative table to a number of Spanish, Basque and Polish folk songs, to a Sephardi melody for a certain *piyyut,* as well as to the well-known motif from Smetana's *Moldau* which found its way into Imber's *Ha-Tikvah.*

KADDISH

Though popularly considered to be a mourner's prayer for the departed, the ancient *Kaddish* was not known in this role until comparatively recent times—from about the thirteenth century. Primarily, it is characterized by an abundance of praise and glorification of God, and an expression of Messianic hope for the speedy establishment of God's kingdom on earth. These themes are common to all forms of this doxology, most of which is written in Aramaic. Its name, too, is an Aramaic word meaning holy. The first of its Hebrew sentences employs eight verbs, all more or less synonymous with praise, and other texts can boast more. On this the Midrash observes: "As Latin is the language of war, and Greek is that of oratory, so is Hebrew the language of prayer."

The Four Forms. The first of the four main forms is the Whole *Kaddish,* the text of which follows: "Glorified and sanctified be His great name throughout the world which He has created according to His will. May He establish His kingdom in your lifetime and during your days, and during the life of the entire house of Israel, speedily and soon; and say, Amen." In reaction to the reader's invitation to join him in praise, the congregation

אמ׳ עשה למען שמך הגדול הגבור
והנורא · שנקרא עלינו ׳׳
אבינו מלכנו חננו ועננו כי אין בנו מעשים ·
עשה עמנו צדקה וחסד · והושיענו ׳׳
יתגדל ויתקדש שמיה רבא ב
בעלמא די ברא כרעותי
וימליך מלכותיה · בחייכון וביומיכון ובחיי
דכל בית ישראל בעגלה ובזמן קריב · ואמרו
אמן ׳׳
יתברך וישתבח ויתפאר ויתרומם
ויתנשא ויתהדר ויתעל
ויתהלל שמיה דקודשא בריך הוא לעלא
מן כל ברכתא · ושירתא תושבחתא · ונחמתא
דאמירן בעלמא · ואמרו אמן ׳
תתקבל צלותהון ובעותהון ד
דכל ישר׳ קדם אבוהון
דבשמיא ואמרו אמן ׳׳
יהא שלמא רבא מן שמיא וח
חיים עלינו ועל כל ישראל
ואמרו אמן ׳׳
עושה שלום במרומיו הוא יע
יעשה שלום עלינו ועל
כל ישראל ואמרו אמן ׳׳
תקיעה שברים תרועה תקיעה ׳׳
תקיעה שברים תרועה תקיעה ׳׳
תקיעה שברים תרועה תקיעה ׳׳
שב׳׳
תקיעה שברים תקיעה ׳׳
תקיעה שברים תקיעה ׳׳
תקיעה שברים תקיעה ׳׳
שב
תקיעה תרועה תקיעה ׳׳
תקיעה תרועה תקיעה ׳׳
תקיעה תרועה תקיעה גדולה ׳׳
אשרי העם יודעי תרועה
יי באור פניך יהלכון

The music shown here is for the *Yigdal* prayer. The example on the left is the famous Leoni *Yigdal* while that on the right is the eastern Ashkenazi version for the High Holy Days. The initial words of each phrase in the *Kaddish* prayer are illuminated in this Italian *maḥzor*. Immediately following the *Kaddish* is the beginning of the service for the blowing of the *shofar* on Rosh Ha-Shanah.

makes the following response, which he in turn repeats: "May His great name be blessed forever and to all eternity." The reader resumes: "Blessed and praised, glorified and exalted, extolled and honored, adored and lauded by the name of the Holy One blessed be He, beyond all the blessings and hymns, praises and consolations that are ever spoken in the world; and say, Amen. May the prayers and supplications of the whole house of Israel be accepted by their Father in heaven; and say, Amen. May there be abundant peace from heaven and life, for us and for all Israel; and say, Amen. He who creates peace in His high places, may He create peace for us and for all Israel; and say, Amen."

This form of the *Kaddish* is recited by the *sheli'aḥ ẓibbur* after each *Amidah* (virtually concluding the whole service), except in the Morning Service when it comes after the prayer *U-Va le-Ẓiyyon.*

The Half *Kaddish* consists of the above text except for the last three sentences. It too is recited by the *sheli'aḥ ẓibbur,* and functions as a link between the sections of each service. In the Morning Service, the Half *Kaddish* is recited after the introductory Psalms of the *Pesukei de-Zimra,* after the *Amidah* (or after *Taḥanun* on those days when that is said), and after the Reading of the Law. In the Afternoon Service it is recited before the *Amidah;* in the Evening Service before *Ve-Hu Raḥum* (when the special Psalms before it are recited) and again before the *Amidah.* It is also recited before the *Musaf* service.

The *Kaddish de-Rabbanan* ("the scholars' *Kaddish*") is identical with the Whole *Kaddish,* except that the third-last sentence is substituted by a prayer "for Israel, for our teachers and their disciples, and all the disciples of their disciples, and for all who study the Torah, in this place and everywhere; may they (and you) have abundant peace, grace, lovingkindness, mercy, long life, ample sustenance and salvation from their Father Who is in heaven; and say, Amen." The prayer then continues with the usual two concluding sentences. This *Kaddish* is recited by mourners, after communal study, and in the synagogue on certain occasions, such as after the reading of *Ba-Meh Madlikim* on Friday nights, after the preliminary readings to the Morning Service, and after *Ein ke-Elohenu.*

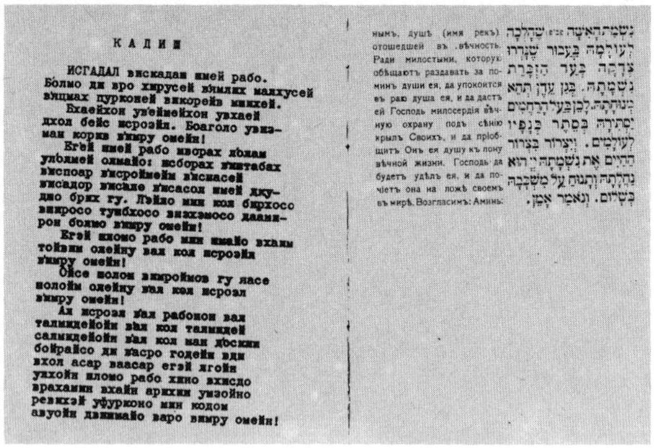

КАДИШ

ИСГАДАЛ вискадаш шмей рабо.
Болмо ди вро хирусей вимлих малхусей
вйцмах пурконей викорейв мшихей.
Бхаейхон увеймейхон увхаей
дхол бейс исроэйл. Боаголо увиз-
ман кориь вимру омейн!
Егэй шмей рабо мворах лолам
улолмей олмайо: исборах вйиштабах
вйспоар вйсроймейм вйснасей
вйсадор висале вйсасол шмей дку-
дшо брих гу. Лэйло мин кол бирхосо
вширосо тушбхосо вихэмосо даами-
рон болмо вимру омейн!
Егэй шломо рабо мин шмайо вхаим
тойвим олейну вал кол исроэйл
вимру омейн!
Ойсе шолом вимроймов гу яасе
шолойм олейну вал кол исроэл
вимру омейн!
Ал исроэл вал рабонон вал
талмидейойм вал кол талмидей
салмидейойм вал кол ман досики
бойрайсо ди васро годейн вди
вхол асар ваасар егэй лгойн
ухлойн шломо рабо хино вхисдо
врахамин вхайн арихин умзойно
ревихэй уфурконо мин кодом
авуойн дившмайо варо вимру омейн!

נשמת האשה שהלכה לעולמה בעבור שנדרו צדקה בעד הזכרת נשמתה. בגן עדן תהא מנוחתה, לכן בעל הרחמים יסתירה בסתר כנפיו לעולמים. ויצרור בצרור החיים את נשמתה, ה׳ הוא נחלתה, ותנוח על משכבה בשלום. ונאמר אמן.

нымъ. душѣ (имя рекъ) отошедшей въ вѣчность. Ради милостыни, которую обѣщаютъ раздавать за поминъ души ея, да упокоится въ раю душа ея, и да дастъ ей Господь милосердія вѣчную охрану подъ сѣнію крылъ Своихъ, и да пріобщитъ Онъ ея душу къ пону вѣчной жизни. Господь да будетъ удѣлъ ея, и да почіетъ она на ложѣ своемъ въ мирѣ. Возгласимъ: Аминь.

The Mourner's *Kaddish* comprises the full text of the Whole *Kaddish* with the exception of the third-last sentence. It is recited by the close relatives of the deceased after the *Aleinu* as well as at the end of each Service, and may be repeated after the reading of additional Psalms.

The practice that mourners recite the *Kaddish* seems to have originated during the 13th century, at a time of severe persecutions in Germany by the Crusaders. No reference is made to it in the *Maḥzor Vitry,* an early prayer book compiled by a disciple of Rashi in the 11th century. According to a late *aggadah,* Rabbi Akiva rescued a soul from punishment after death by urging the sons of the deceased to recite the verse "May His great name be blessed. . . ." The same idea was earlier expressed in Tractate Sanhedrin. The mourner's *Kaddish* is now recited for 11 and not the full 12 months of the mourning period. According to the *Shulḥan Arukh,* the longer period implies a disrespectful view of the parent's piety, since these periods reflect the degree of retribution due to the deceased. The *Kaddish* is also recited on the *yahrzeit,* the anniversary of the demise of the parent or relative. It has been suggested that the *Kaddish* became the mourner's prayer because of the mention of the resurrection of the dead in the messianic passage at the beginning. The phrase, however, no longer occurs in most versions today. In fact, the *Kaddish* is not properly "a prayer for the soul of the departed," but an expression by the bereaved relative of *ẓidduk ha-din* ("justification of judgment"), conforming to the spirit of the talmudic teaching: "A person is obliged to give praise for the evil [that befalls him] even as he gives praise for the good." However, the prayer is popularly thought to be a "prayer for the dead" to the extent that a son, in Yiddish, is often called "a *Kaddish,*" and a childless man is said to have died "without leaving a *Kaddish.*"

All four forms of the *Kaddish* are recited standing, facing Jerusalem. In some communities the whole congregation stands, in others only the mourners. If one is standing at the beginning of the *Kaddish,* however, one should not sit down before the response: "May His great name be blessed. . . ." When the *Kaddish* is recited at the burial service, an addition which stresses the eschatological aspect of the *Kaddish* is made to the opening paragraph. It is also added to the *Kaddish* recited at the celebration marking the conclusion of the study of a Talmud tractate. The added paragraph reads as follows: "May His great Name be magnified and sanctified in the world which He will renew when He will revive the dead and give them everlasting life, when He will rebuild Jerusalem and establish the Temple in it, when He will uproot idolatry from the land and restore the worship of Heaven to its place, when the Holy One, Blessed be He, will rule in absolute sovereignty. May this take place in your lifetime and in your days . . ."—the reader then continues with the usual text of the *Kaddish.*

The sentence "May He establish His kingdom" in the usual Ashkenazi version is expanded by the Sephardim with the phrase: *ve-yaẓmaḥ purkaneih vi-yekarev meshiḥeih* ("May He make His salvation blossom forth and bring His Messiah near"). The congregational response "May His great name be blessed for ever and to all eternity" is the kernel of the prayer. It is akin to an Aramaic phrase in Daniel, to Hebrew verses in the Books of Job and Psalms, and to the formula: "Blessed be the name of His glorious kingdom for ever and ever," which was recited in the Temple (and which was discussed above in connection with the *Shema*). According to Rabbi Joshua ben Levi, a talmudic scholar, "joining loudly and in unison in [this] congregational response" constitutes a prayer of especial efficacy.

History. The simple form in which the pleas for the establishment of the Messianic kingdom are phrased, and the absence of any allusion to the destruction of the Temple, indicate the antiquity of the *Kaddish prayer.* The opening phrase, "Magnified and sanctified be His great name in the world. . . ," stems from a verse in Ezekiel. Similar phrases were apparently used in

Since the *Kaddish* is perhaps one of the most-recited prayers, it has become customary to include a transliteration into the vernacular to help those mourners who are unable to read the Hebrew characters. The illustration on the left is a transliteration into Russian of the *Rabbanan Kaddish* which the mourners are required to recite at certain stages in the service. The music is for the *Kaddish* recited by the cantor before *Barekhu* in the morning service on Rosh Ha-Shanah according to the Sephardi rite. The *Barekhu* invocation is sung to the same melody.

a variety of public and private prayers, including the prayer of thanksgiving for rain. Interestingly, though, the *Kaddish* prayer was not originally part of the synagogue service. The Talmud specifically records that it first served as a concluding prayer to the public aggadic discourse which was also conducted in Aramaic, then the vernacular. The *Kaddish de-Rabbanan,* the *Kaddish* for the scholars, testifies to this connection. At different times, special verses were inserted into this *Kaddish,* invoking blessings on the *nasi,* the *resh galuta* (president or exilarch), and the heads of the academies, or as in Yemen, for such distinguished scholars as Maimonides.

The *Kaddish* is mentioned as part of the prescribed synagogue daily prayers for the first time in the post-talmudic tractate *Soferim.* By geonic times—the period which the world calls the Dark Ages—it had become a statutory synagogue prayer requiring the presence of a *minyan* comprising ten adult males. The name *Kaddish* is first mentioned in this tractate, and it appears that the explanatory passage beginning "Blessed and praised" (which is recited in Hebrew) was added for non-Aramaic speakers. The last three sentences—the plea for the acceptance of the prayer, for the welfare of the supplicants, and the concluding prayer for peace—were all later additions.

The text current in the German and Italian rites, that quoted above, is derived from *Seder Rav Amram,* the pioneering prayer book compiled in the ninth century, but it exhibits local variations. In the Yemenite rite, for example, the phrase *le-eila u-le-eila* ("much beyond all praises") appears in this double form all the year round, and not only during the Ten Days of Penitence. In Jerusalem and Safed and adjective *kaddisha* is added in the *Kaddish de-Rabbanan,* so that the phrase in question reads "in this holy place." At one stage, several additions were made to the passage: "May the prayers and supplication. . . ," and the final invitation to the congregation to respond "*Amen*" appears neither in the *Seder Rav Amram* nor in other old manuscripts.

In Music. The various forms and functions of the *Kaddish* in the service are matched by a variety of musical configurations. Melodies range from simple recitatives to elaborate solo productions, from light tunes in popular taste to the most solemn and impressive compositions. Solomon de Rossi of Venice even set the entire text for a three-and five-part chorus. Nevertheless, some guiding principles may be discerned among the multiplicity of *Kaddish* tunes. In the Ashkenazi rite, the *Kaddish* before the *Amidah* (especially in the *Musaf* service) is distinguished by a striving for sublime melodic expression. Its music is sometimes identical with that of the following *Avot* benediction, for which it sets the mood, the congregation often joining in its singing. The Sephardim emphasize rather the *Kaddish* preceding *Barekhu,* either by means of elaborate coloraturas, or by its melodic identity with that benediction. In the Ashkenazi synagogues, certain liturgical situations evoke *Kaddish* melodies of a definite character or form. The *Kaddish* which closes the *Musaf* prayer is preferably sung to a lively and gay tune, sometimes in a dance-like manner, the earliest known example being that notated by Benedetto Marcello in Venice in the 1720s. During festivals the *Kaddish* recited over the Torah scroll and that before the evening *Amidah* are distinguished by musical motifs that characterize the festival in question. On Simḥat Torah, which closes the cycle of holidays, the characteristic motifs of all the festivals are assembled in some rites in the "Year-*Kaddish.*"

The exotic tunes anchored in local traditions are also worth mentioning, such as the so-called *Trommel* ("drumming") *Kaddish* which used to be sung in Frankfort on Purim Vinz—the 20th of the month of Adar. This is a Special Purim, that is, a local thanksgiving festival, commemorating that day in 1616 when, after the Fettmilch persecutions, the Jews were brought back into the town "with trumpets and drums" in a scene described in Elḥanan Helen's chronicle, *Megillat Vinz.*

The famous "*Kaddish*" of the ḥasidic *rebbe* Levi Isaac of Berdichev, *A Din-Toyre mit Got* ("a lawsuit with God") is a kind of introduction to the liturgical *Kaddish.* In this, the saintly Levi Isaac addresses and rebukes God, appealing to His sense of fair play, as it were, in an extended "prose poem" whose melody comprises elements of the High Holy Day liturgy. Leonard Bernstein's *Kaddish,* an oratorio for narrator, choir and orchestra, first performed in Tel Aviv in 1963, is also a kind of "lawsuit with God" centering on the *Kaddish,* and is thus strongly reminiscent of Levi Isaac's song.

VI the services

origins
ma'ariv
shaḥarit
musaf
minḥah

סדר תפלת

המנחה

של ערב ראש חדש

ש' אומרים בני חברת המתענים

ביום ההוא בפירארה:

IN VENETIA, 1643.

Appresso Ant. Calleoni.

Con Licenza de' Sup.

A prayerbook printed in Venice in 1643 which contains the *Minḥah* service for the eve of Rosh Ḥodesh "which is recited by members of the society who fast on that day in Ferrara (Italy)."

This woodcut, "House of Worship," by Jacob Steinhardt (1887–1968) captures the atmosphere of a ḥasidic synagogue in his native Poland. Although Steinhardt studied under Hermann Struck, his work makes a very different impression.

ORIGINS

The Jewish liturgy contains five communal services to be recited at fixed times during the day: *Ma'ariv* (evening); *Shaḥarit* (morning); *Musaf* (additional); *Minḥah* (afternoon); and *Ne'ilat She'arim* (lit. "closing of the gates"). Of these, only the *Ma'ariv, Shaḥarit* and *Minḥah* are recited on every day of the year. The *Musaf* is added only on Sabbath and festivals; the *Ne'ilat She'arim* service, which was originally recited on all fast days, eventually became restricted to the Day of Atonement (when it is known simply as *Ne'ilah*). Thus, it is only on that occasion that the complete cycle of all five services is now recited during the course of one day.

The general development of the liturgy is discussed in Chapter XII. Although it is recorded that the biblical Daniel prayed three times a day, it is unlikely that that example was based on anything more than the fact that morning, noon and night are natural divisions of the day and the spiritually sensitive person would turn his thoughts to God at those times. There is also no doubt that proper communal prayer services as such were not held in the Temples. It does however seem that a major impetus to the development of a set communal services was provided by the establishment of the *mishmarot* and *ma'amadot* in the Temple service. These were the 24 courses, or divisions, into which the priests and levites were organized for the purpose of performing ritual duty in the Temple. This they did in weekly rotation. This system would appear to have been formalized during the period of the Second Temple. By that time, too, an analogous division had been made of the remainder of the Israelites. They, too, were divided into 24 *mishmarot,* each of which had to take its turn in coming up to Jerusalem for a week. There they served to represent the whole body of the people while the daily (communal offerings were sacrificed for, in the words of the Mishnah, "how can a man's offering be offered while he does not stand by it?" However, not all the members of the *mishmar* were able to go to Jerusalem. They would instead assemble in their own towns and read the story of the Creation. Others would gather at the appointed time for the Temple sacrifices and pray for the welfare of sailors, wayfarers, children, and pregnant women. Even those members of the priestly and Levite *mishmar* who were in Jerusalem but who did not engage in the actual Temple service, would gather to pray that the sacrifices of their officiating brethren (known as the *ma'amad* sector of the *mishmar*) be acceptable.

Long after the destruction of the Temple, memories of the *mishmarot* lingered on. In Ereẓ Israel their names were mentioned each Sabbath in the *piyyutim.* Tablets, fragments of which have survived, were fixed on synagogue walls, engraved with a list of *mishmarot* and their geographical provenance. Karaite liturgy preserved echoes of both the *mishmarot* and the *ma'amadot*. Even as late as 1034, it was still the custom in some communities to announce on each Sabbath: "Today is the holy Sabbath, holy to the Lord. Today is [the Sabbath of] which *mishmeret*? [That of] *mishmeret* . . . May the Merciful One restore the *mishmeret* to its place, speedily and in our days. Amen."

Meanwhile, however, the association which the *mishmarot* had established between sacrificial worship and communal prayer had attained more permanent form. Even during the second Temple period, the time of prayer had been fixed in accordance with that of the Temple sacrifice. Thus, services were held at the time of the morning sacrifice, the additional festival sacrifice (when appropriate), the afternoon offering, and that offered at the close of the Temple gates. Whether a fixed formula also existed for such prayers is difficult to determine. But, with the destruction of the Temple and the consequent discontinuance of sacrifices, a set order certainly emerged. Thus, by the tannaitic period there already existed such a formula, which is found in the Mishnah and the Tosefta and whose composition is attributed to the men of the Great Synagogue.

Recorded is the original prayer formula: i.e. *berakhah* ("the benediction") with its wording *Barukh Attah Adonai* ("Blessed are Thou, O Lord") which serves both for prayers of adoration and of petition; the obligation derived from the Pentateuch, to recite the *Shema* twice daily with its benedictions (three in the morning and four in the evening); and the daily *Amidah,* known as *Tefillah,* comprising 18 benedictions and recited three times daily.

The fixed services with which this chapter will be concerned all reflect the historical development outlined above. In many cases, some of the passages recited during the services appear to have been in use even before the destruction of the Temple. In others, the formulas were not devised until later periods. Only the *Ne'ilah* prayer has lost much of its original context, being restricted solely to the Day of Atonement. For this reason, it will be dealt with in Chapter VIII, which discusses that occasion. In almost every other instance, the services have retained distinct traces of their associations with the sacrificial offerings which they now replace.

MA'ARIV

In this context, the evening service constitutes a striking exception. It is the only fixed service which does not correspond to any set Temple sacrifice. For this reason, its recital was originally regarded as optional by the rabbis of the Talmud. Nevertheless, in view of certain biblical references to the obligation to recite prayers three times a day (Psalms 55:18 and Daniel 6:11), this service too became statutory. Indeed, one tradition, based on Genesis 28:11, attributed the institution of the evening prayers to the patriarch Jacob. Thus, in common with the other services, its recital is the duty of the individual even outside the synagogue and congregational service.

The original Hebrew name for the service is *Arvit* (derived from the root meaning "evening"). As this name implies, ideally the service should be recited after nightfall and before dawn. It may, however, be recited after twilight and, to meet the convenience of worshipers, it is often immediately preceded by the *Minḥah* (afternoon) service on weekdays. The more popular name, *Ma'ariv,* was not in use until about the 16th century. It is derived from the occurrence of this word at the beginning and end of the first blessing preceding the *Shema* during the service.

In its present form the service consists chiefly of *Barekhu* (the invitation to congregational prayer), followed by the *Shema* and its framework of benedictions, and the *Amidah.* When *Arvit* is said after nightfall, the service generally opens with Psalms 134. On weekdays the service opens with Psalms 78:38 and 20:10. According to the Mishnah the reading of the *Shema* is obligatory at nighttime. This view was based on the biblical phrase "when thou liest down," (Deuteronomy 6:7; 11:19) and only the recital of its third section (Numbers 15:37–41) was a matter of controversy.

The theme of the first of the two blessings preceding the *Shema* is the incidence of evening and night. The second blessing (*Ahavat olam;* see Chapter V) is a thanksgiving for the love shown by God for Israel by revealing His Torah to them. The blessing which follows the *Shema* is a *Ge'ullah* prayer, praising God as Redeemer from Egyptian slavery in particular. The two blessings preceding the *Shema* and the one following it thus follow the pattern normal for the recital of this prayer. They are followed by a night prayer *Hashkivenu* ("Grant us to lie down in peace"), imploring God's protection from a variety of dangers and mishaps. The final blessing existed in two versions; one Babylonian and one Palestinian. In the latter a prayer for peace and Zion—Jerusalem· (*ha-pores sukkat shalom;* "who spreads the tabernacle of peace") replaces the more general formula (*shomer ammo Yisrael la-ad;* "who guards His people Israel forever"). The Babylonian version is now used on weekdays; the Palestinian on Sabbaths and festivals.

According to the Ashkenazi rite, a group of scriptural verses beginning with Psalms 89:53 (*barukh Adonai le-olam;* "blessed be the Lord for evermore"), and which originally may have numbered 18, is said between *Hashkivenu* and the *Amidah.* It is a late addition, not found in the Sephardi rite but given in *Maḥzor Vitry.* Later, an additional night prayer (*barukh Adonai ba-yom;* "blessed be the Lord by day") and a benediction expressing messianic hopes (*yiru einenu;* "may our eyes

behold") were attached to this. Elijah of Vilna discontinued this custom and those who follow his *nusaḥ* (e.g. most Ashkenazim in Israel) omit the whole addition.

The *Amidah* is then read silently. This is the service to which the Mishnah and Talmud refer when they speak of *tefillat ha-erev* or *tefillat arvit*. However, in token of its originally optional character, the *Amidah* is not repeated by the reader even in congregational prayer; further blessings could intervene between it, and the *Ge'ullah* blessing, and the half *Kaddish* which originally marked the end of the service is recited before the *Amidah.*

The *Amidah* is followed by the full *Kaddish.* In post-talmudic times this was still preceded by *Taḥanun* and some other additions found in the morning service before the *Kaddish. Aleinu le-Shabbe'aḥ* concludes the service, though in some rites further psalms were added.

SHAḤARIT

Shaḥarit, the daily morning service, is the most elaborate of the three daily prescribed prayers. It is also the only daily prayer during which the *tallit* and *tefillin* are normally worn. The institution of the morning service is traditionally attributed to the Patriarch Abraham (on the basis of Genesis 19:27) and the rabbis later made its recitation obligatory to replace the daily morning sacrifice (*Tamid*) performed in the Temple.

The name *shaḥarit* itself is derived from the Hebrew word *shaḥar,* meaning "dawn." In fact, however, the exact time of the day during which the morning service can be recited is governed by the laws which determine the period for the recitation of the *Shema* and the *Amidah.* The start of the period in which the *Shema* should be recited begins with daybreak and concludes after a quarter of the day has passed. The time for reciting the *Amidah* begins with sunrise and ends after a third of the day has passed. Extremely pious people (*vatikin*) were therefore careful to begin their prayers with daybreak so they could complete the recitation of the *Shema* by sunrise and recite the *Amidah* immediately afterward. If the morning prayers are delayed past their proper time for recitation, they may still be said until midday. If, by accident, the morning *Amidah* was not recited an extra *Amidah* is added at the *Minḥah* service.

Modeh Ani. Even before the set *Shaḥarit* service is begun, the liturgy prescribes a separate prayer to be recited upon waking in the morning. Known as the *modeh ani* (from its initial words), this is a short passage reading: "I give thanks to You, O living and eternal King, who has restored my soul to me in mercy; great is Your faithfulness." Since in the Hebrew version, this passage does not mention any of the Divine Names, it may be said while still in bed and before performing the prescribed morning ablutions. Moreover, because of its brevity and simplicity, it became a favorite morning prayer for very small children before they are capable of reciting the ordinary daily morning service.

This prayer is of late origin, and seems to have been composed during the 17th century.

Mah Tovu. The basic components of the *Shaḥarit* service are (in the order in which they appear), the *Barekhu* introductory; the *Shema;* the *Amidah; Ashrei* and *Aleinu le-Shabbe'aḥ.* However, these prayers and readings are each preceded and followed by a number of supplementary paragraphs.

Thus, in the Ashkenazi rite, a special prayer is recited upon entering the synagogue in the morning. Its initial words, from which it derives the name *Mah Tovu,* are a quotation from Numbers 24:5: "How goodly are your tents, O Jacob; your dwellings O Israel." The Talmud interprets this verse as referring to synagogues and schools, and therefore it is deemed an appropriate opening to public worship. The remainder of the prayer consists of Psalms 5:8; 26:8; 69:14; and 95:6. The reference in the penultimate line to a "time of grace" is taken to mean the time of public worship.

Sephardi Jews recite Psalms 5:8 on entering the synagogue and Psalms 5:9 on leaving.

Morning Benedictions. With the conclusion of *Mah Tovu,* a series of benedictions is recited. Their number and sequence varies in the different rituals, but in all cases they constitute the first portion of the *Shaḥarit* proper.

The first benediction is that recited over the washing of the hands (*al netillat yadayim*) which is obligatory upon waking in

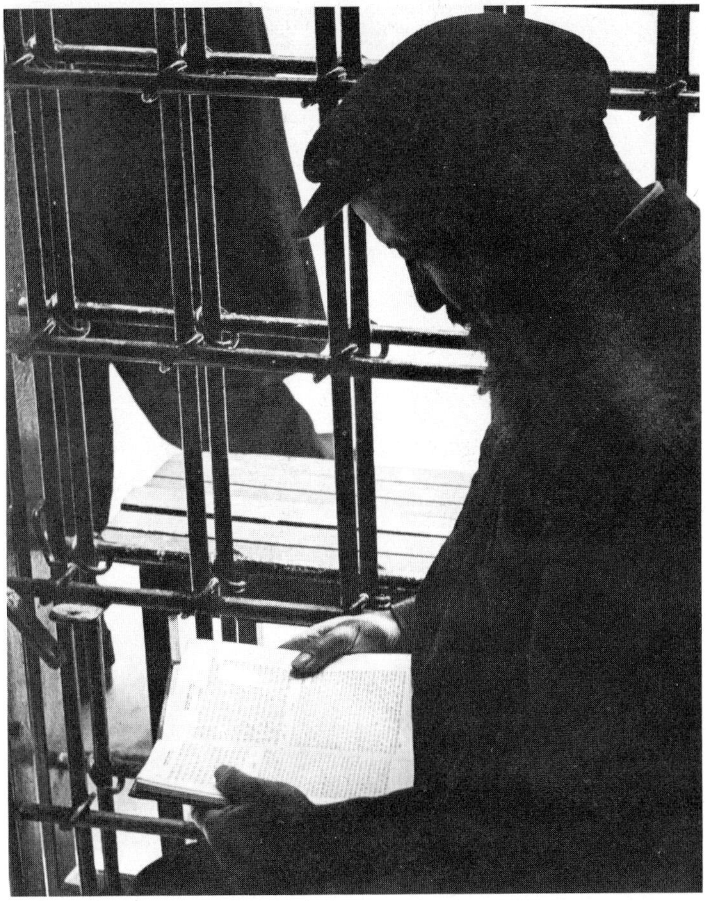

Since the 1967 War and the re-unification of Jerusalem, the Western Wall has become the focus of Jewish prayer. For the soldier, wearing a paper *kippah* given to visitors without headgear, a visit to the Wall is an opportunity to put on *tefillin* and say a prayer. The elderly gentleman—obviously a more frequent visitor—is reciting his daily portion of sacred texts.

the morning. This is followed by a lengthier benediction, which thanks God for creating the harmony of the bodily functions. In many rites, the three Torah blessings are then recited. These, respectively, acknowledge that God has commanded the study of the Torah, beseech that the opportunity to do so may be granted, and thanks God "who gives the Torah." This passage is appropriately concluded with two short passages, one from the Written Law (Torah) and one from the Oral Law (Mishnah). The former consists of the Priestly Blessing, the latter of a quotation from Chapter I of tractate *Pe'ah* which mentions (among other things) the importance of regular synagogue attendance and the primacy of Torah study.

There then follows a short paragraph which acknowledges that man's soul is the gift of God. Based on a talmudic passage, it is known from its opening words as *Elohei Neshama*, "O my God, the soul . . . ." It closes with the formula "Blessed art Thou, O Lord, Who restores the souls unto the dead." A variant reading is: "Who quickens the dead"; some Progressive rites recite: "Who heals the flesh and does wondrously."

There then follows a series of 15 short benedictions (although this number varies in different versions). In some congregations, they are recited aloud by the reader, and the congregants respond "Amen."

These blessings praise God who: (1) "endows the cock with the ability to distinguish between day and night"; (2) "has not made me a heathen"; (3) "has not made me a slave"; (4) "has not made me a woman"; women say: "who has made me according to Thy will"; (these last three blessings are near the end in the Sephardi rite and some ḥasidic rites and are omitted in the Progressive prayer books where the formula "Who has made me a Jew" is said instead by both men and women); (5) "enlightens the blind"; (6) "clothes the naked"; (7) "releases the bound"; (8) "raises them that are bowed down"; (9) "stretches out the earth upon the waters"; (10) "has provided me with all my necessities"; (11) "has ordained the steps of man"; (12) "girds Israel with might"; (13) "crowns Israel with glory"; (14) "gives strength to the weary" (this does not appear in all versions); and (15) "causes sleep to pass from my eyes."

These blessings, most of which are mentioned in the Talmud, were recited originally at home during the various stages of a person's awakening: opening his eyes, standing up, getting dressed, etc. Maimonides opposed their recital at public worship but in the course of time they were incorporated into the morning service in the synagogue, probably because people did not remember by heart their wording or their order.

Further Readings. With the conclusion of the morning benedictions, a number of biblical and talmudic passages are then recited. These begin with several personal prayers of tannaitic and amoraic origin, which are followed by a recital of the confessional prayer attributed by the Talmud to Rabbi Joḥanan. This commences with an admonition that "At all times let a man fear God as well in private as in public, acknowledge the truth, and speak the truth in his heart." It then recites a powerful admission of the insignificance of all men when compared with God. The passage concludes with the recitation of the *Shema* (in some rites, the first two lines only) and with a benediction extolling the sanctity of the Almighty.

In accordance with the sentiments thus expressed, the biblical account of the Binding of Isaac (the *Akedah*; Genesis 22:1–19) is then read. This description of Abraham's faith and God's mercy has been considered an appropriate prayer of intercession from earliest times, and was treated as such in the early rabbinic period. It is apparently for this reason that it was accorded its present place in the liturgy. In many rites this passage is recited before the confessional of Rabbi Joḥanan.

In view of the historical association between the morning prayer and the ancient Temple sacrifices, it is appropriate that reference is also made to the exact nature of the latter. This is done in the form of quotations from the appropriate biblical and talmudic literature. Thus, Numbers 28:1–8 and Leviticus 17:9–10, which describe the morning sacrifices, are recited. On Sabbath, these readings are complemented by Numbers 28:9–10, and on Rosh Ḥodesh by Numbers 28:11–15, which describe the additional sacrifices offered on those days. In most rites, especially the Sephardi, this is followed by a passage from the Babylonian Talmud (*Keritot* 6*a*) known as *Pittum ha-ketoret,* describing the incense offering. In its turn, this is followed by chapter five of tractate *Zevaḥim*. Commencing with the words *Eizehu mekoman shel zevaḥim* ("which are the places where the sacrifices [were offered]?"), this contains a discussion of the sacrificial procedure followed in the Temple. This portion of the service concludes with a recital of the *baraita* of Rabbi Ishmael (Introduction to Sifra, Leviticus), which enumerates the thirteen exegetical principles by which the Torah is expounded.

Pesukei de-Zimra. According to the rabbis of the Talmud, the liturgical pattern requires meditation prior to formal prayer. In order to help the individual worshiper to achieve the required state of mind, and at the same time to overcome the difficulties posed by inarticulate meditation, the recitation of certain Psalms was introduced into the *Shaḥarit* service. Although Psalms were publicly recited in both Temples, their inclusion in the morning service did not become integral to synagogue worship until geonic times. The late development of this custom, which is not mandated in the Talmud, is reflected in the considerable variations in the choice of Psalms to be recited in different rites. The special position which they occupy is further evident from the rabbinic ruling that only a reader and two respondents are required for their recitation. Even the collective name used to describe these Psalms in the Ashkenazi rite—*Pesukei de-Zimra*—is significant. (The Sephardi, Yemenite and Italian designation is *zemirot*—"songs"). Literally translated from the Aramaic, the term means "verses of song/praise." It has been suggested that the expression *pesukei* ("verses") rather than *pirkei* ("chapters") implies that originally not whole Psalms but selections from them were prescribed.

The development is reflected in the *Pesukei de-Zimra* recited in the Ashkenazi rite, where they consist of both whole Psalms and excerpts from cognate biblical passages. On weekdays, they comprise I Chronicles 16:8–36, plus a lectionary of 23 verses from Psalms; Psalm 100; another lectionary, mostly from Psalms, formed by the final verse of Psalms 89, 135, and 72:18–19; I Chronicles 29:10–13; Nehemiah 9:6–11; and Exodus 14:30, 15:18, 19, plus three divine kingship verses. On Sabbaths and festivals, Psalm 100 is omitted while Psalms 19, 34, 90, 91, 135, 136, 33, 92, and 93 are added before *Yehi khevod.*

BARUKH SHE-AMAR. The Ashkenazi practice is to enclose the *Pesukei de-Zimra* between two blessings. The first of these is known by its opening words as *Barukh she-Amar* ("Blessed be He who spoke"). In the Sephardi and other rites some of the *Pesukei de-Zimra* are recited before the *Barukh she-Amar* passage.

Several versions of this passage are extant. In the Ashkenazi rite it consists of 87 words; this number is repeated in the Eastern Sephardi rites—according to the Kabbalah—although there are some slight variations in the text. In the original Sephardi prayer books (Leghorn, Amsterdam, and Vienna), there is a longer version, with additions for Sabbath.

In its present form the *Barukh she-Amar* is a combination of two separate prayers of which only the second part can be considered a benediction. The first part is a hymn praising God, the Creator and Redeemer. In spite of numerous variations and later accretions, the prayer may be talmudic in origin. It is first mentioned by Moses Gaon (c. 820) and is found in the prayer book of Amram Gaon (also ninth century), where the prayer is introduced as follows: "When Jews enter the synagogue to pray, the *ḥazzan* of the congregation rises and begins. . . ." Nathan ha-Bavli reports a century later that at the ceremony of the installation of the exilarch, *Barukh she-Amar* was sung antiphonically, and hence some scholars have suggested that the

The *Ein Ke-Elohenu* prayer translated in the Rabbinical Assembly (Conservative) of America's High Holy Day *maḥzor* (1972). To make things easier for the worshiper, the instructions and notes are printed in a different color than that used for the text to be recited. The passage shown has been somewhat abbreviated.

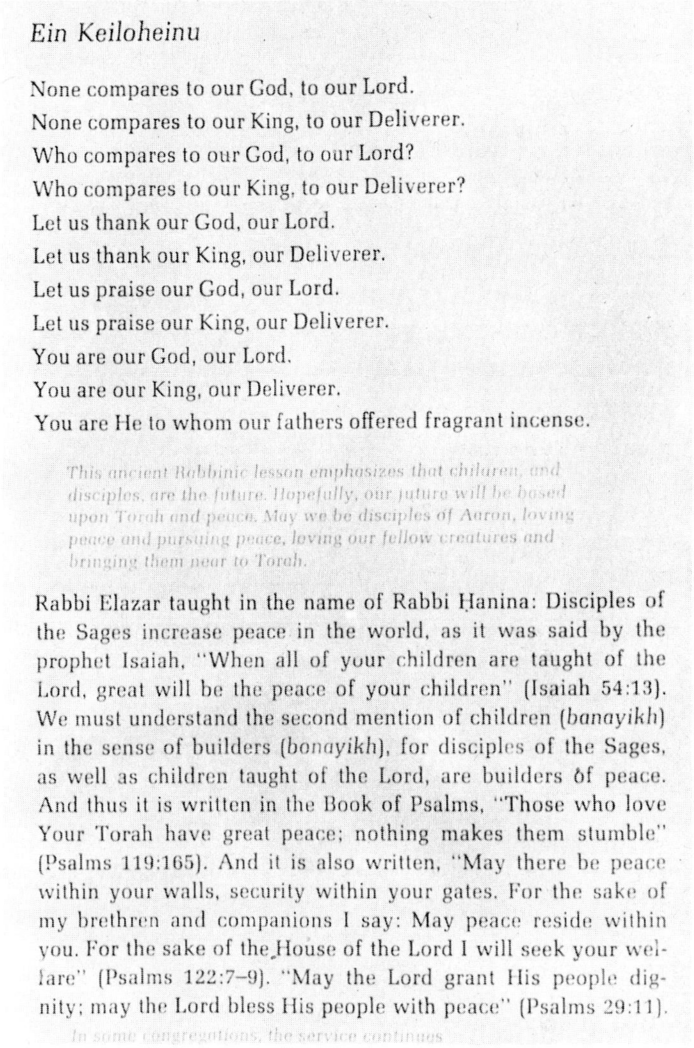

Ein Keiloheinu

None compares to our God, to our Lord.
None compares to our King, to our Deliverer.
Who compares to our God, to our Lord?
Who compares to our King, to our Deliverer?
Let us thank our God, our Lord.
Let us thank our King, our Deliverer.
Let us praise our God, our Lord.
Let us praise our King, our Deliverer.
You are our God, our Lord.
You are our King, our Deliverer.
You are He to whom our fathers offered fragrant incense.

This ancient Rabbinic lesson emphasizes that children, and disciples, are the future. Hopefully, our future will be based upon Torah and peace. May we be disciples of Aaron, loving peace and pursuing peace, loving our fellow creatures and bringing them near to Torah.

Rabbi Elazar taught in the name of Rabbi Ḥanina: Disciples of the Sages increase peace in the world, as it was said by the prophet Isaiah, "When all of your children are taught of the Lord, great will be the peace of your children" (Isaiah 54:13). We must understand the second mention of children (*banayikh*) in the sense of builders (*bonayikh*), for disciples of the Sages, as well as children taught of the Lord, are builders of peace. And thus it is written in the Book of Psalms, "Those who love Your Torah have great peace; nothing makes them stumble" (Psalms 119:165). And it is also written, "May there be peace within your walls, security within your gates. For the sake of my brethren and companions I say: May peace reside within you. For the sake of the House of the Lord I will seek your welfare" (Psalms 122:7–9). "May the Lord grant His people dignity; may the Lord bless His people with peace" (Psalms 29:11).

In some congregations, the service continues

response *Barukh Hu* ("blessed be He"), was repeated as a refrain after every clause, and not only for the first one as in the present text. According to Saadiah's *Siddur* from the 10th century it was recited only on Sabbaths. The style of the hymn is midrashic and most of the phrases are found in various passages of Talmud and Midrash. Eleazer ben Judah of Worms of the 12th–13th centuries, quoting from the *Heikhalot* texts of the early mystics, refers to the esoteric significance of the 87 words contained in *Barukh she-Amar* (at least in the Ashkenazi rite); the extant texts of the *Heikhalot* do not, however, have this passage. The first part of the prayer has been interpreted as an exposition of the various meanings of the Tetragrammaton. In Prague a Barukh she-Amar Society was active from the 16th century until World War II. The members rose early in order to be in the synagogue before the reciting of *Barukh she-Amar*.

With the recitation of the *Barukh she-Amar* prayer, the *shaḥarit* service proper can be said to have begun. This may be indicated by the fact that, according to the codifiers, once the passage has been said, the supplicants are forbidden to speak or to interrupt the prayers until the conclusion of the *Amidah*.

YISHTABBAḤ. The *Pesukei de-Zimra* section of the service concludes with the recitation of another passage of praise. Known by its first word as *Yishtabbaḥ* (lit. "Praised"), it is referred to in the Talmud as "the benediction of song," where it is designated as a conclusion of the *Hallel* recited during the Passover *Seder*. The author of this passage is unknown, as is the date of its composition, although some authorities claim that it was written in honor of King Solomon.

The blessing is one of praise for God, declaring that unto Him "song and praise are becoming, hymn and psalm, strength and dominion, victory, greatness and might, renown and glory, holiness and sovereignty, blessings and thanksgivings from henceforth even for ever." The *Zohar* places great stress on the proper recitation of this prayer since its 13 individual praises of God activate the 13 attributes of God. Thus, *Yishtabbaḥ* should be recited while standing and it is forbidden to interrupt or converse during this portion of the service.

The Daily Psalm. Following *Yishtabbaḥ*, half *Kaddish* is recited in order to mark the distinction between the *Pesukei de-Zimra* and the sections of the service which follow. These consist of the *Barekhu* introduction; the *Shema* and its benedictions; and the *Amidah*. On those days on which *Taḥanun* is recited, this prayer immediately follows the *Amidah*, after which half *Kaddish* is again recited. On those mornings when it is required, the Torah is read, after which the half *Kaddish* is repeated. The service then continues with *Ashrei*, Psalm 20, and the *U-vah-le-zion* paragraph. Thereafter, the reader recites the whole *Kaddish*, after which the *Aleinu* prayer is read.

It is at this point in the service that a Daily Psalm is recited. The exact choice of Psalm to be recited varies from day to day in the week. Thus, on Sundays, Psalm 24 is recited, on Monday Psalm 48, on Tuesday, Psalm 82, on Wednesday Psalm 94 and Psalm 95:1, on Thursday Psalm 81, and on Friday Psalm 93. The origins of this practice have been discussed in Chapter II.

Ein Ke-Elohenu. In the Sephardi and ḥasidic ritual (in Ereẓ Israel, the Ashkenazi too), the morning service is completed by the recital of a hymn which commences with the words *Ein*

The first three of Maimonides' Thirteen Articles of Faith, translated into English for the first time in London, 1770. The decorations have no Jewish significance. It was faith that led these Jewish soldiers serving in the German Army in the field to come together to form a *minyan* so that one of them would be able to recite the mourner's *Kaddish* on the anniversary of his parents' death. Moritz Oppenheim (1799–1882) called his painting "Die Jahrzeit (Minian)."

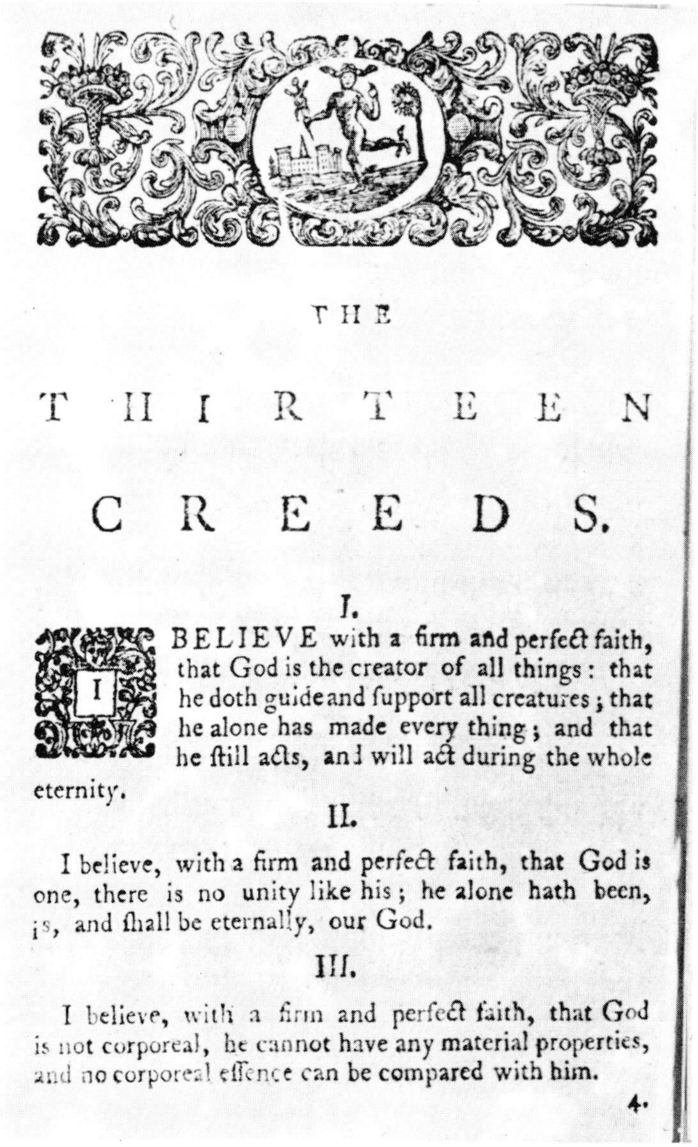

THE

THIRTEEN

CREEDS.

I.

I BELIEVE with a firm and perfect faith, that God is the creator of all things: that he doth guide and ſupport all creatures; that he alone has made every thing; and that he ſtill acts, and will act during the whole eternity.

II.

I believe, with a firm and perfect faith, that God is one, there is no unity like his; he alone hath been, is, and ſhall be eternally, our God.

III.

I believe, with a firm and perfect faith, that God is not corporeal, he cannot have any material properties, and no corporeal eſſence can be compared with him.

4.

Ke-Elohenu ("There is none like our God"). In the Ashkenazi rite this is recited only at the end of the *Musaf* (additional) service, on Sabbaths and holidays.

The practice of reciting *Ein Ke-Elohenu* was current by the medieval period. It is mentioned in the prayer books compiled by Amram Gaon, Maimonides (12th century), and Rashi (13th century), where, however, the order of its stanzas differs from their present sequence. The initial letters of the first three verses form the word "*Amen*" and the other two verses start with "*Barukh*" and "*Attah*," forming the phrase "*Amen Barukh Attah*," ("Amen, Blessed be Thou"). It is possible that originally there was a final verse starting with *Adonai*. Rashi states that *Ein Ke-Elohenu* is recited, in the Ashkenazi ritual, on Sabbaths and holidays only, because on those days the *Amidah* consists of seven benedictions instead of the 19 on weekdays and through this hymn additional praises are recited, making up for those missing. In the *Genizah* fragments, where the stanzas are in a different order from the present text, the hymn is followed immediately by a quotation from Psalms 90:1, which suggests that it may have been recited at the termination of the Sabbath.

Concluding Readings. Many Orthodox prayer books contain a selection of readings inserted at the conclusion of the *Shaḥarit* service. These do not form a part of the communal liturgy, but are recited privately by pious individuals before leaving the synagogue.

In many cases, the first of the readings consists of a private prayer for sustenance, asking that the supplicant might be "enabled to support myself and the members of my household with ease and not with pain, by lawful and not forbidden means." This is followed by a recitation of the six verses of remembrance (*Zekhirot*). These consist of quotations from those portions of the Pentateuch in which the Children of Israel are specifically commanded to "remember" individual items. They refer to the Exodus, the revelation of the Torah, the Amalekite attack on the Israelites in the wilderness, God's anger against His people when they evinced a lack of faith, the divine punishment of leprosy which befell Miriam, and the Sabbath.

In some prayer books these verses are followed by longer quotations from the Bible. These usually contain the Ten Commandments (Exodus 20:1–17), the *Akedah* (Genesis 22:1–19; when not inserted earlier), and the account of the gift of manna in the wilderness (Exodus 16:4–36). The final reading included in this portion of the prayer books is a short creed. Known from its opening words as *Ani Ma'amin* ("I believe"); it consists of 13 separate lines, based on the Thirteen Articles of Faith formulated by Maimonides. Of unknown authorship, they were first incorporated in an Ashkenazi prayer book during the 16th century. The recital of these articles is concluded by the three words of Genesis 49:18 repeated three times in different order, in Hebrew and Aramaic, a custom based on Kabbalah.

The 12th article of the *Ani Ma'amin* expresses "perfect faith

in the coming of the Messiah, and, though he tarry, I will wait daily for his coming." This sentence became the Martyr's Hymn during the Nazi Holocaust, when it was sung to a haunting melody by those about to be taken to their death in the extermination camps.

MUSAF

On Sabbaths, the three pilgrim festivals, Rosh Ha-Shanah, the Day of Atonement, and the New Moon, the *Shaḥarit* service is followed by an additional service, known as *Musaf* (meaning "additional"). This service originated in the biblical injunction to supplement the normal morning and afternoon sacrifices on these days by an additional communal offering (Numbers 28–29). During the period of the two Temples, this obligation was performed, after the regular morning sacrifices. As has been seen, an additional prayer was recited by some persons on these days, even when the sacrificial cult still existed. After the abolition of sacrifice with the destruction of the Temple, this practice was formalized, and the *Musaf* service entered the liturgy. In the process, this service became endowed with the same importance as the regular *Shaḥarit* prayers. The rabbis therefore overruled the opinion of some authorities who regarded the *Musaf* as an exclusively communal service, which could only be recited in the presence of a *minyan* (quorum). Instead, it is considered obligatory even when praying alone.

It is customary to recite the *Musaf* service immediately after the reading of the weekly Torah and *haftarah* portions which follow the morning prayers on Sabbaths and festivals. It is, however, permissible to recite it at any time during the day. Nevertheless, one who negligently postpones its recitation until after the seventh hour of the day is considered a "transgressor."

The *Musaf* is introduced by the reader's recitation of the half *Kaddish*. This is followed by the *Amidah* of *Musaf* which, except on Rosh Ha-Shanah, consists of seven benedictions. The first three benedictions of praise and the last three benedictions of thanks are identical with those of the daily *Amidah*. The benediction *Kedushat ha-Yom* ("Sanctity of the Day") is inserted between these blessings. It consists of an introductory paragraph followed by a prayer for the restoration of the Temple service and concludes with the appropriate selection from the Torah detailing the additional sacrifice for the day.

The precise formula recited during this middle benediction varies from occasion to occasion. It thus accords with both the different sacrifices offered on those days on which *Musaf* is recited and with the distinctive character of each festival being celebrated. Thus, on Sabbaths this benediction includes a recital of both Numbers 28:9–10 (describing the Sabbath sacrifice) and specific invocations referring to the sanctity of the Sabbath and the reward awaiting those who observe the day. On Rosh Ḥodesh, Numbers 28:11, describing the New Moon sacrifice is quoted, and a prayer for a happy and blessed month is recited. On the three Pilgrim festivals, a similar format is followed, with appropriate alterations to suit every individual festival. The *Musaf* recited on Rosh Ha-Shanah and the Day of Atonement is considerably longer. Indeed, the Rosh Ha-Shanah *Musaf* is the longest in the liturgy, and on this occasion three further intermediate benedictions are recited. On the Day of Atonement, the confessional paragraphs form integral portions of the *Musaf* service.

Should either Rosh Ḥodesh or a festival coincide with the Sabbath, further changes are made to the *Musaf* service. In most cases, the alterations necessitated are minor, consisting of the addition of a description of the Sabbath sacrifice and of the words "and this Sabbath day" wherever the individual holiday is mentioned. The one exception is the coincidence of Rosh Ḥodesh with the Sabbath when the normal New Moon formula is considerably altered, and assumes a form very similar to that in use on the festivals.

In communal prayer, the *Musaf Amidah* is generally repeated in full by the *ḥazzan*. In some congregations, however, particularly among the Sephardi Jews, the *ḥazzan* chants the first three blessings aloud with the congregation. This, however, is not done on the High Holy Days, when the entire *Amidah* is always repeated by the *ḥazzan*.

It was customary to interlace the *ḥazzan's* repetition of the *Musaf Amidah* on festivals and special Sabbaths with various *piyyutim*. Except for Rosh Ha-Shanah and the Day of Atone-

Jacob Steinhardt's "Coming from Worship" (1923) has an air of sadness, as though the congregants at the end of the service are reluctantly forced to face the cruel world once again.

ment this is hardly done nowadays. Even on those two holidays most modern congregations recite only selections from the huge volume of *piyyutim* composed throughout the generations.

The *Musaf* services of the first day of Passover and of Shemini Aẓeret are known by special names: the former as *Tal* ("dew"), because prayers for abundant dew are recited during the repetition of the first two blessings by the cantor: the latter as *Geshem* ("rain"), because prayers for rain are recited by the cantor at the same juncture. These are discussed in Chapter VII.

In Reform congregations in the 19th century the *Musaf* service was either entirely abolished or modified since Reform Judaism no longer anticipated the restoration of the sacrificial cult. In the course of time, the tendency was to omit it entirely. Some Conservative congregations have rephrased references to the sacrifices so that they indicate solely past events without inplying any hope for future restoration of sacrifice.

MINḤAH

According to one rabbinical tradition, the afternoon service was instituted by the Patriarch Isaac who, in the words of the Bible, "went out to meditate in the fields at eventide" (Genesis 24:63). A separate tradition attributes the formalization of this service to the desire to commemorate the Temple sacrificial offering of a lamb at dusk. In this respect, it is similar in origin to the *Shaḥarit* and *Musaf* services. There is, however, one difference. In most rites, the afternoon service itself contains no specific reference to this sacrifice. Those which do contain such references place them before the formal commencement of the prayers.

The afternoon service is known in Hebrew as *Minḥah*, a name which is derived from the prophet Elijah's devotions "at the time of the evening (*minḥah*) offering" (I Kings 18:36). It is the shortest of the daily services. It consists of *Ashrei;* the *Amidah; Taḥanun* (when said); and concludes with the *Aleinu*. On Sabbaths and fast days a portion of the Torah is read before the *Amidah*.

In practice, the *Minḥah* service is usually recited in the synagogue as late as possible in the afternoon. This is in order that the congregation might then go on to pray *Ma'ariv* with as little inconvenience as possible. However, the simplicity of this arrangement belies the rather complicated calculations by which the correct time for this service is determined. According to the codifiers, the time for the recitation of the *Minḥah* prayer begins at the conclusion of six and one-half hours of the day. In calculating this time, an "hour" is one-twelfth of the length of the day. *Minḥah* prayed at this time is known as *Minḥah Gedolah* ("major"). *Minḥah* recited after nine and one-half hours of the day is called *Minḥah Ketannah* ("minor"). Rabbi Judah set the final time for the *Minḥah* prayer until midway (*pelag*) through the time designated for the *Minḥah Ketannah,* or until one and one-quarter hours before sunset. The law is, however, in accordance with the opinion that the *Minḥah* may be recited until sunset, which is calculated to occur at the conclusion of the 12th hour of the day. As a precaution lest people forget to pray the afternoon prayer, the rabbis ruled that it is forbidden to commence a large business transaction or sit down to a banquet once the time has begun for the *Minḥah Gedolah,* without having previously recited the prayer. Likewise, it is forbidden to begin a minor transaction or partake of an ordinary meal after the time for the *Minḥah Ketannah*. It seems that some made it a practice to pray both at *Minḥah Gedolah* and *Minḥah Kettanah*. However, the medieval halakhist, Asher ben Jehiel ruled that it is forbidden to do so. According to the *Shulḥan Arukh,* it is permitted to recite the *Minḥah* prayer twice, provided one is recited as an obligatory prayer (*ḥovah*) and the other as a voluntary act (*reshut*). This, however, is only allowed for the extremely pious who are certain that both their prayers will be recited with true devotion. Otherwise, the additional prayer will be considered an unwelcome addition in accordance with the exhortation of Isaiah: "To what purpose is the multitude of your sacrifices unto Me?" (Isaiah 1:11).

VII Days of Rest and Joy

The Sabbath

The Pilgrim Festivals

השומר שבת כהלכתו מוחלין

סדר

תקוני שבת

אמשטרדם

(תעה לפק)

The title page of *Seder Tikkunei Shabbat,* produced in Vienna in 1715 in "Amsterdam letters." The book, which was handwritten on parchment, contains the various invocations compiled by the great kabbalist, Isaac Luria. The sentence running around the central block promises the reader that he who keeps the Sabbath according to its laws will be pardoned for all his sins.

The six-pointed Sabbath lamp was a common feature of Jewish homes in Germany. This example is made of cast-brass and is from the 18th century. The six spouts each contained a wick and thus ensured the Sabbath evening would be spent in more light than the week days. The scene from the Jerusalem kindergarten was photographed on a Friday afternoon. There the children play out the Sabbath home ceremonies.

Perhaps one of the greatest contributions that Judaism has made to the world is the concept of the Sabbath and Festivals. The idea that man needs a retreat from the humdrum of day to day life into the world of the spirit is, in fact, a compliment to the human being in that it sees him as something more than an animal on two legs. One of the great Jewish theologians of this century, Abraham Joshua Heschel, described the Sabbath—a description which also applies by extension, to the festivals—as a Temple in Time and just as there was divine service in the Temple, so too on these "Temple days."

In rabbinic theology the Sabbath—in addition to the benefit it bestows on mankind—is the supreme testimony to the existence of God and the fact that He created the universe. The three Pilgrim Festivals, Passover, Shavuot and Sukkot, are acknowledgments of God's role in human history and are described as the "memorial to the Exodus from Egypt." The High Holy Days—Rosh Ha-Shanah and Yom Kippur—are the manifestation of the individual person's role in the world and the responsibility he bears. All together these days represent the sum total of Judaism's view of human existence and the liturgy for them amply expreses this point. A great deal of the celebration of these festivals takes place in the home. That aspect is discussed in Chapter XI. In this and the following chapter we will consider the liturgical aspects as they are manifested in the synagogue services.

As far as services are concerned, the Sabbath and festivals follow the normal liturgical pattern except for the fact that an extra service, *Musaf*, is added since on those days an additional sacrifice, from which the service takes its name, was offered in the Temple. However, the normal services are embellished with both additional statutory readings and *piyyutim* because of the importance of the occasion and because the congregant has more time to fully savor the flavor of the day. The *Amidot* do not contain the usual petitions but rather benedictions celebrating the theme of Sabbath or the festival. Here we will treat the exceptional aspects of the prayers of these Holy Days.

THE SABBATH

Kabbalat Shabbat. "The Reception of the Sabbath," is the term used to describe the inauguration of the Sabbath in general and, in a more specifically liturgical sense, that part of the Friday evening service which precedes the regular evening service and solemnly welcomes the Sabbath. The inauguration begins considerably before nightfall "so as to add," in the words of the Talmud, "from the weekday to the holy day." Much care

is traditionally lavished on preparing for the Sabbath. All housework that is forbidden on the Sabbath, e.g. cooking, is completed beforehand and before the Sabbath, some people used to read the weekly Torah section, twice in the original Hebrew text and once in the Aramaic (Targum) version. In honor of the day, one should bathe before the beginning of the Sabbath and put on festive clothes. The Talmud tells that Rabbi Ḥanina used to put on his Sabbath clothes and stand at sunset of Sabbath eve and exclaim: "Come and let us go forth to welcome the Queen Sabbath" and that Rabbi Yannai used to don his festive robes at that time and exclaim, "Come, O bride! Come, O bride!" These stories served as the main motif for the Sabbath hymn *Lekhah Dodi* and formed the basis of the custom of the kabbalists of Safed, who welcomed the Sabbath by going into the fields on Fridays at sunset to recite special prayers and hymns in honor of the Sabbath amid nature. This custom is the source for the introductory service that precedes the Sabbath *Ma'ariv* and is known as *Kabbalat Shabbat*. In traditional synagogues it is recited no later than half an hour after sunset. It opens with Psalm 29 (in the Ashkenazi and some other rites with the six Psalms 95–99 and 29 corresponding to the six days of creation or the six weekdays). The hymn *Lekhah Dodi* is then sung, followed by Psalms 92 and 93. In some rituals the evening service is preceded by the recital of the Song of Songs in honor of the Bride (or Queen) Sabbath. In many traditional rituals the hymn *Anna be-Kho'aḥ* is said before the *Lekhah Dodi* (or Psalm 121). Chapter 2 of Mishnah *Shabbat* which is known by its opening phrase, *Ba-Meh Madlikin,* is recited in some rites before the main evening prayer, in other rites following it. In the Yemenite ritual special *piyyutim* are also inserted before the evening prayer on those Sabbaths which coincide with the New Moon as well as for Sabbaths in the *Omer* period. The major deviations from the regular evening service are the elimination of the petitions of the *Amidah* and the substitution of blessings in honor of the Sabbath.

In modern Israel the term, *Kabbalat Shabbat,* is used to designate special ceremonies which are held on Friday at noontime in schools and kindergartens, and before supper in some kibbutzim, where they consist of lighting the Sabbath candles, reciting poetry, and singing songs in honor of the weekly day of rest. In the United States, many Reform and Conservative synagogues have introduced the late Friday evening service, which starts after the end of the business day—not withstanding the actual time of the beginning of the Sabbath—in order to enable a greater number of the congregants to participate. The central feature of the late Friday evening service is the rabbi's sermon; after the service an *Oneg Shabbat* ("Sabbath Reception") is usually held.

ANNA BE-KHO'AḤ. The prayer, called by its opening phrase, *Anna Be-Kho'aḥ* which is recited just before *Lekhah Dodi* is ascribed by tradition to the *tanna* Neḥunya ben ha-Kanah who lived in the second half of the first century C.E. This rabbi was known for the prayers he composed but this prayer was probably composed in the circle of the 13th-century Spanish kabbalists. The hymn, originally part of a group of kabbalistic prayers known under the title *Tefillat ha-Yiḥud,* "The prayer of the unity (of God)," gives expression to the longing of Israel for deliverance from the Diaspora and implores God's support and protection. It consists of seven verses of six words each, the initials of which form the 42-lettered Holy Name of God and similar mystical combinations. The initials of the second verse form the sentence *Kera Satan,* "Rend Satan" i.e. silence the adversary of Israel. The prayer is also recited, according to some rites, in the order of sacrifices contained in the daily morning prayer. Among the rites of Eastern Europe influenced by the Kabbalah it is also recited in the counting of the *Omer.*

LEKHAH DODI. The central feature of the *Kabbalat Shabbat* service is the recitation of a hymn which is known, after the opening phrase of its refrain, as *Lekhah Dodi,* "Come, my friend (to greet the bride)." It consists of nine stanzas; the initial letters of the first eight stanzas form the name of the author Solomon ha-Levi (Alkabez), a Safed kabbalist of the early 16th century. The opening line and refrain is: "Come, my friend, to meet the bride; let us welcome the presence of the Sabbath." Inspired by talmudic accounts mentioned above which describe how the scholars used to honor and welcome the Sabbath identifying it as a princess or bride, *Lekhah Dodi* reflects the

A wall plaque of the *Lekhah Dodi* hymn from Alsace (?), first half of the 19th century. The plaque which is watercolor on paper, has each stanza of *Lekhah Dodi* in a separate window and the Sabbath Psalm at the bottom.

practice of the Safed Kabbalists as well as the kabbalistic identification of the Sabbath with the *Shekhinah,* the mystical archetype of Israel. Hence also the messianic motives in the hymn, echoing talmudic concepts associating redemption with the observance of the Sabbath.

Lekhah Dodi is sung immediately after the recital of Psalms 95–99 and 29, with which the Sabbath eve service starts in Ashkenazi synagogues; the *ḥazzan* stands on the *bimah* (almemar) and not at his regular place to indicate that this part of the service is not in the original order of prayers. It is customary to turn around at the recital of the last stanza ("*Bo'i ve-shalom*") to face the entrance of the synagogue and bow. The "Sabbath bride" is thus symbolically welcomed. *Lekhah Dodi,* among the latest *piyyutim* to be incorporated into the prayer book, is one of the favorite hymns in the Ashkenazi as well as in the Sephardi ritual. In the extant texts, there are only slight variations, although one version has five additional stanzas also attributed to Alkabez. In many rituals, "*Bo'i kallah Shabbat malketa*" ("Come our bride, queen Sabbath") is added at the end of *Lekhah Dodi.*

The Reform ritual has retained only an abridged version of the hymn consisting of the first, third, fourth and the last stanzas. *Lekhah Dodi* has been rendered into most European languages; among the well-known translations are those of the German poets J. G. Herder and H. Heine. In his poem "*Prinzessin Sabbat*" Heine erroneously ascribed its authorship to the poet Judah Halevi. Another version of "*Lekhah Dodi*" was composed by a contemporary of Alkabez, Moses ibn Machir, head of the yeshivah in Ein Zeitun near Safed.

Musical Rendition. The poem was written to be sung, but none of the contemporary sources offers any information about its original melody. In the first printed version of the text, in a Sephardi prayer book, Venice 1583/4, it is headed "To the tune of *Shuvi Nafshi li-Menuḥaikhi,* a poem by Judah Halevi. This heading was taken over by two much later Sephardi prayer books, Amsterdam 1660/1 and Constantinople 1734/5, but apparently nowhere else. No conclusions can be drawn from it about the melody adopted or created in Safed, or about the ancestry of any one of the melodies presently used. Most of the existing melodies—the musicologist A. Z. Idelsohn estimated their number at over 2,000—show no distribution over a larger area and are either demonstrably late or the obvious products of musical styles that could not have been available or acceptable at Safed. Of the remainder there emerge three distinct melodies, one of which may well represent the original setting. One type of melody is found in Ereẓ Israel, southern Syria, Turkey, and the Balkans and has also been notated from North African informants. Another is found in the Sephardi communities of Amsterdam, London, Hamburg, and Leghorn. It is more complex than the first type, and has a definitely oriental flavor. The third type is found in the Sephardi communities of Bayonne and Bordeaux, in the Comtat Venaissin (i.e. Provence, a non-Sephardi community), and has also been notated from informants from Sarajevo (Yugoslavia) and Meknes (Morocco); its variants are extremely divergent, but all of them contain the elements of a Turkish military march. All these communities also have some strictly local melodies for *Lekhah Dodi* and the non-Sephardi Eastern communities have only local and regional melodies. The single example published from Yemen is sung to the general Yemenite pattern of psalm recitation.

In the Western Ashkenazi area, a certain stabilization was attempted by the melodic linking of *Lekhah Dodi* to the particular character of the respective Sabbath, week, or season. There were special melodies for *Shabbat Shuvah* (between Rosh Ha-Shanah and Yom Kippur) and *Shabbat Sefirah* (those between Passover or Shavuot) and the melody used on the eve of *Shabbat Ḥazon* and during the three weeks between the first of the 17th of Tammuz and the 9th of Av was based on that of the lamentation, *Eli Ẓiyyon.* Many of the ostensibly free compositions also begin with a "seasonal reminiscence," such as the *Ma'oz Ẓur* motif for the Sabbath of the Ḥanukkah week. The completely free compositions are in the majority, and the surviving cantorial manuals of the 18th century already contain

סדר ערבית של שבת

A page from a manuscript prayerbook (Italy) of the 15th century. The page shows the beginning of the Sabbath evening service. The text of the *Shema* is not included, it being assumed that the worshiper would know that by heart, and the passage following the *Shema* is a special adaptation for the Sabbath.

hundreds of melodies which for the most part reflect the style of the gentile environments.

They also show the interesting custom of setting each stanza to a different melody, or at least distinguishing the fifth stanza, *Hitoreri* ("Wake Up!") by an energetic melody and the last, *Bo'i ve-Shalom* ("Come in Peace, O Sabbath Queen"), by a lyrical one. Since the "reception of the Sabbath" in the synagogue precedes the "entrance of the Sabbath" itself, it was possible to accompany the ceremony, and especially the singing of *Lekhah Dodi* with musical instruments and there are references to this practice in several communities, notably Prague, in the 17th and 18th centuries.

Psalm 92. The end of the *Kabbalat Shabbat* service proper is the 92nd Psalm, which bears as its superscription the phrase *Mizmor Shir le-Yom ha-Shabbat,* "A Psalm, a Song for the Sabbath Day." The actual contents of this psalm are not particularly connected with the Sabbath but the Talmud records that it was the Sabbath hymn chanted by the Levites in the Temple. Besides its place in *Kabbalat Shabbat* it is also recited in the *Pesukei de-Zimra* on Sabbath morning and serves as the daily psalm for the Sabbath day. In the Sephardi rite and some Ashkenazi rites it is chanted at the Sabbath *Minḥah* service. In *Kabbalat Shabbat* and *Pesukei de-Zimra,* Psalm 93 is added.

Some aggadic sources attribute Psalm 92 to Adam who offered it as a hymn of thanksgiving on hearing that Cain would not be punished by death for killing Abel and that repentance could avert harsh judgment. According to this legend, in the course of time the Psalm was forgotten until Moses reintroduced it with ten other psalms.

Ba-Meh Madlikin. The second chapter of the Mishnah tractate *Shabbat* consisting of seven paragraphs is recited, according to traditional practice, during the Friday evening service either before the start of the *Ma'ariv* prayer (Sephardi and Ashkenazi ritual in Ereẓ Israel) or at the end of it (Ashkenazi ritual). Known by its opening words, *Ba-meh madlikin* ("with what may one kindle?") the chapter discusses the oils and wicks which may be used for the Sabbath lights as well as what must be done on Fridays before the commencement of the Sabbath. Some ḥasidic rites do not recite it at all but substitute a passage from the *Zohar,* known as *ke-galua,* dealing with the Sabbath. The reading of the chapter of the Mishnah was instituted in the geonic period as a reminder of the duty of kindling the Sabbath lights, as a precaution against any unintentional desecration of the Sabbath caused by adjusting the lamp, and as a safeguard for latecomers to the synagogue (the recital of this chapter by the congregation made it possible for latecomers to finish their prayers with the other congregants and to leave for home together without fear of injury in the dark). *Ba-Meh Madlikin* is not recited on a Sabbath falling on or immediately following a holiday because latecomers to the service would be few.

Magen Avot. The *Amidah* of the evening service is followed by the recitation of one of its sections comprising Genesis 2:1–3 and by a short summary of all the seven benedictions which make up the *Amidah.* This summary is popularly known, after its opening phrase, as *Magen Avot,* "The Shield of the Patriarchs," but in rabbinic parlance it is called *Me-Ein Sheva,* "The Condensation of the Seven [Benedictions]."

The recital of Genesis 2:1–3 is, in fact, a kind of *Kiddush* although it does not contain the actual *Kiddush* benediction. Normally, the evening service *Amidah* is not repeated by the *ḥazzan;* in this case the "condensation" was added to delay the completion of the service to enable to late-comers to catch up with the rest of the congregation and not have to go home alone.

Shaḥarit

Nishmat Kol Ḥai. An ancient and beautiful adoration rich in its poetical imagery is recited at Sabbath and festival morning services at the conclusion of the *Pesukei de-Zimra.* Known by its initial words, *Nishmat Kol Ḥai,* "The soul of every living being," the prayer expresses the gratitude men owe to God for His mercies in sustaining them. In talmudic literature it is called *Birkat ha-Shir,* "Benediction of the Song." Based upon the opinion of Rabbi Johanan, *Nishmat* also became part of the Passover *Haggadah.*

Nishmat consists of three main sections. The first contains an avowal of God's unity: "Besides Thee we have no King,

The *Nishmat* prayer is a liturgical addition for Sabbaths and festivals. It is also recited in the Passover night home *seder* ceremony, and the page here is from the *Schocken Haggadah*, early 15th century Italy. The illustration is a hunter with a falcon on horseback; hunting is the occupation for the month of May, the time of the year when Passover falls. The other illustration is a page from an 18th-century Carpentras *maḥzor* containing the prayer for the welfare of the pope, who is not named.

Deliverer, Savior, Redeemer . . . We have no King but Thee." Some scholars believed that this passage was composed by the apostle Peter as a protest against concepts foreign to pure monotheism. Rashi, the famous tenth century scholar and leading commentator of the Bible and Talmud, indignantly repudiated this legend and attributed its authorship to Simeon ben Shetaḥ, the outstanding sage of the century. The second section starting with the words: "If our mouths were full of song as the sea . . ." originated in the tannaitic period. It is similar to the formula of thanksgiving for abundant rain recited in that period. The passage: "If our eyes were shining like the sun and the moon . . . we could not thank God for the . . . myriads of benefits He has wrought for us" especially, is thought to substantiate this ascription to the tannaitic period since it reflects the opinion of Rav Judah that God has to be praised for each drop of rain. The third section, starting with the words: "From Egypt Thou hast redeemed us," is believed to have originated in the geonic period (c. tenth century C.E.). There is considerable disagreement among scholars about the original version of the *Nishmat*. There is, however, a general consensus that there existed an ancient but shorter version, called *Birkat ha-Shir*, which was later amplified and enlarged. This view is supported by the fact that the *Nishmat* in the Ashkenazi and in the Sephardi ritual, respectively, differ only in the wording of two or three sentences. In most prayer books the words at the end, *Ha-Melekh, Shokhen ad* and *Ha-El* are printed in large type, since the *ḥazzan* starts the central part of the morning service at these places, on High Holy Days, Sabbath, and festivals respectively. In the section *Be-fi yesharim* ("By the mouth of the upright") some prayer books mark an acrostic of the names Isaac and Rebekah, which was not customary in Jewish liturgical poetry prior to the Middle Ages. Some scholars consider it a later addition, but it could also be coincidental.

EL ADON. After the cantor's invitation to public worship, *Barekhu*, the *Shaḥarit* service follows much the same pattern as that of weekdays. The main difference is the addition of *piyyutim* into the first of the two benedictions that precede the *Shema*. The outstanding one is *El adon al kol ha-ma'asim*, "God, Lord over all works" which is an alphabetical acrostic, each phrase beginning with a consecutive letter of the alphabet. According to some scholars the hymn contains another acrostic in the last line, namely the initial letters of the Hebrew names of the planets, Saturn, Venus, Mercury, Jupiter and Mars.

It has been suggested that this hymn was written by the Essenes, a sect in Second Temple times at the beginning of the common era. This group was known for its ascetic way of life and its mystical approach to nature. Thus *El Adon* which is both mystical and nature oriented would fit the Essene philosophy. However, most authorities agree that the hymn was the product of a group of mystics of the eighth century C.E.

El Adon is followed by another *piyyut* known as *Ha-El Asher Shavat*, "To God who rested on the seventh day," which may date back to talmudic times. It is based on the Midrash which has it that the Sabbath day itself gave thanks to God.

YEKUM PURKAN. Perhaps the central and halakhically most important part of the Sabbath morning service is the Reading of the Torah. The history and development of the Torah reading has been discussed in Chapter V since it is a component of the liturgy which does not only apply to the Sabbath. However, after the reading, some prayers are recited which are unique to the Sabbath and for the festivals. Besides the Announcement of the New Moon which is treated together with Rosh Ḥodesh in Chapter IX, the congregation recites two prayers for the well-being of rabbis, students and the general congregation—in the Ashkenazi rite—immediately after the reading of the *haftarah* on the Sabbath. Written in Aramaic, the prayers derive their name from their opening words, "May deliverance arise." Both are very similar in form. The first consists of a prayer for the welfare of the students in the academies of Ereẓ Israel and Babylonia, their teachers, the exilarchs, and the judges. Many of the phrases of this prayer resemble those of the *Kaddish de-Rabbanan* ("the scholars' *Kaddish*"). In modern times, some communities have added the phrase *Ve-di be-khol arat galvatana* ("and all that are in the lands of the dispersion") in order to make this prayer more meaningful. The second is a more general prayer for the welfare of the congregation, similar in content to the Hebrew prayer *Mi she-Berakh* which follows it. The prayers are not found in the Babylonian *siddurim*

ואנחה : וְעוֹד כְּתִיב פִּצְחוּ רַנְּנוּ יַחְדָו חָרְבוֹת יְרוּשָׁלָיִם
כִּי נִחַם יְיָ עַמּוֹ גָּאַל יְרוּשָׁלָיִם : וְעוֹד כְּתִיב חָשַׂף יְיָ אֶת
זְרוֹעַ קָדְשׁוֹ לְעֵינֵי כָּל הַגּוֹיִם וְרָאוּ כָּל אַפְסֵי אָרֶץ אֵת
יְשׁוּעַת אֱלֹהֵינוּ :

פּוּמוֹן לִמְצַלְאִין לַאֲדֹנֵינוּ הַפַּפְיוֹר יִרֵה

לָנוּ׳ חוֹדוּ רַעְיוֹנִי

יַקִּירוֹן מֵי בְרָכוֹת׳ תְּהִלּוֹת הֶגְיוֹנֵנוּ׳ וְעַל גּוֹיִם וּמַמְלָכוֹת׳
נְשַׁחֵר פְּנֵי קוֹנֵנוּ׳ וְלִמְעוֹן הַבְּרָכוֹת׳ נַמְלִיךְ מִמְּעוֹנֵנוּ׳
וְנָבִיא שִׁירוֹת עֲרוּכוֹת׳ לְבָרֵךְ אֶת אֲדוֹנֵנוּ :

מְצַלְאִין אֲנַחְנָא וְתָבְעִין רַחֲמֵי מִן קֳדָם אֱלָהּ שְׁמַיָּא
מָרֵי דְרַחֲמֵי לְחַיֵּי אַב הֲמוֹן אֲדוֹנֵנוּ הָאַפִּפְיוֹר
פָּאפָּא פְּלוֹ׳ אֲנַחְנָא בְּנֵי גָלוּתָא עַבְדּוֹהִי לִמְלוֹךְ שְׁמַיָּא
דִי קְשׁוֹט מֶעֶבְדּוֹהִי׳ אָתוֹהִי כַּמָּה רַבְרְבִין וְכַמָּה
תַּקִּיפִין תִּמְהוֹהִי :

כַּכָּתוּב יְיָ יְיָ אֵל רַחוּם וְחַנּוּן אֶרֶךְ אַפַּיִם וְרַב חֶסֶד
וֶאֱמֶת נוֹצֵר חֶסֶד לָאֲלָפִים נוֹשֵׂא עָוֹן וָפֶשַׁע
וְחַטָּאָה וְנַקֵּה :

הַנּוֹתֵן לַמְּלָכִים תְּשׁוּעָה׳ הַפּוֹצֶה אֶת דָּוִד עַבְדּוֹ
מֵחֶרֶב רָעָה׳ הַנּוֹתֵן רוֹזְנִים לְרוּם וְכוֹכְבֵי
מֶמְשַׁלְתּוֹ יִנְהוּ׳ וְאֶת מְלָכִים לַכִּסֵּא וְיוֹשִׁיבֵם לָנֶצַח וַיִּגְבָּהוּ׳
הוּא בְּרַחֲמָיו יַגְבִּיהַּ וִירוֹמֵם וְיִנַּשֵּׂא מַעְלָה מַעְלָה אֲדוֹנֵנוּ
הָאַפִּפְיוֹר פָּאפָּא פְּלוֹ הוּא יִשְׁלַח מַלְאָכוֹ אִתּוֹ וְכָל פֶּגַע
רַע יִשְׁמְרֵהוּ׳ מוֹשִׁיעַ וָרַב יַטְּלֵהוּ וִינַשְּׂאֵהוּ׳ וְכִסָּא
כָבוֹר

---

of Amram Gaon and Saadiah Gaon, although they were probably written in Babylonia. The first is found in the *Maḥzor Vitry*, and the second in the halakhic work, *Roke'aḥ*, of Eleazar ben Judah of Worms (1160–1238). Both prayers are absent from the Sephardi rite, although a similar but more lengthy prayer entitled "Prayer for the Congregation" is found in some Yemenite prayer book manuscripts.

These prayers are not recited on festivals. A reason given for this is to enable the worshiper to leave the synagogue earlier and enjoy the meals which they are permitted to cook on the holidays.

After *Yekum Purkan* a Hebrew prayer is recited invoking blessings on the congregation and particularly those who devote themselves to communal and synagogal activities.

PRAYER FOR THE GOVERNMENT. The prayer for the welfare of the government forms part of the synagogue ritual on Sabbath mornings and on the festivals. Its inclusion in the service is based on the Mishnah: "Rabbi Ḥanina, Segan ha-Kohanim said: 'Pray for the welfare of the government; since but for fear thereof, men would swallow each other alive." The idea is found as early as Jeremiah; the prophet counseled the Jews who were taken into the Babylonian captivity: "Seek the peace of the city whither [i.e. the Lord] have caused you to be carried away captive, and pray unto the Lord for it; for in the peace thereof shall ye have peace."

The prayer for the welfare of the ruling powers of the State (king, government, etc.) and petitions for the welfare of the congregation, belong to the morning service and are recited before the Scrolls of the Law are returned to the Ark. The Sephardim recite it on the Day of Atonement after *Kol Nidrei*. The traditional version of the prayer starts: "May He Who dispenseth salvation unto kings and dominion unto princes, Whose kingdom is an everlasting kingdom, Who delivereth His servant David from the destructive sword . . .[etc.] . . . may He bless, preserve, guard, assist, exalt, and highly aggrandize our Sovereign . . ." the titles following.

In non-monarchic countries the prayer is recited for the welfare of the head of the state (the president) and the government. In modern times the prayer is recited in most synagogues in the vernacular. The wording has frequently been modified in accordance with the circumstances. The difficulties of Jewish life in Exile can be demonstrated by the Prayer for the Government. An 18th-century Carpentras *maḥzor* has an elaborate prayer for the welfare of the pope and in the Moscow synagogue a wall plaque bears the following invocation: "Our Father in heaven! Bless the USSR, guardian of peace in all the world. Amen, Amen."

In Israel a new version of this prayer was formulated and approved by the Chief Rabbinate after the establishment of the

One of the familiar melodies for the *Anim Zemirot* hymn.

State in 1948; it also includes a prayer for the welfare of all Jews in the Diaspora. The prayer is also recited in the U. S. at public services on special occasions such as Thanksgiving Day, July 4, and Armistice Day.

AV HA-RAḤAMIM. Before the Torah scroll is returned to the ark, many communities recite a memorial prayer for Jewish martyrs and martyred communities. This prayer, known by its first words, "O Merciful Father . . .," was composed by an unknown author in memory of the martyrs massacred in Germany during the First Crusade. It is first known from a prayerbook dated 1290. The prayer emphasizes the merit of the martyrs who died for *Kiddush ha-Shem* ("Sanctification of God"). Several scriptural verses are quoted, and God is asked to remember the martyrs, to avenge them, and to save their offspring. The wording of the last part of the prayer, invoking Divine retribution on the persecutors, has undergone many changes. Originally this prayer was recited in southern Germany only on the Sabbaths preceding Shavuot and the Ninth of Av and at the conclusion of the *Hazkarat Neshamot* memorial service. In the Ashkenazi ritual it became part of the Sabbath morning service. In the Polish rite it is recited either every Sabbath (except when the Prayer for the New Moon is said. When Sabbath falls on a New Moon, or when a circumcision takes place), or only on all the Sabbaths of the *Omer* period between Passover and Shavuot, and on those of the Three Weeks between the Fast of Tammuz and the Ninth of Av. Another short prayer of the same name "May the Father of mercy have mercy upon a people that has been borne by him," etc. is recited in Orthodox synagogues immediately before the reading from the Torah.

Musaf. The *Musaf* service of the Sabbath follows the normal structure, i.e., the central benediction describes the additional Sabbath sacrifice in the Temple. This description is introduced by a poetic prayer in which the initial letters of the first 22 words form an alphabet in inverted order. In the modern era objections have been raised to those parts of this central benediction which pray for the restoration of the sacrificial cult in the Temple. The Reform movement has deleted the prayer whereas the official Conservative prayer book has emended the text from ". . . lead us in joy unto our land where we will offer unto Thee the obligatory sacrifices . . ." to ". . . lead us in joy unto our land where they [our ancestors] did offer unto Thee . . ."

ANIM ZEMIROT. Following the *Aleinu* on Sabbaths and festivals, the ark is opened, and a special hymn known by its opening words *Anim Zemirot* ("let me chant sweet hymns") is chanted in alternate verses by the Reader and the congregation. Also called *Shir ha-Kavod* ("Song of Glory"), this synagogue hymn has been ascribed to Judah he-Ḥasid, of Regensburg (d. 1217) and, with less probability, to a number of other medieval authors. The hymn is an alphabetical acrostic of 31 lines, the first and last four being a prologue and epilogue respectively. Each line consists of two half-lines which rhyme. The first three of the last four lines may not be part of the original poem.

The theme is a fervent paean of God's greatness and might, drawing upon Bible and Midrash but also showing the influence of philosophical ideas. The metaphors used are bold to the point of anthropomorphism. Though the hymn is recited in Ashkenazi rites at the end of the Sabbath and festival services, in some synagogues it is said before the Reading of the Law after *Shaḥarit*. The custom to recite it daily is disappearing although it has appeared at the end of the daily *Shaḥarit* in most editions of the prayer book since that of Venice in 1547. *Anim Zemirot* and all the Songs of Unity (*Shir ha-Yiḥud*) are recited at the conclusion of the *Kol Nidrei* service in some Orthodox synagogues. Objections against the recital of *Anim Zemirot* in general were voiced by Solomon Luria, and against its daily use by Mordecai Jaffe, Judah Loew of Prague, Jacob Emden, and Elijah ben Solomon of Vilna, because they considered it an extremely holy poem. A variety of tunes have been composed for the hymn.

A Purim parody of the hymn was composed by Aryeh Leib Cordovero of Torczyn. The custom has developed of having *Anim Zemirot* recited by a child at the close of the Sabbath morning service.

Minḥah. The Sabbath afternoon service is introduced by a

Left: Partly gilt *Havdalah* spice box, Germany, 17th century. Jerusalem, Israel Museum.
Below: The table is laid at the onset of the Sabbath and the housewife recites "The Blessing over the Candles," in this painting by Isidor Kaufmann. New York, Oscar Gruss Collection.

Left: Spice box used during the *Havdalah* ceremony, silver filigree with semi-precious stones and enameled panels. France or Germany, late 17th century. The illustrations on the panels are of biblical scenes.
Below: An engraved silver gilt *Kiddush* cup, Germany, 18th century. The word *Zakhor* in the center refers to the Fourth Commandment: "Remember the Sabbath day to keep it holy." Jerusalem, Sir Isaac and Lady Wolfson Museum, Hechal Shlomo.

The spirit of the day of rest in a wealthy Sephardi household around the turn of the century is captured in this painting entitled "Shabbat in Safed," c. 1940, by Moshe Castel, himself a member of an old Sephardi family in Jerusalem, who lived in Safed. Tel Aviv Museum.

Left: A rare English silver Sabbath oil lamp by Abraham d'Oliveria, 1734, designed to burn safely throughout the entire Sabbath day. London, The Jewish Museum.
Below: Several articles used in the *Havdalah* ceremony. Left to right: silver candle holder, Germany, early 18th century; gold wine goblet, Germany, early 17th century; silver and gilt spice box, Austria, 1817. Jerusalem, Israel Museum.

brief Torah reading, to which three persons are called. The first section of the following Sabbath's portion is read. After the *ḥazzan's* repetition of the *Amidah,* a short passage made up of three verses from the Book of Psalms (119:142, 71:19, 36:7) each of which begins with the word *Ẓidkatekha,* "Thy righteousness." The traditional explanation is that these sentences comprise a sort of abbreviated funeral service (*Ẓidduk ha-Din,* "Submission to Divine Judgement") which is recited in honor of Moses who died on the Sabbath. However, a more acceptable explanation is that the *Ẓidkatekha* prayer is a Sabbath substitute for the *Taḥanun* prayer and indeed on those days when *Taḥanun* would not be recited, *Ẓidkatekha* is also omitted.

ATTAH EḤAD. The intermediate benediction of the Sabbath afternoon *Amidah* is introduced by a section named after its opening words, *Attah Eḥad,* "Thou art One." The prayer emphasizes the Oneness of God: "Thou art One, Thy Name is One," and the uniqueness of Israel: "and who is like Thy people Israel, a unique nation on earth." In the prayer, the Sabbath is called "a crown of distinction and salvation" which God gave to His people as a day of rest and holiness. The patriarchs Abraham, Isaac and Jacob all found joy and rest on the Sabbath. The prayer closes with the invocation: "May Thy children know that from Thee cometh their rest, and by their rest they hallow Thy name." This prayer, which originated with the *geonim* (eighth-tenth century C.E.) is based upon the Midrash that God, Israel, and the Sabbath mutually testify to the Oneness of God, the peerlessness of Israel His people and the uniqueness of the Sabbath as a day of holy rest.

BAREKHI NAFSHI. According to traditional Ashkenazi custom a series of psalms are recited on Sabbath afternoon between Sukkot and Passover. Referred to as *Barekhi Nafshi,* "Bless the Lord, O my soul" the initial words of Psalm 104, the psalm bespeaks the glorification of God as the Creator of the universe, the majesty and beauty of which testify to the wisdom of the Master of all creatures. This psalm is regarded as one of the loftiest and most beautiful examples of ancient Hebrew poetry and a magnificent expression of monotheism. The psalm is recited together with the 15 "Psalms of Ascent" (120–134). The reason for this custom may well be the analogy of this psalm with the account of creation given in Genesis and read on the Sabbath following the Sukkot festival (*Shabbat Bereshit*). After Passover the recitation of *Pirkei Avot,* "Ethics of the Fathers," replaces that of the Psalms. The praise of the Creator and the creation is also the reason why Psalm 104 is recited on New Moons after the morning service (and in the Sephardi rite also before the evening service).

PIRKEI AVOT. A treatise of the Mishnah commonly referred to as "Ethics of the Fathers" (*Pirkei Avot,* lit. "The Chapters of the Fathers") is studied on Sabbath afternoons between Passover and Rosh Ha-Shanah. The treatise is located toward the end of the fourth order, *Nezikin,* but once perhaps was found at the very end of the sixth order, *Tohorot,* as a sort of epilogue to the Mishnah as a whole. *Avot* is a unique mishnaic treatise in at least three respects: 1) From beginning to end it is aggadic, with no *halakhah* in it at all. 2) By tracing (in its first two chapters) the uninterrupted transmission of tradition from the Sinaitic revelation through the leading *tannaim* of the generation after the destruction of the Second Temple, the treatise provides the credentials, as it were, of these teachers and their subsequent students. In effect, it declares that in these teachers and their loyal disciples will be found the unbroken and authoritative instruction which began at Sinai. Thus *Avot* serves as the underpinning of the authority of the Mishnah as a whole. 3) The sages in this continuous tradition from the Men of the Great Assembly are not merely listed in "genealogical" or roll-call fashion but their "platforms" are also quoted. Along with the editorial report (in the first two chapters) that Master B took over from Master A, an important statement is also attributed to each master. This statement, originally, was not an expression, however, of just one more personal view, *bon mot,* or some general moral maxim, but apparently a formulation of a fundamental principle or policy or program the Pharisaic leader and (later) the leading *tanna* directed to his own generation. Taken together, these sayings reveal the convictions which shaped the Pharisaic and the early dominant tannaitic schools: that the principal task was to raise many disciples; that the pillars on which society rests are the Scrip-

The tractate *Avot* begins with the train of transmission of the Torah from Moses down to the sages of the Mishnah. The *Rothschild Siddur* (15th-century Italy) shows Moses standing on Mt. Sinai while Joshua and the Jews eagerly await his return with the Divine Word.

tures, worship, and acts of piety; that the duty of man, regardless of consequences, is to serve God; that the company of the sages is to be preferred above all; that a household is to be governed by certain proprieties; that proper associations are to be cultivated, proper procedures are to be followed in the administration of justice; that one must engage in work rather than seek power and political influence; that it is no light responsibility teachers assume; that priests have social obligations over and above their ritual ones; that consistency and practice and decency toward all men are what count; that study of Torah is of prime significance; that there are right ways of human conduct to adopt and wrong ways to avoid. To these statements, which constituted the original core of the treatise were added later reflections and teachings of the sages who were the students of Johanan ben Zakkai's most outstanding students, and those of other sages too (some famous from the period before the destruction of the Temple, many from the middle of the second and the following century). In this way, the first four chapters of *Avot* preserved those teachings and emphases of the *tannaim* which reflected what most concerned classical Judaism: the claim of high antiquity for the Oral law; the nature and destiny of man; the permanent centrality of Torah; the doctrine of reward and punishment; the approved course for man in his life in this world in expectation of the world to come.

The fifth chapter of *Avot* may also have been part of the original core; at all events, its statements were early attached to that core. These statements are anonymous; their distinguishing feature is a number—ten, seven, or four. The sixth chapter, called *Kinyan Torah* ("On the Acquisition of Torah"), is a *baraita* (external Mishnah) added to the five chapters. Also found in the post-talmudic tractate *Kalla Rabbati* (8) and in *Seder Eliahu Zuta* (17), this *baraita* consists of a selection of sayings in praise of the Torah and the sages. It was added to *Avot* for liturgical reasons, when it became customary to recite the treatise in the Babylonian academies and synagogues on the Sabbath. This custom may well be pre-geonic. Since a favorite season for reciting *Avot* was the period between Passover and Shavuot, the addition of the sixth chapter provided the reading matter for the sixth Sabbath between these two holidays. The Sephardi tradition still continues the custom of reasing *Avot* only during this period. Most Ashkenazi congregations, however, repeat the entire treatise three times each year. *Avot*, therefore, is read until the Sabbath before the New Year. When studied on the Sabbath, each chapter is introduced with the Mishnah of *Sanhedrin* 10:1 and concluded with the the Mishnah of *Makkot* 3:16.

Because *Avot* became a text for recital in the synagogue, it has been reproduced and reprinted more often than any other talmudic work. It is included in editions of the traditional prayer book. Since it furnishes teachings of what the Jewish sages considered fundamental aspects of life, and because these teachings were expressed in polished epigrams, *Avot* has been the best known talmudic treatise among non-Jews. It has been translated into Latin, English, French, German, Italian—

probably into every language into which the prayer book has been translated. The most valuable edition, although it is outdated, is that by C. Taylor, *Sayings of the Jewish Fathers* (Cambridge, 1877, reprinted 1969). There is no Talmud (*Gemara*) on *Avot*. The two most influential commentaries on *Avot* are (1) the one in *Maḥzor Vitry* and (2) Maimonides' commentary; in one way or another, all subsequent commentators are indebted to these two.

The Conclusion of the Sabbath. Just as additional prayers accompany the *Ma'ariv* service at the start of the Sabbath, so too the *Ma'ariv* at the close of the Sabbath is accompanied by various psalms. In many congregations of the Ashkenazi rite, Psalm 144 and Psalm 67 are recited usually to a lively martial traditional melody before the actual start of the service. In the general Sephardi rite, only the latter psalm is recited. This custom is very ancient and probably predates the geonic period.

Ma'ariv is said a little later than usual in order to add some of the sanctity of the Sabbath to the weekday. A folkloristic explanation for this delay is that on the Sabbath the wicked who are being punished in Hell, are released only to be returned after *Ma'ariv*. By delaying the service a little we are thus able to extend their "holiday."

The actual *Ma'ariv* is as usual for a weekday except that the text of the fourth benediction is changed to be a *Havdalah* prayer distinguishing between the holy Sabbath and the profane weekday. That the insertion of a *Havdalah* prayer in the *Amidah* is an exceedingly ancient custom from before mishnaic times is clear from a discussion in the Mishnah as to exactly where in the *Amidah* it should be put. According to the discussion in the Talmud, the prayer was instituted in the times of the Men of the Great Synagogue just after Ezra and the return from Babylon. When times were bad and people did not have enough money to buy wine over which to recite the *Havdalah* they inserted it in the *Amidah* instead. Later, the economic position improved and they stopped saying it in the *Amidah* and recited it as a separate ceremony over wine. Later again, when their lot deteriorated, they wanted to put it back into the *Amidah* but were not sure where it should go. Nowadays therefore, the Talmud concludes, it should be recited both in the *Amidah* and as a separate ceremony. As a home ceremony, *Havdalah* is discussed in Chapter X.

After *Ma'ariv*, Psalm 91 is recited. This was known as the Psalm of Blessing and was therefore chosen to start the new week and invoke divine protection throughout it. Therefore, if a festival falls during the week it is omitted since the festival is considered sufficient protection. The psalm is followed by a collection of biblical verses which make up the *Kedushah de-Sidra* which is recited at the end of weekday *Shaḥarit* services. Many rites then continue with a large collection of biblical verses, known as *Ve-Yiten lekha*, "May God give thee," of a very optimistic nature presumably to put the worshiper in a good frame of mind for the struggles of the coming week.

In most synagogues, the regular *Havdalah* ceremony is recited for the benefit of those congregants who will not recite it at home.

Special Sabbaths. Throughout the year there are several Sabbaths which have a special character. Of these the most important are four of the Sabbaths preceding Passover because of the special Torah readings which are added. The other special Sabbaths are special insofar as they fall either before or after a festival and are usually marked by a special *haftarah*. In many rites there are *piyyutim* which have been composed for these Sabbaths and in all rites minor liturgical changes are made. Two such Sabbaths which recur on several occasions throughout the year are: *Shabbat Mevarekhin*, the Sabbath that immediately precedes a new month, and *Shabbat Rosh Ḥodesh*, a Sabbath which coincides with Rosh Ḥodesh. Both of these are described in Chapter IX.

The other Sabbaths (listed here chronologically according to the Jewish calendar) are:

SHABBAT SHUVAH, "Sabbath of Repentance," also called (erroneously) *Shabbat Teshuvah*, the Sabbath which occurs during the Ten Days of Penitence (between Rosh Ha-Shanah and the Day of Atonement). The name is derived from the initial word of the *haftarah* "Return [*Shuvah*] O Israel, unto the Lord" (Hosea 14:2) read on that Sabbath. One main feature of *Shabbat Shuvah* is the sermons on repentance delivered by the congregational rabbis.

SHABBAT ḤOL HA-MO'ED, the Sabbath of the Passover and

Moritz Oppenheim's serene family scene, the *Havdalah* ceremony, conveys an atmosphere of dignified sorrow at the departure of the beloved Queen Sabbath. It is customary for the youngest member of the family to hold the candle. In the Sabbath lamp in the background only two of its wicks are still burning.

Sukkot intermediary days. The liturgy includes *piyyutim* appropriate to the festivals and special Torah readings, instead of the regular weekly Torah portion. Song of Songs during Passover and Ecclesiastes during Sukkot are also recited.

SHABBAT ḤANUKKAH, the Sabbath (sometimes two) during Ḥanukkah. It is marked by an added Torah reading for the festival and, if it coincides with Rosh Ḥodesh Tevet, also for the New Moon.

SHABBAT SHIRAH, "The Sabbath of the Song," the Sabbath on which the Torah reading is Exodus 14–17. The name is derived from Exodus 15, which includes "The song of Moses and of the children of Israel" at the Red Sea. In some rituals special *piyyutim* are also recited. This Sabbath does not occur on a specific date but depends on when the Torah portion is read.

SHABBAT SHEKALIM, the first of four special Sabbaths, which are

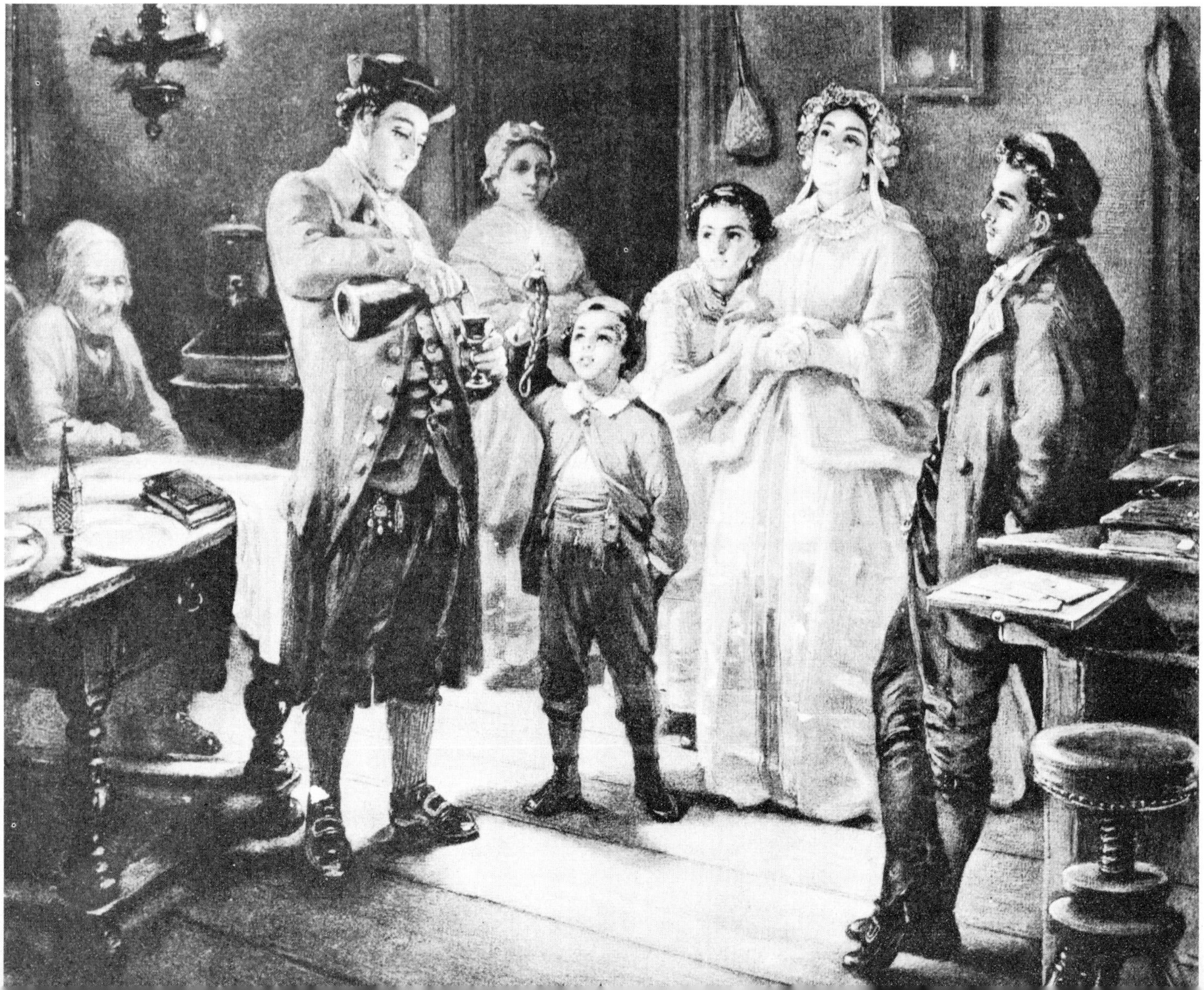

also called *Arba Parashiyyot* ("the four pericopes"), and which occur in spring. *Shabbat Shekalim* is observed on the Sabbath immediately preceding the month of Adar (in a leap year, the second month of Adar). In addition to the weekly Torah portion, Exodus 30:11–16, whose theme is the duty of donating half a shekel toward the upkeep of the Temple, is also read. It commemorates the custom according to which on the first of Adar special messengers were dispatched to all Jewish communities to collect these donations. Special *piyyutim* are included in the ritual of the Sabbath.

SHABBAT ZAKHOR, "Sabbath of Remembrance," the second of the four special Sabbaths. It is the Sabbath before Purim. The name derives from the additional Torah portion read from Deuteronomy 25:17–19 whose theme is the duty "to remember" (*zakhor*) what Amalek did to Israel. The traditional belief is that Haman the Agagite, the villain of the Purim story, was a direct descendent of Agag, the king of the Amalekites. In some rites special *piyyutim* are recited.

SHABBAT PARAH, "Sabbath of the Red Heifer," the third of the four special Sabbaths. It is the Sabbath preceding *Shabbat ha-Ḥodesh*. An additional portion is read from the Torah (Numbers 19:1–22) whose theme is the ritual purification with the ashes of the red heifer. The purification was compulsory in Temple times for all those who had been defiled by contact with a corpse. *Shabbat Parah* commemorates the custom of everyone who would participate in the Passover pilgrimage to Jerusalem having to cleanse himself in due time. Special *piyyutim* are also added to the liturgy in some rites.

SHABBAT HA-ḤODESH, the last of the four special Sabbaths. It precedes, or falls on the first day of, the month of Nisan. On it, in addition to the weekly Torah portion, Exodus 12:1–20 is also read. It states that the month of Nisan "shall be the beginning of the months [of the Jewish year]" and includes many details on the ritual laws concerning the Passover sacrifice and the interdiction to eat leavened bread, *ḥamez,* on the festival. Special *piyyutim* are also recited in some communities.

SHABBAT HA-GADOL, the Sabbath immediately preceding Passover. This Sabbath is discussed in Chapter VII.

SHABBAT ḤAZON, "Sabbath of Vision," the Sabbath that precedes the Ninth of Av. The name is derived from the initial word of its *haftarah,* "The vision of Isaiah" (Isaiah 1:1–27), in which the afflictions which God will visit on Israel in punishment of its sins are prophesied. The Yemenites call this Sabbath "*Shabbat Eikhah,*" and read Isaiah 1:21 ff. for the *haftarah* portion. *Shabbat Ḥazon* occurs during the period of mourning for the destruction of the Temple and the *haftarah* is therefore appropriate since its theme is destruction and redemption. The destruction is understood as a punishment for the sins of Israel and repentance is a prerequisite for the restoration of the Temple. It was customary not to dress in festive clothes during that period including (except in a few communities) the Sabbath.

SHABBAT NAḤAMU, the Sabbath immediately following the Ninth of Av. It is named after the first word of the *haftarah*: "Comfort ye [*naḥamu*], comfort ye My People" (Isaiah 40:1).

On most special Sabbaths the memorial prayer for the dead is not recited and the *Ẓidkatekha* prayer at *Minḥah* is also omitted. In the Reform ritual some of these Sabbaths (such as *Zakhor* and *Parah*) are not marked. On the other hand modern, special Sabbaths, such as Brotherhood Sabbath, Sisterhood Sabbath and United Unions Sabbath, have been instituted.

THE PILGRIM FESTIVALS

General Liturgy. The liturgy of the festivals reflects the joy and gratitude to God that it is their purpose to inspire. The main addition to the Services is the recitation of the *Hallel,* the psalms of thanksgiving. Since the *Hallel* is said on other occasions as well, it is discussed in Chapter V. The *Amidah* of each festival service is adjusted to the occasion; the benedictions of petition are replaced by a benediction celebrating the sanctity of the day which is introduced by the *Ya'aleh ve-Yavo* prayer in which the name of the festival is inserted. This prayer, which is also discussed in Chapter V, is not recited in the special *Musaf Amidah* since that is totally relevant to the festival in that it describes the Temple sacrifices of the day and begs for their restoration. *Ya'aleh ve-Yavo* is inserted into the Grace after Meals during the festivals.

THE SECOND DAY. Outside Ereẓ Israel, the actual festival is kept

for a second day. This is because of the uncertainty in the Diaspora as to when Rosh Ḥodesh, the first day of the month, was proclaimed in Jerusalem. Rosh Hodesh, which was fixed according to the testimony of eye witnesses as to the reappearance of the moon, could be either 30 or 31 days after the previous one. A permanent calendar based on astronomical calculations was established by the middle of the fourth century C.E. and since that time there is no uncertainty. However, the second day of the festival in the Diaspora had become a firmly entrenched custom and is still observed today in Orthodox communities. The Reform movement has discarded the custom, claiming that the original reason is no longer valid and the Conservative movement leaves the decision to the individual congregations.

In the communities that do observe the second day, the liturgy is exactly the same as for the first day.

ḤOL HA-MO'ED. Passover and Sukkot have intermediate festival days. The first and last days of these festivals are full holidays and the days in between are known as *Ḥol ha-mo'ed,* "the weekdays of the festival" on which most of the work prohibitions do not apply. However, they do have a festive atmosphere. In all rites in Israel and in the *ḥasidic* rites in the Diaspora, *tefillin* are not worn, and even in those Diaspora rites which do wear *tefillin* the benedictions are not recited. A *Musaf Amidah* is added into the service and *Ya'aleh ve-Yavo* is recited in the other *Amidot* which are of the ordinary weekday type. *Taḥanun* is not recited. During *Ḥol ha-Mo'ed* of Passover only the "half *Hallel*" is said whereas on *Ḥol ha-Mo'ed* Sukkot the entire *Hallel* is recited.

YIZKOR. A feature of the festival liturgy which has become exceedingly popular is the recitation of a prayer in memory of the departed. In Sephardi usage it is known as *Ashkavah,* "laying to rest" and in the Ashkenazi as *Hazkarat Neshamot*, "mentioning the souls." Amongst Ashkenazim, however, it is more popularly known by its first word, *Yizkor,* "May [God] remember . . ." In the Ashkenazi ritual, it is said after the reading of the Torah, during the morning service of the last day of Passover, Shavuot, and Sukkot and on the Day of Atonement. In the Sephardi rite it is recited also on the Day of Atonement eve before *Ma'ariv.*

The prayer is divided into three sections; the principal part opens the prayer with the words, "*Yizkor Elohim*" ("May God remember . . . the soul . . . "). *Hazkarat Neshamot* expresses the fervent hope that the departed souls will enjoy eternal life in God's presence. These is evidence that this custom dates back to the period of the Hasmonean wars (c. 165 B.C.E.) when Judah Maccabee and his men prayed for the souls of their fallen comrades and brought offerings to the Temple in Jerusalem, as atonement for the sins of the dead. The belief that the meritorious deeds of descendants can atone for the departed appears frequently in aggadic literature. However, Hai Gaon and his pupil Nissim ben Jacob (C. 1000 C.E.) opposed the custom of praying for the departed on festivals and on the Day of Atonement, and of donating to charity on their behalf. They believed that only the actual deeds performed by a person during his lifetime count before God. Nevertheless, the memorial prayer became one of the most cherished customs, especially in the Ashkenazi ritual. Historically, it gained its significance through the Crusades and through the severe persecutions that took place in Eastern Europe during the 17th century when thousands of Jews died as martyrs. They were all inscribed in the death rolls (called *kunteres* or *memorbuch,* or *yizkor-bukh*) of their communities and commemorated in the memorial prayers held on the three festivals, on the Day of Atonement and, in some congregations, on the Sabbaths during the *Omer* period (between Passover and Shavuot). In time, the death rolls came to include names not only of martyrs, but also of other members of the community, and the custom of memorial prayers for individuals evolved. After the memorial prayer for relatives, in the Ashkenazi rite the prayer *El Maleh Raḥamim* is recited for those who have died. Nowadays, a special prayer is frequently added for the victims of the Nazi Holocaust and for the Jewish soldiers who died in wars, particularly in Israel. The traditional memorial service concludes with the recital of *Av ha-Raḥamim.* The Torah Scroll(s) which had been taken out for the Reading of the Law is (are) returned to the ark and the *Musaf* service follows. In the Sephardi ritual, instead of reciting the *Hazkarat Neshamot* after the Torah service, everyone who is called to the Torah, after blessing it, recites a memorial prayer for his rel-

The memorial page of a German *memorbuch*. The right-hand page is a prayer in memory of all the rabbis who had passed away, while the left-hand page is in memory of the martyrs of the Jewish communities listed. In quite a different tone is the *piyyut* for *Shabbat ha-Gadol* from the *Worms Maḥzor*. The illustration shows a bridegroom motioning to his bride to draw near, after the opening words of the *piyyut*: "With me from the Lebanon, O bride."

atives. *Hazkarat Neshamot* mentions charitable offerings "for the repose of the departed souls" and in Orthodox synagogues, it is customary to promise donations during the service. It is also customary that those whose parents are still alive leave the synagogue during the entire *Hazkarat Neshamot* prayer. In the Conservative ritual, several introductory readings and appropriate Psalm verses in Hebrew and in the vernacular, as well as sections for meditation and special responsive readings in that language, were added to the traditional text of *Hazkarat Neshamot*. In the Reform ritual, the memorial service is held only on the last day of Passover and on the Day of Atonement as part of the late afternoon service before *Ne'ilah*. The service consists of a shortened version of the traditional text, the recital of Psalm 23 and of selected poems by Ibn Gabirol, Judah Halevi, and Bahya ben Joseph, and of readings and meditations expressing the transience and evanescence of life and the merits of those who have lived an exemplary life. Solemn music accompanies this *Hazkarat Neshamot* service which concludes with the entire congregation reciting the *Kaddish*. Synagogues are usually well attended by both men and women on the days that *Hazkarat Neshamot* is said; in some congregations these days have become occasions for major sermons by the rabbi.

The Thirteen Attributes of God. In the Ashkenazi rite a feature common to all the Pilgrim Festivals and the High Holy Days is the recitation of the thirteen attributes of God as they are recorded in Exodus 34:6–7. These verses, beginning with *Adonai Adonai El Raḥum ve-Ḥanun,* "O Lord, O Lord, the merciful and gracious God . . ." are chanted three times by the congregation when the ark is opened to take out the Torah scrolls for the public reading. This is followed by a private devotion praying for success in life both spiritual and temporal. When a festival coincides with the Sabbath, both the Attributes and the devotion are omitted since they are both of a petitionary nature which is forbidden on the Sabbath.

One of the main aspects of the festival liturgy is the addition of *piyyutim* to the service. Furthermore, three of the five books of the Bible known as scrolls—Song of Songs, Ruth, Ecclesiastes—are recited during Passover, Shavuot and Sukkot. The other two scrolls, Esther and Lamentations, are read on Purim and the 9th of Av respectively. The special features of each festival will be discussed below.

Passover. The spring festival which commemorates the Exodus of the Israelites from Egyptian bondage is known in Hebrew as *Ḥag ha-Pesaḥ*, the Festival of *Pesaḥ*. The word *Pesaḥ* derives from the root meaning "to pass over" (thus the English name) which God did to the Israelite homes when he slew the Egyptian first-born. *Pesaḥ* is also the name of the lamb which the Jews used to slaughter and eat in the Passover night ceremony known as the *Seder*, in Temple times. The Samaritans still observe the Paschal Lamb ceremony. For normative Judaism, this ceremony ceased with the destruction of the Temple but is remembered in many of the symbols in the *Seder* which is discussed together with other home ceremonies in Chapter XI.

Shabbat Ha-Gadol. The liturgical signs of Passover start on the Sabbath preceding it. This is known, according to some opinions, as the Great Sabbath because of the declaration in the *haftarah* (Malachi 3:4, 24) "Behold, I will send you Elijah the prophet before the coming of the great [*gadol*] and terrible day of the Lord." This *haftarah* was selected in accordance with the popular belief that the messianic redemption of Israel will occur in the same month as its deliverance from the Egyptian bondage. Another opinion on the institution of the "great Sabbath" before Passover is that it was influenced by the Christian concept of the Saturday before Easter. Another explanation is that on this Sabbath only the greatest scholar (*ha-gadol*) in the community is allowed to preach. In some ancient rabbinic sources the Sabbaths preceding Shavuot and Sukkot were also called *Shabbat ha-Gadol*. On this Sabbath it is customary to read the greater part of the Passover *Haggadah* during the afternoon service. In traditional synagogues, the rabbi delivers a sermon devoted almost exclusively to the rites and the dietary laws pertaining to Passover.

Ma'ariv. Besides the normal adjustments to the Passover *Ma'ariv* service, many rites—ḥasidic in the Diaspora and nearly all in Ereẓ Israel—have the custom of reciting the whole *Hallel* immediately after the service. Since the *Hallel* is also said during the *Seder* ceremony at home as well as during the

These three beautiful silver items are all connected with Passover. The silver and glass three-tiered Passover dish is from Copenhagen where it was produced in 1918. The tiers are for the three *mazzot*. The silver holder was specially created by Ilya Schor (c. 1950) for the candle used when searching for the leaven on the eve of Passover. The inscriptions and illustrations all have Passover significance. The magnificent English silver *seder* plate is also a 20th-century production.

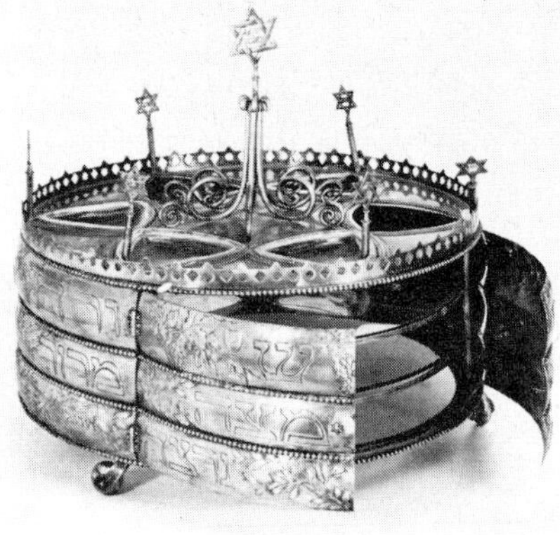

Shaḥarit service this means that it is in fact recited three times in one day. This proliferation is understandable because most of the *Hallel* relates directly to the Exodus from Egypt.

SHAḤARIT. Of all the *piyyutim* composed for Passover, most are not recited. This is in line with the general tendency to limit the *piyyutim* because they unduly lengthen the service and are often unintelligible except to the scholarly. However, one *piyyut* is included in many rites before the *Shaḥarit Amidah*. The poem is known as *Beraḥ Dodi,* "Make haste my beloved," and consists of three stanzas based upon the allegorical interpretation of the central motif of Song of Songs according to which "the beloved" is the people of Israel and the "lover" is God. Israel implores the "lover" to hasten his return to his "beloved." It made use, at the end of each stanza, of the text of Song of Songs: "Behold he standeth behind our wall" (2:9); "Hark! my beloved! behold, he cometh" (2:8); "This is my beloved, and this is my friend" (5:16). On the basis of the initials interwoven in this *piyyut* the authorship has been ascribed to the tenth-century liturgical poet Solomon ben Judah ha-Bavli. Another *ge'ullah piyyut* in the morning prayer of the second day of Passover recited outside Ereẓ Israel (Ashkenazi rite) and composed by Meshullam ben Kalonymus (c. 1000 C.E.), bears the same name. This *piyyut* of four stanzas is based upon the same motif as the aforementioned one. A third *piyyut* by the same name is recited on the Sabbath during the Intermediate Days of Passover. This was composed by Simeon ben Isaac, who also lived in the tenth century.

THE TORAH READINGS. On the first day of Passover the Torah reading is Exodus 12:21–51. This tells the story of the Exodus from Egypt and how the Israelites obeyed the commandment of the Paschal Lamb. As usual, the *maftir* treats the *Musaf* sacrifice (Numbers 28:19–25). The *haftarah* (Joshua 5:2–6:1) is the description of the first Passover the Israelites celebrated in the Promised Land. The reading for the second day is Leviticus 22:26–23:44 which is the listing of the festivals; the *maftir* is the same as the first day. The *haftarah* (in the Diaspora) is II Kings 23:1–9, 21–25 describing the major celebration of Passover in the days of King Josiah. On the seventh day of Passover, the reading is Exodus 19:1–20:23. This day is

traditionally the day of the crossing of the Sea of Reeds and the reading describes that event and the ecstatic song the Israelites sang on their successful escape from the house of bondage. The Song of the Sea is also recited more festively than usual in the morning liturgy. The *maftir* for the day describes the *musaf* sacrifice. A full list of the Torah readings for all the days of Passover can be found in Chapter V.

PRAYER FOR DEW. Another special Passover addition is the Prayer for Dew. This prayer was incorporated into the liturgy because Ereẓ Israel depended on the moisture of dew during the long, dry summers. As with rainfall, dew was held to be a heavenly blessing, and its absence a divine punishment. The end of the rainy season and the beginning of summer is therefore liturgically marked by a special prayer for dew, called *Tefillat Tal* (among Ashkenazim) or *Tikkun Tal* (among Sephardim), which forms part of the *Musaf* of the first day of Passover, since it was held that the "stores of dew" are opened on this day. The prayer is recited at the reader's repetition of the *Musaf Amidah*. In the Ashkenazi ritual the prayer consists of a series of acrostic *piyyutim* (the central one is *Taḥat Eilat Ofer* by Eleazar Kallir) and an invocation in six stanzas ending with: "For Thou art the Lord our God, who causes the wind to blow and the dew to descend," and with the plea: "For a blessing and not for a curse; For life and not for death; For plenty and not for famine; Amen." Nowadays, the *piyyutim* are generally omitted and in Israel the prayer is sometimes said after the Torah scrolls are returned to the ark and before the Additional Service. In Israel all rites have adopted the Sephardi custom of inserting the phrase: "Thou causest the dew to descend" (*morid ha-tal*) in every *Amidah* at the beginning of the second benediction in the period beginning with the first day of Passover and ending with Shemini Aẓeret when the Prayer for Rain is said. The Prayer for Dew and the Prayer for Rain are part of the service in all Jewish rituals including the Conservative and Reform trends who recite them, however, in shortened versions. In traditional Ashkenazi synagogues the reader wears a *kittel* ("shroud") for the Prayer for Dew (as he does on the Day of Atonement) and intones the *Kaddish* before the *Musaf* service in the melody of the Day of Atonement.

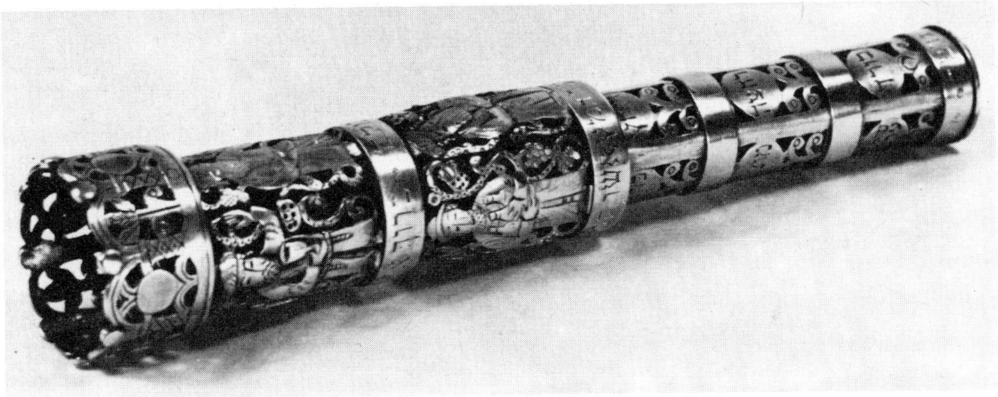 

THE OMER. On the second night of Passover after the *Ma'ariv* service a brief ceremony which will be repeated on each of the following 48 evenings takes place. This is the Counting of the *Omer*. *Omer* (literally "sheaf [of grain]") was an offering brought to the Temple on the 16th of Nisan, the second day of Passover and it became the name of the 49 day period between Passover and Shavuot.

The Bible prescribes that "when you enter the land which I am giving to you and reap its harvest, you shall bring the first sheaf of your harvest to the priest . . . the priest shall wave it on the day after the Sabbath." After the waving, a burnt offering together with a meal offering and a libation were made at the altar and after that had been done it was permissible to eat of the new harvest: "Until that very day, until you have brought the offering of your God, you shall eat no bread or parched grain or fresh ears." The exact meaning of "the day after the Sabbath" in the biblical passage was a major point of controversy between the Pharisees and their opponents, the Boethusians and, later, the Karaites. The latter argued that the ceremony was to be performed on the day after the Sabbath immediately following the first day of Passover whereas the rabbis argued that in this context the word "sabbath" was to be understood not as the weekly Sabbath but as a "holy day" and meant the first day of Passover itself. Since the passage quoted continues with the law "And from the day on which you bring the sheaf of wave offering—the day after the sabbath—you shall count seven weeks" and the fiftieth day is Shavuot it follows that according to the sectarians the festival of Shavuot always fell on a Sunday. It has been suggested that this was a major factor in the dissidents' view, as having the festival always on a Sunday was far more convenient for the Temple cult.

The rabbis, in the light of Exodus 16:36—"The *Omer* is a tenth of an *ephah*"—interpreted the word as a measure of grain and also ruled that it was to be brought of barley only. The *ephah* was three *se'ot* and thus on the 16th of Nisan three *se'ot* of barley were reaped, brought to the Temple, ground and sifted, and of this, one tenth (the *omer*) was "waved" by the priest. The Mishnah describes the ritual in detail. It was celebrated with a great deal of ceremony and festivity in order to stress the opinion of the rabbis that the 16th of Nisan was the correct date. The ceremony, including the reaping, took place even if the 16th of Nisan was a Sabbath. If the barley was ripe it was taken from the vicinity of Jerusalem; otherwise it could be brought from anywhere in Israel. It was reaped by three men, each with his own scythe and basket. The grain was then brought to the Temple where it was winnowed, parched, and ground into coarse flour. It was then sifted through 13 sieves and one tenth was given to the priest who mixed it with oil and frankincense for "a pleasing odor to the Lord" and "waved" it "before the Lord." This was done by the priest taking the offering on his outstretched hands and moving it from side to side and up and down. This ceremony was interpreted as a prayer to God to protect the harvest from injurious winds and other calamities. After the waving ceremony a handful was burnt on the altar and the rest was eaten by the priests.

Counting the Omer. The injunction to count the 49 days from the 16th of Nisan until Shavuot is considered to be of biblical authority as long as the *Omer* itself was offered; thus at present time it is of rabbinic authority only. The 49 days themselves are commonly known as the *sefirah*.

The counting is preceded by a special benediction ". . .concerning the counting of the *Omer*." Since the Bible states that "You shall count off seven weeks. They must be complete" and "You must count . . . fifty days," the counting must mention both the number of days and the number of weeks. Hence the standard formula runs as follows on the first day, "Today is the first day of the *Omer*"; on the eighth day, "Today is the eighth day, making one week and one day of the *Omer*," and so on. The time for the counting, which is to be done standing, is after the evening service, that is, when the new day begins. One who forgets to count in the evening may count during the following day, without however reciting the blessing. He may then count again the following evening, saying the blessing. But if he fails to count for one complete day, he is not permitted to resume the utterance of the blessing for the whole duration of the *Omer*. And since the sole stipulation of the commandment is that the number of the particular day of the *Omer* is to be

Many communities and even private homes have a special *Omer* calendar to remind them which day of the *Omer* to count. The example here is from the Shearith Israel synagogue in New York and was made before 1713. Moritz Oppenheim's Shavuot scene shows the synagogue lavishly decorated with plants and flowers. Of interest is the obviously oriental figure to the right; perhaps he was an emissary from the Holy Land.

spoken aloud, one should avoid uttering it inadvertently once the time for counting has arrived; for example, if one has not yet counted and is asked what the number of the day is, one should reply by giving the number of the previous day.

The kabbalists used the 49 days (7 × 7) to form permutations of various *sefirot* denoting the ascent out of the 49 "gates" of impurity of the Egyptian bondage to the purity of the revelation at Sinai. In many prayer books these combinations are printed at the side of each day listed. Because the days counted "must be complete" it has become customary not to recite the evening service for Shavuot until after nightfall of the 49th day, whereas for other festivals it is permissible to start some time before nightfall.

In order not to forget the count of the day it was fairly common practice to have an "*Omer* calendar" in the home with movable numbers on it. These "calendars" even developed into an art form and several early specimens show intricate work and lettering.

The *Omer* period is one of mourning during which certain festive activities such as marriage are forbidden. However, there are days—Lag ba-Omer and others—when these restrictions are lifted. The special liturgy for these days is discussed in Chapter IX.

THE SONG OF SONGS. On the intermediate Sabbath of Passover the Song of Songs is read in the synagogue before the Torah is taken from the ark. Should the first day of the festival coincide with the Sabbath, it is read—in Israel—on the first day; in the Diaspora on the eighth day. Under kabbalistic influence it was also instituted as a voluntary reading before the regular Friday evening service and Sephardim, particularly, recite it on the Sabbaths between Passover and Shavuot.

Song of Songs or *Shir ha-Shirim* as it is known in Hebrew is composed entirely of a series of love lyrics. According to Jewish tradition, it was written by King Solomon in his youth. In middle-age he wrote Proverbs and in his old age, Ecclesiastes. Modern critical scholarship, however, sees it as a collection of love songs from various periods.

The Talmud records a controversy as to whether the book should be included in the Canon of the Bible. No less an eminent authority than Rabbi Akiva insisted that it should, claiming that the Song of Songs is the Holy of Holies. His opinion prevailed. Judaism sees the book as an allegory for the love between God and His people, Israel. As such it is considered sacred and the same Rabbi Akiva warned that "He who trills his voice in chanting the Song of Songs in banquet halls and makes it a secular song has no share in the world to come."

The reason for reading the Song of Songs on Passover is that the whole "action" of the book takes place in the spring and Passover is the Festival of the Spring.

Shavuot. The festival of Shavuot, as it is described in the Bible, is an agricultural festival celebrating the end of the barley harvest and the beginning of the wheat harvest. Its name means "weeks" and signifies the fact that it falls seven weeks (49 days, see above *Omer*), after Passover; in English it is known as Pentecost, i.e. "the 50th day." In the Bible it is also called *Ḥag Ha-Kaẓir*, the Harvest Festival. In Temple times the main celebration was the bringing of two loaves (*shetei ha-leḥem*) to the Temple to be "waved before the Lord." These loaves had to be made of the finest wheat from produce grown that year in Ereẓ Israel.

In rabbinic times a remarkable transformation of the festival took place. Based on the verse: "In the third month after the children of Israel were gone forth out of the land of Egypt, the same day came they into the wilderness of Sinai," the festival became the anniversary of the giving of the Torah at Sinai. The description of the feast in the liturgy therefore is "*zeman mattan toratenu*" ("the time of the giving of our Torah"). The transformation was in accord with a process to be observed in the Bible in which the ancient agricultural feasts were transformed into festivals marking the anniversary of significant historical events in the life of the people. Both Passover and Sukkot are connected with the Exodus; it was natural to link Shavuot with this event.

The earliest clear references to Shavuot as the anniversary of the giving of the Torah are from the third century, e.g. the saying of the Talmud sage, Rabbi Eleazar, that all authorities agree that it is necessary to rejoice with good food and wine on Aẓeret (the rabbinic name for Shavuot) because it was the day on which the Torah was given.

The ancient *bikkurim* ceremony is nowadays observed in a more modern context; these two Israeli children are bringing symbolic First Fruits.

In some medieval communities it was customary to introduce children to the Hebrew school on Shavuot, the season of the giving of the Torah. At this initiation ceremony the child, at the age of five or thereabouts, was placed on the reading desk in the synagogue and from there was taken to the school where he began to make his first attempts at reading the Hebrew alphabet. He was then given cakes, honey, and sweets "that the Torah might be sweet on his lips." In many modern synagogues, particularly Reform, the confirmation of older children takes place on Shavuot.

It is customary to adorn the synagogue with plants and flowers on Shavuot because, tradition has it, Sinai was a green mountain, and with trees, because Shavuot is according to the Mishnah, judgment day for the fruit of the tree. Some authorities disapproved of the custom because of its similarity to certain church rites. It is a home custom to eat dairy products on Shavuot because, in the Bible, the Torah is compared to milk. In some communities it is customary to eat triangular pancakes stuffed with meat or cheese because the Torah is of three parts (Pentateuch, Prophets and Hagiographa) and was given to a people of three parts (priests, Levites, and Israelites) on the third month through Moses who was the third child of his parents.

RUTH. The biblical "scroll" for Shavuot is the Book of Ruth. It is read before the Torah reading and in the Diaspora it is recited on the second day of the festival. In the Sephardi and Italian rites, it is divided into two parts and read on both mornings (or afternoons).

The book tells a story that took place in the days of the Judges. Elimelech, of Beth-Lehem in Judah, migrated with his wife Naomi and his two sons Mahlon and Chilion to Moab on account of famine. He died there and so did his two sons, who had married Moabite women, Orpah and Ruth. Left without either husband or sons, Naomi decided to return to Beth-Lehem. The two daughters-in-law wanted to move to Judah with her, but she bade them stay in their homeland. Orpah obeyed but Ruth vowed that she would share the fortunes of her mother-in-law. Arriving in Beth-Lehem at the beginning of the grain harvest, Ruth took advantage of the privilege of gleaning which custom accorded the poor. The field she came to glean in belonged to a prosperous farmer by the name of Boaz. When Naomi learned that Boaz had shown Ruth special kindness out of appreciation for her devotion to her mother-in-law, she was doubly delighted because Boaz was a kinsman of Elimelech and hence of Ruth's dead husband Mahlon, and the old woman could see a prospect of a levirate marriage for Ruth. The levirate marriage with Ruth involved the redemption of the land of the dead husband, which Naomi had sold. Boaz consented to marry Ruth and to redeem the land and he thus fulfilled the ancient patriarchal duty of "establishing the name of the dead upon his inheritance." Through this marriage Boaz became the ancestor of King David. The book concludes with the genealogy of David (4:17–22), which seems to have been the ultimate purpose of the author.

Among the reasons given for the choice of the Book of Ruth on Shavuot are: that the events recorded in Ruth took place at harvest time; that Ruth was the ancestor of David who, traditionally, died on Shavuot; that Ruth's "conversion" to Judaism is appropriate reading for the festival which commemorates the giving of the Torah; and that Ruth's loyalty is symbolic of Israel's loyalty to the Torah.

AKDAMUT. The portion of the Torah read in the synagogue on Shavuot is the account of the theophany at Sinai (Exodus 19:1–20:26) when God spoke to the assembled Israelites. This stresses the rabbinic view of the festival as the anniversary of the giving of the Torah. The reading includes the Ten Commandments. Although the Mishnah states that the Ten Commandments were recited each day in the Temple, the rabbis discouraged their recitation outside the Temple to refute the claims of the "sectarians" that only these, and not the whole Torah, were given to Moses at Sinai. During the Middle Ages there were some protests against the practice of standing while the Ten Commandments were read on Shavuot. But the custom for the whole congregation to stand is still followed on the grounds that the talmudic objection to any special significance being attached to the Decalogue cannot apply to congregational reading from the Scroll since the whole of the Torah is written in the Scroll. The account of the revelation on Mount Sinai is usually sung to a specially solemn tune.

The Torah reading is introduced by a lengthy Aramaic poem, called *Akdamut Millin,* "Introduction." It was written by Meir ben Isaac Nehorai (also called Sheliaḥ Ẓibbur, i.e. "cantor") who lived in the 11th century in northern France. The poem was originally recited in the synagogue on Shavuot as an introduction to the Aramaic translation (*targum*) of the reading. Exodus 19:1 was read aloud in Hebrew, "*Akdamut Millin*" was then read, followed by the next few verses in the Hebrew, and after that the same verses in Aramaic. The remainder of the reading was finished in the same sequence: two to three verses of the Hebrew text followed by the Aramaic translation of the preceding verses. The recitation of *Akdamut Millin* now generally precedes the Reading of the Torah, in deference to the objections of later halakhic authorities against interrupting the Reading of the Torah, particularly since it is no longer customary to read the Aramaic translation.

The poem consists of 90 acrostic lines forming a double alphabet followed by the author's name. It praises God as creator and lawgiver, expiates on Israel's fidelity to God despite all sufferings and temptations, and ends with a description of the apocalyptic events at the end of days and the future glory of Israel. The poem is recited in the Ashkenazi rite only. A similar work by the same author, introducing the reading of the Aramaic version of the Song of Moses (Exodus 15:1–10) on the seventh day of Passover, is found in some medieval manuscripts. *Akdamut Millin* has been translated into English in various prayer books, notably by Joseph Marcus (Silverman, Prayer Book) and Raphael Loewe (*Service of the Synagogue*). There are also several versions of the *Akdamut* in Hebrew. A similar poem, *Yeẓiv Pitgam,* is recited on the second day of Shavuot before the reading of the *haftarah*. Some scholars identify the author of that *piyyut* with Rashi's grandson Jacob ben Meir of Orleans.

In East European folk tradition the origin of the *Akdamut Millin* is connected with the widespread legend that Meir ben Isaac saved the Jewish community of Worms by invoking the help of a miraculous emissary of the Ten Lost Tribes from across the Sambatyon. In many versions of the legend, extant in manuscripts and still alive in oral tradition, the hero is identified with Meir Ba'al ha-Nes who is well-known from the Talmud and the *Akdamut piyyut* celebrates a victory over the Jew-baiters.

The poem has been given two musical settings which have become well-known in Ashkenazi synagogues. One of these can claim great antiquity by its psalmodic style of recitation; the simple but expressive declamation suits the narrative character of the poem. Its identity in the Western and Eastern branches of the Ashkenazi rite, and its use for the *Kiddush* and other prayers, indicates its age. Another melody is found only in the West, and apparently is of a later date, although its motifs were already incorporated in cantorial works of 1744 and 1796. Moreover, this second tune serves as a motto theme of the Feast of Weeks and is applied in the *Hallel,* the Blessing of the Priests, and other prayer texts.

AZHAROT. The festival of Shavuot has a special type of liturgical poem created for it. These are known as *azharot* (singular, *Azharah,* "warnings") and are practical enumerations of the 613 commandments of the Torah. The term originates from the opening of the early *piyyut, Azharah reshit le-ammekha nattata* ("Thou gavest thy people a preliminary warning"); and also because the numerical value of the word *azharot* is 613. At first, the style of the *azharot* was simple and devoid of embellishments, but with time they were infused with the spirit of *piyyut*. First mentioned by Natronai Gaon, the *azharot* were already accepted in his day, even though there were some who, then and later, opposed them. One reason for this opposition was that the composers were *paytanim* and not halakhists.

Occasionally the poems dealt with subjects other than the 613 commandments, e.g. the number of paragraphs in the Mishnah,

the 70 names of God, etc. Since no composer's name is found on the early *azharot* they are known as *azharot de-rabbanan* ("*azharot* of the rabbis") or *azharot de-metivta kaddisha de-rabbanim de-Pumbedita* ("the *azharot* of the holy yeshivah of the rabbis of Pumbedita"). *Azharot* are known in the liturgy of Ereẓ Israel, Babylonia, Spain, Italy, Germany, Provence, and Romania (i.e. Byzantium), and have also been included in other liturgies. Saadiah Gaon, two of whose *azharot* were printed in his *Siddur*, wrote in his introduction that he composed his *azharot* because his contemporaries were accustomed to such poems, in particular *attah hinḥalta* ("Thou hast bequeathed"), and also because the existing *azharot* did not mention all the 613 commandments and were repetitious and longwinded. Subsequent *azharot* were composed by many outstanding poets. In later generations, "Introductions to *azharot*" were also composed; and, since the language of the *azharot* was often difficult and complicated, scholars wrote commentaries on them. *Azharot* were usually said at the *Shaḥarit* or at the *Musaf* Service, while among northern Sephardim they were also said at the *Minḥah* Service. Beside the *azharot* for Shavuot which include the 613 commandments,

there are *azharot* for other times of the year, e.g. for the Sabbath before Sukkot, the Sabbath before Shavuot, the Sabbath before Passover, and also Rosh Ha-Shanah, Ḥanukkah, Purim, and the New Moon. These include sections pertaining to their particular season. In most Ashkenazi rites, *azharot* are not recited at all, even though they are printed in the festival prayer book. The Sephardim and Yemenites recite the *azharot* by Solomon ibn Gabirol—on the first day of Shavuot, the positive commandments, and on the second day, the negative commandments. Over 60 *azharot* are known.

THE VIGIL. Under the influence of the Kabbalah it became customary to stay awake for the whole of the first night of Shavuot and recite the beginnings and ends of all the Jewish classical books. This compilation is known as *Tikkun Leil Shavuot*. According to tradition the ancient Israelites remained awake all night in anticipation of receiving the Torah and thus it is fitting to imitate them and recite the whole Torah, in the wider sense of the term. Many synagogues arrange study sessions throughout the night and start the *Shaḥarit* service at the crack of dawn. In Jerusalem, the Western Wall is a favorite location for this early service.

A less observed custom is to spend the second night of Shavuot in the Diaspora reciting the Book of Psalms since that day is the anniversary of King David's death who, according to the tradition, was the author of the bulk of the book. In many congregations Psalm recitation takes place in the afternoon of the second day.

Sukkot. The distinctive features of the Festival of Sukkot which begins on the 15th day of Tishrei is the commandment to live in specially constructed booths (after the Hebrew term *sukkah* for which the festival is named) and to "take for yourselves" four species of plants which play a central role in the liturgy. Sukkot is the last of the three Pilgrim Festivals and because it occurs after the summer, in the fall, the main theme is a good rainfall for the winter which the farmers need so badly.

Alphons Levi's lithograph of an old Jew making the benediction for the Four Species stands in sharp contrast to the 1968 photograph of Sukkot at the Western Wall. We can assume that it was *ḥol ha-mo'ed* since photography is forbidden there on the Sabbath and festivals. The central European 19th-century *etrog* container was obviously made to resemble the fruit it is meant to hold.

Most of the rites of Sukkot revolve around this central motif. The festival lasts for seven days and the eighth day (in the Diaspora, also the ninth) is really a separate festival. However, in popular view, the eighth (and ninth) day is seen as the concluding day of the festival.

THE SUKKAH. For the duration of the festival (not including the eighth day) it is a positive duty for the male Jew to spend as much of his time as he possibly can in the *sukkah*. This is a temporary dwelling which must have at least three walls and of which the roof is made out of twigs and leafy branches. Many pious men, particularly in warm climates, sleep in the *sukkah*; everybody is supposed to at least eat his meals in it.

No special benediction or prayer is recited for the construction of the *sukkah*. However, on the first night at the *Kiddush* ceremony which is celebrated in the *sukkah*, the *She-heḥeyanu* benediction is also intended for the *mitzvah* of *sukkah*. Furthermore, at every meal after the appropriate blessing a special one is recited to God "Who has sanctified us by His commandments and Who has enjoined us to sit in the *sukkah*." This benediction is recited every time a person eats in the *sukkah* throughout the seven days. On the last day of Sukkot a special farewell prayer is said in the *sukkah* expressing the hope that in the coming year we will also merit being able to perform this mitzvah.

USHPIZIN. According to kabbalistic tradition, seven mystical "guests"—Abraham, Isaac, Jacob, Moses, Aaron, Joseph and David—visit the *sukkah* during the festival. These are known by the Aramaic word for guests, *Ushpizin*, which may derive from the Latin *Hospes*. According to the *Zohar* Joseph comes after Moses and Aaron, but in most Ashkenazi *maḥzorim* and prayer books the order is chronological. The spiritual guest of each day is invited before the meal and the text of this invitation in Aramaic, "Enter, exalted holy guests . . . " is found in several Ashkenazi and Sephardi prayer books. The custom was adopted by the Ḥasidim and many pamphlets entitled *Seder-Ushpiz*, including liturgy based upon the practices of certain *ẓaddikim* (e.g., the rabbis of Belz, Zunz, etc.), began to be published in the 19th century. Decorating the *sukkah* wall with a plaque which bears an inscription including the names of the seven guests has also become an accepted practice and the decoration itself is also called *ushpizin*. Moroccan Jews have a special compilation of prayers in honor of the *ushpizin*, called *Ḥamad Elohim*, from which special sections are recited each day of the festival.

THE FOUR SPECIES. An obligatory part of the rite of Sukkot according to the biblical commandment is to take four different plants: "And ye shall take you on the first day [of Sukkot] the fruit of goodly trees, branches of palm trees, and boughs of thick trees, and willows of the brook, and ye shall rejoice before the Lord your God seven days." "Ye shall dwell in booths for seven days" is also enjoined, despite the fact that it would appear that in the time of Nehemiah, the plants in the first verse were regarded as referring to the materials from which the *sukkah* mentioned in the second verse, was to be constructed, the traditional interpretation sees it as a separate and distinct commandment from the injunction of the *sukkah*.

Two of the species are described explicitly: the "branches of palm trees" are the *lulav*, and the "willows of the brook," the *aravot*. Tradition has universally identified the "fruits of goodly trees with the *etrog* (the citron) and the "boughs of thick trees" with *hadassim* ("myrtle"). The four species are made up of three sprigs of myrtle and two of willow, which are bound to the *lulav* with strips of palm, the former on the right and the latter on the left of the *lulav*. They are held in the right hand and the *etrog* is held separately in the left.

During the Temple period the main ceremonial of the four species took place in the Temple. They were taken and waved during the seven days of Sukkot whereas elsewhere, the rite was confined to the first day only. They were waved in a prescribed manner: toward the east, south, west, north, upward, and downward, in acknowledgment of the divine rule over nature. This took place during the recitation of Psalms 118:1–2 and 25 of the *Hallel*. After the *Musaf* sacrifice of the day had been offered, the four species were again taken, this time in procession around the altar while Psalms 118:25, or the words *ani va-hu hoshi'ah na*, a popular version of that verse, were chanted. On the first six days, only one circuit of the altar was made; on the seventh day, seven circuits. After the destruction

These Israel soldiers are celebrating the festival of Sukkot in a *sukkah* made from discarded crates. The scene was in the Golan Heights in October 1973 during the Yom Kippur War.

of the Temple, Johanan ben Zakkai ordained the Temple ceremonial as universal practice "in remembrance of the Temple," all the features of the Temple rite were included in the synagogue service.

The popularity of the ceremony during the period of the Second Temple is reflected in the fact that Ḥanukkah was celebrated by the Maccabees as a second Feast of Tabernacles, as well as in the incident in which the vast throng of worshipers in the Temple pelted King Alexander Yannai with their *etrogim* during the festival, in protest against his disregard of the Feast of Water Drawing. The remarkable hold which the four species had on the sentiments of the people during the Second Temple period, and immediately afterward, is evidenced by the fact that even during the rigors of war, Bar Kokhba took special care to see that his warriors were supplied with them.

In the Bible no attempt is made to explain the symbolism of the four species. They probably symbolized the fertility of the land as evidenced in the harvest just concluded, and as desired for the coming season, especially with a view to the fact that the rains are due immediately after Sukkot. The Midrash gives a number of moral and homiletic interpretations; the most popular is based on the qualities of the four trees. The *etrog* has both "taste and odor," the date (palm) only taste, the myrtle only odor, the willow neither: "taste and odor" symbolize "Torah and good works" respectively. The four species represent four categories of Jews insofar as they possess both, one, or none of these virtues. But Israel is regarded as a whole, and the failings of one are compensated for by the virtues of the others.

Another interpretation is based on the shape of the species. The *lulav* resembles the spine, the *etrog* the heart, the myrtle leaves the eye, and the willow leaves the mouth. Therefore one should submit these organs, and all the others, to the service of God, in accordance with Psalms 35:10, "All my bones shall say, Lord, who is like unto Thee." It has also been suggested that the four species represent the four agricultural areas of Israel: the *lulav*, the lowland; the *aravot*, the river; the *hadassim*, the mountains; and the *etrog*, the irrigated areas. Kabbalistic symbolism interprets the four species in terms of the doctrine of the *Sefirot*.

In the ritual of the Four Species as it is today a special benediction is recited on taking them. This is: "Who has sanctified us with His commandments and has enjoined us concerning the taking of the *lulav*." That plant being the tallest is singled out for the benediction. On the first day, the *Sheheḥeyanu* blessing is also recited. In order not to "take" the Four Species before the benediction it is customary to hold the *etrog* upside down and to turn it around after the blessing. Then the Four Species are shaken in the four directions of the compass and up and down. With regard to when this is done there are different customs. Some do it early in the morning before *Shaḥarit* in the *sukkah*. Others do it in the synagogue before the *Hallel* prayer. The Four Species are not taken on the Sabbath even if it is the first day of the festival. In the synagogue the Four Species are taken in the same manner as they were in the Temple as described above.

THE TORAH READINGS. On the first (and, in the Diaspora, the second) day of Sukkot Leviticus 22:26–23:44 is read. This is the listing of all the festivals of the year. The *maftir* is the commandment regarding the *Musaf* sacrifice (Numbers 29:12–16). The *haftarah* for the first day is Zechariah 14:1–21 which describes the Day of the Lord and inter alia states that God will smite the nations "that go not up to keep the festival of Sukkot." In the Diaspora, the *haftarah* for the second day is I Kings 8:2–21 which is the dedication of Solomon's Temple which took place on Sukkot. In Israel, on each day of the festival the verses dealing with the sacrifice for that day are repeated four times, once for each of the *aliyot*. A full listing of the festival readings can be found in Chapter V.

ECCLESIASTES. Known in Hebrew as *Kohelet*, the Book of Ecclesiastes is recited on the intermediary Sabbath of Sukkot, or on the eighth day of the festival (Shemini Aẓeret), if the latter coincides with a Sabbath. It is read during the morning service before the reading of the Torah. In some oriental rites, it is read in the *sukkah*. Among the many reasons put forward

Right: *Ushpizin* plaque for the *sukkah* with depictions of the "invited guests." Abraham is symbolized by a house with many open doors to illustrate his generous hospitality; Isaac by the scene of his binding where the ram which was ultimately sacrified in his place is also shown; Jacob by the heavenly ladder of his dream, with angels ascending and descending; Moses by the Tablets of the Law being given on Mount Sinai; Aaron by appurtenances and actions of the priestly service; Joseph by his dreams of the sheaves of corn and the moon and stars; and David by the royal throne and a musical instrument, this time from the violin family rather than the traditional harp. Mishkan le-Omanut, Kibbutz Ein Harod.
Below: A permanent collapsible *sukkah* from Fischach, South Germany, c. 1800, decorated with traditional motifs of Jerusalem, the Temple, and the Western Wall. It is exhibited at the Israel Museum, Jerusalem.

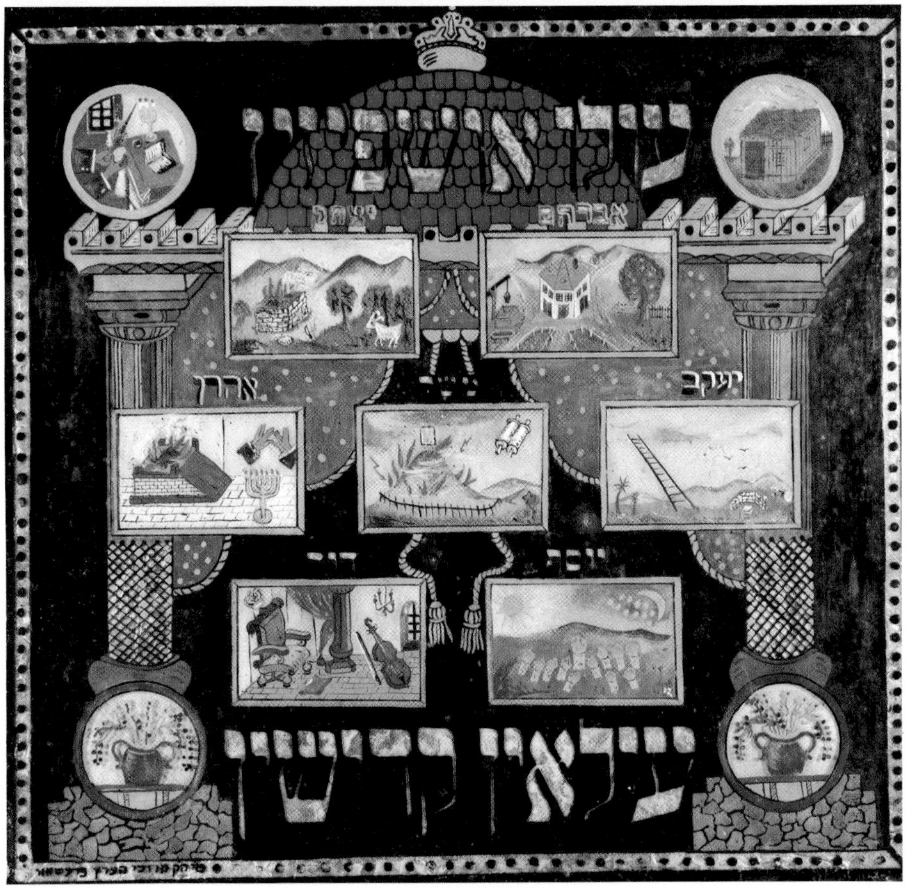

Right: "Descendant of the High Priest" by Isidor Kaufmann, c. 1903, which depicts a young ḥasidic boy holding the Four Species used on Sukkot. London, William Margulies Collection.
Below: Embroidered hanging for a *sukkah*, silk, gold, and silver thread on taffeta, Italy, 18th century. It depicts the Simḥat Bet ha-Sho'evah, the Feast of Drawing the Water, and shows three men performing dances and acrobatics as described by Simeon ben Gamaliel, head of the Sanhedrin. Washington, D.C., Smithsonian Institute.

A papercut *Omer* counting chart with the benediction and the formula for the first day of the counting in the center. The formulas for the remaining 48 days are in the medallions around the borders. Around the inside border are additional prayers connected with the counting of the *Omer*. The chart is from Poland and is dated 1866. Jerusalem, Israel Museum.

Three aspects of Shavuot. A *piyyut* for the festival, illuminated with flowers, animals, and human figures wearing medieval Jewish hats; the *Worms Maḥzor*, South Germany, 1272. J.N.U.L. Manuscript Hebrew 4°781, Vol. I, folio 39v. The wooden *Omer* calendar, a useful aid to remembering which day of the *Omer* to count, is from Germany, 18th century. Jerusalem, Israel Museum. In the 20th century, Jerusalem pre-kindergarten children with their floral crowns and baskets of first fruits celebrate Shavuot in Independence Park, 1973. Photo Murray Bloom, Jerusalem.

for its reading on Sukkot is the fact that chapter 11, verse 2 has been interpreted by some commentators as an allusion to the duty to rejoice during the eight days of Sukkot. The warning not to defer the fulfillment of vows (including donations to the poor and to the sanctuary) was also thought to be particularly appropriate at the last festival of the annual cycle. Others have suggested that the somber and pessimistic outlook of Ecclesiastes fits the atmosphere of autumn.

Simḥat Bet ha-Sho'evah. Rabbinic authorities mention a special ceremony of "water-libation" during the seven days of Sukkot. The Sadducees rejected the ceremony because they could find no support for it in Scripture. The special rites of "water-liberation," accompanied by the playing of the flute. took place only on *Ḥol ha-mo'ed* (except on the Sabbath), not on *yom tov*. The ceremony was known as Simḥat Bet ha-Sho'evah ("the rejoicing of the place of water-drawing"), based evidently on Isaiah 12:3 "Therefore with joy shall ye draw water out of the wells of salvation." There were said to be three huge golden candlesticks in the Temple court which were lit on these occasions "and there was not a courtyard in Jerusalem that did not reflect the light of the Bet ha-Sho'evah." "Men of piety and good works used to dance before them with burning torches in their hands, singing songs and praises." It was further said that whoever had not seen the Simḥat Bet ha-Sho'evah, had never witnessed real joy in his life. It was disregard of the water libation that led the populace to throw their *etrogim* at the king-priest, Alexander Yannai.

During *Ḥol ha-mo'ed* of Sukkot it has become customary to hold festive gatherings which are called by the name of this ancient ceremony. In the Orthodox quarters of Jerusalem this is an especially joyous time.

Hoshanot. When the circuits with the Four Species are made in the synagogue, special *piyyutim* are recited. The circuits are made around the *bimah* either after the *Shaḥarit* service or after the *Musaf* service. The prayers are called *hoshanot,* because of the recurring phrase *Hoshana* or *Hoshi'a ha,* "Save, I pray . . ." The origin of the prayers and the procession lies in the Temple ritual: "Every day [of Sukkot] one circles the altar once and says, 'Pray! O Lord, save, I pray! Pray, O Lord, give success, I pray!'; and Judah says, 'I and He save, I pray,' . . . and on that day [i.e. the seventh] one circles the altar seven times." The first references to this practice in the synagogue come from the period of the *geonim*.

Already in ancient times, the words *hosha na* were linked into one word *hoshana*. The word served as a response, or a call, after every rhyme or section of prayers which were composed in later generations for this purpose. Of these prayers (usually alphabetic acrostics) many are undefined in content (e.g. "For the sake of Thy truth, for the sake of Thy covenant"); others are supplications for water or for a blessing for the produce (e.g. "Save, I pray! the land from being cursed, the animal from losing its offspring"); while still others are concerned with salvation from exile and with redemption.

In all prayer books—from those of Rabbi Amram Gaon and Rabbi Saadiah Gaon to those of the present day—there are *hoshanot* on various subjects and in different forms. It can be assumed that several of the *hoshanot,* which are signed with the name "Eleazar," were written by Rabbi Eleazar Kallir. There is insufficient evidence, however, to determine the authorship of other *hoshanot*. Some were also written for the Sabbath of Sukkot, and include topics pertaining to the Sabbath. But on that day there is no procession. In some rites *hoshanot* are not recited on the Sabbath of Sukkot at all. The *hoshanot* of the seventh day, Hoshana Rabba, are of a special character. Seven processions take place; in some rites the *hoshanot* of all the previous days are repeated while others recite *hoshanot* written specially for this day. Under the influence of the Kabbalah, *piyyutim* dealing with the seven guests, *Ushpizin,* have been supplemented to the *hoshanot* of this day. Indeed, the seven processions allude to them.

Hoshanot is also the name of the special willow branches taken on Hoshana Rabba, from which the expression "a beaten *hoshana*" derives (applied, for example, to a man who has come down in the world). In the Babylonian Talmud the myrtles which are bound to the *lulav* (palm branch) together with the willows are referred to as *hoshanot*.

Hoshana Rabba. Although all the last six days (five in the Diaspora) of Sukkot are imbued with the sanctity of *Ḥol ha-*

The Sukkot scene of the North London synagogue is noteworthy because only the wardens and the cantor have the Four Species. In the frontispiece to the Sukkot *maḥzor* from Sulzbach (1826) which depicts the processions in the synagogue on Sukkot, all the congregants are suitably equipped.

mo'ed, the last of them has a special character. It is known as Hoshana Rabba, "The Great Hoshana" because on that day seven circuits are made with the Four Species as opposed to the one circuit on each of the other days.

In Temple times, the day was also distinguished by the fact that willow branches, which on this day were specially cut at the village of Moza near Jerusalem, were stood around the side of the altar with their leaves overlapping the top. In the Mishnah the day is therefore known as *yom ha-shevi'i shel aravah* ("the seventh day of the willow"). According to Joḥanan ben Beroka palm twigs were beaten on the ground and thus the day is known as *yom ḥibbit harayot* ("the day of the beating of the palm twigs"). It is generally known as Hoshana Rabba because of the numerous *hoshanot* which are recited and is thus referred to already in the Midrashim. The ceremony of the willow took place even if this day occurred on the Sabbath in order to publicize the obligatory nature of the practice. In Second Temple times this was a source of controversy between the Boethusians and the Pharisees who gave the ceremony biblical authority even though it is nowhere mentioned in the Bible. They considered it to be *halakhah le-Moshe mi-Sinai,* i.e., as having been instructed verbally to Moses during his stay on Mt. Sinai. According to the tradition of many rabbinic authorities the calendar was fixed in such a way that the New Year would not occur on a Sunday so that Hoshana Rabba should not fall on the Sabbath, which would cause the taking of the willow to be canceled. Today, the obligation of taking the willow on the seventh day of Sukkot remains and it is the "custom of the prophets" or the "principle of the prophets" to beat it on the ground or on some object. The custom of circling the interior of the synagogue seven times while reciting prayers and supplications is known from the period of the *geonim* (see above). Already in the Talmud Hoshana Rabba is mentioned as one of the two days ("the day of blowing of the *shofar* and the day of the willow") on which all attend the synagogue service.

In the period of the *geonim,* the celebration of Hoshana Rabba acquired considerable solemnity and religious-mystic significance. In Jerusalem a large gathering used to take place on the Mount of Olives which was circled seven times; official announcements (such as fixing the coming year) were proclaimed; philanthropists and communities received blessings; and public excommunications were issued. The *piyyut* of Hoshana Rabba which opens with the words, "the power [or, the truth] of Thy salvation cometh," which deals with the splitting open of the Mount of Olives (according to the prophecy of Zechariah, 14:4) and the resurrection of the dead, probably had its origin in this ceremony. From the 13th century onward, there is evidence regarding special popular beliefs connected with Hoshana Rabba. There was a very widespread belief that he who did not see the shadow of his head on the night of Hoshana Rabba would die during that year, for Hoshana Rabba was the day of the "seal," wherein the verdict of man (passed on the Day of Atonement) is "sealed," or the day on which the "notices" of the verdict were sent out. It is probable that the view of Hoshana Rabba as a day of judgment was originally connected with the ancient belief that "during the festival [i.e. Sukkot], the world is judged for the water to be received," whether the coming year would be blessed with rain or be one of drought and Hoshana Rabba is the conclusion of Sukkot. This would explain the numerous *hoshanot* of Hoshana Rabba in which the motif is water. There is also an allusion in medieval halakhic literature to a Prayer for Rain on Hoshana Rabba.

Over the generations, the conception of Hoshana Rabba as a day of judgment has been expressed by a series of distinct customs, all or some of which have been included in the prayer service of the day in the various rites; numerous candles are kindled in the synagogue, as on the Day of Atonement; in some rites the *ḥazzan* wears a white robe; the *Pesukei de-Zimra* of the Sabbath and the *Nishmat* prayer are added to the service; the sentences (of the Ten Days of Penitence), "Remember us unto life," and "Who is as Thou," are included in the *Amidah; Avinu Malkenu,* the Great *Kedushah,* and *U-Netanneh Tokef* are said in the *Musaf* prayer; and the *shofar* is blown during the processions. In some rites *seliḥot* are recited. The *Amidah* and the Reading of the Law, however, remain the same as on the other intermediate days of the festival. There is a widespread custom to stay up during the night of Hoshana Rabba, and to read the whole of the Pentateuch or the books of Deuteronomy

and Psalms, and the like. This custom does not go back further than the 13th century. Its original intention was probably to ensure that even those who were not particular concerning the reading of the Pentateuch during the whole of the year would complete it together with the public on Simḥat Torah. This custom later assumed the character (probably through the kabbalists of Safed) of a *tikkun* ("purification"; *Tikkun Leil Hoshana Rabba, "Tikkun* of the night of Hoshana Rabba").

Shemini Aẓeret and Simḥat Torah. "On the eighth day ye shall have a solemn assembly (*aẓeret*); ye shall do no manner of servile work." The eighth day of Sukkot is treated by the rabbis as a separate festival, *regel bifenei aẓmo* and is known as Shemini Aẓeret, "the Eighth Day of Solemn Assembly." In the liturgy it is also called by this name although in some rites it is referred to as "The Eighth Day, The Festival of Solemn Assembly." The Memorial service and a special prayer for rain (*Tefillat Geshem*) are recited during *Musaf* (in Israel before it), in the synagogue. Simḥat Torah, "The rejoicing of the Torah," is the last day of the holy days begun by Sukkot. In the Diaspora Simḥat Torah falls on the 23rd of Tishrei, the second day of Shemini Aẓeret, the festival which concludes Sukkot. In Israel, it coincides with Shemini Aẓeret. On this festival, the annual reading of the Torah scroll is completed and immediately begun again. Simḥat Torah, as a separate festival, was not known during the talmudic period. In designating the *haftarah* for this day, the Talmud refers to it simply as the second day of Shemini Aẓeret. Similarly it is termed Shemini Aẓeret in the prayers and the *Kiddush* recited on this day. Its unique celebrations began to develop during the geonic period when the one-year cycle for the reading of the Torah (as opposed to the triennial cycle, discussed in Chapter V), gained wide acceptance.

The Talmud already specified the conclusion of the Torah as the portion for this day (i.e. Deuteronomy 33–34). The assignment of a new *haftarah*, Joshua, is mentioned in the ninth-century prayer book, *Seder Rav Amram*. Later it also became customary to begin to read the beginning of the Book of Genesis again on Simḥat Torah. This was done in order "to refute Satan" who might otherwise claim that the Jews were happy only to have finished the Torah, but were unwilling to begin anew.

During the celebrations, as they continue to be observed by Orthodox and Conservative congregations, all the Torah scrolls are removed from the ark and the *bimah* ("pulpit") is circled seven times (*hakkafot*). All the men present are called to the Torah reading (*aliyyot*); for this purpose, Deuteronomy 33:1–29 is repeated as many times as necessary. All the children under the age of bar mitzvah are called for the concluding portion of the chapter; this *aliyah* is referred to as *kol ha-ne'arim* ("all the youngsters"). A *tallit* is spread above the heads of the youngsters, and the congregation blesses them with Jacob's benediction to Ephraim and Manasseh (Genesis 48:16). Those who are honored with the *aliyyot* which conclude and start the Torah readings are popularly designated as the *ḥatan Torah* and *ḥatan Bereshit*, the Bridegroom of the Torah, and the Bridegroom of Genesis; they often pledge contributions to the synagogue and sponsor banquets for their acquaintances in honor of the event. In many communities similar ceremonies are held on Simḥat Torah eve; all the scrolls are removed from the ark and the *bimah* is circled seven times. Some communities even read from the concluding portion of Deuteronomy during the evening service, the only time during the year when the Torah scroll is read at night.

The Simḥat Torah festivities are accompanied by the recitation of special liturgical compositions, some of which were

Bernard Picart's engraving of Simḥat Torah in the Portuguese synagogue of Amsterdam is called "The Joy for the Law." However it can hardly match the joyous spirit of the 1970 photograph of a mass procession down to the Western Wall in Jerusalem in which the Torah scrolls are being carried under a *ḥuppah* consisting of an upheld *tallit*. The venerable figure in the center is Isaac Nissim, the former Sephardi chief rabbi of Israel.

written in the late geonic period. The *ḥatan Torah* is called up by the *piyyut Me-Reshut ha-El ha-Gadol*, and the *ḥatan Bereshit* by *Me-Reshut Meromam*. Both of these poems praise the Torah and the "bridegrooms." The return of the Torah scrolls to the ark is accompanied by the joyful hymns "*Sisu ve-Simḥu be-Simḥat Torah*" and "*Hitkabbeẓu Melakhim Zeh el Zeh.*" A central role in the festivities is allotted to children. In addition to the *aliyah* to the Torah, the children also participate in the Torah processions; they carry flags adorned with apples in which burning candles are placed. There have even been communities where children dismantled *sukkot* on Simḥat Torah and burned them.

Ḥasidim also hold Torah processions on Shemini Aẓeret eve. Reform synagogues observe these customs, in a modified form, on Shemini Aẓeret, which is observed as the final festival day. In Israel, where the second day of the festival is not celebrated, the liturgy and celebration of both days are combined. It has also become customary, there, for public *hakkafot* to be held on the night following Simḥat Torah, which coincides with its celebration in the Diaspora; in many cities, communities, and army bases, seven *hakkafot* are held with religious, military, and political personnel being honored with the carrying of the Torah scrolls.

In the U.S.S.R. among Soviet Jewish youth seeking forms of expressing their Jewish identification, Simḥat Torah gradually became, during the 1960s, the occasion of mass gatherings in and around the synagogues, mainly in the great cities, Moscow, Leningrad, Riga, and others. At these gatherings large groups of Jewish youth, many of them students, sang Hebrew and Yiddish songs, danced the *hora*, congregated and discussed the latest events in Israel, etc. In the beginning, the Soviet authorities tried to disperse these "unauthorized meetings," but when Jewish and Western public opinion began to follow them and press correspondents as well as observers from various foreign embassies began attending them, the authorities largely reverted their attitude and even instructed the militia to cordon off the synagogue areas and redirect traffic, so as not to cause clashes with the Jewish youngsters, whose numbers swelled rapidly in Moscow into the tens of thousands. In many cities in the West, notably in Israel, England, the United States, and Canada, Simḥat Torah was declared by Jewish youth as the day of "solidarity with Soviet Jewish youth," and mass demonstrations were staged voicing demands to the Soviet authorities for freedom of Jewish life and the right of migration to Israel.

HAKKAFOT. Although the term *hakkafot* is used to designate any ceremonial processional circuits both in the synagogue and outside it, on various occasions, it usually refers to the circuits made on Simḥat Torah.

Such circuits are mentioned in the Bible. There were, for instance, seven circuits around Jericho—once a day for six days, and seven times on the seventh day. The Mishnah records that the *lulav* was carried around the Temple altar during the seven days of Sukkot. The custom of carrying the Torah scrolls around the synagogue in processional circuits during both the *Ma'ariv* and *Shaḥarit* services on Simḥat Torah is first mentioned by Rabbi Isaac Tyrnau, 14th–15th century.

Hakkafot are also performed on a number of other occasions. For instance, Torah scrolls are carried around in a processional circuit during the dedication of both synagogues and cemeteries. In a number of communities, it is customary for the bride to make either three or seven *hakkafot* around the bridegroom during the wedding ceremony. The Sephardim and Ḥasidim walk around a coffin seven times prior to burial. It is also customary to walk around the cemetery when praying for the sick.

On all of these occasions one may note the juxtaposition of the "magic circle" with the mystical figure of seven, and the implied attempt to dissuade *shedim* ("evil spirits") from intruding upon the object of attention. With regard to the funerary *hakkafot* it has been suggested that the purpose is to ward off the spirits of the dead man's unborn children and to appease them with symbolic gifts of money. It is also significant that the miracles of Ḥoni ha-Me'aggel, a wonder-worker of talmudic fame, were performed after he had made a circuit (in the form of a drawn circle) around the place on which he stood.

THE PRAYER FOR RAIN. Sukkot marks the end of the summer and the start of the winter. The water motif that runs through the whole festival reaches its climax on Shemini Aẓeret with the *Tefillat Geshem*, Prayer for Rain, or the *Tikkun Geshem*, as it is known in Sephardi parlance. Prayers for rain are offered on various occasions. God is acknowledged as the power causing rain and the change of seasons, and petitioned for the fertility of the fields and for preservation from famine. The principal prayer for rain, however, is recited during the *Musaf* service on Shemini Aẓeret as part of the second benediction in the reader's repetition of the *Amidah* (Ashkenazi tradition). The Sephardim recite it before *Musaf*. The *piyyutim* of which this prayer is composed vary according to the different rites. Those in the Ashkenazi rite are by Eleazar Kallir; the last of the six *piyyutim* invokes the remembrance of Abraham, Isaac, Jacob, Moses, Aaron, and the Twelve Tribes, and culminates in the invocation: "In their merit favor us with abundant water (rain) . . . For a blessing and not for a curse, for life and not for death, for plenty and not for famine. Amen." From this service on Shemini Aẓeret until that of the first day of Passover when the prayer for dew is said, the sentence *mashiv ha-ru'ah u-morid ha-geshem* ("cause the wind to blow and the rain to fall") is included in every *Amidah* prayer at the beginning of the second benediction. This insertion is called by the Mishnah *gevurot* (meaning "the Powers of God"). In traditional synagogues following the customs of Eastern Europe the *ḥazzan* officiates in a white robe at the *Musaf* service when the prayer for rain is read as on the Day of Atonement, and recites the *Kaddish* before the *Musaf* service to the solemn melody of the High Holy Days. In Israel, the *Tefillat Geshem* is recited after the Torah scrolls have been returned to the ark and before the *Musaf* service so as to avoid an "interruption" in the statutory *Amidah;* however, the ḥasidic rite in Israel recites it in the reader's repetition of the *Amidah*. The *Tefillat Geshem* (like the prayer for dew) is part of the service in all Jewish rituals including the Conservative and Reform where it appears in a shortened version.

Another prayer for rain is the petition (*she'elah*) "and give dew and rain for a blessing" (*ve-ten tal u-matar li-verakhah;* in the Sephardi rite this is a different and longer petition) inserted in the ninth benediction of the *Amidah* for weekdays. This petition is recited only from a date two weeks or more after the *Tefillat Geshem* on Shemini Aẓeret because the pilgrims in Temple times had to return from Jerusalem to their homes and traveling during a rainy season would have caused them hardship. Thus, in Ereẓ Israel the insertion is made from the evening prayer of the seventh of Ḥeshvan; elsewhere, from the 60th day after the autumnal equinox, that is, from the fifth or sixth of December. This petition for rain appears in the ninth benediction (the "Blessing of the Years"), rather than in the second benediction of the *Amidah*, because the first three benedictions of the *Amidah* should contain the praise of God only and no petitions.

Besides rejoicing with the Torah, Jews have always seen it as their most honored possession. This painting by Tully Filmus is called "Preserving the Torah," and depicts Jews who have been expelled from their homes taking the holy Torah scrolls with them on their wanderings.

Prayers for rain are among the earliest liturgical texts and withholding of rain is regarded in the Bible as a punishment from God. In the time of the Second Temple, the high priest recited a special prayer for rain on the Day of Atonement based upon Solomon's prayer (I Kings 8:35–36). During periods of drought, special prayers and supplications combined with fasting were ordained. These prayers entered the liturgy as it evolved in the time of the Mishnah and thereafter.

The dates for the special fasts and prayers for rain were fixed by the rabbis with a view to the climate and agricultural needs of Palestine; later rabbinic authorities decreed that wherever rain is beneficial during the summer, appropriate prayers for rain may be inserted, even during this season, in the 16th benediction of the *Amidah.*

VIII Days of Awe

Elul

Rosh ha-Shanah

The Day of Atonement

מחזור
ספרדים
מימים נוראים
וסדר סליחות ללילי אשמורות
וסדר תפלות לראש השנה וליום הכפורים
ולצום גדליה :
מסודרים באופן שאין צריך לחזור לאחוריו
ולחפש שום דבר אלא הכל מסודר בכל תפלה
ותפלה כפי ענינה :
והשמטנו הדברים שלא נהגו לאמרם
להקל כובד הכרך :
נדפס באמשטרדאם
בבית הגביר אורי הלוי יצ״ו :
בשנת כי טל אורות טלך

The title page of a Sephardi *maḥzor* for the High Holy Days and the *Seliḥot*. This prayerbook was printed in Amsterdam in 1679 and the title page announces that among its advantages is the fact that the user will find everything in order without having to turn back and forward, and that "the things which it is not customary to say have been omitted in order to decrease the weight of the volume."

The recitation of the *Seliḥot* during the month of Elul is made in a spirit of weariness; weariness at one's own spiritual inadequacy and perhaps because of the early hour at which the *Seliḥot* are recited. The *Seliḥot* are often published as separate prayerbooks including selections according to the local rite. The title page shown here is of a *Seliḥot* prayerbook printed in 1677 in Amsterdam by Joseph Athias. Its illustration shows the patriarch Jacob meeting his long-lost son Joseph, which scene was the printers' mark of this particular firm.

The atmosphere of the High Holy Day period is one of somber soul-searching. The motif of these days is man's inadequacy in view of his potential and God's demands on him, and this motif is strongly felt in the liturgy. Some of the services for Rosh Ha-Shanah and Yom Kippur are structured quite differently from the normal services and they are all embellished with *piyyutim* of one kind or another. From a month before Rosh Ha-Shanah, from Rosh Ḥodesh Elul the synagogue liturgy is adapted to start creating the mood for the High Holy Days themselves.

ELUL

A rabbinic homily sees in the very name of the month an allusion to its importance. The letters of Elul, said the rabbis, make up the initial letters of *Ani le-Dodi ve-Dodi li,* "I am my beloved's and my beloved is mine," a verse in the Song of Songs in which tradition identifies the beloved as God. Furthermore, the *aggadah* has it that Moses' 40 days on Mt. Sinai started from the first of Elul and lasted till Yom Kippur. During the month the *shofar* is sounded at the end of every *Shaḥarit* service except on the Sabbaths and the day before Rosh Ha-Shanah. The reason for the abstention on the Sabbath is that the Sabbath law forbids sounding musical instruments and for the day before Rosh Ha-Shanah to distinguish between a voluntary sounding out of custom and the obligatory sounding on Rosh Ha-Shanah itself. At the end of the *Shaḥarit* and *Ma'ariv* (*Shaḥarit* and *Minḥah* in the Sephardi and ḥasidic rites), Psalm 27 is recited from the beginning of Elul until Hoshana Rabba. This Psalm which stresses reliance on divine protection, was considered especially fitting for this period of the year. Sephardim recite the *Seliḥot* service every day for the whole month; Ashkenazim start toward the end of the month.

Seliḥot. The word *seliḥah* means "forgiveness," and in the singular is used to indicate a *piyyut* whose subject is a plea for forgiveness for sins. In the plural, the word is used for a special order of service consisting of non-statutory additional prayers which are recited on all fast days, on occasions of special intercession and during the Penitential season which begins before Rosh Ha-Shanah and concludes with the Day of Atonement.

The Mishnah gives the order of service for public fasts, usually proclaimed during periods of drought. It provided, inter alia, for the addition of six blessings to the normal eighteen of the daily *Amidah,* and gives the concluding formula before the actual blessing for each:

> May He Who answered our father Abraham on Mt. Moriah answer you . . . may He that answered our fathers at the Red Sea . . . Joshua in Gilgal . . . Samuel at Mizpah . . . Elijah in Carmel . . . Jonah in the belly of the whale . . . David and his son Solomon . . .

The first mention of a distinct order of *Seliḥot* occurs in *Tanna de-Vei Eliyahu Zuta,* which has been variously dated between the third and the tenth centuries:

> David knew that the Temple was destined to be destroyed and that the sacrificial system would be abolished as a result of the iniquities of Israel, and David was distressed for Israel. With what would they effect atonement? And the Holy One blessed be He said, "When troubles come upon Israel because of their iniquities, let them stand before Me as one band and confess their iniquities before Me and recite before Me the order of *Seliḥot* and I will answer them" . . . Rabbi Johanan said, "The Holy One blessed be He revealed this in the verse 'and the Lord passed before him and proclaimed, the Lord, the Lord God, manifest and gracious etc.' (Exodus 34:6 which gives the thirteen divine attributes). This teaches that the Holy One blessed be He descended from the mist like a *sheli'aḥ ẓibbur,* enveloped in his *tallit* and stood before the ark and revealed to Moses the order of *Seliḥot.*

It was not until the ninth century that such an order of *Seliḥot* is found—the *Seder* of Rav Amram—and these two passages, the "May He Who answered" and the scriptural verse quoted above, together with a number of others, are the essential elements in it, as in all subsequent *Seliḥot.*

During the course of time, however, a considerable number of *piyyutim,* of which the *Seliḥah* is the most important, were

added to this basic formula. There are a great number of different rites; many individual communities, as distinct from countries, evolving their own order of *Seliḥot*. *Seliḥot* composed by such great personalities as Saadiah Gaon, Gershom ben Judah, Rashi and Solomon ibn Gabirol are included in orders of *Seliḥot*. In all rites the main theme is contained in a petitional prayer called, after its first words, *El Melekh Yoshev*. This prayer is recited in a standing position after each of the individual *Seliḥot piyyutim*. It is thought to have originated in the sixth century C.E. and contains the Scriptural verse of God's thirteen attributes.

The *Seliḥot* were at first inserted, as indicated by the Mishnah, after the appropriate sixth blessing of the *Amidah* (the prayer for forgiveness for sins), but the Palestinian custom of reciting them after the *Amidah* prevailed and became the almost universal custom. The Italian and Roman rites, however, retain the old custom. Originally *Seliḥot* were recited only on fast days, both statutory and special, proclaimed in times of trouble, their recitation being a form of *ẓidduk ha-din,* the justification of God. Since God was just, the calamities were the result of Israel's sins, and the evil could be averted by confession and praying for forgiveness for those sins. Their extension to what is at the present time the most widespread recital of *Seliḥot,* those of the Penitential days, derived from the custom of fasting on the six days before Rosh Ha-Shanah, when *Seliḥot* were said in connection with the fast, and the custom of saying *Seliḥot* was then extended over the Ten Days of Penitence (including the Day of Atonement, but not Rosh Ha-Shanah). The Sephardim follow the custom of reciting *Seliḥot* for the 40 days from Rosh Ḥodesh Elul to the Day of Atonement, but the Ashkenazi custom is to commence reciting them on the Sunday before Rosh Ha-Shanah or of the preceding week should Rosh Ha-Shanah fall on Monday or Tuesday. The *Seliḥot* for the first day are usually recited at midnight and thereafter before the morning service.

In addition to statutory fast days and the Penitential season, *Seliḥot* have been composed for semi-official voluntary fasts undertaken by pious individuals. They are the "Behab"—fasts undertaken on the Monday, Thursday and Monday following the festivals of Passover and Sukkot and, during a leap year, on the Thursday of the eight Sabbaths during which the scriptural portions from *Shemot* to *Teẓavveh* (called from their initial letters *Shovavim Tat*) are read, and on Yom Kippur Katan. These fasts are discussed in Chapter X. *Seliḥot* are also recited by the members of the *ḥevra kaddisha* at their annual service, and to avert plague affecting children.

סליחות
שירות ותושבחות׳ לאל כל הדורות׳
חרים אביון מאשפות׳ והפך יגון ואנחות׳
לששון ולשובע שמחות׳ והם מעט
הכמות אכן רב האכיות׳ אשר חיבר
במחברת הקודש נ״י פ״ה האב״ד דמדינת
מוינשטר ואנפיה כבוד שמו
מוהר״ר אברהם ברבי יצחק
אויערבך בקוספעלד
נדפס כדפוס המשובח והמהולל של
הגביר והטפסר יוסף עטיאש
באמשטירדאם
ת זל כטל אמרתי לפ'ק

Erev Rosh Ha-Shanah. The spiritual preparations for the High Holy Days reach one of their peaks with the day before Rosh Ha-Shanah. It was a custom of the pious—mainly disregarded nowadays—to fast on this day. Still widely practiced is the ritual of *Hattarat Nedarim,* the absolution of vows. This subject is discussed later in this chapter with regard to *Kol Nidrei.* The pre-Rosh Ha-Shanah custom stems from the person's desire

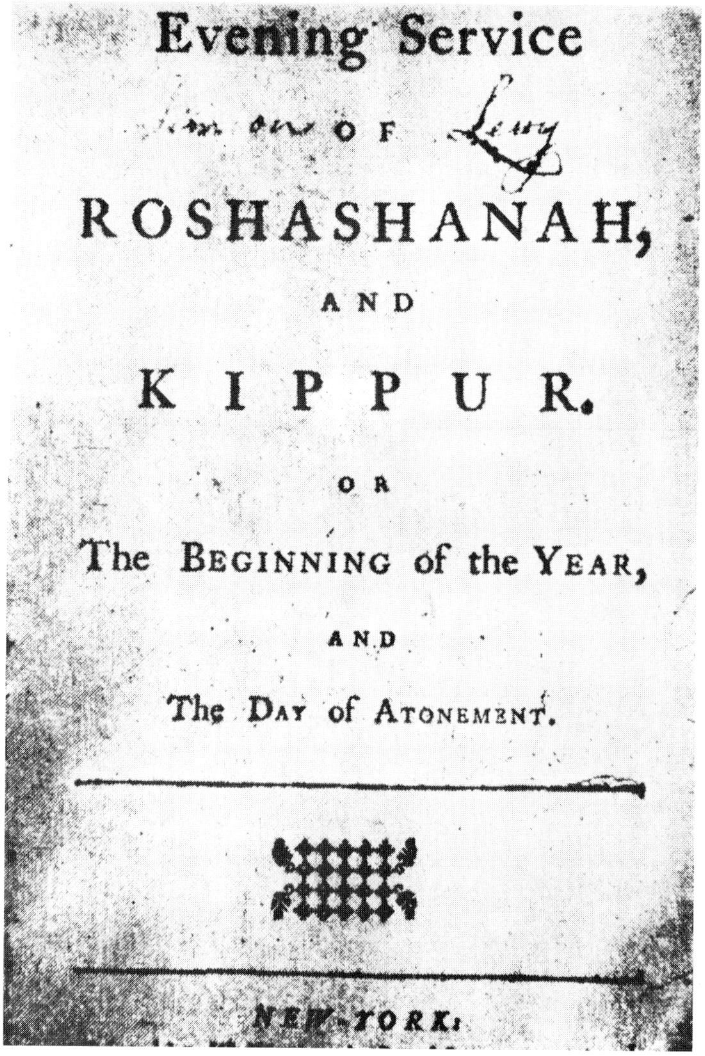
Evening Service

OF

ROSHASHANAH,

AND

KIPPUR.

OR

The BEGINNING of the YEAR,

AND

The DAY of ATONEMENT.

NEW-YORK:

The first Jewish prayerbook for the holy days published in the American colonies appeared in New York in 1761. Interestingly enough, no Hebrew appears on the title page. The lavish illustrated page from *Kirschliche Verfassung* (1748) by Johann Christoph Bodenschatz, a Protestant theologian, shows several Yom Kippur scenes. The center illustration is the synagogue for *Kol Nidrei* with all the congregants wearing *tallitot.* The top right panel shows the traditional pre-Yom Kippur visit to the cemetery; bottom right shows the *kapparot* ceremony; bottom left is a group of Jews at the cemetery giving charity; and top left is the symbolic administration of lashes which was customary on the eve of the Day of Atonement. The top center panel might possibly be a scene of the comforting of mourners.

not to enter the day of judgment with vows outstanding towards God. Immediately after the *Shaḥarit* service, the congregation divides into groups of four men or more. Three of the group act as the *Bet Din* (the court hearing the supplicant) and the fourth stands before them and recites a Hebrew formula requesting that any religious obligations he assumed but did not fulfil should be cancelled. The court then pronounces a stylized decision indicating its agreement. Each member of the group takes his turn as the supplicant. In some rites *Hattarat Nedarim* is performed on the day before Yom Kippur.

ROSH HA-SHANAH

The first day of the month of Tishrei is described as a day of "memorial proclaimed with the blast of horns" and as "a day of blowing the horn." The Mishnah lists four days during the year which it describes as Rosh Ha-Shanah, the Head of the Year: The first of Nisan is the New Year for Jewish kings and for the religious calendar; the first of Elul is the New Year for tithing cattle; the 15th of Shevat is the New Year for trees; and the first of Tishrei is the New Year for the civil calendar, for the Sabbatical and Jubilee years. On this last day, according to the Mishnah, "the whole world is judged." One rabbi in the Talmud, Rabbi Eliezer, believed that the world was created on the first of Tishrei and although another sage has it that that happened on the first of Nisan, Eliezer's view was accepted.

These motifs dominate the period which starts with Rosh Ha-Shanah and ends with Yom Kippur. Rabbinic theology sees these days—which are also known as the Ten Days of Penitence, or as the *Yamim Nora'im,* the Days of Awe—as the time when man's fate is fixed on high. In the words of a famous talmudic homily:

> Three books are opened on Rosh Ha-Shanah, one for the completely righteous, one for the completely wicked, and one for the average persons. The completely righteous are immediately inscribed in the book of life. The completely wicked are immediately inscribed in the book of death. The average persons are kept in suspension from Rosh Ha-Shanah to the Day of Atonement. If they deserve well, they are inscribed in the book of life, if they do not deserve well, they are inscribed in the book of death.

Since the overwhelming majority of people are neither completely righteous nor completely wicked, the Ten Days of Penitence should be used for an intensive spiritual effort to better one's lot. A concomitant of this theology is the doctrine of repentance, which teaches that if a man repents his sins, they will be forgiven. This is the meaning of the Ten Days of Penitence. In this period God is seen as King, that is, as the Supreme Ruler who sits in judgment.

In the liturgy, therefore, several changes are made to express this idea. The third benediction of the *Amidah* ends with "the Holy King" instead of "the Holy God" and the 11th with "the Just King" instead of "the King who loves justice and judgment." Furthermore, several additions are made to the *Amidah.* In the first benediction, "Remember us for life, O King who delights in life, and inscribe us in the book of life for Thy sake, O God of Life," is added and in the second, "Who

p. 216. §. 10

This medieval woodcut showing the blowing of the *shofar* appeared in *Judenbeichte,* an anti-Semitic tract by Johannes Pfefferkorn, one of the most notorious apostates of the Middle Ages. The book appeared in 1508. Pfefferkorn was an ignoramus as is quite obvious from the various postures adopted by the congregants—postures which might have been in place in a medieval monastery but hardly in a synagogue.

is like Thee, merciful Father? Thou rememberest thy creatures in mercy for life." In the penultimate benediction of the *Amidah* the insertion is, "Inscribe all the people of Thy covenant for a good life," and in the last benediction, "May we and all Thy people Israel be remembered and inscribed before Thee in the book of blessing, peace and prosperity for a good life and for peace." These changes and additions are made throughout the Ten Days of Penitence.

Ma'ariv. The evening service for Rosh Ha-Shanah follows the usual festival pattern. The third benediction is greatly expanded and elaborates on the idea of God sitting in judgment. *Ya'aleh ve-Yavo* is inserted and the central benediction celebrating the sanctity of the day closes with "King over all the world who sanctifies Israel and the Day of Remembrance."

AḤOT KETANNAH. In the Sephardi ritual a special *piyyut* is recited before the *Ma'ariv* service. The poem consists of eight metrical stanzas of four or five lines, each ending with the refrain "May this year and its curses end." The last stanza ends, "May the year and its blessings begin." The acrostic gives the name of the author "Abram Ḥazzan" who was Abraham Gerondi, a *paytan* who flourished in 13th-century France. The opening words, "Little sister" are taken from the Song of Songs which, according to the traditional interpretation, is a love song between God and His people Israel. In that context the "little sister" is the *Shekhinah,* the Divine Presence.

The poem has been adopted in the Yemenite rite as well as in many Ashkenazi rites especially in kabbalistic circles.

TRADITIONAL GREETINGS. On the first night of Rosh Ha-Shanah it is customary to greet one's friends with: "May you be inscribed (in the book of life) for a good year." The Sephardi version of the greeting is "May you be inscribed for a good year; may you be worthy of abundant years." At the festive meal, it is customary to dip the piece of bread, over which grace has been recited, into honey as a token of the sweet year it is hoped will come. For the same reason, a piece of apple is dipped in honey and before eating it, the prayer is recited: "May it be Thy will O Lord our God and God of our fathers, to renew unto us a good and sweet year." Nuts should not be eaten on Rosh Ha-Shanah because they produce phlegm, and make it more difficult to recite the prayers of the day; also because the numerical value of the Hebrew for "nut" (*egoz*) is the same as that of "sin" (*ḥet*). In some communities, the loaves for the festival meal are baked in the form of ladders to symbolize the fortunes of men in the year ahead: some ascending, others descending life's ladder.

Shaḥarit. The morning service for Rosh Ha-Shanah follows the normal basic pattern. The *Shaḥarit ḥazzan* takes over the service at the word "*Ha-Melekh*" towards the end of the *Nishmat* prayer and traditionally he starts the melody and sings the word to a special tune at his seat. Only then does he proceed to the lectern. Between *Barekhu* and the *Shema* various *piyyutim* are inserted. These vary from rite to rite and many synagogues do not recite them. The *Shaḥarit Amidah* is the same as that for *Ma'ariv* except that *Sim Shalom* is substituted for *Shalom Rav*. It is in the cantor's repetition of the *Amidah* that all rites insert *piyyutim*; some more and some less. Before he actually starts the *piyyutim,* the *ḥazzan* recites a *reshut,* "permission," in which he admits his spiritual inadequacy for the task he is about to undertake. The melodies for the *piyyutim,* as for all the Rosh Ha-Shanah and Yom Kippur services,

Andante religioso
'A - vi - nu mal - ké - nu ḥon-
-né - nu waʿă - né - nu 'a - vi - nu mal-
-ké - nu ḥon-né - nu waʿă - né-nu ki én ba-nu ba - nu maʿă-
-śim ʿă - śé im - ma - nu zĕ - da - qa wa-
-he - sed ʿă - śé im - ma- nu zĕdaqa wa - ḥe- sed
wĕ - ho - ši - ʿé - nu ʿă- -ʿé - nu.
1.
2.

The *Avinu Malkenu* prayer is an outstanding characteristic of the High Holy Day period. A custom has developed for the entire congregation to sing the last stanza to a plaintive melody, the notation of which is shown here.

are traditional and very distinctive particularly in the Ashkenazi rite. For some *piyyutim* the ark is opened and the congregation stands; the choice of the *piyyutim* for which this is done seems to be arbitrary. There are different *piyyutim* for each of the two days of Rosh Ha-Shanah. Because of the somber atmosphere of judgment, the festive *Hallel* is not recited.

AVINU MALKENU. At the end of the *Shaḥarit* service a prayer is recited that is said after the *ḥazzan's* repetition of the *Amidah* at every *Shaḥarit* and *Minḥah* for the Ten Days of Penitence; on Yom Kippur itself it is recited at the *Ne'ilah* service instead of *Minḥah*. It is also recited in some rites on fast days. Each line begins with the words *Avinu Malkenu* (Our Father, Our King), and ends with a petition. The number and order of the verses vary considerably in the different rites: in *Seder Rav Amram Gaon* there are 25 verses, in the Sephardi rite 29, 31 and 32, the German 38, the Polish 44, and in that of Salonika 53. According to one medieval authority Amram Gaon's *Avinu Malkenu* consisted of 22 verses arranged in alphabetical order. The prayer is not found in the prayer books of Saadiah Gaon and Maimonides. The origin of *Avinu Malkenu* is Rabbi Akiva's prayer on a fast day proclaimed because of a drought: "*Avinu Malkenu,* we have no King but Thee; *Avinu Malkenu,* for Thy sake have compassion upon us." Other such litanies containing some of the same petitions but opening with *Avinu she-ba-Sha-mayim* ("Our Father who art in Heaven") are still in use in some rites. *Avinu Malkenu* now opens, in the Ashkenazi rite, with "Our Father, our King, we have sinned before Thee" and contains petitions such as "Inscribe us in the book of good life; inscribe us in the book of redemption and salvation; inscribe us in the book of prosperity and sustenance." In the *Ne'ilah* service of the Day of Atonement "seal us" is substituted for "inscribe us," and on fast days "remember us" is used. In the Ashkenazi rite *Avinu Malkenu* is not recited on the Sabbath, since supplications should not be presented on that day. If the Day of Atonement occurs on a Sabbath, *Avinu Malkenu* is recited only during the *Ne'ilah* service. In Spain, though, it was the custom to recite it on the Sabbath of the Ten Days of Penitence, presumably on the grounds that this was warranted by the gravity of the period. Originally, the words *Avinu Malkenu* were chanted by the congregation and the rest of each verse was recited by the Reader who could add verses freely. It became the custom for the congregation to recite the whole prayer in an undertone except for some of the middle verses, which are repeated individually after the Reader. In many congregations the last verse is sung to a popular tune. The ark is opened for the prayer. The opening appeal to God as both "Our Father" and "Our King" expresses two complementary aspects of the relationship between God and man, striking a balance between the intimacy of the one and the awe of the other.

The Torah Reading. On Rosh Ha-Shanah a special plaintive melody is used for the Torah readings. On the first day Genesis 21 is read and on the second, Genesis 22. These two chapters tell the story of the birth of the patriarch, Isaac, and his binding by his father Abraham. According to tradition, both of these events took place on Rosh Ha-Shanah and the *Akedat Yizḥak,* the Binding of Isaac, is a theme of many of the prayers and *piyyutim*. It is on the merit of Abraham's willingness to sacrifice his son that their descendents beg mercy in spite of their own sins. On the first day, the *haftarah* is I Samuel 1:1–2:10 which parallels the Torah reading with the story of the birth of the prophet Samuel and on the second day the *haftarah* is Jeremiah 31:2–20, a passage full of hope for Israel's ultimate redemption.

The main feature of the two days of Rosh Ha-Shanah is the sounding of the *shofar*. The Oriental Jew performing the *mitzvah* is obviously completely absorbed in the act. Ben Shahn's mosaic mural "The Call of the Shofar" (1959) is in the vestibule of Temple Ohabai Shalom, Nashville, Tennessee. The artist sees the sound of the *shofar* as a symbol of the brotherhood of man.

The Shofar. The essential ritual of Rosh Ha-Shanah is the sounding of the *shofar*. The Mishnah rules that the horn of any animal (e.g. sheep, goat, antelope), except the cow, may be used as a *shofar* on Rosh Ha-Shanah. One of the reasons why the horn of a cow is not used is its reference to the golden calf and a "prosecuting counsel cannot act for the defense." At a later period, the ram's horn was preferred in order to recall the Binding of Isaac for whom a ram was substituted. It is considered meritorious to use a curved *shofar*, symbolic of man bowing in submission to God's will. The silence of the Scriptures as to why the horn is blown on this day left room for a wide variety of interpretations among later teachers. There are ten frequently quoted reasons, which scholars have attributed to Saadiah Gaon: (1) Trumpets are sounded at a coronation and God is hailed as King on this day. (2) The *shofar* heralds the beginning of the penitential season (from Rosh Ha-Shanah to the Day of Atonement). (3) The Torah was given on Sinai accompanied by blasts of the *shofar*. (4) The prophets compare their message to the sound of the *shofar*. (5) The conquering armies that destroyed the Temple sounded trumpet blasts. (6) The ram was substituted for Isaac. (7) The prophet asks: "Shall the horn be blown in a city, and the people not tremble?" (Amos 3:6). (8) The prophet Zephaniah speaks of the great "day of the Lord" (Judgment Day) as a "day of the horn and alarm" (Zephaniah 1:14–16). (9) The prophet Isaiah speaks of the great *shofar* which will herald the messianic age (Isaiah 27:13). (10) The *shofar* will be sounded at the resurrection. Maimonides writes: "Although it is a divine decree that we blow the *shofar* on Rosh Ha-Shanah, a hint of the following idea is contained in the command. It is as if to say: 'Awake from your slumbers, ye who have fallen asleep in life, and reflect on your deeds. Remember your Creator. Be not of those who miss reality in the pursuit of shadows, and waste their years in seeking after vain things which neither profit nor save. Look well to your souls and improve your character. Forsake each of you his evil ways and thoughts.'"

On Rosh Ha-Shanah, Psalm 47 is recited seven times before the sounding of the *shofar*. This is symbolic of the seven circuits that the Israelites made around Jericho before the wall fell down at the blasts of the *shofar*, and of the seven heavens through which prayers must penetrate in order to reach the throne of God. There are two series of blasts: for the first, which is sounded before the *Musaf*, the congregation may sit before they rise to hear it, and hence it is called *teki'ot meyushav* ("sitting *teki'ot*"; to distinguish it from the second series, which is heard during the *Musaf Amidah*, for which the congregation has been standing all the time). This first series is preceded by two benedictions: (1) "Blessed art Thou O Lord our God King of the universe, Who has sanctified us by Thy commandments and has instructed us to hear the call of the *shofar*"; (2) "Blessed art Thou . . . Who has kept us in life, has sustained us and privileged us to reach this season of the year." The second series, the *teki'ot me'ummad* ("standing *teki'ot*") is heard three times during the reader's repetition of the *Musaf*

(in the Sephardi rite also in the silent *Amidah*) at the conclusion of each one of its major sections (*Malkhuyyot*—the kingship of God; *Zikhronot*—the remembrance of the merit of our ancestors; and *Shofarot*—hope for the coming of the Messianic Era to be ushered in by the sound of the *shofar*). Each time a series of ten notes is sounded. At the end of the *Musaf* service another series of 30 notes is sounded and, to round out the number to 100, a further ten notes are blown.

The *shofar* may be sounded only in the daytime. Women and children are exempt from the commandment to listen to it, but such is its place in the Rosh Ha-Shanah ritual that nearly all do. When Rosh Ha-Shanah occurs on the Sabbath, the *shofar* is not blown, the traditional reason being "lest he carry it (the *shofar*) from one domain to another (in violation of the Sabbath)." When the Temple stood it was sounded there even on the Sabbath, but not elsewhere. After the destruction of the Temple, Johanan ben Zakkai permitted its use on the Sabbath in a town where an ordained *bet din* sat. This, however, is not the normal practice in our times. The congregant sounding the *shofar* is called a *ba'al teki'ah* and anyone capable of doing so is permitted to blow it. The prompter, or caller, is the *makri*.

The particular *shofar* sounds blown on Rosh Ha-Shanah have an extended development. "A day of blowing the horn" is, in Hebrew, called *yom teru'ah,* and is rendered by the Targum as *yom yabbava*. The phrase concerning the mother of Sisera who is said to have "looked through the window" (*va-teyabbev;* Judges 5:28) is interpreted by the rabbis as "and she wept." Hence the *shofar* blast is said to be a weeping sound. According to rabbinic tradition, however, the *teru'ah-yabbava* sound must always be followed and preceded by an extended, unbroken note, *teki'ah.* Since there are three references to the *teru'ah-yabbava* sound, it follows that three *teru'ah-yabbava* sounds are required, each preceded and followed by a *teki'ah.* There are doubts as to whether the weeping sound means three groaning notes (*shevarim*) or a series of nine very short wailing notes (*teru'ah*). Is the biblical *teru'ah-yabbava,* then, a *shevarim* note, or a *teru'ah* note, or both together? In order to eliminate all doubt, the practice arose, and is still followed, of sounding all three notes. The order became:

teki'ah shevarim teru'ah teki'ah (3 times)
teki'ah shevarim teki'ah (3 times)
teki'ah teru'ah teki'ah (3 times)

The final *teki'ah* is especially long and drawn out, and is known as *teki'ah gedolah,* "the great *teki'ah.*"

The sounding of the *shofar* in the synagogue is an occasion of great solemnity at which God is entreated to show mercy to His creatures. The Midrash remarks: "Rabbi Josiah said: It is written: 'Happy is the people that know the sound of the trumpet' (Psalms 89:16). Do not the nations of the world know how to sound the trumpet? They have numerous horns, sirens and trumpets, and yet it is said: 'Happy is the people

This page from the *Great Maḥzor of Amsterdam* (13th/14th century Germany) shows the beginning of the *U-Netanneh Tokef piyyut.* It also contains intonation signs for the sounding of the *shofar* which are quite common in manuscript prayerbooks but rare in printed ones.

that know the sound of the trumpet.' This means that Israel is the people which knows how to win over their Creator with the blasts of the *shofars* so that He rises from His throne of judgment to His throne of mercy and is filled with compassion for them and turns His quality of judgment into the quality of compassion."

Musaf. After the Torah scrolls have been returned to the ark, the *ḥazzan* recites a special prayer that his rendering of the *Musaf* should be acceptable to God and that he should prove worthy of his mission to represent the congregation in this fateful hour. This prayer, *Hineni He-Ani Mi-Ma'as,* "Behold, I the poor in deeds . . .," is recited only on Rosh Ha-Shanah and Yom Kippur and in it the *ḥazzan* confesses his imperfection and prays that he be worthy despite his own shortcomings to be the congregation's delegate to bring its supplications before God. The prayer, of anonymous authorship, originated in Europe during the Middle Ages, and is recited to a somber melody which is traditional in all Ashkenazi communities. In the Reform ritual main parts from it were chosen as *The Rabbi's Prayer,* to be recited at his discretion.

TEKI'ATA. The contents of the *Musaf* service for Rosh Ha-Shanah are already described in the Mishnah. According to that source the *Musaf* should contain a central body of three benedictions, each of which is to be made up of ten verses from the Bible in a certain order. Thus altogether, the *Musaf Amidah* contains nine benedictions. The first of these central three is called *Malkhuyyot* and celebrates the sovereign kingship of God. *Zikhronot,* the second of the series, praises God who remembers everything and begs Him to remember the good deeds of the patriarchs, particularly the Binding of Isaac. The last of the series is called *Shofarot* and describes the events that have—and will—take place to the sound of the *shofar*. During the repetition of the *Musaf Amidah,* the *shofar* is sounded at the end of each of these benedictions. In some rites, it is also sounded at these points in the silent recitation. The benedictions are thus known as *Teki'ata,* from the note *teki'ah* which is sounded.

The *teki'ata* are first mentioned in the Mishnah of Rosh Ha-Shanah. According to the first opinion of the Mishnah, each of the series comprises ten verses—three from the Pentateuch, three from the Prophets, three from the Hagiographa, and a final verse from the Prophets. Another view expressed in the Mishnah, that of Yose ben Ḥalafta, is that the final verse may also be from the Pentateuch. Rabbi Johanan ben Nuri maintained that each *teki'ata* should contain only three verses—one from the Pentateuch, one from the Prophets, and one from the Hagiographa. Halakhic practice conforms to Yose ben Ḥalafta's opinion; and each *teki'ata* contains ten verses, the final one being from the Pentateuch. The Ashkenazi and French custom differs, however, in that the hagiographic verses in each series precede those from the Prophets. In the course of time, introductory *piyyutim* were added to the *teki'ata*: *Aleinu le-Shabbe'aḥ* and *Ve-Al Ken Nekavveh* before the *malkhuyyot. Attah Zokher* before the *zikhronot,* and *Attah Nigleita* before the *shofarot*. These introductions are attributed to Rav (second and third centuries C.E.) and are therefore called *Teki'ata de-Rav* or *Teki'ata de-Vei Rav.*

In the age of the *paytanim* more *piyyutim* were added, corresponding to the theme of each *teki'ata.* It may be assumed that these *piyyutim* were first used as alternatives to those of Rav, but eventually both old and new were incorporated jointly into the liturgy. The oldest *piyyutim* are those of Yose ben Yose (fourth or fifth century C.E.). Saadiah Gaon praised them in his *siddur* stating that he chose them in preference to all others. They have been adopted into the Ashkenazi and French rites; and so also have the *piyyutim* of Eleazar Kallir. *Teki'ata* by Solomon ibn Gabirol beginning *Ansikhah malki* are also well known. Several *teki'ata* were discovered in the Cairo *Genizah,* outstanding among them being those composed by a Palestinian *paytan,* Mishael, who lived after Kallir; and still other *teki'ata* exist in manuscript.

U-NETANNEH TOKEF. Of the *piyyutim* added in the *ḥazzan's* repetition of the *Musaf Amidah,* perhaps the best known is *U-Netanneh Tokef,* "Let us declare the mighty importance [of the holiness of this day] . . ." It is recited before the *Kedushah* of the *Musaf* on both Rosh Ha-Shanah and Yom Kippur and it epitomizes the significance of the High Holy Days as "the day of judgment" on which all creatures pass, one by one,

before God, like a flock before the shepherd who decrees their fate. It emphasizes man's precarious and painful lot and his futile strivings. Following an enumeration of the manifold fates which may be decreed for a man during the year to come, the prayer, however, goes on to stress the belief that "repentance, prayer and charity avert the severe decree"; God is full of forgiveness toward man who "came from dust and who shall return to dust" and whose days are "as a fleeting shadow, as a passing cloud . . . and as a dream that vanishes." Because this prayer, in simple yet very expressive words, voices the basic idea of the Day of Judgment, it came to be one of the most popular pieces in the High Holy Day liturgy. In the Ashkenazi liturgy of Rosh Ha-Shanah (and in its eastern branch, of the Day of Atonement also), the recital of the hymn is invested with great solemnity. In some traditional *maḥzorim* an instruction is given in Yiddish at a certain point: "This is where you should cry." It has been adapted by many Sephardi communities of the Mediterranean, in some of which it is recited before *Musaf* in a Ladino translation. It is also in the Italian rite. Written in its present form by Kalonymus ben Meshullam Kalonymus, the 11th-century *paytan* of Mayence, a well-known legend ascribes it to Amnon of Mainz. *U-Netanneh Tokef* is actually older; for it is found in old liturgical manuscripts and in *Genizah* fragments. It apparently derives from a very early Palestinian prayer which was later attributed to Amnon.

Amnon of Mainz (tenth century) was a martyr and legendary figure. He is known mainly through Isaac ben Moses of Vienna (12th–13th century) who quotes Ephraim ben Jacob (12th century) as speaking of Amnon as "a leader of his generation, wealthy, of distinguished ancestry, and pleasing appearance." The legend is that after repeated attempts by the bishop of Mainz to persuade Amnon to accept Christianity, he finally asked for three days to consider the matter. His conscience troubled, Amnon failed to appear at the appointed time and was brought by force. Asked why he had failed to keep his promise, Amnon pleaded guilty and requested that his tongue should be cut out for not refusing at once. The bishop thereupon replied: "Not your tongue, but your legs, which did not bring you at the agreed time." Amnon's legs and arms were barbarously amputated, and salt poured on the wounds. However, he bore the torture with fortitude. He was brought back to his home, and on Rosh Ha-Shanah was carried into the synagogue. As the *Kedushah* prayer was about to be recited Amnon asked the *ḥazzan* to wait while he "sanctified the great name (of God)," and thereupon recited the hymn "*U-Netanneh Tokef Kedushat ha-Yom*" ("Let us tell the mighty holiness of this day"), after which he died. Three days afterward, he appeared in a dream to Kalonymus ben Meshullam and taught him the entire prayer, asking him to circulate it throughout the Diaspora for recital in synagogues on Rosh Ha-Shanah. This legend, which gained wide credence during the time of the Crusades, inspired many to martyrdom. In Johanan Treves' commentary on the Roman *maḥzor* (Bologna, 1540) and in various editions of the Ashkenazi rite, the story is repeated with slight changes.

Tashlikh. On the afternoon of the first day of Rosh Ha-Shanah, towards evening, a special ceremony, called *Tashlikh,* "Thou

shalt cast," is held near a sea or a running stream. When the first day occurs on the Sabbath, the ceremony is deferred to the second day, to ensure that no prayer book be carried to the riverside on the Sabbath. The name itself is derived from Micah 7:19: "Thou shalt cast all their sins into the depths of the sea." The core of the ceremony is the recitation of Micah 7:18–20. Psalms 118:5–9; 33; 130; and Isaiah 11:9 are added in some rites. Kabbalists added quotations from the *Zohar* and there were other variants in different communities (e.g. in Kurdistan Jews actually entered the water; in certain parts of Bulgaria the ceremony was performed on the afternoon of the Day of Atonement).

The origin of the custom— not mentioned by talmudic, geonic, or early authorities—is uncertain. Some scholars sug-

Two scenes of the *tashlikh* ceremony. Ideally the ceremony should be performed near running water. However, many of the residents of Tel Aviv go to the beach and perform the ceremony there. Others perform it near any body of water, even at a cistern.

gest a pagan origin. There is no direct reference to the custom, however, until Jacob Moellin (died 1427) explains it as a reminder of the midrashic tale of Abraham's refusal to be deterred from his mission to sacrifice Isaac even after Satan had transformed himself into a brook obstructing his path. Other authorities suggest that, as fish never close their eyes, so the ceremony is symbolic of God's eyes, ever-open; or, as the fate of fish is uncertain, so is the ceremony illustrative of man's plight. Moses Isserles saw the ceremony as a tribute to the Creator, to Whose work of creation (this actually starting on Rosh Ha-Shanah) the fish were the first witnesses. Thus it was recommended that the ceremony be performed on the banks of a river where living fish are found. However, when this is impossible the ceremony is performed even by a well of water as is customary in Jerusalem.

The custom of shaking out the pockets of one's garments during the ceremony is popularly taken as a rite of transferring the sins to the fish, but other authorities connect it with the talmudic saying that cleanliness of garments is a sign of moral purity. To feed the fish during the ceremony, however, is forbidden. Oriental-Sephardi Jews have practiced the custom since the time of Isaac Luria in the 16th century.

THE DAY OF ATONEMENT

The theme of Yom ha-Kippurim (or Yom Kippur as it is popularly known) is clear from its name. Although man can atone for his sins throughout the whole year, this day is especially auspicious for repentance. One talmudic sage was of the opinion that the very day itself atones for sin irrespective of whether the sinner repents or not. Although this interpretation was not accepted, and the general view is that the day is not efficacious without a spiritual effort, it is believed that repentance is more readily accepted on high on the Day of Atonement. In the Bible the day is described as the "Sabbath of Sabbaths" and thus all the laws of an ordinary Sabbath apply on it; the normal penalties for transgression, however, are suspended and the punishment is "in the hands of heaven."

Yom Kippur is the holiest day of the year; most of the day—if not all of it—is spent in the synagogue. Since it is a fast day on which all labor is prohibited, there is no need to take the length of the services into account and so it is on this day that most *piyyutim* are recited. The officiants in the synagogue—and many of the congregants—wear white robes, known as the *kitel,* which is the shroud in which the Jew is buried. Besides symbolizing the purity that man seeks after on this day, the ultimate death of every man is evoked thus contributing to an atmosphere of contrition. On this day the wearing of leather shoes is forbidden, which too adds a quietness to the synagogue. Many explanations have been offered for this prohibition; perhaps the most appealing is that when man begs for forgiveness he should not stand on the skin of another living creature.

The prayers on Yom Kippur are recited to traditional melodies which are very well known to the congregants and, on more than any other occasion, they participate and help the *ḥazzan* along. As far as the statutory prayers are concerned, Yom Kippur is outstanding because it contains the last vestige of the *Ne'ilat She'arim* service which in ancient times was recited on every fast day. However, because of the various types of *piyyutim* and confessional prayers recited, the liturgy of Yom Kippur stands by itself.

Kapparot. On the day before Yom Kippur the *Hattarat Nedarim* ceremony which was described in the Rosh Ha-Shanah section is observed by some. In the past a widespread ritual was the *Kapparot,* "Expiation," a ceremony in which the sins of a person are symbolically transferred to a fowl. The custom is practiced in certain Orthodox circles also on the day before Rosh Ha-Shanah or on Hoshana Rabba. Psalms 107:10, 14, 17–21, and Job 33:23–24 are recited; then a cock (for a male) or a hen (for a female) is swung around the head three times while the following is pronounced: "This is my substitute, my vicarious offering, my atonement; this cock (or hen) shall meet death, but I shall find a long and pleasant life of peace." The fowl is thought to take on any misfortune which might otherwise befall a person in punishment of his sins. After the ceremony, it is customary to donate the fowl to the poor, except for the intestines which are thrown to the birds. Some rabbis

Eve of Yom Kippur scene depicted in a woodcut which appeared in *Der ganz Judische Glaub*, Augsburg 1530. The upper part is a depiction of the *kapparot* ceremony, whereas the lower seems to be a pre-holiday immersion in the *mikveh* and the final meal before the fast. Another depiction of the *kapparot* is the oil painting by Jesekiel David Kirszenbaum (1900–1954), an artist of the Paris school.

recommended that money, equivalent to the fowl's value, be given instead.

This custom is nowhere mentioned in the Talmud. It appears first in the writings of the *geonim* of the 9th century, who explain that a cock is used in the ritual because the word *gever* means both "man" and "cock"; the latter can, therefore, substitute for the former. In Babylonia, other animals were used, expecially the ram since Abraham offered a ram in lieu of his son Isaac, or plants, e.g. beans, peas. After the destruction of the Temple, no animals used in sacrificial rites could serve similar purposes outside the Temple, and therefore cocks or hens were employed in the *Kapparot* because they were not used in the Temple sacrifical cult. Solomon ben Abraham Adret, one of the outstanding rabbinic authorities of 13th-century Spain, strongly opposed *Kapparot* because it was similar to the biblical atonement rites; he also considered the ritual be a heathen superstition. This opinion was shared by other authorities who called the *Kapparot* "a stupid custom." The kabbalists, however, invested the custom with mystical interpretations. These appealed strongly to the masses, and it became very popular when the rabbis acquiesced to it. Isserles made it a compulsory rite and enjoined for it many ceremonials similar to those of the sacrifical cult; e.g., the laying of the hands upon the animal, its immediate slaughter after the ceremony, prayers of confession, etc.

If a cock, or hen, cannot be obtained, other animals, fish or geese, may be used instead. A white cock or hen was especially desirable but some authorities forbade the use of a white cock on the grounds that it was a pagan rite. *Kapparot* is not practiced with a fowl at all in some traditional and many modern congregations. Money is substituted for a cock and the formula is changed accordingly ("this coin shall go to charity but we . . ." etc.). In Yiddish and popular Hebrew parlance the word *kapparot* may also refer to financial or material loss, a regretted waste, or a vain effort.

Confession of Sins. In line with the motifs of repentance, one of the outstanding features of Yom Kippur is the confession of sins since without confession there can be no repentance. According to the Talmud it is sufficient for the penitent to declare: "Truly, we have sinned" but over the ages elaborate formulas have gradually evolved. Of these, two—*Ashamnu* and *Al Ḥet*—are combined and recited in every silent *Amidah* and in every reader's repetition throughout Yom Kippur.

Though statutory on "the eve of the Day of Atonement close to nightfall," confession is made both prior to the last meal before the fast ("lest he become confused while eating and drinking"), and after it ("lest some mishap occurred during the meal"), as well as at each of the Day of Atonement services, the individual saying it after the *Amidah* proper and the reader in the middle of it. Confession is now said once in the afternoon prayer on the eve of the Day of Atonement and ten times during the Day itself, although in the *Ne'ilah* service it is somewhat abbreviated.

ASHAMNU. The shorter form of confession is known by its opening word, as *Ashamnu*, "We are guilty." Besides Yom Kippur it also forms part of other penitential services, such as *Seliḥot*, the daily morning and afternoon prayers (according to most Sephardi and some Ashkenazi rites), and the prayer service recited on the day preceding the New Moon, according to the Ashkenazi rite. Its origin is in the confession recited by the high priest on the Day of Atonement. In later periods it was expanded in the more elaborate medieval style. The *Ashamnu* confession lists trespasses of a moral nature only and consists of 24 or more words in alphabetical order, the last letter of the Hebrew alphabet being repeated three times. In the Reform ritual *Ashamnu* appears in an abridged form.

The melody of *Kol Nidrei* is perhaps the best-known of all synagogue music. It is highly evocative for all Jews, even those farthest removed from religious observance. In fact this music has, to some extent, become the symbol of Jewish music.

Ashamnu is also used as the form of confession at the approach of death as well as by the bridegroom and bride before their wedding, that day being considered a sort of "Day of Atonement" for them.

Al Ḥet. The longer confession is called *Al Ḥet* after the first words, "For the sin [we have sinned] . . ." of each of its 53 lines. It is not recited at the *Ne'ilah* service.

Al Ḥet contains a list of sins in alphabetical order, two sins being allotted to every letter. After the forty-four sins in alphabetical order, another nine lines are added enumerating sins according to their prescribed punishments. The recitation is divided into four parts. After each, the formula, "And for all these, O God of forgiveness, forgive us, pardon us, grant us atonement," is chanted during the reader's repetition. The list of sins embraces the specific (e.g. unchastity) and the general (e.g. those committed "unwittingly"), but sins of a ritual nature are not included. The whole confession, like the *Ashamnu,* is in the first person plural, perhaps as an expression of the doctrine of collective responsibility.

The authorship of the *Al Ḥet* is unknown. It is first mentioned in the *She'iltot* of Aḥai Gaon (eighth century) and an abbreviated and probably more original form is found in the *Seder Rav Amram.* The Christian *Didache* (second century) also contains traces of an earlier Jewish alphabetical confession suggesting that this arrangement is very ancient. In the Sephardi rite the alphabetical arrangement is only one letter for each sin, but in some this is followed by a reverse-order alphabetical arrangement. The Yemenites use a shortened version. There are many textual variants of *Al Ḥet* according to different rites. It is customary to recite *Al Ḥet* while standing with the head bowed, and to beat one's breast at the mention of each sin. In Reform usage the *Al Ḥet* has been considerably shortened.

Kol Nidrei. The evening service for Yom Kippur is preceded by a liturgical ceremony known as *Kol Nidrei* "All the vows," and because of its hold on the popular imagination the whole evening service is generally called by that name.

In *Kol Nidrei* the worshipers proclaim—in Aramaic—that all personal vows, oaths, etc., that they made unwittingly, rashly, or unknowingly (and that, consequently, cannot be fulfilled) during the year should be considered null and void. The recitation must begin while it is still daylight and must be prolonged until sunset. Since the Middle Ages the *tallit* is put on before the service and worn till the end of *Ma'ariv.* It is the custom to repeat *Kol Nidrei* three times in order to accommodate latecomers. In *Kol Nidrei* only vows affecting the self, i.e. vows made between man and God are comprehended. Not formally a prayer, *Kol Nidrei* nevertheless became

Left: An illuminated Rosh Ha-Shanah *piyyut* showing the blowing of the *shofar* and a ram caught in a thicket, representing the binding of Isaac by Abraham. From Volume II of the *Leipzig Maḥzor*, South Germany, c. 1320. Leipzig, University Library.
Below: "Yom Kippur," a Day of Awe in which man's fate for the coming year is sealed, is depicted in this stirring painting by Leopold Pilichowski. Mishkan le-Omanut, Kibbutz Ein Harod.

Left: "Jews at Prayer on the Day of Atonement" by Maurcycy Gottlieb, 1878. Tel Aviv Museum.
Below: This four-dimensional painting is the conception of Yaacov Agam, a modern Israeli artist, of "Rosh Ha-Shanah." The illustration shows three different views of the same painting.

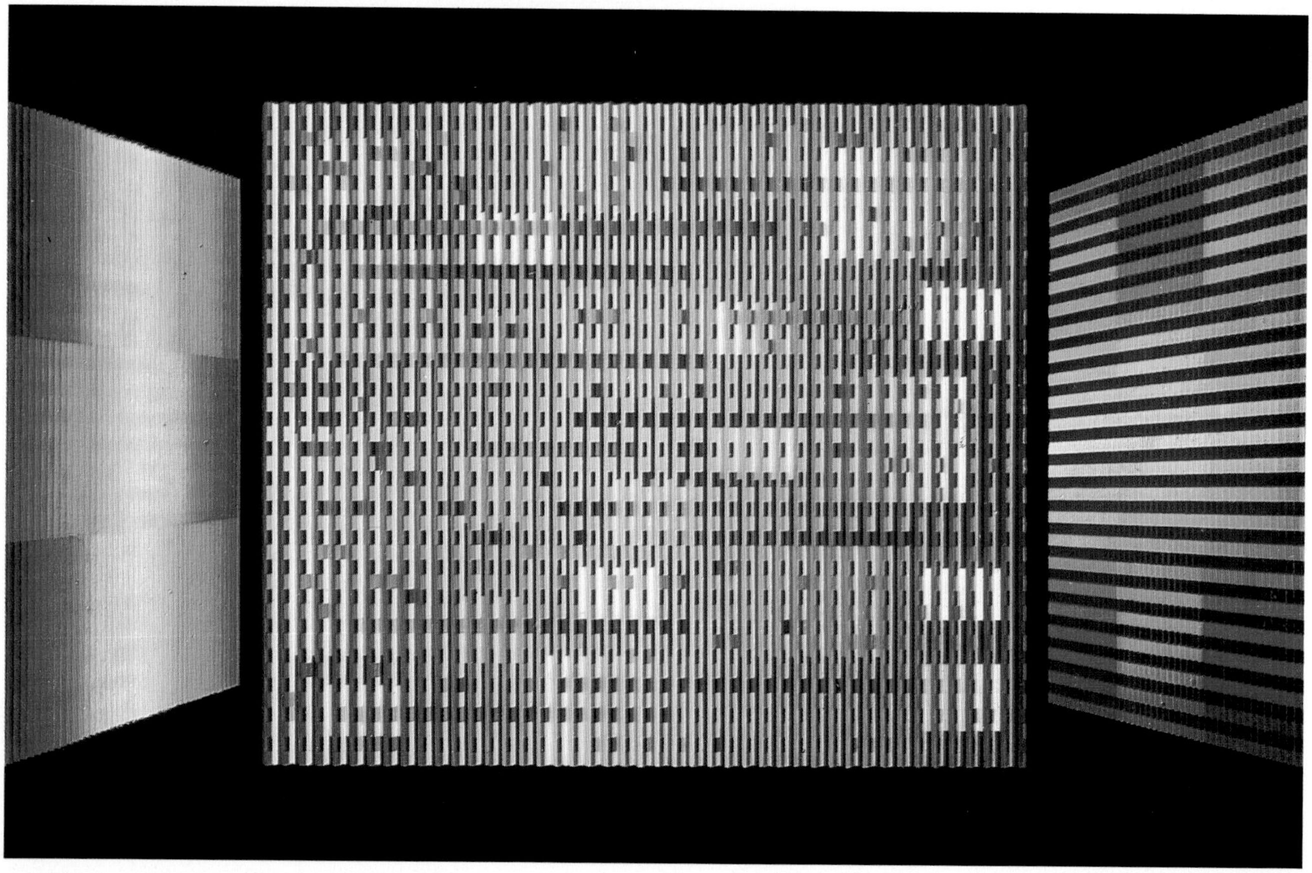

The *shofar* has taken on varying shapes and sizes in different Jewish communities throughout the ages. The detail from a page of the *Rothschild Miscellany*, written and illuminated in Ferrara, c. 1470, shows a man blowing the *shofar* for women listeners. The inscription reads *Avinu Malkeinu*, "Our Father, Our King," from the High Holy Day liturgy. Jerusalem, Israel Museum. The Ashkenazi *shofar* and method of blowing are illustrated in the photograph taken at the Western Wall in Jerusalem; also at the Western Wall is a Yemenite Jew blowing a spiral *shofar* in the typical Sephardi manner. The *shofar*-maker of Haifa shown apparently caters primarily for the Ashkenazi trade. Photos Werner Braun, Jerusalem.

Top left: Rosh Ha-Shanah plate from Delft, Holland, c. 1700, used for the apple dipped in honey which is eaten during the festival as a portent for a sweet year. New York, Jewish Museum.
Bottom left: Decorated earthenware plate from Delft, 18th century, used to serve the *ḥallah* and honey eaten during the festive meal preceding the Yom Kippur fast. One of the Hebrew words is misspelled. Jerusalem, Israel Museum.
Right: The *kapparot* ceremony on the eve of the Day of Atonement is performed in this picture by a father over his son in Safed, 1972. In this ceremony the sins of a person are symbolically transferred to a fowl, which is waved around the head. Photo Werner Braun, Jerusalem.

the most beloved ritual of the Day of Atonement. It alleviated anxiety which was especially intense in the Rosh Ha-Shanah season because of possible violation of the sanctity of pledges. Sensitive to inherent juridical and ethical difficulties, the rabbis set definite conditions and restrictions on the annulment procedure. Vows could only be abrogated by a *bet din* or by an expert scholar, after careful investigation of their nature and bearing. The Mishnah permits the nullification of the vows of an individual; its extension to an entire community, however, taxed the ingenuity of later authorities and aroused bitter controversy.

The origins of *Kol Nidrei* are unknown; none of the many theories is conclusive. The first reference to *Kol Nidrei* as a collective declaration is found in the responsa of the Babylonian *geonim* (beginning in the eighth century). It is stated that *Kol Nidrei* was familiar to them from "other lands"; but the *geonim* (especially of Sura) sharply condemned it for many generations. The "other lands" are not identified. An obvious possibility is Palestine, yet none of the extant sources of the old Palestinian liturgy has *Kol Nidrei*. Some scholars nevertheless contended that congregational recitation of *Kol Nidrei* originated in Palestine, as a reaction to Karaite attacks on the Rabbanite practice. Another suggested that the *geonim* opposed *Kol Nidrei* because of possible innovations by mystical circles for whom it assuaged a magic fear of vows that might have been unwittingly broken, while still another, citing parallel Aramaic formulas found inscribed on incantation bowls from the time of talmudic Babylonia, proposed that the original function of *Kol Nidrei* had been "the annulment of curses or oaths . . . that touch off evil forces in the community."

The *geonim* of Pumbedita were more lenient than those of Sura, probably in response to popular demand. About the time of Hai Gaon (c. 1000 C.E.), general acceptance had been gained for a *Kol Nidrei* formula; it invoked divine "pardon, forgiveness, and atonement" for the sin of failing to keep a solemn vow (or, possibly, for having vowed at all). The period envisioned was "from the previous Day of Atonement until this Day of Atonement." The tosafists of 12th-century France and Germany did not accept the geonic version but reworded *Kol Nidrei* as an annulment of vows which may possibly be made "from this Day of Atonement until the next Day of Atonement." This (Aramaic) version has remained standard for Ashkenazim. The geonic (Hebrew) version was adopted by the Rumanian and Italian rites. Western Sephardim recite only the geonic text referring to vows of the past year, while oriental Sephardim and Yemenites add in that of the tosafists.

Anti-Semites have frequently taken *Kol Nidrei* as evidence that the oath of a Jew is worthless. In the Disputation in Paris in 1240 it was attacked by Nicholas Donin and defended by Rabbi Jehiel ben Joseph. Suspicion about the effects of *Kol Nidrei* on testimony given by Jews influenced the wording of the *more judaico*, the special oath that Jews were forced to take in medieval courts. It appeared too in the attacks of anti-Semitic writers such as Eisenmenger, Buxtorf, and Wagensei. To counteract these accusations, Jewish apologists have cited the severe limitations that the *halakhah* has imposed on *Kol Nidrei*. In 1860 a Hebrew introduction to *Kol Nidrei* was included in prayer books in Russia on the recommendation of a rabbinic commission. It explained that *Kol Nidrei* was not meant to apply to oaths taken before courts of law. In Germany in 1844, a synod of the Reform movement recommended that *Kol Nidrei* be expunged from the liturgy; later Reformers, however, offered substitute versions. The 1961 edition of the Reform Union Prayer Book (U.S.) restored the full Aramaic text. *Kol Nidrei*'s persistent popularity is partly attributed to emotional factors, especially in association with Jewish martyrdom.

MUSICAL RENDITION. The standard Ashkenazi melody for *Kol Nidrei* is deservedly famous as a superior example of the musical tradition of the Diaspora, and, with much justification, of "Jewish music" as such. It is not a melody in the conventional sense, but an artistic concatenation of motifs, stylistically related to the general melodic conventions of the High Holy Days. The motifs alternate between solemn syllabic "proclamations" as in the opening, intensely devotional wave-like phrases, and virtuoso vocal runs. It may even be asked whether the musical rendition of *Kol Nidrei* was shaped by the solemnity of the liturgical and ideological status of the

The beginning of the *Avodah* service from a manuscript prayerbook written in Fez, Morocco, in the 15th century. The page shows the "permission *piyyut*" (*reshut*) recited before the actual service. The belt buckle was specially created to be worn on Yom Kippur over the *kitel*. It is of silver and the inscription is the central motif of the day: "For on this day He shall atone for you to purify you from all your sins. Before the Lord shall you be cleansed."

prayer, or whether the latter did not come about in a great measure, at least, during the last two centuries, through the extraordinary effect of the melody. The source of the melody is still a subject of research, and the frequent attempts to relate it to Sephardi traditions (because of the presumed connections of the text with the Spanish Marranos) are highly hypothetical. In the Sephardi traditions *Kol Nidrei* is rendered by the entire congregation, which alternates with the *ḥazzan,* and the rendition is, therefore, more syllabic in character: there seems to be no standard melody common to the entire Sephardi Diaspora. In the Carpentras (Provencal rite) the *Kol Nidrei* is said in a whisper and therefore has no melody.

The Ashkenazi version of *Kol Nidrei* was arranged in 1880 by the non-Jewish composer Max Bruch for cello and orchestra, on commission from the Jewish community of Liverpool, and it became his most popular work. Arnold Schoenberg's *Kol Nidrei* for speaker, chorus, and orchestra, opus 39 (1938) is based on a text by Jacob Sonderling, and some of the traditional motifs are reworked there in Schoenberg's twelve-tone technique. The text itself, written in close collaboration with the composer, is a personal philosophic reinterpretation of the prayer.

Shir Ha-Yiḥud. After the *Amidah* of *Ma'ariv,* a *Seliḥot* service is recited. This consists of several *piyyutim* which alternate with the recitation of the 13 attributes of God. At the end of the *Seliḥot,* the confession is recited. In many communities it is customary to recite the *Shir Ha-Yiḥud,* "Hymn of [God's] Unity" at the end of the statutory service. This is a lengthy medieval liturgical poem divided into seven parts, one for each day of the week, praising God, extolling His uniqueness, and emphasizing the smallness of His creatures. Poetic beauty and sublimity of religious thought have placed the poem among the foremost liturgical compositions. Each line is divided into rhymed couplets, with four repeats in each couplet. From the fourth line on, each verse throughout the remainder of the poem contains 16 syllables. The first three lines serve as an introduction, a free translation of which reads:

I will sing to my God as long as I live,
The God who has sustained me all through my life,
To this day Thou hast taken me by the hand,
Life and loving kindness hast Thou given me.
Blessed be the Lord, blessed be His glorious name,
For His wondrous kindness shown to His servant.

The identity of the author is uncertain and no trace of his name is to be found in any acrostical combination in the poem. One scholar ascribes its authorship to Samuel ben Kalonymus he-Ḥasid, the father of Judah he-Ḥasid of Regensburg, the founder of the medieval mystical sect, Ḥasidei Ashkenaz.

Originally, the appropriate portion of the *Shir ha-Yiḥud* was recited in many congregations after the conclusion of the daily service. Some congregations only recited it on the Sabbath. Its elimination from the daily and Sabbath services was probably due to the desire not to lengthen the service unduly, though some authorities also quoted the talmudic dictum that no mortal is capable of properly praising the Almighty. "It is as if an earthly king had a million denarii of gold, and someone praised him as possessing silver ones. Would it not be an insult to him?" A custom of the pious was to remain awake in the synagogue the whole night reciting the Book of Psalms.

Shaḥarit. Like all the other services of Yom Kippur, *Shaḥarit* is embellished with many *piyyutim* which vary in the different rites. As on Rosh Ha-Shanah the *Shaḥarit ḥazzan* takes over the service at the word *Ha-Melekh* and the *piyyutim* begin after *Barekhu.*

The Torah Reading. Six men are called to the reading of the Torah which is the description of the Yom Kippur sacrificial ritual in Leviticus 16. A seventh person is called to the *Maftir* which is Numbers 29:7–11 which deals with the *Musaf* sacrifice for the day. Isaiah 57:14–58:14 is the *haftarah;* it describes the ideal fast.

Avodah. After the Torah scrolls have been returned to the ark

the *ḥazzan* recites the same personal prayer as on Rosh Ha-Shanah and the *Musaf* service begins. The silent *Amidah* follows the normal structure. The third benediction is expanded as on Rosh Ha-Shanah and the central blessing celebrates Yom Kippur as a day of forgiveness. Mention is made, as usual, of the *Musaf* sacrifice. The *Amidah* ends with the confession. The *ḥazzan*'s repetition of the *Musaf* includes many *piyyutim,* some of which are also recited on Rosh Ha-Shanah and within the repetition is a kind of independent service known as the *Avodah,* "Service" which describes in *piyyut* fashion, the Yom Kippur ritual in the Temple as it is described in the Talmud.

After the destruction of the Second Temple, the description of this ancient ritual became the core of the *Musaf* service on the Day of Atonement, and in early times it was also recited during *Shaḥarit* and *Minḥah.* The Day of Atonement was the only occasion during the year when the high priest entered the Holy of Holies in the Temple, and he had to make special preparations for the ritual. Seven days prior to the Day of Atonement, the high priest was moved to a special apartment in the Temple court (*palhedrin*) where he studied with the elders every detail of the sacrificial cult for the Day of Atonement. A deputy priest was appointed to take the place of the high priest should he be prevented by defilement or death from performing his duties. The day before the Day of Atonement, the high priest was escorted by the elders to his chamber in the Temple compound where he joined the other priests. The elders earnestly entreated him to perform all the minutiae of the sacrifical cult carefully as interpreted by the Pharisaic school, and took leave of him. On the Day of Atonement, the high priest himself performed the offering of the daily sacrifice, the incense offering, and the other sacred duties. After a series of immersions and ablutions he offered a bull as his personal sin-offering. He confessed his own and his family's sins, the sins of the tribe of Aaron (the priests) and those of all Israel. Every time he uttered the holy name of God, the Tetragrammaton which was uttered only on the Day of Atonement, the people prostrated themselves and responded: "Blessed be His Name whose glorious kingdom is forever and ever."During the service of the high priest, this procedure was repeated ten times or, according to another source, 13 times.

The high priest then drew two lots from a wooden box, one inscribed "For Azazel" and the other "A sin-offering for the Lord." The role of each of two he-goats participating in the ritual was determined by the lots. The high priest sent the goat "For Azazel" into the desert and he offered the other as a sin-offering. After a special incense-offering in the Holy of Holies, the high priest recited a prayer that the climate in the coming year be moderate, neither too hot nor too wet; that the sovereignty of Judah be preserved; that Israel be prosperous; and that no earthquake harm the inhabitants of the Sharon Plain.

This traditional, and to some extent idealized, account of the ceremony served as the base for the subsequent development of the *Musaf* liturgy of the Day of Atonement. Originally, the *Avodah* was of a simple nature, being an unadorned description of the Temple service following the Mishnah. The main section was composed, at latest, in the fourth century C.E. but was enriched in the Middle Ages by elaborate *piyyutim,* most of them of an acrostic pattern. The *Avodah* texts currently in use contain compositions by Yose ben Yose, Solomon ibn Gabirol, Judah Halevi, and Moses ibn Ezra. The *Avodah* service, according to the Sephardi rite, opens with the *piyyut* "*Attah Konanta Olam*" by an unknown *paytan,* or with an introductory poem "*Be-Or Divrei Nekholot*" (Roman rite), followed by a series of acrostics where the initial letter is repeated up to eight or even 16 times. The Piedmont rite opens with another *piyyut* entitled "*Attah Konanta Olam*" by Yose ben Yose. The Yemenite *Avodah* is similar to the Piedmont rite. In the Ashkenazi rite the Avodah opens with an introductory *piyyut,* "*Amiẓ Ko'aḥ*" by the poet Meshullam ben Kalonymus, which gives a short account of biblical history, the creation of the world, the sinfulness of the early generations, the election of the Patriarchs and of Israel, up to the priestly ritual of atonement in the Holy of Holies in the Temple. These themes are found in all of the later *Avodah* services. Next follow detailed descriptions of the sacrifical cult on the Day of Atonement in the Temple. There is also an opening

"The Day of Atonement in the Country," is the title of this lithograph by Alphons Levy. Jews who lived in small villages made every effort to get a *minyan* together for the High Holy Day services or alternatively to go to the nearest Jewish center which had a synagogue.

Avodah piyyut, called "*Asoḥe'aḥ Nifle'otekha*" found in the ancient French rite and attributed to Meshullam ben Kalonymus. In both the Ashkenazi and the Sephardi rite (but not the Yemenite), the order of the confession of the high priest is recited three times as is the response of the people: "And when the priests and the people that stood in the court (of the Temple) heard the glorious Name (of God) pronounced out of the mouth of the high priest, in holiness and purity, they knelt and prostrated themselves, and made acknowledgement to God, falling on their faces and saying: Blessed be His name, whose glorious kingdom is forever and ever." This response is recited a fourth time in the Sephardi rite. At this passage, it is still customary in the Orthodox Ashkenazi rite and in some Sephardi communities for worshipers to prostrate themselves on the floor of the synagogue.

Other parts of the *Avodah* (e.g. *Tikkanta Kol Elleh le-Khevod Aharon,* "All this didst Thou establish for the glory of Aaron" in the Sephardi and Yemenite rites) then describe in great detail the high priest's actions, including the counting of the blood-sprinklings of the sacrifices, which are recited in solemn melody "And thus he counted: One, One, and One, One and Two . . ." etc.

This elaborate poetic description of the sacrificial cult of the Day of Atonement closes with an account of the festivity which the high priest arranged for his friends in gratitude for the successful performance of the Day of Atonement ritual "in peace and without harm." After a free poetic rendition of the high priest's prayer for the welfare of the people of Israel, this section of the *Avodah* closes with the nostalgic *piyyut,* "*Ashrei Ayin Ra'atah Kol Elleh*" ("Happy is the eye that saw these glorious services . . ."), based on a hymn in Ben Sira 50.

This is followed by a series of acrostic *piyyutim* deploring the misfortune of Israel, now deprived of the Temple and its sacred cult, and subjected to the sufferings and persecutions of exile. This cycle of *piyyutim,* which closes with an ardent prayer for the reestablishment of the Holy Temple, its cult and institutions, destroyed because of the sins of Israel, is immediately followed by the penitential *Seliḥot* prayers of *Musaf,* thus linking up again with the main motif of the Day of Atonement service.

In the Reform ritual, only the confession of the high priest "*Anna Adonai Kapper Na,*" is recited, in Hebrew and the vernacular. The details of the ancient sacrificial cult are not dwelt upon and the congregation does not prostrate itself during the service. In that ritual the prayers inserted instead of the traditional *Avodah* emphasize the moral duties to which Israel has to consecrate itself anew to bring about the kingdom of God among all mankind. In the Conservative ritual, most parts of the traditional Hebrew *Avodah* service are retained, but, instead of their exact rendition in English, new meditations and prayers of contemporary relevance are inserted as well as modern interpretations of the symbolism of the ancient sacrificial cult.

MUSICAL SETTINGS. The descriptions and emotional content of the *Avodah* has always been a challenge to musical inventiveness. It was set to especially solemn melodies in many Jewish communities, for example that of Rome. The most distinguished *Avodah* tunes, however, can be heard in Ashkenazi synagogues. These possess a uniform tradition for the chapter *Ve-ha-kohanim ve-ha-am;* less distinctive tunes are given to the texts *Ve-khakh hayah omer* and *Ve-khakh hayah moneh.* In addition, the cantors of Eastern Europe used to perform their own versions of certain sections.

The *Ve-ha-kohanim* tune is common to all Ashkenazi communities, both eastern and western, and belongs to the cycle of unchangeable *Mi-Sinai* melodies. Its musical character is that of a "cantorial fantasia," in which sustained passages of vocalise are inserted between short groups of words. In *Ve-ha-kohanim,* the brief textual statements are interrupted by almost explosive coloraturas which are intended to give expression to the vision of the overwhelming power of the former atonement ritual.

Elleh Ezkerah. Following the *Avodah* service a particularly poignant *piyyut* is recited. It is called *Elleh Ezkerah,* "These, do I remember . . ." and tells the story of the ten great rabbis of the Talmud who were put to death by the Romans in the time of Hadrian, for having defied the ban on teaching Torah.

Imre Szigeti (1897–) is an Australian graphic artist known for his line drawings. "Blowing the Shofar" has a certain oriental atmosphere created by the minarets in the background. Bernard Picart in his engraving showed Yom Kippur "as it is celebrated at the German Jews." One can assume that it is the *Kol Nidrei* service from the fact that the candles have not burned low. Why one of the congregants is sitting on the floor, however, is not clear.

The ten martyrdoms are depicted as having taken place on one day. The *piyyut* is based on several midrashic stories which date from geonic times and which constitute a literary composition about martyrdom. According to the story, the emperor condemned them to death because of the ten sons of Jacob who sold their brother Joseph into slavery and were never punished for it. One of the sages ascended to heaven and learned that the decree had been irrevocably sealed, so the ten sages accepted their fate. The legend has many mystical overtones and the Ten Martyrs served during the Middle Ages as a model for contemporary martyrs especially from the times of the First Crusade. In some congregations a description of the fate of a group of Polish Jewish girls in the Holocaust is also read. These girls, students at Orthodox religious schools, were taken to a brothel for Nazi soldiers. They committed suicide.

Minḥah. At the *Minḥah* service, three men are called to the Torah from which Leviticus 18 is read. This section deals with the prohibitions concerning incest which is a continuation of the morning reading according to the ancient custom which still exists in Italy. One explanation for reading this particular section on Yom Kippur is that even at the peak of religious spirituality, the human being must still remember that he is heir to all the temptations of the flesh. As *haftarah* the entire Book of Jonah is read. This book whose subject is ideal repentance and God's forgiving mercy, is particularly apt for the day. The *Amidah* for *Minḥah* is the same as for *Shaḥarit*. In its repetition *Seliḥot* are inserted as well as the confessional prayers.

Ne'ilah. The fifth prayer service of Yom Kippur is introduced with the *Ashrei* psalm which is moved from its usual place before *Minḥah*. Originally a fifth service was recited on all fast days, today it remains only on Yom Kippur. The full name of the service is *Ne'ilat She'arim* ("Closing of the Gates"), referring to the daily closing of the Temple gates. On the Day of Atonement this literal closing was associated with the symbolic closing of the heavenly gates, which remained open to prayer until sunset. Throughout the year, according to the Talmud, *Ne'ilah* was recited one hour before sunset,

when the Temple Gates were closed; on the Day of Atonement, because of its length, *Ne'ilah* did not begin until close to sunset. Once *Ne'ilah* was limited to the Day of Atonement, it began before twilight and ended at nightfall.

By the third century *Ne'ilah* consisted of an *Amidah* of seven benedictions, parallel to the other statutory services of the day. It likewise featured confession of sins. *Ashamnu* however, and *Al Ḥet* were replaced by two prayers unique to the confession in the *Ne'ilah* service: *Attah noten yad le-foshe'im* ("Thou stretchest forth Thy hand [in forgiveness] to sinners") and *Attah hivdalta enosh* ("Thou has distinguished man [from the beast]"). These recapitulate the biblical-talmudic doctrine that God eagerly forgives the truly penitent. In accordance with the rabbinic idea that the divine judgment, inscribed on Rosh Ha-Shanah, is not sealed until the Day of Atonement ends, the word "inscribe" (in the Book of Life) is amended to "seal." To set it off from the preceding *Minḥah* service, *Ne'ilah* is prefaced by *Ashrei* (Psalms 145) and *U-Va le-Ẓiyyon Go'el,* which ordinarily introduce *Minḥah.*

Ne'ilah was eventually embellished with sacred poetry, especially *Seliḥot.* Impressive melodies heightened the emotional impact of *Ne'ilah.* The central motif is exhortation to make a final effort to seek forgiveness before the heavenly gates close at sunset. Yet the overall tone is one of confidence, especially in the final litany. In most communities the ark remains open for the whole of *Ne'ilah* and the congregation stands. In Israel the Priestly Blessing is recited at *Ne'ilah* if the appropriate point in the service is reached before sunset. The service proper concludes with *Avinu Malkenu* and *Kaddish.* The entire ritual culminates in responsive proclamations of *Shema,* followed by *Barukh shem kevod malkhuto,* and "The Lord, He is God" (I Kings 18:39). A single *shofar* blast announces the end of the "Sabbath of Sabbaths."

A pious practice is to begin building the *sukkah* for the Sukkot festival five days later immediately after *Ne'ilah.* Cleansed of sin, the new life is started with a *mitzvah.*

IX Days of Commemoration

Rosh Ḥodesh

Yom ha-Aẓma'ut

Lag ba-Omer

Yom Yerushalayim

Tu be-Av

Ḥanukkah

Tu bi-Shevat

Purim

מי כמכה

להחכם המשורר רבי יהודה
הלוי זכרו לברכה

והוא פיוט

אדון חסדך

שנוהגים לאומרו בשבת
טלפני פורים בין מי
שברך לאשרי

כדפס פה

ויניציאה

צמות זוטן דינגרס סנת הטמו ליצירה

Con licentia de'Superiori ·

Title page of a prayerbook printed in Venice in 1586. The book contains a piyyut called *Adon Ḥasdekha* which was composed by Judah Halevi, and which was recited in the synagogue on the Sabbath before Purim "between *Mi she-Berakh* and *Ashrei*."

Calendars are of the utmost importance for the maintenance of a Jewish life. The example shown here (for 5719—1959) originates from the Soviet Union. The printing and publication of any Jewish books was forbidden; this calendar was written by hand.

The Minor Festivals of the Jewish calendar differ from the Sabbath, the three Pilgrim Festivals and the High Holy Days in origin, function and form of celebration. Indeed, of all the festivals with which this chapter is concerned, only Rosh Ḥodesh, the New Moon, is mentioned in the Torah; all the others are of considerably later origin. Some were introduced into the calendar in commemoration of a specific and important historical experience; others grew out of indigenous or borrowed folk customs. They are regarded, therefore, less as sacred institutions than as popular celebrations which have acquired a particularly strong hold on the imagination of the Jewish people. This attitude is readily apparent in the rituals appertaining to these days. The elaborate ceremonies and abstention from work, which are characteristic of the Sabbath, the Pilgrim Festivals and the High Holy Days, do not apply to the minor festivals and the liturgical peculiarities of these days are similarly muted. As will be seen, each of the minor festivals does indeed possess its own wealth of ceremony and custom. Yet the changes which their commemoration necessitates in the prayer book are, although significant, almost invariably restricted to limited additions or omissions.

In view of the diverse nature of the minor festivals, and their number, the arrangement adopted in this chapter will follow that of the Jewish calendar itself. With the exception of Rosh Ḥodesh (which is the most frequent minor festival) each of them will be discussed in the order in which they appear during the course of the year.

ROSH ḤODESH

The ancient Israelites attached considerable importance to the celebration of the first day or beginning of each month. Indeed, in the Book of Numbers the New Moon is mentioned together with the festivals as a day on which "you shall blow with your trumpets over your burnt offerings." Later books of the Bible mention various other practices observed on this day, including festive meals, abstention from business transactions and visits to the prophet. It is, moreover, significant that when Hosea wished to illustrate the calamities about to befall the Jewish people, he specifically mentioned a cessation of "the joys of the New Moon."

The rabbis of the Talmud somewhat modified ostensible biblical practice. In particular, they permitted work on the New Moon. Nevertheless, it did become customary for women to abstain from such difficult labor as weaving on this day, which, according to talmudic tradition, they were allowed to observe as a semi-festival in recognition of their not having surrendered their jewelry for the creation of the golden calf. Moreover, the rabbis also forbade fasting on this day and ruled that any funeral service taking place on it should be abbreviated. It was also considered meritorious to partake of a festive meal on Rosh Ḥodesh.

The liturgy for Rosh Ḥodesh contains a similar amalgam of biblical and later elements. Thus, since the addition of a special *Musaf* sacrifice on the New Moon is ordained in the Bible (Numbers 28:11–15), the normal daily service is now complemented by a formalized *Musaf* prayer. This begins with the words: "You did assign the beginnings of the months unto Your people as a season of atonement throughout their generations." However, when Rosh Ḥodesh coincides with a Sabbath, this formula is replaced by a blessing containing mention of the two additional sacrifices due in the Temple in this circumstance. Further reference to the New Moon sacrifice is also made in the Torah reading designated for the day, which consists of Numbers 28:1–15. Should Rosh Ḥodesh coincide with the Sabbath, two scrolls are taken from the ark. Seven persons are called to the first, from which the normal weekly portion is read; an eighth is called to the second, for *maftir,* which consists of Numbers 28:9–15. The *haftarah* is read from Isaiah 66:1–24.

As early as talmudic times, the Rosh Ḥodesh liturgy was further distinguished by a recitation of the *Hallel.* However, since this day was not biblically sanctified by the prohibition of labor, some portions of the *Hallel* were omitted on this occasion. Furthermore, the later codifiers differed as to whether the usual blessing that "Who has hallowed us by Your commandments and has commanded us to read the *Hallel*" should be recited on Rosh Ḥodesh. In most communities the blessing is recited, but Shneur Zalman, the founder of Ḥabad Ḥasidism,

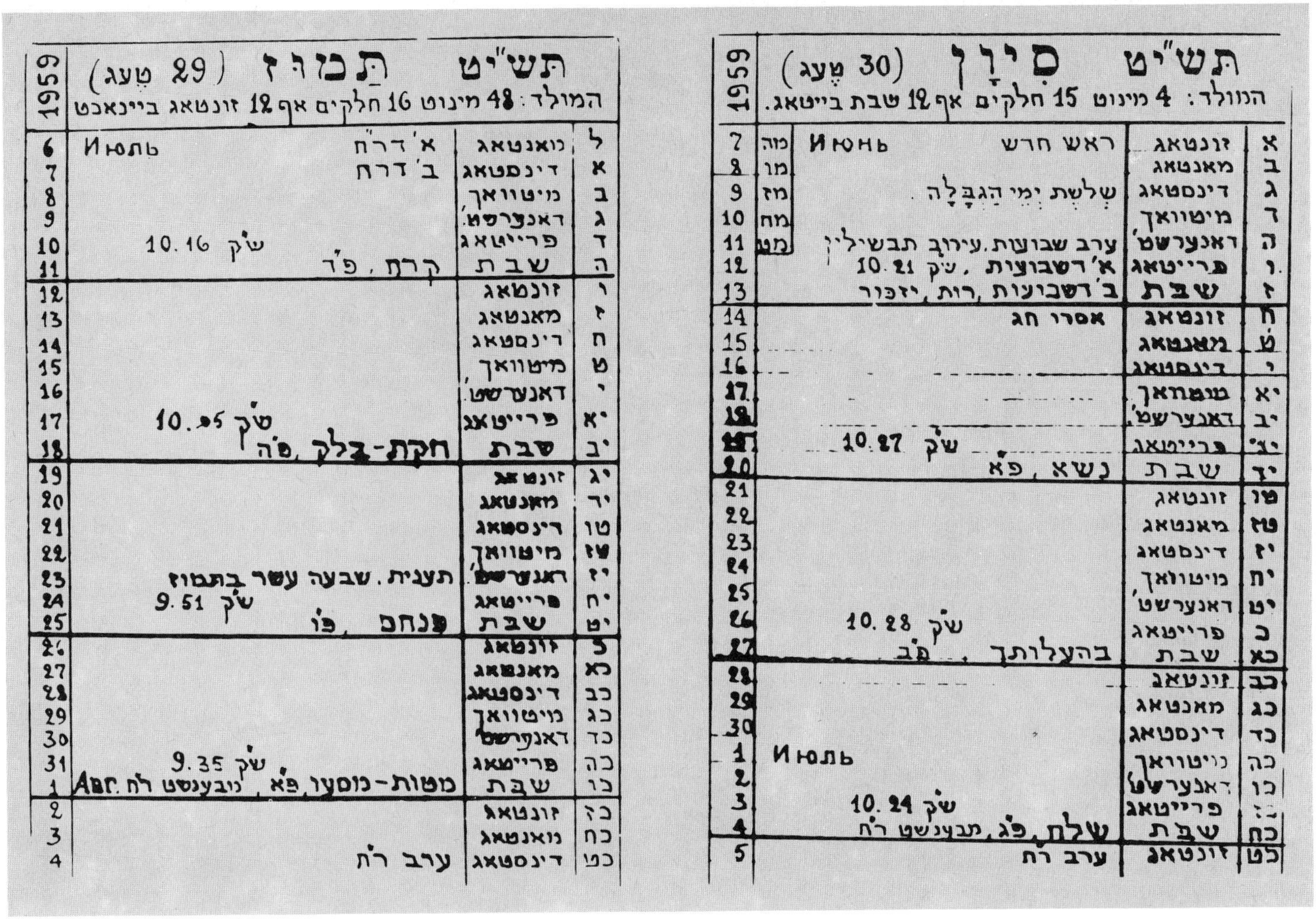

1959				
		תשי"ט סיון (30) טעג		
	המולד: 4 מינוט 15 חלקים אף 12 שבת ביטאג.			
7	מוה	שבת **И НОН** ראש חדש	זונטאג	א
8	מו		מאנטאג	ב
9	מז	שלשת ימי הגבלה	דינסטאג	ג
10	מח		מיטװאך	ד
11	מט	ערב שבועות.עירוב תבשילין	דאנערשט	ה
12		א' דשבועות , שק 10.21	פרייטאג	ו
13		ב' דשבועות, רות, יזכור	שבת	ז
14		אסרו חג	זונטאג	ח
15			מאנטאג	ט
16			דינסטאג	י
17			מיטװאך	יא
18			דאנערשט	יב
19		שק 10.27	פרייטאג	יג
20		נשא, פא	שבת	יד
21			זונטאג	טו
22			מאנטאג	טז
23			דינסטאג	יז
24			מיטװאך	יח
25			דאנערשטאג	יט
26		שק 10.28	פרייטאג	כ
27		בהעלותך , פב	שבת	כא
28			זונטאג	כב
29			מאנטאג	כג
30			דינסטאג	כד
1			מיטװאך	כה
2			דאנערשטאג	כו
3		שק 10.24	פרייטאג	כז
4		שלח, פג, תבענשט רח	שבת	כח
5		ערב רח	זונטאג	כט

1959				
		תשי"ט תמוז (29) טעג		
	המולד: 48 מינוט 16 חלקים אף 12 זונטאג ביינאכט			
6		חתם **И НОН** א' דר"ח	מאנטאג	ל
7		ב' דרח	דינסטאג	א
8			מיטװאך	ב
9			דאנערסט.	ג
10		שק 10.16	פרייטאג	ד
11		קרח , פד	שבת	ה
12			זונטאג	ו
13			מאנטאג	ז
14			דינסטאג	ח
15			מיטװאך	ט
16			דאנערשט.	י
17		שק 10.15	פרייטאג	יא
18		חקת-בלק , פה	שבת	יב
19			זונטאג	יג
20			מאנטאג	יד
21			דינסטאג	טו
22			מיטװאך	טז
23		תענית. שבעה עשר בתמוז	דאנערשט.	יז
24		שק 9.51	פרייטאג	יח
25		פנחס , פו	שבת	יט
26			זונטאג	כ
27			מאנטאג	כא
28			דינסטאג	כב
29			מיטװאך	כג
30			דאנערשט	כד
31		שק 9.35	פרייטאג	כה
1		מטות-מסעי, פא, תובענסט רח נאט	שבת	כו
2			זונטאג	כז
3			מאנטאג	כח
4		ערב רח	דינסטאג	כט

ruled that only the cantor is to recite the blessing, while the congregation merely responds "Amen."

Two further additions are made to the normal daily liturgy on this day. The first is the insertion of the special festive prayer, *Ya'aleh ve-Yavo,* in the *Amidah* and in the Grace after Meals. The second is the recital of Psalm 104, which is read after the morning service. In the Sephardi ritual it is also inserted before the evening service. *Taḥanun* is not recited on Rosh Ḥodesh.

Announcement of the New Moon. The changes in the liturgy which the celebration of the New Moon necessitates on Rosh Ḥodesh itself form only one portion of the liturgical references to the occasion. The arrival of a new month is also marked by several other, associated, customs and rituals during the normal service, which have often attained importance in their own right.

Chronologically, the first such liturgical addition consists of the announcement of the New Moon. This takes place on the Sabbath before Rosh Ḥodesh is due to fall. Following the reading of the *haftarah,* the cantor leads the congregation in announcing and blessing the coming month.

This custom was introduced by the *geonim,* and its main purpose was to make a public pronouncement of the exact day(s) on which the New Moon will fall. It is possible that this practice was based upon the statement of Rabbi Yose, that he did not pray the *Musaf* service (on the Sabbath before the New Moon) until he knew exactly when the New Moon was to occur. The announcement is made after a special prayer for the house of Israel, and in the Ashkenazi rite begins: "He Who wrought miracles for our fathers, and redeemed them from slavery into freedom, may He speedily redeem us and gather our exiles from the four corners of the earth, even all Israel united in fellowship: and let us say, Amen." The exact time of the *molad* (the point in time in which the moon is directly between the earth and the sun) is then announced and the reader proclaims the day(s) of the week on which the first day of the coming month falls; and the blessing concludes with the prayer that the New Moon be for life, peace, gladness, salvation, and consolation for the house of Israel. Prior to the proclamation of the New Moon, the Ashkenazi ritual contains an introductory prayer, *Yehi Raẓon* which is substantially the private petition recited daily by the Talmud authority Rav upon the completion of the *Amidah*. In order to adjust this prayer to the occasion, the sentence "to renew unto us this coming month for good and for blessing" was inserted. This introductory prayer was first recited in the Polish ritual during the first part of the 18th century. It then gradually spread to all Ashkenazi rituals. In some rites the words "*bi-zekhut tefillat Rav*" ("by the merit of the prayer of Rav") appear at the end of the prayer. It has been suggested that this is a mistake for a marginal note which originally read *berakhot, tefillat Rav* ("Tractate *Berakhot*, the prayer of Rav") to indicate the source and authorship of the prayer. These words were later erroneously incorporated in the liturgy, *berakhot* being changed to *bi-zekhut*. One scholar has asserted that a further mistake in some rites changed *Rav* to *rabbim* making it end "by the merit of congregational prayer." Many Sephardi and oriental rituals contain introductory prayers for the ingathering of the exiles and the well-being of the rabbis. It became customary to recite the announcement of the New Moon while standing, in remembrance of the original sanctification of the New Moon by the *bet din* in Jerusalem, which was done when standing. It is also customary for the reader to hold the Torah scroll while reciting this prayer. The Sabbath on which the New Moon is announced is popularly known as *Shabbat Mevarekhim* ("the Sabbath of the Blessing"), or in Yiddish, "*Shabbos Rosh Ḥodesh bentshn.*" A special sermon in honor of the event is preached in some communities. The New Moon of Tishrei is not announced in advance since it is also Rosh Ha-Shanah and everyone knows when it will occur.

Yom Kippur Katan. Many Jews celebrate the day preceding Rosh Ḥodesh in a totally different fashion—by fasting and penitential prayers. It is for this reason that the eve of the New Moon is known as Yom Kippur Katan (lit. "the minor Day of Atonement"). Although the custom of observing this day is a late one (which is not mentioned in the Shulḥan Arukh) it earned many rabbinical commendations. It therefore became popular among the pious, who observed this day as though it were sanctioned by *halakhah*. In fact, the practice of fasting on the eve of Rosh Ḥodesh began among the kabbalists of Safed in the second half of the 16th century. They regarded the waning of the moon as a symbol of the exile of the *Shekhinah* ("Divine Presence") and the dimunition of the power of holiness during the Exile, and its renewal as a symbol of the return to perfection in the age of Redemption. They based this conception on the talmudic legend, according to which God had said to Israel: "Bring atonement upon me for making the moon smaller."

The liturgical additions made to the normal services on Yom Kippur Katan reflect its penitential character. In addition to the reading of the Torah and other prayers and *seliḥot*, customary for a fast day, special *seliḥot* were written for the afternoon service (*Minḥah*) of this day. They are based on the themes of Exile and Redemption. A special liturgy, *Tikkun Yom Kippur Katan*, was first printed in Prague in 1662. Later it appeared in different versions and in special books which were very popular until the 19th century.

Kiddush Levanah. The announcement of the New Moon and the celebration of Yom Kippur Katan, as well as the rituals of Rosh Ḥodesh itself, are all observed before the monthly reappearance of the moon's crescent. However, a special prayer of thanksgiving is also recited once the latter event has occurred. Known in Hebrew as either *Birkat ha-Levanah* ("the blessing of the moon") or *Kiddush Levanah* ("sanctification of the moon"), this rite originated in the time of the Second Temple (and may even be older). The rite takes the moon as a symbol of the renewal in nature as well as of Israel's renewal and redemption.

The basic text of the ritual is given in the Talmud, but many additions were subsequently made. In the present Ashkenazi ritual, the blessing is introduced by the recital of Psalms 148:1–6 (in the Sephardi rite also Psalm 8:4–5), after which a benediction praising God as the creator and master of nature is pronounced. In the mishnaic period, the proclamation of the new month by the rabbinical court was celebrated with dancing and rejoicing. It is still customary to rise on the tips of the toes in the direction of the moon while reciting three times "As I dance toward thee, but cannot touch thee, so shall none of my evil-inclined enemies be able to touch me." (It was suggested

This page from the *Harrison Miscellany* (18th-century Italy) is the beginning of the Announcement of the New Moon. The manuscript contains many biblical scenes which are not necessarily connected with the text. In this one, the patriarch Abraham is being visited by the three angels.

after the first moon landing that this text should be emended.) This is followed by "Long live David, King of Israel" (also pronounced three times) and by the greeting *Shalom aleikhem* ("Peace be to you") which is extended to those standing around who respond *Aleikhem shalom* ("to you be peace"). This part of the ceremony is reminiscent of the days of Judah ha-Nasi when the Romans abrogated the authority of the rabbinical court to consecrate the new moon which therefore had to be carried out clandestinely. "Long live David, King of Israel" served as a password between Judah ha-Nasi and his emissary Ḥiyya. It also voiced Israel's continuous hope for redemption by the Messiah, a descendant of David whose kingdom would be "established forever as the moon" (Psalm 89:38). The ceremony concludes with the recital of several scriptural verses, a quotation from the Talmud, "In the school of Rabbi Ishmael it was taught: Had Israel merited no other privilege than to greet the presence of their Heavenly Father once a month, it were sufficient," which is followed by a plea that God readjust the deficiency of the light of the moon caused by the moon's complaint against the sun (a reference to an aggadic passage, Ḥullin 60b) and a prayer for the fulfillment of the promise of the restoration of the Kingdom of Israel when the Jews will "seek the Lord their God, and David their King."

The *halakhah* specifies the time and manner in which the ritual of *Kiddush Levanah* should be observed. Thus, the prayer can only be recited from the third evening after the appearance of the new moon until the 15th of the lunar month; after that day, the moon begins to diminish. Furthermore, the prayer is recited only if the moon is clearly visible (not when it is hidden by clouds) and it should preferably be said in the open air. According to the Talmud, "Whoever pronounces the benediction over the new moon in its due time welcomes, as it were, the presence of the *Shekhinah*" and hence it is recommended to pronounce the benediction, if possible, on the evening after the departure of the Sabbath when one is still in a festive mood and clad in one's best clothes. The blessing of the new moon in some rites is delayed in the month of Av, until after the Ninth of Av, in Tishrei, until after the Day of Atonement, and in Tevet until after the fast of the tenth of Tevet. A mourner does not bless the moon until after *shivah* ("the first week of mourning"); in the rainy season, however, when the moon is often hidden by clouds, he recites it whenever possible. The blessing of the moon is not recited on Sabbath and holiday eves, mainly because of the prohibition to carry prayer books outside the house or synagogue building when no specific provision is made for this purpose in accordance with rabbinical requirements (*eruv teḥumim*).

YOM HA-AẒMA'UT

While Rosh Ḥodesh is the most ancient of the minor Jewish festivals, Israel Independence Day (Yom ha-Aẓma'ut) is one of the more recent. It is celebrated each year on the fifth of Iyyar, the anniversary—according to the Jewish calendar—of the day in 5708 (May 14, 1948) when the Declaration of Independence was promulgated and the State of Israel established. When the anniversary falls on a Sabbath or a Friday, it is celebrated on the preceding Thursday. This occasion is preceded by Remembrance Day (Yom ha-Zikkaron) for all those who have fallen in defense of Israel's independence and security.

The Chief Rabbinate of Israel recognizes Yom ha-Aẓma'ut as a Thanksgiving Festival to be celebrated in both the synagogue and the home. One of its members wrote: "The date of this anniversary is indeed appropriate, in that it marks the day on which the essence of the miracle took place—when we went forth from slavery to freedom through the proclamation of independence." Thus, despite the coincidence of this holiday with the *Omer* period of mourning, the Chief Rabbinate has permitted the holding of all celebrations connected with this occasion.

Prayers for Yom ha-Aẓma'ut were first formulated by the Israel Chief Rabbinate in 1949. The festive evening service is introduced by thanksgiving Psalms (107, 97, 98) and concludes with the sounding of the *shofar*, to the accompaniment of the

petition: "May it be Thy will, that as we have been deemed worthy to witness the beginning of redemption, so also may we be deemed worthy to hear the *shofar* announcing the Messiah, speedily in our days." The morning service includes the Sabbath festival introductory Psalms, *Nishmat*, the *Hallel* and the *haftarah* (Isaiah 10:32–11:12) that is read on the last day of Passover in the Diaspora, but without the accompanying benedictions. *Taḥanun* is also omitted as on all festive days.

From the moment of publication many religious elements in Israel felt that the Chief Rabbinate's order of service represented an inadequate and halfhearted expression of the historic nature of the occasion. Criticism was directed against the

Three quite different Yom ha-Aẓma'ut scenes. The day is, to a large extent, celebrated in the streets, and the top photograph shows the municipal building of Tel Aviv and the square in front of it on the eve of the festival. The day is celebrated in the synagogues as well and in Jerusalem the main service takes place in the Yeshurun synagogue. Among the dignitaries in the front row is the late Chief Rabbi Herzog. Members of the Neturei Karta do not see Yom ha-Aẓma'ut as any occasion for happiness. On the contrary the day is observed by them as one of fasting and, for some, the wearing of sackcloth.

Lag ba-Omer is traditionally celebrated by bonfires. These two scenes from Meron, the traditional burial place of Simeon bar Yoḥai, illustrate the tremendous appeal that the day has, particularly for Ḥasidim.

omission of the benedictions before the *Hallel* and *haftarah*, of the *She-heḥeyanu*, and of the reading of a special portion of the Torah. These omissions have been demonstratively remedied in some orthodox congregations in Israel, chiefly those of Ha-Kibbutz ha-Dati (the religious kibbutz movement) and the Army rabbinate. The former has printed its own *maḥzor* under the imprimatur of the Army chief chaplain (and now the Chief Rabbi of Israel), Rabbi Shlomo Goren, and Rabbi Elimelech Bar-Shaul of Rehovot, prescribing the recital of *She-heḥeyanu* at *Kiddush* and *Al ha-Nissim* in the *Amidah*. Three persons are called to the Torah, the portion read being Deuteronomy 7:1–8:18. Some synagogues read Deuteronomy 30:1–10.

Although these changes were sanctioned by several authorities, the order of service ultimately adopted by a specially appointed council of the Israel Chief Rabbinate represented an attempt to placate the objections of the more orthodox circles to any changes in the liturgy. The religious establishment continued to maintain this "no-change" attitude even after the Six-Day War when the demand grew to give appropriate expression to the restoration and the Temple site in the daily prayers and even to the abolition of the fast days commemorating its original wresting from Jewish rule.

Special Independence Day services in the synagogue are a feature of almost all Jewish communities today, though practices are far from uniform. Among the differing customs may be mentioned that of proclaiming the number of years since the establishment of the State, before the sounding of the *shofar* in the evening service. The wording is adapted from the proclamation of the years since the destruction of the Temple which is read out in Sephardi and Yemenite synagogues on Tishah be-Av. It reads: "Hear ye, our brethren . . . today . . . years have elapsed since the beginning of our redemption marked by the establishment of the State."

LAG BA-OMER

Whilst Yom ha-Aẓma'ut constitutes one pause in the *Omer* period of mourning between Pesaḥ and Shavuot, Lag ba-

Omer provides a second such occasion. The name itself denotes that this is the 33rd day (ל״ג in Hebrew denoting 33) of the counting of the *Omer,* a date which coincides with the 18th of Iyyar. As a mark of the festive nature of this day, the *Taḥanun* prayer is omitted during the morning and afternoon services. The liturgical alteration parallels the fact that on Lag ba-Omer the traditional mourning customs of abstention otherwise observed during the *Omer* (abstention from haircutting and shaving, the non-performance of marriage ceremonies etc.) are relaxed.

Although it has been celebrated as a semi-holiday since the time of the *geonim,* the original reason for merrymaking on this occasion is obscure. Some sources maintain that the manna began to fall in the wilderness on Lag ba-Omer; other traditions state that this was the date on which a plague, which had struck down 24,000 of Rabbi Akiva's students, ceased. In medieval times it was therefore recognized as a "Scholar's Festival" and in present day Israel is known as "Students' Day."

The kabbalists attach particular significance to Lag ba-Omer. They hold this date to be the anniversary of the death of Rabbi Simeon bar Yoḥai, regarded by them as the author of the *Zohar,* the classic kabbalistic work. Called *Hillula de-Rabbi Shimon bar Yoḥai,* it is celebrated in Israel in the village of Meron (near Safed) where Simeon ben Yoḥai is traditionally buried. The celebrations are carried out with songs and dances by the thousands who gather there. A special hymn, *Bar Yoḥai . . . Ashrekha,* consisting of ten stanzas corresponding to the ten *sefirot* in the Kabbalah, is sung on this occasion. Three-year-old boys are given their first haircut (*ḥalakah*) while their parents distribute wine and sweets. The same rites are observed at the grave of Simeon the Just, in Jerusalem. Elsewhere in Israel, the festival is marked by the lighting of bonfires and family outings to the countryside.

YOM YERUSHALAYIM

The third festive day to fall during the period of the *Omer* is Yom Yerushalayim (Jerusalem Day), which falls on the 28th of Iyyar. This day marks the liberation of the eastern section of Jerusalem from Arab occupation during the Six-Day War of 1967. It is therefore the newest holiday in the Jewish calendar.

The Israel Rabbinate has proclaimed Yom Yerushalayim to be a day of thanksgiving, and has directed that the *Shaḥarit* service that day include the *Hallel,* Psalm 107, and a verse by verse reading of the "Song of the Sea" (Exodus 15:1–18), which praises God for His triumph over Israel's enemies. The day is also to be celebrated with a joyous festive meal. Moreover, despite the coincidence of Yom Yerushalayim with the period of the *Omer,* the restrictions appertaining to the latter are lifted for the occasion "because of the importance of the miracle which the Lord caused for His people Israel in the liberation of Jerusalem."

In Jerusalem itself, the celebration of Yom Yerushalayim is a blend of solemnity and joy. The day begins with a thanksgiving service at the Western Wall, where eighteen torches are lit in memory of the soldiers who fell in the battle for Jerusalem. The Western Wall is also the scene of a mass *Minḥah* service on the following afternoon.

TU BE-AV

By comparison with the popular celebrations associated with Lag ba-Omer, Yom ha-Aẓma'ut and Yom Yerushalayim, the festival of Tu be-Av has an almost neglected air. As its name implies, it falls on the 15th day (ט״ו in Hebrew denoting 15) of Av. But this date has not gained any real hold on the popular imagination. The only liturgical changes made on this day are the omission of the *Taḥanun* prayer from the daily service, and the absence of eulogies from funeral services.

The celebration of Tu be-Av as a minor festival dates from the period of the Second Temple, when it marked the beginning of the vintage season. According to the Mishnah, on this day (as on the Day of Atonement) the daughters of Jerusalem dressed in white clothes (which they borrowed so that the daughters of poor families should not be ashamed of not having suitable dresses) and went out to dance in the vineyards chanting songs. This was also the day of the wood offering when

Right and below right: Two parts of a panel of the west wall in the ancient synagogue of Dura-Europos depicting Purim scenes. Ahasuerus, with Queen Esther enthroned at his side, receiving a report about the number of people killed by the Jews in Shushan (Esther 9:11).
Below: Ḥasidic family in Jerusalem carrying the traditional gifts of food to be delivered to friends during Purim. Photo Peter Larsen, Jerusalem.

Three Ḥanukkah lamps. Top left: An English Ḥanukkah lamp made by John Ruslen in 1709. The decoration shows Elijah and the ravens surrounded by scroll, foliage, and shell motifs. It was probably a wedding gift to Elias Lindo on his marriage at the Bevis Marks synagogue in London on February 2, 1708/9. The lamp is owned by Felix Nabarro and is on loan to the Jewish Museum, London.
Top right: A pewter candelabrum from Horb, Germany, dating to the 18th century. Mishkan le-Omanut, Kibbutz Ein Harod.
Bottom: An artillery shell-case was the material from which this Ḥanukkah lamp was made. The Hebrew words along the side are the blessing for the lighting of the Ḥanukkah candles and the *Al ha-Nissim* prayer. On top is a dedication to Herbert Samuel, the first High Commissioner for Palestine. Made by Eliezer ben Menaḥem, London, The Jewish Museum.

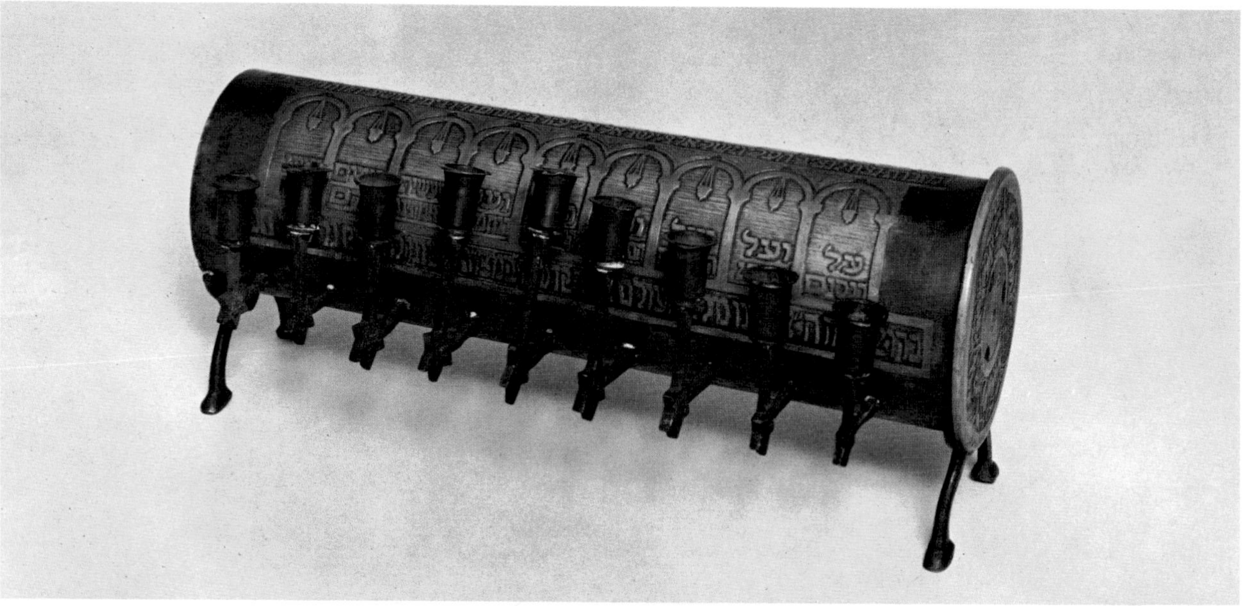

Typical Ḥanukkah scenes. Clockwise from right: Children in a Jerusalem kindergarten preparing for the Festival of Lights with typically seasonal artwork. Photo Werner Braun, Jerusalem. Moroccan candelabra from the 17th-18th centuries. Every evening throughout the festival the Ḥanukkah lights are kindled at the Western Wall, Jerusalem. Photo: Werner Braun, Jerusalem. The Israel Scout movement takes part in the ceremonial lighting of the Ḥanukkah torch at Modi'in, home of the Maccabees. The torch is then carried by relay runners to the home of the president of Israel in Jerusalem and other locations throughout the country and is used to kindle the first candle of the festival. Jerusalem, Keren Kayemet le-Israel Photo Archives.

Carved wooden doors from an 18th-century Polish Ark of the Law. The Hebrew inscription reads: "Strong as a leopard; swift as an eagle; springs like a deer; brave as a lion," which are qualities required, according to a saying in the *Ethics of the Fathers*, in the service of God. Jerusalem, Sir Isaac and Lady Wolfson Museum, Hechal Shlomo.

Besides the *seder* ceremony on Passover, Ḥanukkah is a festival particularly for children. From a very early age the boys—and the girls too—are encouraged to light their own Ḥanukkah lights, which exercise is always exciting. In many families the children are given gifts or Ḥanukkah *gelt* after the lighting of the lights.

all people brought kindling wood for the Temple altar. The Talmud offers half a dozen other historical events which occurred on that day, and which justify the celebration of Tu be-Av as a minor festival. Since this holiday was celebrated by torches and bonfires, some scholars believe that it originated in a pagan festival of the summer solstice.

In recent years attempts have been made in various kibbutzim to revive the festival of Tu be-Av. Called *Hagigat ha-Keramim* (the "Festival of the Vineyards"), the celebrations include music, dancing, poetry and love songs.

ḤANUKKAH

The lengthiest of the minor festivals in the Jewish calendar is Ḥanukkah. It is also that which has most successfully retained its popularity. This festival is celebrated for eight days, beginning on the 25th of Kislev. Of post-biblical origin, the name of the festival means "dedication." It commemorates the heroic struggle of the Jews against pagan forces and the religious persecution of the Greco-Syrians during the second century B.C.E. This struggle proved decisive in forming the character of the Jewish people. The victories achieved by the Jewish forces led by the family of the Maccabeans against overwhelming odds in 168–165 B.C.E., brought about the religious freedom and national independence which was to last until Roman times. It has therefore inspired many subsequent generations to face persecution with triumphant courage.

The oldest historical source for these exploits are the first and second books of the Maccabees. Both works are written in Greek, although the first is probably a translation of the Hebrew original, and was apparently written as an eye-witness account of the events described. These works form a section of the apocrypha (i.e. books not included in the sacred canon of the Bible).

Kindling the Lights. The central ceremony of the Ḥanukkah liturgy is the kindling of lights. On each of the eight days of the festival, oil lamps or candles are kindled in a specially constructed *menorah* (candelabrum) in the synagogue and the home. The candelabrum is also known as the *ḥanukkiyah.* Several reasons have been advanced to explain this ceremony. The most popular tradition (which is cited in the Talmud) associates the kindling of the lights with one of the miracles which occurred to the Maccabean warriors. It relates that when they reconquered Jerusalem and entered the Temple, they discovered that the Greeks had defiled all the oil necessary for the daily lighting of the candelabrum there. They found only one small jar of oil whose seal was still intact. That small jar contained enough oil to keep the candelabrum burning for one day only. However, by a miracle, it sufficed to last for the eight days which it took to prepare a supply of pure, fresh oil.

It was with this story as their model that the mishnaic school of Shammai ruled that: "On the first day eight lights should be kindled; thereafter they should be progressively reduced" until only one light is lit on the last day of the festival. But this view was overruled by the school of Hillel, who objected to

any suggestion that one lessen the sanctity of the holiday on each day. Instead, they maintained that: "On the first night one light should be kindled, thereafter they should be progressively increased." The latter practice is that which is followed today. The Hanukkah lights are kindled as soon after nightfall as possible. On the first night of the festival one light is set at the extreme right of the menorah. On each successive night, one more light is added on its left side. In addition, a separate light, known as the *shammash,* is placed apart from and at a different height to, the other lights. The function of the *shammash* is to provide the flame from which the Ḥanukkah lights are themselves kindled. Each night, the most recent of the lights

Two Ḥanukkah scenes. The Chief Rabbi of the State of Israel, Rabbi I. J. Unterman, lighting the first light of Ḥanukkah in a very elaborate silver Ḥanukkah lamp at the Western Wall in 1968. Lighting the lights in newly-unified Jerusalem is an act of great symbolism. No less symbolic, however, for the participants was the ceremony performed in the Nazi transit camp in Westerbork, Holland, in 1942. Most, if not all, participants in that ceremony did not survive the nightmare of terror into which they were plunged.

is that which is lit first, the order of kindling thus being from left to right.

Two benedictions are recited before the lights are kindled. The first mentions the commandment "to kindle the Ḥanukkah light"; the second recalls the historical origins of the festival itself ("Blessed art Thou . . . who wrought miracles for our fathers in days of old at this season.") On the first night *Sheheḥeyanu* (the blessing for the season) is added.

On Friday evening the Ḥanukkah lights are lit before the Sabbath candles. On Saturday night in the synagogue the Ḥanukkah lights are lit before the *Havdalah* ceremony, in order to proclaim the miracle of the festival as early as possible and also in order to postpone the formal departure of the Sabbath for as long as possible. At home, however, *Havdalah* is recited before the Ḥanukkah lights are lit, because *Havdalah* is made every week and therefore takes precedence over the Ḥanukkah candles which are lit only one week a year. Since women, too, were included in the original miracle, they are also obliged to kindle the Ḥanukkah lamp.

The rabbis of the Talmud went to some lengths to emphasize that the major motivation for kindling the Ḥanukkah lights is the desire "to proclaim the miracle" which occurred at the time of the Maccabees. Consequently they taught that this ceremony should be performed as openly, and as opulently, as is practical. Thus, "the lamp should be placed outside the entrance of the house. If a person lives on an upper storey, it should be set on the window nearest to the street. If he is in fear of the gentiles, the lamp may be placed inside the inner entrance of the house, and in times of danger, the precept is fulfilled by setting it on the table." Moreover, because of the importance of publicizing the miracle, if a man of limited means has to choose between purchasing oil for the Ḥanukkah lights and wine for *Kiddush,* he is to buy the oil. So that the miracle may be known to all, the lights are kindled before any member of the household, adult or child, goes to sleep. The lamp itself may be filled with any kind of oil, but olive oil is preferred. Nowadays, when it is common custom to light candles, one must choose a candle that will burn for at least half an hour. Finally, since the Ḥanukkah candles are a *mitzvah* it is not permitted to make use of them for any practical purpose. The *shammash* is therefore left alight in the *menorah,* so that in case of need the light from that particular candle will be considered that which is being used.

Several of these regulations are listed in a short paragraph which begins with the words *Ha-nerot hallalu* ("these lights"). This is recited or sung immediately after the lights have been kindled.

Ma'oz Ẓur. In the Ashkenazi rite, the ceremony of kindling the Ḥanukkah lights concludes with the singing of a popular hymn whose opening words are *Ma'oz ẓur yeshua'ti,* "O Fortress, Rock of my salvation." The words were written in Germany, probably in the 13th century, by an author whose name was Mordecai; an acrostic spelling his name is formed from the first letter of each stanza. The first stanza expresses Israel's messianic hope for the reestablishment of the ancient Temple worship. The following three stanzas praise God for the deliverance of Israel from Egyptian bondage, from the Babylonian exile, and for the Purim miracle. The fifth stanza summarizes the miracle of Ḥanukkah itself. A sixth stanza, which is said to refer to the German emperor Frederic Barbarossa (12th century) is rarely sung. The Sephardim recite Psalm 30: "A song at the dedication of the House of David," which was perhaps sung at the rededication of the Temple by the Maccabees themselves.

Al ha-Nissim. The various other changes which the festival of Ḥanukkah causes in the liturgy are similarly designed to stress the miraculous nature of the Maccabean victory. However, it is the religious message of the triumph which is stressed; the military aspect of the episode is underplayed. This is particularly marked in the *Al ha-Nissim* ("For the miracles") passage, which is inserted in the *Amidah* and the Grace after Meals during the festival. Although mentioning the delivery of "the strong into the hands of the weak, the many into the hands of the few," this summary passes over the military campaigns that followed the Maccabean reconquest of the Temple, and which heralded the rebirth of an independent Judean state. A similar order of priorities is revealed in the *haftarah* chosen to be read on the Sabbath during Ḥanukkah. Containing Zechariah's

vision of the *menorah,* the passage pointedly concludes: "Not by might, not by power, but by My spirit, saith the Lord of hosts."

Hallel and the Torah Reading. On each of the eight days of the Ḥanukkah festival, the complete *Hallel* (Psalms 113–118) is recited during the morning service. Immediately thereafter special readings are made from the Torah. On a weekday, three persons are called to the Torah. The portion read is taken from Numbers, chapter seven, which describes the gifts that the princes of the twelve tribes brought for the dedication of the altar in the new Tabernacle in the wilderness. When Rosh Ḥodesh Tevet falls on a weekday, two scrolls are taken from the ark; three people are called to the first for the normal Rosh Ḥodesh reading, and a fourth is called to the second for the appropriate Ḥanukkah reading. When Rosh Ḥodesh Tevet falls on a Sabbath three scrolls are taken from the ark; six people are called to the first for the normal Sabbath reading; a seventh is called to the second for the Rosh Ḥodesh portion; and an eighth is called to the third for the *maftir,* which consists of the appropriate Ḥanukkah portion. In this case, the *haftarah* is as for a normal Sabbath Rosh Ḥodesh (Isaiah 66:1–24). Otherwise, on the Ḥanukkah Sabbath, two scrolls are taken from the ark; seven people are called to the first for the weekly Sabbath reading and an eighth is called to the second for *maftir,* consisting of the appropriate Ḥanukkah portion. The *haftarah* is Zechariah 2:14–4; 7. Should a second Sabbath fall during Ḥanukkah, the *haftarah* is I Kings 7:40–50, which describes the *menorah* and other vessels made for the Temple of King Solomon in Jerusalem. *Taḥanun* is omitted throughout Ḥanukkah.

The Scroll of Antiochus. During the Middle Ages it was customary to read the *Scroll of Antiochus* in the synagogue on Ḥanukkah. This scroll is a popular—partly historical, partly fictional—account of the events surrounding the holiday. It was handed down in several Aramaic versions, probably dating from the late talmudic period (fifth and sixth centuries C.E.) and was then translated into various languages which the Jews spoke in different countries. The custom of reading this scroll has now been discontinued.

Since the development of modern Jewish nationalism, the festival of Ḥanukkah has been endowed with additional importance. In particular, its themes of the preservation of the minority's values, and the victory of the small band of stubbornly courageous Jews over a mighty empire, have been stressed by the Zionists. Thus, because of its "relevance" the observance of this festival has spread to secular Jewish circles in which other religious festivals were minimized or ignored. At the same time, these groups have helped to add to the festivities normally associated with Ḥanukkah. Thus, in recent years Israelis have begun to make pilgrimages to Modi'in, the city in which the Hasmonean revolt began, and the eight days of the festival are generally marked by parties, gala concerts and torchlight parades. Giant *menorot* are also lit on the roofs of public buildings and, since 1967, at the Western Wall.

TU BI-SHEVAT

Within less than two months of the completion of Ḥanukkah, the Jewish calendar reveals a completely different type of festival. On the 15th day of Shevat (Tu bi-Shevat in Hebrew), Jewish attention is concentrated, not on the heroism and valor of the Maccabees, but on nature. That day is known as the "New Year for Trees," and is considered to mark the beginning of the process whereby the sap in the trees becomes active, thus bringing new life to nature. According to the Talmud, this date was chosen because most of the heavy winter rainfall has come to an end by then in Ereẓ Israel.

Tu bi-Shevat is regarded as a minor holiday for liturgical purposes; neither *taḥanun* nor any other penitential prayers are said, and fasting is forbidden.

In the Ashkenazi communities of Europe it was customary to eat 15 different kinds of fruit on Tu bi-Shevat, special

The *piyyut, Ma'oz Ẓur,* is now common among all Jewish communities, even the Sephardi. The melody to which it is sung is usually a rousing march shown here on the far left. A far more tender melody is that which was used by the "Tedesco," German-Italian Jews. At the bottom of that music is Benedetto Marcello's setting for voice and two instruments. The Tel Aviv kindergarten children are about to plant saplings in celebration of Tu bi-Shevat. They seem fascinated by the tiny plants they are holding, while an onlooker would most probably be equally as fascinated by their symbolic floral headdresses.

preference being given to the seven particular species grown in Ereẓ Israel. The eating of fruit was accompanied by the recital of Psalm 104, which describes God's greatness as manifested in nature, and of the 15 "Songs of Ascent" (Psalms 120–134).

The Sephardim attached greater significance to the day and under the influence of the kabbalists of Safed in the 16th century, the Sephardi liturgy and customs for this festival were expanded. The Sephardim know Tu bi-Shevat as The Feast of Fruits. Special poems, called *complas,* were recited on this day, which was also the occasion for festive home meals. The customs and liturgical changes of the day were further expanded by the kabbalists. They recited additional poems, *piyyutim,* during the *Amidah* and readings from the Scriptures and the midrashic literature. These selections appear in a special booklet called *Peri Eẓ Hadar,* "The Goodly Fruit." They also conducted a special meal, modeled on the Passover *seder,* which included drinking four cups of wine.

Tradition has it that Tu bi-Shevat is the day on which the fate of trees and fruits is decided. Accordingly, on that day the Ḥasidim pray that the *etrogim* (citrons) may grow in beauty and perfection in order to be enjoyed during the festival of Sukkot.

Since the establishment of the agricultural settlements in Palestine in the last decades of the 19th century, the New Year of Trees has acquired great significance symbolizing the revival and redemption of the land by the conquest of the desert. In Israel Tu bi-Shevat is celebrated with children's songs in honor of the feast of the trees and with tree-planting ceremonies by kindergarten schoolchildren under the auspices of the afforestation department of the Jewish National Fund.

PURIM

The rabbis enjoined that with the commencement of the month of Adar, Jews are to increase their happiness. This happiness reaches its height on the 14th of Adar, the date of the festival of Purim, the most joyous of the Jewish holidays.

The festival commemorates the triumph of Esther and Mordecai over the wicked Haman who sought to exterminate all the Jews of the Persian empire. These events (which are difficult to date with any precision) are related in the Scroll of Esther, known in Hebrew as *Megillat Esther* which constitutes one of the Hagiographa sections of the Bible. The name Purim itself means "lots," and recalls the lots which Haman cast in order to determine the day on which the destruction of the Jews was to be effected.

Because the Jews of the capital city of Shushan, which was encircled by a wall, did not celebrate Purim on the 14th of Adar as did those in the provinces, but rather marked the day on the 15th, Jews living in towns that are considered to have been walled in the days of Joshua (such as Jerusalem) fulfill the laws of Purim on the 15th of the month. That day is called Shushan Purim.

The Megillah. The most distinctive liturgical feature of the Purim festival is the public reading of the *Megillah* on the 14th of Adar. Two such readings take place: one on the evening of the festival and the second during the morning. Women, as well as men, are obliged to hear the *Megillah,* which is read from a parchment scroll. This it is customary to fold over and spread out before the reading since it is called a "letter" (cf. Esther 9:26, 29).

Three benedictions of thanksgiving are recited before the *Megillah* is read. The first acknowledges the fact that one has been held worthy to read the sacred book. The second recognizes that God miraculously delivered our ancestors in those days. The third, the *She-ḥeheyanu* benediction recited on

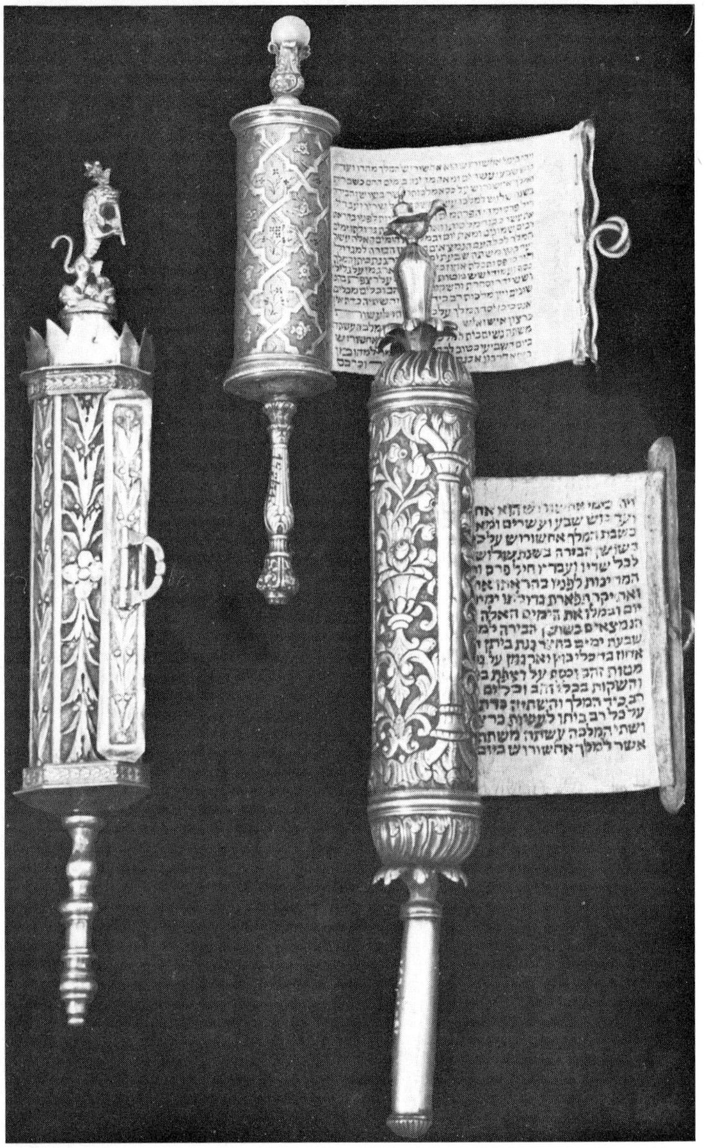

every festival, expresses gratitude for being alive to celebrate the event.

A special blessing also follows the *Megillah* reading. This praises God the Savior for having fought our battles, judged our disputes, avanged our injuries and punished our enemies. At the evening reading, this is followed by an alphabetical poem beginning "He who brought the counsel of the heathen to nought" which recounts the story of Purim with poetical and midrashic embellishments.

The reading itself follows a special cantillation or melodic pattern. This, too, however, has certain distinctive features. Thus, ever since the geonic period it has been customary for the reader to raise his voice, and for the entire congregation to join him, when reciting the four verses of "redemption" that tell of Mordecai's origin and of his triumph over Haman (2:5; 8:15–16; and 10:3). Another practice is for the reader to recite the tongue-twister names of the ten sons of Haman in one breath (9:7–9). Finally, long usage has almost hallowed the practice whereby the congregation, and especially the younger members, make a loud noise whenever the name of Haman is read. Although this practice is frowned upon as indecorous by some authorities, it still persists and is said to exhibit zeal in the fulfilment of the commandment to "blot out the memory of Amalek," from whom Haman was descended (cf. Deuteronomy 25:19; Esther 3:1; and I Samuel 15:8–9).

The Torah Reading. The association between Purim and Amalek also determined the choice of Torah reading on Purim. The Mishnah established that this was to consist of three sections (to each of which one person is called) from Exodus chapter 17, which describe the attack of the Amalakites upon

A great deal of love is lavished on the containers for the Scroll of Esther. The various examples shown here are all made of silver with lavish decoration. Another popular material is carved olive wood. In Moritz Oppenheim's "Purim at Home," a typical Purim scene of the 19th century is shown. The family is enjoying a Purim skit performed by strolling players, usually yeshivah students.

Here the Purim story is depicted in embroidery on paper with various inscriptions. The last part illustrates the hanging of the villain, Haman, while his ten sons await the same fate. Every time Haman's name is read in the *megillah*, it is customary for the congregants—particularly the children—to make a great deal of noise, symbolically "blotting out Haman's name." The Purim *gregger* illustrated here was specially manufactured for this purpose and bears the inscription "Cursed be Haman."

the Israelites in the wilderness. The same association is recalled by the reading of the law which takes place on the Sabbath preceding the festival. Indeed, this Sabbath has been designated Shabbat Zakhor (the Sabbath of Remembrance). The name is derived from the first word of the additional reading (*maftir*) for this day, which commences: "Remember what Amalek did to you on your journey after you left Egypt" (Deuteronomy 25:17). The *haftarah* for this Sabbath echoes this theme. It is I Samuel, chapter 15, which begins: "Thus says the Lord of hosts: I remember that which Amalek did to Israel . . . when he came up out of Egypt."

Al ha-Nissim and Hallel. The remaining liturgical changes occasioned by the festival have a more direct relationship with the traditional story of Purim itself. This is particularly so of the *Al ha-Nissim* ("For the miracles") passage, which is inserted into both the *Amidah* prayer and the Grace after Meals. Containing the identical introduction to the passage of the same name used on Ḥanukkah, this paragraph contains a brief recital of the story of Purim.

However, in contrast with the sharing of *Al ha-Nissim* by both Ḥanukkah and Purim, the *Hallel* which is said on Ḥanukkah, is not recited on Purim. The traditional explanation is that *Hallel* is appropriate for the spiritual redemption marked by Ḥanukkah, the feast of the Rededication of the Temple, but not for Purim, which marks the purely physical salvation of the Jews.

The morning service on Purim concludes with the reading of Psalm 22. This Psalm is prefaced by the dedicatory phrase: "For the leader upon *ayelet ha-shaḥar* (the morning star)." It is traditionally held that "morning star" refers to Queen Esther (who was as beautiful as the morning star), and that this was the prayer she offered before supplicating the Persian king for the redemption of her people.

Other Celebrations. The remaining customs associated with Purim do not possess any liturgical expression. In many communities, special Purim plays (known in Yiddish as *shpiels*) were composed for the festive meal which it is obligatory to eat on the day itself. Several further customs have become associated with the unique rabbinic encouragement to imbibe large quantities of alcohol on this occasion. The obligation to despatch gifts of food to one's neighbors and friends (*mishlo'aḥ manot*) has also attained the status of a ceremonial, as has the distribution of charity and the traditional consumption of choice culinary delights. However, none of these actions is accompanied by either a blessing or a standard prayer. *Taḥanun* is not said on Purim.

Purim Katan. In a leap year, Purim is celebrated during the second month of Adar. However, the 14th and 15th days of the first month of Adar are in this case known as Purim Katan (The Minor Purim). These days have none of the liturgical or ritual features of Purim itself: the *Megillah* is not read and the *Al ha-Nissim* passage is not recited. However, since these days are also considered minor occasions of rejoicing, fasting and funeral eulogies are prohibited and *Taḥanun* is not recited.

Special Purims. The rabbis of the Talmud taught that one must recite a special thanksgiving benediction on returning to the place where one was miraculously saved from danger. Following this injunction, the custom evolved for Jewish communities to celebrate the anniversary of their salvation by reciting special prayers and with a ritual similar to that of Purim itself. Thus, on such special Purims, the story of the personal or communal salvation was often read from a scroll in the course of a synagogue service in which special prayers of thanksgiving, in the style of *piyyutim*, were offered. Sometimes the *Hallel* was inserted into the service, and an imitative form of *Al ha-Nissim* recited during the *Amidah* and the Grace after Meals.

X DAYS OF SORROW

liturgical changes
the destruction of the temple
other historical fast days
penitential fast days

The title page of the volume of *Seliḥot* to be recited on various fast days to God "Who desires repentance at all times." The book was printed in Luneville in 1799 and the woodcut of the title page shows the three Patriarchs, Abraham, Isaac and Jacob as well as the prophet Jonah.

A long drought is perhaps the worst catastrophe that can befall any country, and in the ancient world in particular, before the development of modern methods of irrigation, drought was the cause for serious concern and the Mishnah describes the series of fast days imploring God to supply the life-giving rain. This photograph, which was taken in Israel in 1963 during a period of drought, shows earth which was once arable.

The periods of mourning and fast days which occur in the Jewish calendar have been developed over the long years of Jewish history. These days are generally characterized by an abstention from food and drink and, in several instances, from washing (for pleasure), anointing, the wearing of shoes (for comfort) and cohabitation as well. Nevertheless, the Jewish fasts vary widely in their origin, purpose and application. Thus, although several fast days are mentioned in the Bible, only the Day of Atonement is commanded by biblical statute. The vast majority of fast days are of post-biblical origin. Moreover, the various fast days do not serve one, cohesive, purpose. Some commemorate a particular misfortune or disastrous event, which is duly mourned. Others are dominated by the theme of repentance; they are characterized by the expression of present remorse and of future good intention, rather than the recollection of past tragedy. At a third level, particular fasts are designed to complement a process of purification; a period of self-denial is considered to help conquer the material aspect of man's nature and accentuate the spiritual. Finally, the various fast days also differ in their applicability. Some are private in origin and intention, and thus apply exclusively to specific groups or individuals at particular times. Amongst this category are the private penitential fasts (such as that observed by Ahab; I Kings 25:27), or the fasts observed by a bride and bridegroom on the day of their wedding, or by firstborn sons on the day before Passover. Others are public fasts which, although observed by the whole community, take place at irregular intervals or even on single occasions. Common amongst this category in mishnaic times were the public fasts held at times of drought, or on the death of a sage. Finally there exists in the Jewish calendar a group of fasts which are both binding on every Jew and which also occur annually. It is with this latter group that the present chapter will be concerned.

In view of the variety of the fasts to be discussed, and even their differing duration, this chapter will not follow a chronological arrangement. Rather, for the sake of convenience, the annual public fasts will be discussed under three separate headings. The first is the group of fasts associated with the destruction of the Temple. The second is the remaining fasts of historical origin. The final group to be discussed will be those fasts which have particularly penitential associations. This discussion will be preceded by a survey of the development of the principal liturgical features common to these days.

LITURGICAL CHANGES

Ever since biblical times, fasts have been accompanied by public prayer and confessions of sins. During the First Temple period sacrifices were offered, and from the Second Temple period onward, the public fast has been accompanied by a public reading of the Torah. On solemn fasts four prayers—*Shaḥarit, Ḥazot* ("noon"), *Minḥah,* and *Ne'ilat She'arim*—were recited as well as *Ma'ariv*. The *Amidah* of the fast day consisted of 24 benedictions—the eighteen of every day, to which another six were added—and the liturgy was elaborated with special passages of supplication, *seliḥot,* and prayers for mercy. The central part of the service was the sounding of the *shofar* or the *ḥaẓoẓerot* ("trumpets") or trumpets (as main instruments) accompanied by horns. During the Middle Ages, in some Jewish communities, *shofarot* were sounded, in others, trumpets.

Seliḥot. Echoes of these ancient practices are to be found in the alterations necessitated to the present liturgy by fast days. Of these, one of the most noticeable is the recital of *Seliḥot*. These special prayers, usually of poetic form (they are discussed in Chapter II), are normally recited immediately following the repetition of the *Amidah*. Certain congregations, however, say the *Seliḥot* during the repetition itself. On each of the fast days, the *Seliḥot* are interspersed with a declamation of the 13 attributes of God found in Exodus 34:6–7. However, the *Seliḥot* to be recited on each fast day vary, since those with allusions to past events and the meaning of the specific fast are selected for the occasion.

Aneinu. On all fast days a special prayer is inserted in the *Amidot* of both the *Shaḥarit* and *Minḥah* services. The prayer is known by its opening word, *Aneinu* ("Answer us") and consists of a plea for the Almighty's help "on this day of the

Jewish theology does not recognize the concept of original sin. However it does see the sin of the Golden Calf as having effects far beyond itself. This painting by Nicolas Poussin, "Adoration of the Golden Calf" (1635) shows Moses descending the mountain and breaking the two tablets of stone when he saw what his people were doing.

Most of the statutory fasts have some connection with the destruction of the Temples in Jerusalem. These events have been the motif for artists throughout the ages. On the left is a 17th-century Dutch etching which depicts Jerusalem and the Temple surrounded by besieging armies. To the right is a 15th-century French miniature by Jean Fouquet showing Nebuchadnezzar's army attacking the Temple. The medieval savagery in this picture is most probably indicative of the type of battle which was fought in Europe at that time.

fast of our affliction." The *ḥazzan* inserts this prayer between the seventh and eighth benedictions. Individuals recite the prayer in the 16th benediction of the silent *Amidah*. However, custom varies in respect to the latter point. In the Ashkenazi rite, *Aneinu* is only recited individually in the *Minḥah* service, while other rites recite it in *Shaḥarit* as well.

One old form of the *Aneinu* prayer is found in the Talmud. However, each of the ancient versions of the prayer contain different formulas, none of which is identical to that in use today.

The Priestly Blessing. In Jerusalem, where the priestly blessing is recited daily during the morning service, on a fast day it is recited during the afternoon *Minḥah* service. In other communities the priestly blessing has been replaced (except during the *Musaf* service on festivals) with an equivalent recital by the reader. On a fast day this too is transferred to the *Minḥah* service.

Avinu Malkenu. Following the *Amidah* or the *Seliḥot*, another special prayer is recited, *Avinu Malkenu*. This prayer, which is a series of supplications each beginning with the refrain "Our Father, our King," can also be traced to ancient times, to the prayer uttered by Rabbi Akiva: "Our Father, our King, we have no king but Thee; our Father, our King, have mercy on us for Thy sake." The *Avinu Malkenu* prayer is recited at both the morning and the afternoon service. Frequently this is done in chorus; the reader reading each or a part of the supplication, one by one, to be followed by the congregation.

Torah Reading. On all the regular fast days the Torah is read both during the morning and the afternoon service. At both times the same portion is read. This is from Exodus 32:11–14 and 34:1–10. The first part of this portion relates how Moses prayed for Israel after the sin of the Golden Calf, when God threatened to destroy the whole people except for Moses himself. Moses reminds God of His oath to the patriarchs. The second part relates how God ordered Moses to prepare a new set of stone tablets. Moses ascends Mount Sinai with the tablets and perceives God's glory. As this happens he hears the 13 attributes of God. Immediately Moses begs for mercy for Israel. Certain verses—when Moses asks for mercy and the 13 attributes—are recited by the congregation and then read by the reader. This in itself is a prayer which the congregation attributes to itself. In the afternoon, according to Ashkenazi rite only, a portion from the Prophets is also read (*haftarah*) containing Isaiah's call to seek God and repent (Isaiah 55: 6–56–8).

THE DESTRUCTION OF THE TEMPLE

The destruction of the two Temples in Jerusalem constituted the most disastrous single events to occur in ancient Jewish history. Consequently, the period surrounding the anniversaries of these tragedies has become recognized as the most outstanding time of national Jewish mourning. This is especially so since, according to tradition, the destruction of the Second Temple occurred on the exact anniversary of the fall of the first—the ninth of Av. Not surprisingly, therefore, the fast of Tishah be-Av (meaning "the ninth of Av" in Hebrew), has attained an importance among the fast days second only to the Day of Atonement. Two other fasts (those of the 10th of Tevet and the 17th of Tammuz) also have associations with the events surrounding the destruction of the Temple. Although these are less severe than that of Tishah be-Av itself, the rabbis did make efforts to ensure that these fasts were not neglected. Thus, as in the case of Tishah be-Av, they deliberately enumerated all the various other tragedies which had befallen the Jewish people on those days. More particularly, the three weeks between the fast of the 17th of Tammuz and Tishah be-Av are known as a general period of mourning, which is observed with attendant rites. These become more pronounced after the first of Av. The liturgical changes on these occasions thus serve further to emphasize the sense of national disaster which is apparent from Jewish behavior and ceremony on these days.

Asarah be-Tevet. According to the biblical account of the destruction of the First Temple, it was on the 10th of Tevet (in Hebrew: Asarah be-Tevet) that Nebuchadnezzar first laid siege to the city of Jerusalem. Since the fast observed on that day commemorated the beginning of the tragic process,

Quant. Ezechie roy
de deux lignes. Auou
ia tenu quatorze ans
le royaume. le roy des
assyriens nomme sennacherib a
tresgrant main mist les tentes cotre

li. et par fort bras prist toutes les ci
tez de iuda et de beniamin. Et ainsi
comme il aloit en ierusalem. Eze
chie envoya legats au devant de
li. En li promettant quil li obei
roit et quil paieroit les treux telz q

Since the 1967 war between Israel and her neighbors, and the subsequent re-unification of Jerusalem, Jews have been able to visit the Western Wall, which is the last remaining vestige of the Temple. On Tishah be-Av particularly, the Wall has a special attraction and here a young Ḥasid can be seen seated on the ground reciting the traditional *kinot* in mourning for the destruction.

it was also the first fast to be abolished by the Messianic sect led by Shabbetai Ẓevi in 1665.

The liturgy for this day is the same as that for a regular fast. However, the Karaite sect made certain additions to this rule. In their rite, special *seliḥot* passages are recited throughout the month of Tevet, and special prayers added on the Monday, Thursday and Monday preceding the fast. Moreover, on the Sabbath preceding the 10th they refrain from the customary Torah reading.

In recent years, the Chief Rabbinate of Israel has proclaimed Asarah be-Tevet as a commemorative fast for the six million Jews who perished during the Holocaust in Europe. Memorial candles are lit, and the mourners' *Kaddish* is recited. Special Psalms and the *El Maleh Raḥamim* prayer are also said. The

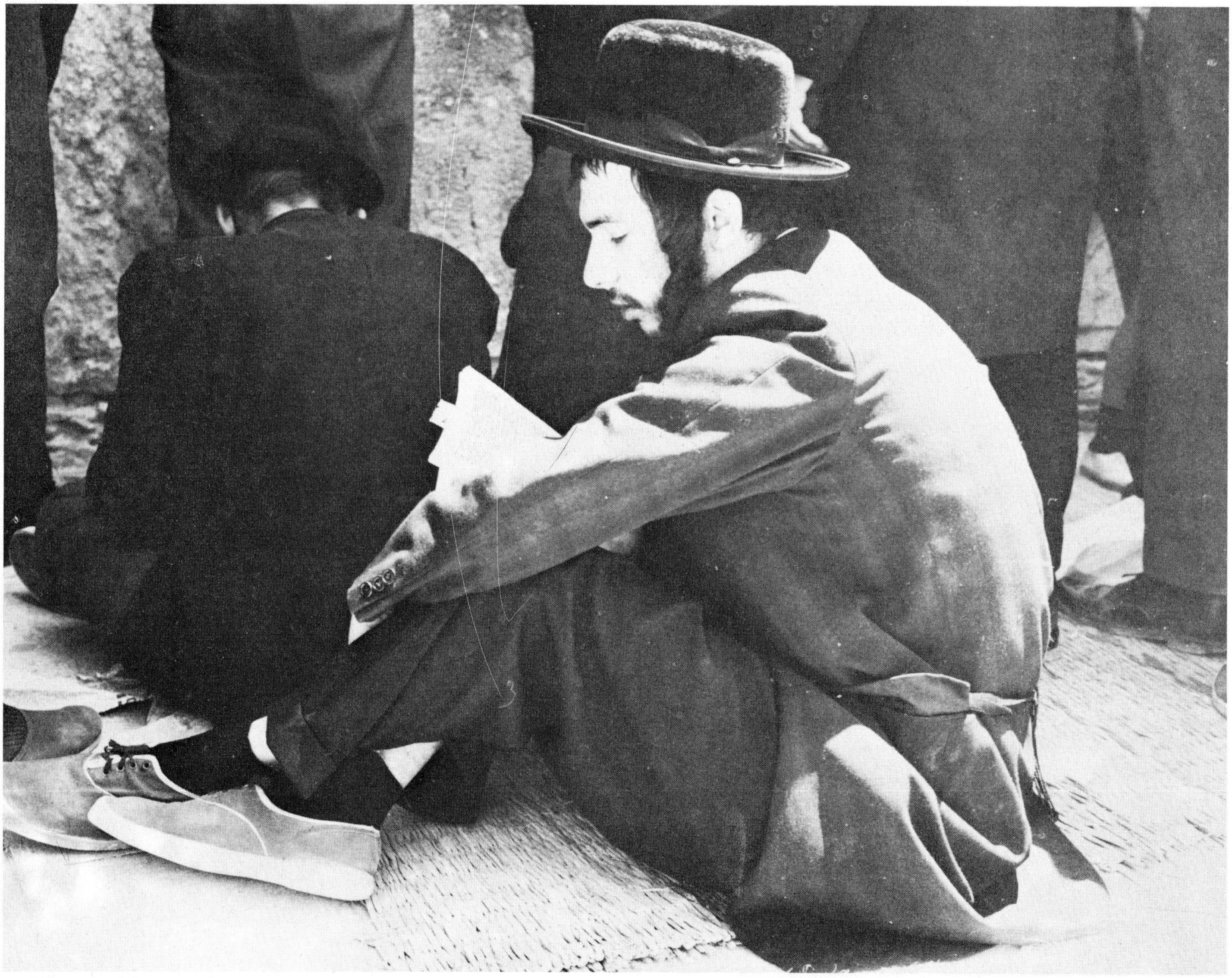

Knesset, however, passed a law in 1951 marking the 27th of Nisan as Remembrance Day for the Holocaust.

According to the regulations of the Jewish calendar, Asarah be-Tevet can never fall on a Sabbath. It thus never needs to be postponed. It can, however, fall on a Friday. It is unusual in that in this case it is not then postponed, but must be observed until nightfall.

Shivah Asar be-Tammuz. The fast observed on the 17th day of Tammuz commemorates the second stage of the process leading to the destruction of the Temple. On that day (translated in Hebrew as Shivah Asar be-Tammuz) the Roman soldiers breached the walls of Jerusalem. Although in the case of the First Temple, a similar breakthrough had occurred on the ninth of the month, the 17th was ultimately accepted as a joint anniversary, except by the Karaites. The liturgy for this day is the same as that for a regular communal fast day.

The Three Weeks. Shivah Asar be-Tammuz commences the three week period of mourning known as Bein ha-meẓarim ("between the straits," i.e. the 17th of Tammuz and the 9th of Av). This commemorates the time it took for the invading armies to battle their way through the streets of Jerusalem to the Temple compound. The old custom of fasting during this period has practically fallen into disuse. However, certain rituals of mourning are still observed. During the first nine days of Av especially, no weddings are performed; the consumption of meat and wine (except on the Sabbath) is forbidden; such comforts as bathing are relinquished. Ashkenazim observe many such rites throughout the three week period.

The last Sabbath of the three week period (i.e. the Sabbath immediately preceding the fast of Tishah be-Av) is known as Shabbat Ḥazon (literally, "Sabbath of Vision"). This is discussed in the Special Sabbaths section of Chapter VII.

The only other liturgical alteration made during this period (in some communities) is the recital of the *Av ha-Raḥamim* prayer before the Torah is returned to the ark after being read on Sabbath morning.

Tishah be-Av. Because of its special origin, the fast of Tishah be-Av occupies a special place in the *halakhah*. With the exception of the Day of Atonement, it is the only fast which begins before sunset on the previous day, and lasts for over 24 hours. Moreover, although work is not absolutely forbidden on Tishah be-Av, it is frowned upon and the general custom is to refrain from work at least until midday. Even the study of Torah is forbidden on this day, since "Torah gladdens the heart."

MA'ARIV. The liturgy of Tishah be-Av also differs from that of other fasts. In particular, whereas on the other fasts the theme of mourning is relegated in favor of repentance, on Tishah be-Av the atmosphere of mourning is constantly stressed. The opening *Ma'ariv* service is the same as usual, until the completion of the *Amidah*. But already one can sense that this is not an ordinary service. In Ashkenazi synagogues the curtain which always covers the ark with the Torah scrolls, is removed. The bare ark gives the synagogue somber appearance. In some Sephardi communities the ark and Torah scrolls are covered in black. The atmosphere of mourning is usually enhanced by the subdued lighting instead of the usual bright lights with their festive effect. Following the *Amidah* the congregants seat themselves on the ground, or else use low stools or upturned benches. In Sephardi communities the number of years since the destruction of the Temple is announced. Then the Book of Lamentations is recited. In Israel Lamentations is frequently read from a kosher (handwritten parchment) scroll. In this case the recital is preceded by the benediction" . . . Who has commanded us concerning the reading of the scroll (*megillah*)." The *She-heḥeyanu* benediction, usually recited before reading from a *megillah* is not said on this occasion.

Lamentations is read in low tones, to a dirge-like tune. The congregation reads quietly together with the reader, who with each chapter, raises his voice slightly. The last sentence but one, "Turn Thou us unto Thee, O Lord, and we shall be turned. Renew our days as of old," is read in a loud voice and is again repeated aloud by the whole congregation at the end of the recital. Then further mourning prayers are said. These are called *kinot* and are similar to the *seliḥot* except that they are not supplications but lamentations. The style, however, is also poetical. The earliest *kinot* that have come down to us were

B.SATT

"Tishah be-Av" by Berel Satt, a wooden bas-relief, shows a scene which is very typical of that day. Seated on a low stool as though in mourning, the lady is holding a candle in her hand by which to read the prayers, because the normal lighting has been dimmed to add to the sorrowful atmosphere of the day. The page from the *De Castro Pentateuch* (14th-century Germany) is the beginning of the Book of Lamentations which is recited on Tishah be-Av. The universal Jewish custom nowadays is for the reader to sit on the ground during the recitation, but the reader pictured here is standing at a lectern.

composed by Eleazar ha-Kallir (seventh century), and many more were added by later *paytanim*. Following the recital of several *kinot* the evening prayers are concluded.

SHAḤARIT. From the Middle Ages it became customary except among certain oriental communities to wear *tallit* and *tefillin* during the morning *Shaḥarit* service. (They are considered to be ornaments, and the *tefillin* in particular are held to be Israel's "crown of glory.") They are worn instead during the *Minḥah* (thus the blessing "who crowns Israel with glory" is omitted from the Morning Benedictions, because it refers to the *tefillin*).

In the Sephardi rite the Song of Moses in Deuteronomy 32 is substituted for the Song of Moses in Exodus 15 which is normally recited after the morning Psalms. During the *Amidah* prayer, the *Aneinu* supplication is added, as on all fast days.

THE TORAH READING. The Torah reading is from Deuteronomy 4:24–40. This deals with Moses' warning of the misfortunes that will befall the people if they do not remain faithful to God. The portion also contains the promise that God will not desert Israel. For the prophetic portion Jeremiah 8:13–9:23 is read to the same tune which is used for Lamentations. This is a recital of the woes which Israel suffers and the state of utter despair in which the people find themselves. The passage ends on a high moral note: ". . . let him that glorieth in this, that he understandeth and knoweth Me, that I am the Lord who exercises mercy, justice and righteousness in the earth; for in these things I delight, saith the Lord."

THE KINOT. The Torah reading is followed by the recital of *kinot*. According to Sephardi custom these precede the Torah reading. The congregants seat themselves on the ground, as on the previous evening. In some communities the rabbi reads each *kinah* aloud while the congregation recites it silently. In other communities the *kinot* are recited aloud by all the congregants, the reader only beginning the correct *kinah* and terminating it.

The *kinot* vary from rite to rite: Polish, Lithuanian, Italian and others. Thus, the Sephardi rite contains one *kinah* modeled on the four questions in the Passover *Haggadah*. Its opening stanza reads: "I will ask some questions of the holy congregation; How is this night different from all other nights? Why on Passover eve do we eat *mazzah* and bitter herbs, while this night all is bitterness . . . ?" Another interesting *kinah* recited by the Sephardim is *Bore ad anna*. The fifth verse of the original version contains a derogatory reference to the Trinity, and was modified in some western communities. In some congregations the *kinah* is recited in Ladino, under the title *La Paloma* ("The Dove").

The *kinot* recited in the Ashkenazi rite exhibit a similar compound of local variation and widespread popularity. Thus, they include *Sha'ali Serufah be-Esh* by Meir of Rothenburg, which commemorates the burning of the Talmud in Paris in 1242. Also recited is *Arzei ha-Levanon* ("the cedars of Lebanon"). This describes the death of ten rabbinical martyrs, and parallels the account recited on Yom Kippur towards the end of the *Musaf* service. However, probably the most well-known *kinot* are the Odes to Zion. These begin with the famous *Ẓiyyon Halo Tishali* by Judah Halevi, and conclude with *Eli Ẓiyyon ve-Areha* ("Wail Zion and its cities.") This dirge, written in the Middle Ages, but of anonymous authorship,

consists of 12 stanzas which enumerate the cruelties suffered by Judea and its inhabitants during the destruction of the Second Temple. *Eli Ẓiyyon* is sung by the congregation while standing. The melody is of an elegiac character and has become, for all Ashkenazi communities, a symbol of the yearly commemoration of the Destruction. It therefore came to be used also for some other *kinot* and also for *Lekhah Dodi* in the Friday evening service during the "Three Weeks." In Israel, a new *kinah* with the same meter as *Eli Ẓiyyon* and chanted to the same melody, is recited mourning the fate of the Jews in the Holocaust. Recital of the *kinot* continues until about midday. When these are completed, the final morning prayers are said. In many communities the Book of Lamentations is then read again.

MINḤAH. The *Minḥah* service on Tishah be-Av takes the normal form, with, however, certain commemorative additions. The Torah reading is as for a normal fast day and consists of Exodus 32:11–14 and 34:1–10, and, as *haftarah*, Isaiah 55:6–56:8. The Sephardi *haftarah* is Hosea 14:2–9. In some rituals the person called up to the Torah says: "Blessed be the righteous Judge"—the verse by which mourners are greeted.

During the *Amidah*, a special prayer is inserted into the 14th blessing, the benediction for the restoration of Jerusalem. Known, from its opening word as *Naḥem* ("Comfort"), this paragraph probably dates back to the era of the Babylonian Talmud. Containing expressions of grief for the Destruction,

it concludes with the prayer that the Lord will comfort Zion and rebuild Jerusalem.

Since the *tallit* and *tefillin* were not worn during *Shaḥarit*, they are worn during *Minḥah*. Should Tishah be-Av fall on a Sunday, *Havdalah* is recited after the Sunday evening service before breaking the fast.

The other mourning customs practices on Tishah be-Av vary in origin and application. In Jerusalem, it is customary to visit the Western Wall on this day. Visits to cemeteries, especially to the graves of martyrs and pious men, were frequent in order to implore the deceased to intercede for the speedy redemption of Israel. In Algiers, the *shofar* was blown in memory of the ancient fast day ceremonies in Temple times. In the State of Israel, public places of entertainment and restaurants are closed on the eve of Tishah be-Av. In the evening after the fast, some people greet each other with the formula: "May you soon enjoy the comfort of Zion."

The music is for the *Eli Ẓiyyon* lamentation which is recited at the end of the morning service for Tishah be-Av. The plaintive melody has become symbolic of the day and is also used in many congregations for the *Lekhah Dodi* hymn on the Sabbath eve before Tishah be-Av. The dirge which was written in the Middle Ages consists of 12 stanzas each closing with the refrain, "Wail, Zion and its cities, as a woman in labor pains . . . " A modern dirge in commemoration of the Holocaust is recited in many Israel synagogues to the same melody. Quite out of keeping with the spirit of a fast day are these naked putti which adorn the page from the *Rothschild Maḥzor* dealing with the fast of the Tenth of Tevet. The seal shown here comes from a papyrus letter sent from Jerusalem to Lachish in 587/6 b.c.e. It is inscribed "To Gedaliah who is in charge of the house," who may in fact be that Gedaliah in memory of whose murder the fast is observed.

Classical Reform Judaism of the 19th century did not observe the mourning ritual of Tishah be-Av. In recent decades, however, Reform circles have come to feel that this day should not be ignored but rather it should be reinterpreted to make it relevant and meaningful in modern times.

SHABBAT NAḤAMU. The Sabbath immediately following the fast of Tishah be-Av is known as Shabbat Naḥamu ("The Sabbath of comfort"). This too is discussed in Chapter VII in the section dealing with Special Sabbaths.

OTHER HISTORICAL FAST DAYS

The fasts associated with the destruction of the Temples form only one group (albeit the most important) of the historical fasts in the Jewish calendar. The Jewish community is also called upon to commemorate by public fasts other past tragedies and thereby to attain a degree of empathy with other emergencies of former years.

Ẓom Gedaliyah. The first of these, in the order in which they appear in the Jewish calendar, is Ẓom Gedaliyah (The Fast of Gedaliah). Occurring on the third day of Tishrei, it commemorates the murder of Gedaliah, the governor of the Jews appointed by Nebuchadnezzar after the destruction of the First Temple. This event dashed every hope of a peaceful Jewish settlement in Ereẓ Israel under Babylonian rule, and led to the mass flight of the Jewish remnant to Egypt.

The fast itself was first instituted during the years of exile, and is mentioned by Zechariah together with the other three fasts commemorating the Temple destruction. Discontinued during the period of the Second Temple, it was reinstituted after that, too, was destroyed. The liturgy for this day is as for a normal fast day.

The Seventh of Adar. According to talmudic tradition, the seventh of Adar commemorates the anniversary of both the birth and the death of Moses. In oriental communities it became widespread as a day of fasting and commemoration for the pious because of the belief that a spark of the soul of Moses is found in every righteous person. Sephardi Jews therefore still light candles on this day for the "ascension of the

souls of the righteous." Some communities also recite specially composed *piyyutim* on this day (some of which are repeated on *Simḥat Torah,* when the biblical account of Moses' death is read in the synagogue). In the 17th century, Samuel Aboab (d.1694), the rabbi of Venice, compiled a collection of selected passages from Scripture, Mishnah and the *Zohar* to be recited in the synagogue on the seventh of Adar.

In Eastern and Central Europe, as well as in the United States, this day was observed as the annual fast day for the *ḥevra kaddisha* (burial society). It was customary for members to go to the graves of those who had died during the year and ask for forgiveness in case the last rites had not been properly observed. Rabbis would also eulogize Moses, as well as the famous rabbinical scholars who had died during the previous year. The fast would be terminated by a festive meal at which new members would be admitted to the society and a new board elected.

The death of Moses is observed by members of the burial society with a fast. This illustration from the *Leon Bible*, Spain, 1162, shows Moses on his deathbed surrounded by the Children of Israel who are tearing their cheeks in grief. A different expression of grief is "Zion's Elegy" by Jules Leon Butensky (1871–1947), showing the great poet Judah Halevi mourning over the ruins of the Temple.

In Israel, the seventh of Adar has been officially designated as memorial day for those soldiers of the Israel Defense Forces whose last resting place is unknown.

Ta'anit Esther. One week after the anniversary of the death of Moses, Jewish communities throughout the world celebrate the festival of Purim. That minor feast day is, however, also preceded by a fast occurring one day earlier, on the 13th of Adar. Known as Ta'anit Esther ("The Fast of Esther"), its supposed origin is Esther's call for a public gathering on that day (Esther 9:18). The practice of fasting on this day is almost

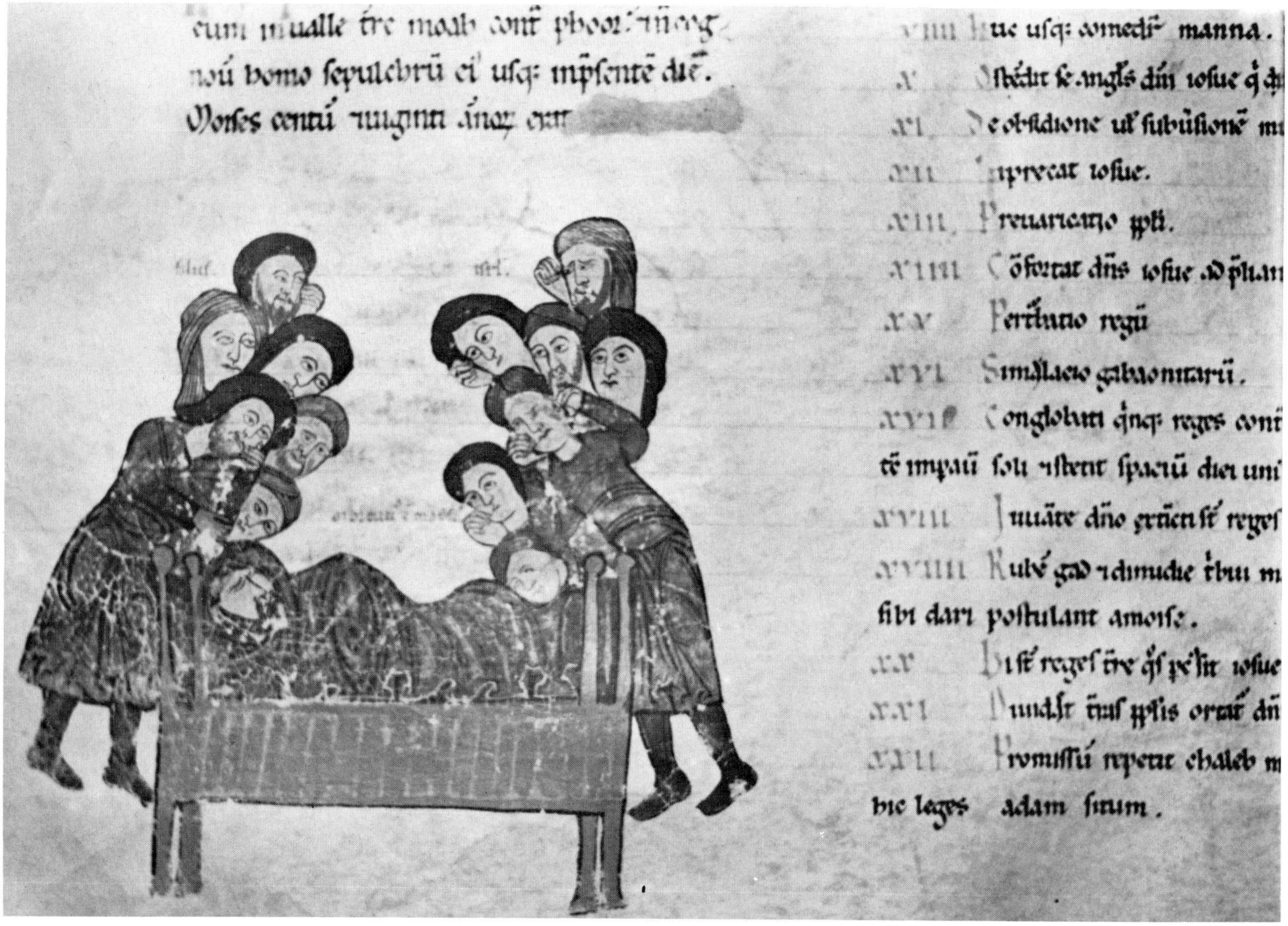

certainly of post-mishnaic origin, since until the festival of the Second Temple the 13th of Adar was observed as a minor festival on which fasting was forbidden; it was known as Nicanor's Day, commemorating the Hasmonean victory over the Seleucid general of that name.

Ta'anit Esther is peculiar in that it is the only one of the fast days not to be postponed to a Sunday should it fall on the Sabbath (Yom Kippur is the only fast to be observed on the Sabbath itself). Rather, because the fast decreed by Esther was considered to be an essential preliminary to the ultimate deliverance of the Jewish people on Purim, Ta'anit Esther is moved forward to the preceding Thursday. In a leap year, when an additional month of Adar is intercalated, the fast (like Purim itself) is observed only in the second Adar.

On Ta'anit Esther, special *Seliḥot* are recited in addition to those of a normal fast day. Moreover, in anticipation of the Purim joy, *Taḥanun* is omitted from the *Minḥah* service. Otherwise the normal fast day liturgy is observed.

The 20th of Sivan and Erev Shabbat Ḥukkat. The practice of commemorating national tragedies by a public fast (such as Ẓom Gedaliyah) was occasionally imitated on a wide scale during more recent periods of Jewish history. This was particularly the case with the fast celebrated throughout Europe on the 20th of Sivan. This day marks the anniversary of both the massacre of the Jews of Blois in 1171, and of the destruction of the community of Nemirov, in the Ukraine, by Chmielnicki's cossacks in 1648. The eve of the Sabbath reading of Ḥukkat (in the Book of Numbers) was also declared a fast, in commemoration of the public burning of the Talmud in Paris in 1242.

Although these fasts have now fallen into disuse, they were once marked by liturgical changes in the normal services. Thus, specially composed *Seliḥot* describing these events were recited in the synagogue. The 20th of Sivan, in particular, was considered so important that David ben Samuel Halevi (Taz) (1586–1667) ruled that, should it fall on a Monday or Thursday, the special Torah reading for fast days would then take precedence over the normal Torah reading.

PENITENTIAL FAST DAYS

Besides those fasts commemorating the destruction of the Temple and other historical events, the Jewish calendar also contains a third group of public fast days—those specifically associated with the theme of repentance. The two themes of national mourning and individual penance are, of course, interrelated. Thus Maimonides, when discussing the reasons for fasting on such days as Tishah be-Av, states: "These are days on which all Israel fasts because of the disasters which occurred on these days, in order to rouse the hearts to find ways of repentance. And this should be a reminder of our bad deeds and the (bad) deeds of our fathers . . . which caused them and us these woes. By remembering these matters we mend our ways." Nevertheless, certain days of the Jewish year are specifically devoted to penetential fasting without any particular reference to an historical event. While the Day of Atonement is the most outstanding of these, several other occasions have been set aside for this purpose.

When he witnessed Jews in Russia observing Tishah be-Av Napoleon Bonaparte is reputed to have said that "a people who can mourn the destruction of a Temple for so many years will surely ultimately see its rebuilding." "Tishah be-Av" by Leopold Horowitz was a common scene on that day in thousands of prayer houses throughout central and eastern Europe. The 17th-century engraving shows Jews mourning the destruction of the Temple while it is actually burning in the background.

Yom Kippur Katan. The most regular of such occasions is the eve of every Rosh Ḥodesh which has been discussed in the previous chapter. The penitential character of these days is apparent from their collective name—*Yom Kippur Katan,* meaning "Minor Yom Kippur."

Shovavim Tat. During the months between Ḥanukkah and Purim a separate series of fasts is added to the Jewish calendar. They are known as ShOVaVIM TaT, an acrostic composed of the initial letters of the weekly Torah portions denoting the weeks when the fasts take place. They begin in the week when the first portion of the Book of Exodus is read, and continue six to ten weeks. During this period, it became customary to fast on either the Thursday before every Sabbath (Ashkenazi rite) or on both the Monday and Thursday (Italian rite).

The penetential aspect of the Shovavim fasts was stressed by the kabbalist school of Isaac Luria. They attributed to these days a purpose similar to that which they associated with Yom Kippur Katan: the restoration of the universe to perfection. In more popular form, these fasts were also regarded as opportunities to request divine assistance in the avoidance of disease and miscarriages during the hard winter months.

Very few communities still observe the Shovavim fasts. In those which do, *Selihot* are recited in *Shaḥarit* (in the Ashkenazi rite) or during *Minḥah* (in the Italian rite).

The Behab Fasts. The intention and form of the Shovavim fasts are paralleled by similar commemorations of the period immediately following the festivals of Passover and Sukkot. The Monday, Thursday and Monday after these festivals are known collectively as the BeHaB fast days, an acrostic formed by the Hebrew letters denoting the second, fifth and second days of the week.

The practice of fasting on these days was interpreted as an atonement for possible sins committed while in a state of drunkenness and gluttony during the holidays. Certain pious individuals fasted after Shavuot too, even though that festival was considered to be too short to let a person forget himself. The fasts would be announced in the synagogue during the service on the previous Sabbath. They were accompanied by the recital of *Seliḥot,* and the special Torah reading for fast days, both in the morning and afternoon services.

Today the Behab fasts are generally unknown or ignored. However, in some communities *Seliḥot* are still recited. During the Yom Kippur War of 1973 the Israel Chief Rabbinate ordained a fast on the first Monday of the Behab fasts, following Sukkot. This was widely observed, together with special prayers and even the traditional Torah reading.

Erev Rosh Ha-Shanah. The outstanding penitential period in the Jewish year commences with Rosh Ḥodesh Elul, and reaches its climax on Yom Kippur. Fasting has sometimes been practiced for the whole, or a part of this period. Within this context, the eve of Rosh Ha-Shanah has attained particular significance, because it is the last day of the year and the last before the Day of Judgment begins. As such, it has been widely observed as a fast, ever since talmudic times. Even children were enjoined to participate once they reached the age of understanding the meaning of the fast.

Because of the incoming festival, the fast of Erev Rosh Ha-Shanah is not observed until nightfall, for which reason the special Torah reading does not take place. It is customary for those who observe the fast to do so until after the *Minḥah* service, which is held early, about half an hour after noon. The special *Aneinu* prayer is recited by the individual at this service, but not by the reader when he repeats the *Amidah.*

XI In the Family

Daily Domestic Ceremonies

The Sabbath and the Festivals

A Time to Mourn and a Time to Rejoice

At least 3,000 different editions of the Passover *Haggadah* have been printed. The title page shown here is that of one of the most famous, printed by Solomon Proops in Amsterdam, 1712. The page shows Moses at the Burning Bush and Moses and Aaron, the high priest. Rays of light emanate from the former's head and Aaron is dressed in his priestly vestments. The copper engraved illustrations used in this *Haggadah* for the first time were widely copied.

The illustration from the 13th-century *Birds' Head Haggadah* shows a celebrant reciting the benediction after he has washed his hands. The *Copenhagen Seder Birkot ha-Mazon* page is the blessing to be recited before the consumption of wine and the shortened form of Grace to be said after it.

At one level, the complete cycle of the Jewish liturgy can be considered as one series of domestic ceremonies. The reason for this is that there are very few prayers which cannot be recited by the individual in his own home. Admittedly, the rabbis of the Talmud did maintain that communal prayer is of greater significance than private prayer, and that regular synagogue worship is a boundless virtue. Nevertheless, the centrality of the synagogue has never been allowed to displace the importance of the home in Jewish life. Rather, several significant portions of the Jewish liturgy are pre-eminently domestic ceremonies. Of these, some have been reproduced in the normal communal service, and thus possess a dual habitat. This is true, for instance, of the lighting of the Ḥanukkah candles, which is performed in both the synagogue and the home. Other liturgical ceremonies, however, have retained their domestic and private associations, and are therefore performed exclusively in one's private abode. It is with these that the present chapter is primarily concerned.

DAILY DOMESTIC CEREMONIES

Grace Before and After Meals. The rabbis laid great stress on the obligation to recite a blessing before partaking of food, since they considered it sacreligious to enjoy of this world without giving prior thanks to Him whose bounty has provided us with the means of sustenance. They therefore instituted separate blessings to be recited before eating the various species of food, of which those over bread and wine are considered the most important. The latter, "Who creates the fruit of the vine" (*Bore peri ha-gafen*) is recited even when wine is drunk during the course of the repast, and not at the beginning. The blessing for bread, "Who brings forth bread from the earth" (*Ha-moẓi leḥem min ha-areẓ*), when recited at the start of a meal exempts one from the obligation to recite most additional blessings for the remaining courses. Since this blessing is thus often the only one recited before a meal, the formula for the entire Grace before meals has become popularly known as *moẓi*.

Washing the Hands. When the blessing over bread is to be recited, the *moẓi* is preceded by another ceremony. In this case, the rabbis made it obligatory to wash the hands, and to recite a benediction. Its text, which is also recited after washing one's hands when rising from sleep, reads: ". . .and commanded us concerning the washing of the hands." This ceremony is sometimes performed before the recitation of the Grace after Meals too (when it is known as *Mayim Aḥaronim,* "the latter water"). Then, however, no blessing is recited.

The washing of the hands before and after the meal is designed to serve a ritual purpose; these acts must therefore not be confused with washing for the sake of cleanliness. This is evident from the rabbinic requirement that the hands must be clean before the ritual ablution. The custom of *netillat yadayim* seems to have originated with the priestly custom of washing hands before eating consecrated foods. Indeed, many persons emphasize the sacred nature of the practice by reciting the verse: "Lift up your hands to the sanctuary, and bless the Lord" (Psalm 134:2) during the washing. The reason given in the Talmud for the practice of *mayim aḥaronim* is to remove any salt adhering to the fingers, which could cause serious injury to the eyes. It is also possible that this washing derived from ancient Roman table manners.

The Text. The recitation of Grace after Meals is considered a biblical ordinance. It is inferred from the verse: "You shall eat and be satisfied and bless the Lord your God for the good land which He has given you." (Deuteronomy 8:10.) After a meal at which bread has been eaten, a rather lengthy grace is recited, consisting of four blessings. The first *(Birkat ha-Zan)*, praises God for providing food for all His creatures. The second (*Birkat ha-Areẓ*) expresses Israel's particular gratitude for the "good land" God has given it, the redemption from Egypt, the covenant of circumcision, and the revelation of the Torah. The third benediction, called *Boneh Yerushalayim* and also *Neḥamah* (Consolation) asks God to have mercy on the Kingdom and to restore the Temple and the kingdom of David. To these three benedictions which form the core of the Grace, a fourth (*Ha-Tov ve-ha-Metiv*) was added after the destruction of Bethar, the last Jewish fortress to continue Bar Kokhba's resistance to Rome in 135 C.E. Despite the national

tragedy which that event symbolized, the rabbis ordained that God had to be thanked in times of sorrow as well as of joy. The benediction itself therefore combines thanks for God's goodness with the prayer that He may fulfill specific desires. It is followed by several petitions which each begin with the word *Ha-Raḥaman* ("May the All-Merciful. . ."). Originally phrased to suit individual desires, the supplication has now become standardized, and contains supplications for the continuation of God's rule and mercy, and for personal sustenance and blessing. The number of these petitions varies greatly in different rites; the general Sephardi rite has some 15, while the Ashkenazi has nine. It is at this point in the Grace that some persons now add a petition for the State of Israel.

The collective term for the Grace after Meals is known as *Birkat ha-Mazon*. However, more popular designations have evolved. Thus, among Portuguese Jews it is known as *bencao,* and among Ashkenazim by the Yiddish term *benshn,* a corruption of the Latin "benedictio" (by way of Old French).

THE INVITATION. Although a characteristically domestic ceremony, the *Birkat ha-Mazon* formula is also changed in accordance with the number of participants. In particular, the rabbis ordained that when three or more have eaten bread together, one of them must summon the others to say Grace with him. This introductory formula is known as *Zimmum*. In reply to the invitation "Gentlemen, let us say Grace," (in Sephardi usage "with your permission"), the others reply "Blessed be the name of the Lord henceforth and forever." The leader repeats the statement and then continues, "With your consent (in Sephardi usage "with the permission of Heaven") let us now bless Him of whose food we have eaten." The others then respond: "Blessed be He whose food we have eaten and through whose goodness we live." This formula, according to the Talmud, must even be recited by three women who eat together. According to one opinion in the Mishnah, the *zimmun* formula becomes increasingly elaborate as the number of participants grows to ten, a hundred, a thousand, and ten thousand; more numerous and more solemn epithets are added every time. According to the accepted opinion, when ten or more men

ברוך אתה יי אלהינו מלך העולם המוציא לחם מן הארץ:
ברוך אתה יי אלהינו מלך העולם אשר קדשנו במצותיו וצונו על אכילת מצה:
ברוך אתה יי אלהינו מלך העולם אשר קדשנו במצותיו וצונו על אכילת מרור:
כן עשה הלל בזמן שבית המקדש קיים היה כורך מצה ומרור ואוכל ביחד לקיים מה שנאמר על מצות ומרורים יאכלהו:
סדר ברכת המזון
נברך אלהינו שאכלנו משלו ברוך אלהינו שאכלנו משלו ובטובו חיינו: ברוך אלהינו שאכלנו משלו ובטובו חיינו:
נברך שאכלנו משלו ברוך שאכלנו משלו ובטובו חיינו: ברוך שאכלנו משלו ובטובו חיינו: ברוך הוא וברוך שמו:
ברוך אתה יי אלהינו מלך העולם הזן את העולם כלו בטובו בחן בחסד וברחמים הוא נותן לחם לכל בשר כי לעולם חסדו: ובטובו הגדול תמיד לא חסר לנו ואל יחסר לנו מזון לעולם ועד: בעבור שמו הגדול כי הוא זן ומפרנס לכל ומטיב לכל ומכין מזון לכל בריותיו אשר ברא ברוך אתה יי הזן את הכל:
נודה לך יי אלהינו על שהנחלת לאבותינו ארץ חמדה טובה ורחבה ועל שהוצאתנו יי אלהינו מארץ מצרים ופדיתנו מבית עבדים ועל בריתך שחתמת בבשרנו ועל תורתך שלמדתנו ועל חקיך שהודעתנו ועל חיים חן וחסד שחוננתנו ועל אכילת מזון שאתה זן ומפרנס אותנו תמיד בכל יום ובכל עת ובכל שעה:

The beginning of Grace after Meals as it appears in the *Erlangen Haggadah* (Germany, 1748). The engravings around the letters of the word *Barukh* make up a pastoral scene. The instructions in the *Haggadah* are in both Hebrew and Yiddish.

are present "our God" is added to the response which then reads: "Let us now bless our God of whose food we have eaten."

THE FINAL BENEDICTION. When bread is not eaten, there are two other forms of grace (known as *Berakhah Aḥaronah*—"final benediction") to be recited, depending on the nature of the food consumed. The first is a shortened form of the usual Grace after Meals, and is recited after eating food prepared from the five species of grain (wheat, barley, rye, oats and spelt), wine, or the fruits of Ereẓ Israel (grapes, figs, olives, pomegranates and dates). For any other food a short benediction (called in the Talmud *Ve-lo-Khelum,* "nothing," but popularly known by its first two words, *Bore Nefashot*) is recited.

On extraordinary occasions, the "complete" *Birkat ha-Mazon* recited after bread might also be shortened. Most shortened versions retained the first blessing, but tend to telescope the remaining three benedictions. It is hence known as *Me'ein Shalosh* ("The Essence of the Three"). Among those permitted to recite the shortened form were workmen who eat during working hours, children, and persons in a position of danger or emergency.

In the United States, the Conservative movement has evolved a shortened version of the Grace after Meals based on the traditional formula. The Reform prayer book has a shortened version made up of two English paragraphs and concluding with the Hebrew ending of the traditional first blessing.

Night Prayers. Once *Ma'ariv* became established as a community prayer to be recited in the early evening, an individual night prayer became the concluding liturgical ceremony of the day. The Hebrew name for this prayer, *Keri'at Shema al-ha-Mittah* reflects the fact that its central feature is the recitation of the first paragraph of the *Shema*. It also reflects the rabbinic concept that sleep is akin to a state of minor death; just as one is obliged in the last hour of life to recite the *Shema* and bless the unity of God, so one should recite the *Shema* at night and commend one's spirit to God before succumbing to sleep. The prayer also has a prophylactic significance. The recitation of the *Shema* is followed by a paragraph known as *Ha-Mappil* ("Who causes the bands of sleep to fall on my eyes. . .") This invokes God's protection against the various dangers that might befall man at night and during sleep, and especially against sin. This paragraph also reflects the notion that the night prayers are a prophylactic against *shedim* (evil spirits) which were believed to be abroad at night. In post-talmudic times, additional scriptural passages (e.g. Psalms 91 and 3) and liturgical passages were added to the night prayer. It is customary not to recite these additional prayers and texts on the first night of Passover. Since this is a "night of watching unto the Lord" (Exodus 12:42), it is believed that God Himself guards the Jews from the dangers of this night.

THE SABBATH AND THE FESTIVALS

The features which best characterize the celebration of the Sabbath and the festivals in the Jewish home are not necessarily liturgical. As days of rest and rejoicing, they are distinguished by the particular atmosphere of festivity and sanctity to which Jews aspire on these occasions. Nevertheless, the celebration of the Sabbath and festivals does also attain liturgical expres-

Imre Szigeti's pencil drawing of the housewife lighting the Sabbath candles. It is an old, widely accepted custom to cover the eyes while reciting the benediction. Many women cover their heads with a kerchief for the ceremony.

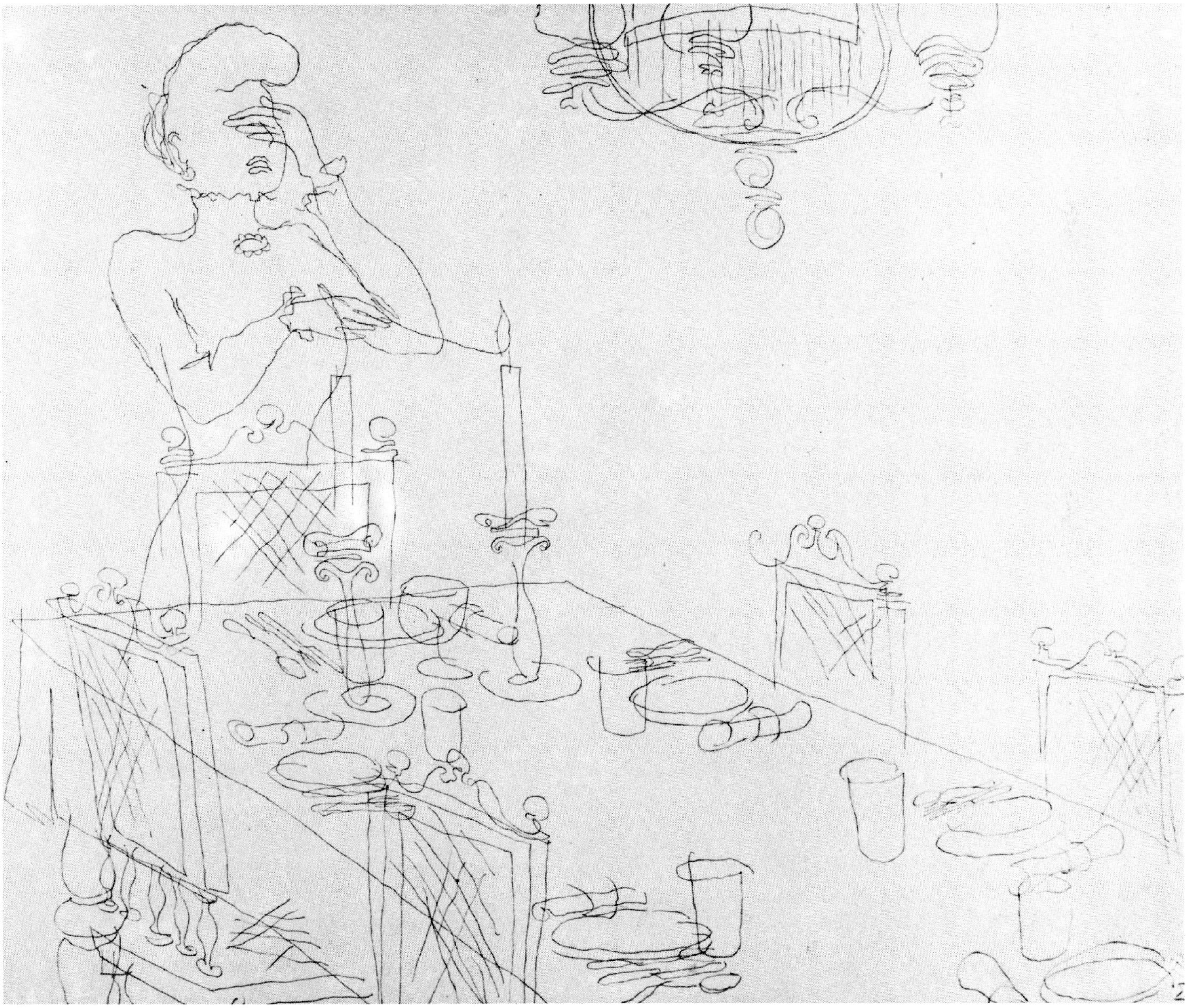

These young ladies are obviously enjoying the lesson in how to bake *ḥallot* for the Sabbath. On the Sabbath table a goblet of wine always appears together with the *ḥallot*. The *Kiddush* goblet has become an art form. The example on the left is 18th-century Russian; the other is from Augsburg, Germany, and dates from 1753–55.

sion in domestic ceremonies and prayers. While some of these are reflections, and even repetitions, of the changes which these days necessitate in the synagogue service, others are unique to the home.

Kindling of the Lights. This is most obviously so in the case of the kindling of the Sabbath or festival lights, the ceremony which inaugurates these days. Thus, at dusk on Friday evening, the mistress of the house kindles at least two candles, one corresponding to "remember the Sabbath day" (Exodus 20:8), the other to "observe the Sabbath day" (Deuteronomy 5:12). After so doing, she recites the benediction ". . .who has commanded us to kindle the Sabbath light." The same ceremony is performed just before the advent of a festival, when the formula of the blessing is changed to refer to "the festival light." On the first evening of the festivals, this benediction is followed by the *She-heḥeyanu* blessing; and when the Sabbath and festival coincide, the formula is again changed to read: "The Sabbath and the festival light."

The rabbis of the Talmud considered this ceremony so important that they warned that the omission of its performance was one of the sins for which women die in childbirth. The respect and affection which it has attained in Jewish imaginations can be seen in the elaborate decorations often designed to adorn the Sabbath and festival candlesticks. In some communities there is a custom for the mistress of the house to light one additional candle for every one of her children.

The Angels. The lighting of the candles on the Sabbath and festivals precedes the departure of the members of the household to the synagogue. According to one talmudic statement, they are accompanied on their return home by two ministering angels, one "good" and one "bad." Should they find the household prepared to celebrate the Sabbath, the "good" angel expresses the wish that the family celebrate the next week's Sabbath in the same fashion. The "bad" angel is then forced to respond "Amen." However, should the household not be prepared to welcome the Sabbath, the two angels reverse their roles when reciting the same formula. It is on this basis that many families, as soon as they enter home on Friday evenings, sing a special hymn known as *Shalom Aleikhem*. Consisting of four stanzas, each of which is usually recited three times, it welcomes the angels into the household and asks for their blessing. At the conclusion of this hymn, in some communities, the children of the family are then assembled in order to receive the parental blessing. The father lays his hands on the head of each child, and invokes the patriarchal blessing: for a boy, he recites the verse "May God make thee like Ephraim and Menasseh" (Genesis 48:20); and for a girl the verse "May God make thee like Sarah, Rebekah, Rachel and Leah" (cf. Ruth 4:11). This is followed by the priestly benediction (Numbers 6:24–26). These formulas, which are also recited on the eve of the Day of Atonement and prior to a child's wedding ceremony, are sometimes recited in the synagogue.

In many families, the husband (together with his children) then pays homage to the housewife and mother of the family by reciting Proverbs 31:10–31. This passage, which is known by its opening words as *Eshet Ḥayyil* ("a woman of valor"), enumerates the virtues of the ideal wife and mother. The laudations reach a climax in the statement that "Grace is deceitful and beauty is vain. But a woman who fears the Lord, she shall be praised. . ." Although the customs of reciting this passage originated in kabbalistic circles, who referred to the Divine Presence (*Shekhinah*) as the mystical mother and wife, it has since been adopted as a specific tribute to wives.

Kiddush. In the atmosphere of family unison thus induced,

the members of the household then proceed to the dining table. There, the master of the house recites a prayer over a cup of wine. Known as *Kiddush* (lit. "sanctification"), this prayer consists of both scriptural quotations and a prayer passage. Kiddush is also recited on Sabbath and festival mornings. The precise formula then used, however, varies from that recited before the evening meal. Thus, the text of the standard evening *Kiddush* for Sabbaths consists of an introductory paragraph from Genesis 1:31 and 2:1–3; the blessing over wine; and the blessing for the sanctification of the day. On festival evenings, the introductory scriptural passage is omitted, and after the blessing over wine a different blessing for the sanctification of the day is recited. (This is suitably altered when the festival coincides with a Sabbath.) On all full festivals, except for the last days of Passover, the *She-heḥeyanu* blessing is then recited. The Sabbath morning *Kiddush* consists of an introductory paragraph from Exodus 31:16–17 and 20:8–11, and the blessing over wine. On festival mornings, the passage preceding the blessing over wine is replaced by Leviticus 23:4 and 44, the two verses which respectively introduce and conclude the festival laws as outlined in the Bible.

In some Ashkenazi communities, *Kiddush* is also recited in the synagogue at the conclusion of the Sabbath and festival evening services. Despite the opposition of some rabbis to this practice, it was defended on the grounds that at one time travelers were housed and fed in a room adjoining the synagogue, and could only thus perform the obligation of sanctifying wine before their meal.

Havdalah. The recital of the *Kiddush* at the commencement of Sabbaths and festivals is paralleled by the recital of *Havdalah* at the conclusion of these days. Meaning "distinction," the main theme of this prayer is the distinction between the sanctity of the holy day now ending and the ordinary nature of the days to follow. This distinction is first mentioned during the *Amidah* in the *Ma'ariv* recited at the conclusion of the Sabbath and festivals. However, it is in the home ceremony of *Havdalah* that the idea attains its clearest expression.

Havdalah is one of the most ancient blessings, originating in pre-talmudic times. However, the text of the ceremony has developed over a long period of time. In the Ashkenazi version, the ceremony commences with the recital of a number of scriptural verses, of which the first is: "Behold, God is my salvation" (Isaiah 12:2–3). This introduction is then followed by three blessings. The first, over wine, derives from the duty to use this drink in the ceremony (although where wine is not available any other national beverage may be used). The second, "Who creates the light of the fire," is recited over a specially lighted candle, which contains at least two wicks. The purpose of this blessing is to indicate that work is now permitted and to stress the departure of the Sabbath. A separate blessing is then made over spices, which are handed round among the participants. Although the origin of this portion of the ceremony is not clear, it has been interpreted as an attempt to offer the Jew some compensation for the loss of the "additional soul" which traditionally accompanies him throughout the Sabbath. The ceremony then concludes with the *Havdalah* blessing proper, which enlarges upon the distinction between the holy and profane.

In all rites, including the Karaite, the ceremony is followed by the recitation of a hymn known, from its opening word, as *Ha-Mavdil* ("Who distinguishes"). Probably composed in Spain during the 11th century, it asks God to pardon our sins (some versions add: "and our wealth") and to multiply our offspring as the sand and the stars at night. In all likelihood, it was originally intended to be recited at the *Ne'ilah* service on Yom Kippur, where it is still to be found in the Algerian rite. In many communities, this hymn is then followed by several others, perhaps the most famous of which implores Elijah the Prophet speedily to herald the promised redemption.

Havdalah is also recited at the conclusion of a festival. Then, however, the blessings over the candle and spices are omitted. A special case arises when a festival commences on Saturday night, since it is then obligatory to recite both the *Havdalah* (commemorating the conclusion of the Sabbath) and the *Kiddush* for the festival. The formula to be adopted in this instance is indicated by the talmudic mnemotechnic aid, *yaknehaz*. This stipulates that the order to be adopted is: blessing over wine (*yayin*); the festival *Kiddush;* the *havdalah* blessing over the candle (*ner*), the fourth "distinction" blessing in the *Havdalah* (*Havdalah*); and then the *She-heḥeyanu* blessing for the season (*zeman*).

The Meal. The lighting of the candles, the *Kiddush* and the *Havdalah* are all performed at either the commencement or

The hare hunt in the *Joel ben Simeon Haggadah* (15th century) represents the mnemonic for the order of *Kiddush* plus *Havdalah* to be recited on a festival that starts on Saturday night. The Hebrew word is *Yaknehaz* which sounds like the German *"jag'n Has."* The woodcut from the *Venice Minhagim* book (1601) shows the *Havdalah* blessing over light; the very elaborate silver holder for the *Havdalah* candle was made in Vienna in 1819.

the conclusion of the Sabbath and festival. The remaining home ceremonies associated with these days are all connected with the meals eaten on these occasions. This is not accidental, since participation in a festive banquet on these occasions is regarded as a religious duty. Indeed, the Talmud laid it down as a precept that three meals must be eaten on the Sabbath. In order to distinguish the festive nature of these meals, it has become customary in both Ashkenazi and Sephardi communities to sing specially composed table hymns (*zemirot*) during or after the repast. Some of the *zemirot* still sung date from as early as the tenth century; many have been printed in standard prayer books, while others have been published in special collections. The tunes to which they are sung are often borrowed versions of popular folk songs, and numerous different compositions have thus survived. Curiously, two of the most popular *zemirot, Yah Ribbon Olam* ("Lord, Master of the Universe") and *Ẓur Mi-shelo* ("Rock from whose store [we have eaten]"), contain no reference to the Sabbath. Nevertheless, they have been reserved for recitation on that day alone. Among *Ḥasidic* circles, particular importance was attached to the singing of *zemirot* as well as wordless melodies at the third meal on the Sabbath (*Se'udah Selishit*). Elsewhere, it has also become customary to chant Psalm 23 at this meal.

No comparable *zemirot* have been composed for the festival meals. Nevertheless, these are also regarded as obligatory (*se'udot shel mitzvah*), as are the special banquets on Purim and the eve of the Day of Atonement. It has thus become customary to adorn the table on these occasions by the singing of appropriately joyous verses from the Scriptures.

The particular character of these days also finds expression in the Grace after Meals then recited. On the Sabbath and festive days this is preceded by the chanting of Psalm 126. The rabbis considered that the optimistic vision contained in this chapter was better fitted to a festive occasion than the sentiments expressed in Psalm 137, which at one time preceded the Grace after Meals on a weekday. Moreover, specific reference is made to the holy day in question during the course of the grace itself. Thus, on Ḥanukkah and Purim, the *Al-Hanissim* prayer already added to the *Amidah* is also inserted during

The children in Moritz Oppenheim's "Seder Night" are already a little sleepy. The master of the house is dressed in his High Holy Day *kitel,* a widespread custom which adds to the festive air of the occasion. The family has presumably reached the end of the *seder* and one of the sons is opening the door for the final declaration.

the second blessing of the Grace. On the Sabbath a special prayer asking God to grant us repose on this day (*reẓeh*) is added to the third blessing. At this point, too, the *Ya'aleh Ve-Yavo* paragraph is inserted on festivals. Moreover, special supplications are on these occasions also inserted towards the end of the Grace. On the Sabbath, the All-Merciful is asked "to let us inherit the day which shall be wholly a Sabbath and rest in the everlasting life." On the festivals, He is asked to "let us inherit the day which is altogether good." Particular formulas of these prayers are also inserted here for Rosh Ḥodesh, Rosh Ha-Shanah and the intermediate days of Sukkot. Finally, on all these occasions, an alteration is made to the subsequent acclamation: "Great salvation giveth He to his King." This quotation from Psalms 18:51 is, on festive days and Sabbaths, changed to the alternate reading found in the Second Book of Samuel (22:51), "He is a tower of salvation to his king."

The Seder. The most popular festive meal in the Jewish calendar is the Passover *Seder*. On the first night of Passover, Jews the world over congregate with their families or in other groups in order to commemorate the deliverance of the Israelites from Egypt over 4,000 years ago. Indeed, it is the recounting of that story from a prescribed text (the *Haggadah*) which forms the central element of that ceremony. The duty to narrate this episode is of biblical origin, and in the days when the Paschal sacrifice formed the central part of the celebrations, the story was told at the Paschal meal. Thus, parts of the text of the *Haggadah* are very old, and much of it appears in the Mishnah. It was probably compiled as a separate book in the eighth century.

In its present form, the *Haggadah* consists of a conglomeration of various elements. The narrative itself, which is composed of exerpts from the Bible, Mishnah and Midrash, is preceded and followed by ritual passages, and is interspersed with added songs of thanksgiving and joy. Moreover, the *Seder* service is replete with various symbolic rituals and many unfamiliar actions. The latter are intended to fill the participants, and especially the children, with amazement and curiosity, in the hope that they will be stimulated into asking for an explanation. Their questions will provide the cue for the unfolding of the story of the liberation from Egypt. "And it shall come to pass when your son shall ask you: 'What means this service to you?'. . .And you shall tell your son on that day: 'Because of what the Lord did for me when I went out of Egypt.'" (Exodus 12:26 and 13:8).

The Bible itself specifically lists three essential ingredients to be eaten during the *Seder* service—the paschal sacrifice; *maẓẓah* (unleavened bread); and *maror* (bitter herbs). During the course of time, this list has been supplemented by several other dishes. Some have their origin in local community savories, others have been specifically ordained by the rabbis. Of the latter, the most important is the injunction to drink four cups of wine during the *Seder*. Indeed, the *Seder* ceremony itself commences with the recitation of *Kiddush*. The formula pronounced is that used on all the festivals, except for a specific reference to Passover as "the season of our liberation."

Immediately thereafter, reference is made to the *maẓẓah*. The master of the ceremony points to "This. . .bread of affliction," and expresses the conviction that, just as the Israelites who ate it were redeemed from Egypt, so may all those present at the ceremony be freed from bondage. It is at this point that the narrative itself begins. The youngest member of the gathering is invited to ask four set questions concerning the peculiar foods and the unusual behavior which he sees around him, and in answer to these enquiries is informed that "We were slaves to Pharaoh in Egypt." After a further prologue which emphasizes the importance of telling the narrative, comes a brief survey of Jewish history prior to the Exodus. This concludes with an account of that miraculous event itself; a Mishnah explaining the significance of the Passover sacrifice, the unleavened bread and the bitter herbs; and the recitation of the first two chapters of the *Hallel*. This portion of the ceremony then concludes with the drinking of a second cup of wine.

At this point, various actions are performed preliminary to the eating of the main meal. These begin with *netillat yadayim* (washing of the hands), accompanied by the appropriate benediction. Then, attention is again turned to the *maẓẓah*. Since the basic components of this substance are identical

This very ornate silver *seder* plate originates from Vienna (1807). The trays are designed each to hold one *mazzah*; the figures on the top include Moses, Aaron and Miriam, and the small dishes are for the symbolic foods eaten during the ceremony. The European pewter *seder* plate (1773) is far less ornate. The center engraving is of the four sons discussed in the *Haggadah* and the plate also bears the name of the artist, Leib Segal, and another name, Esther the daughter of Alexander, presumably the owner.

with those of bread, throughout Passover it is the normal benediction over bread which is recited. However, during the *Seder* service, this blessing is immediately followed by another, "over the eating of *mazzah*," in order to emphasize the religious duty of partaking of *mazzah* on this night. Attention is then turned to the dish of bitter herbs, the second ingredient of the *Seder* meal which is specifically prescribed in the Bible. The company recites the blessing, "over the eating of *maror*" after which each person present eats a portion of lettuce or horse-radish equivalent to an olive's bulk. This done, another piece of *maror* is taken and placed, in the form of a sandwich, between two pieces of *mazzah*. This is a custom derived from the practice of Hillel the Elder (first century C.E.), and an explanatory formula is recited to this effect. In both the cases when *maror* is eaten, the bitter herbs are dipped into *ḥaroset*, a paste made of fruit, spices, wine and *mazzah* meal. The word *ḥaroset* may be connected with *ḥeres*, meaning clay, which it is supposed to resemble in color, and symbolizes the mortar that the Jews made in Egypt. However, no specific formula is recited to this effect.

During the meal which then follows, it is often customary to sing appropriate songs of praise and thanksgiving. But it is after the recitation of the Grace after Meals and the consumption of a third cup of wine that a specific set of hymns of praise is sung. Rather incongruously, however, this portion of the *Seder* is preceded by a short collection of verses commencing with the words *Shefokh Ḥamatkha* ("Pour out Thy wrath"). Their theme is a supplication for vengeance on the nations that have oppressed Israel. Since medieval times, this paragraph has been accompanied by the act of opening the doors of the house in order to welcome the prophet Elijah, the harbinger of redemption, for whom a special cup of wine has been placed on the table.

The ceremony then continues with the chanting of the second half of the *Hallel* (Psalms 115–118), followed by the "great *Hallel*" (Psalm 136), and the *Nishmat* hymn normally recited during *Shaḥarit* on the Sabbath. With the consumption of another cup of wine, the *Seder* service proper is then concluded, and all the participants signify the fact by the recitation of a paragraph to this effect which ends with the call: "Next year in Jerusalem." If they are already in Jerusalem, they say "Next year in Jerusalem the rebuilt."

In Ashkenazi communities further hymns are sung. These were included in the *Haggadah* as an incentive to encourage children to stay awake for the singing at the end. Of these, probably the most famous is the last song, *Ḥad Gadya* (An Only Kid). Written in Aramaic, and possibly based on a medieval German folksong, it recites the tale of destruction which ensued from the fact that a cat ate the only kid which father bought for two coins. Although it was probably originally intended as an amusement, this song has since become the subject of several allegorical interpretations, all of which regard it as an expressed prayer for Divine redemption of Israel.

These sentiments, which provide one of the central themes of the whole *Haggadah*, are not the exclusive preserve of traditionally orthodox Jews. Rather, the motifs of personal freedom and national liberation which are distinctive to the traditional *Haggadah*, have been adapted and borrowed by several other groups. Thus, in non-religious kibbutzim in Israel an elaborate public *Seder* is held with music and dancing for members, children and guests, at which their own Kibbutz *Haggadah* is read. The *Haggadah* compiled by Kibbutz Yagur is the prototype for all kibbutzim. It is based on the theme of the Exodus from Egypt, but also includes events of a similar nature pertinent to modern Jewish history and kibbutz life, as well as appropriate passages from modern Hebrew literature. Many radical groups in America have also compiled their own

haggadot, including additional passages from various sources on topics that are considered appropriate: liberation and freedom are popular themes.

A TIME TO MOURN AND A TIME TO REJOICE

The domestic ceremonies with which this chapter has been hitherto concerned are regular occurrences. With the exception of those performed daily, their timing is determined by the fixed cycle of the Jewish calendar, whose Sabbaths and festivals they are designed to adorn. Over and above these occasions, however, the liturgy also designates a place of unique importance to those domestic ceremonies which occur at irregular intervals in the life of the Jew. In so doing, it also attributes a new dimension to the very concept of prayer in Jewish philosophy. At this level, prayer can be regarded as much more than a "fixed task" and a regular obligation, which might degenerate into a deadeningly familiar recital. Rather, it can answer to the specific desires of an individual to communicate with his Maker before embarking on a new stage in the life which He has given him. Since such experiences, by their nature, are invariably highly personal, it is fitting that the appropriate prayers then recited form part of the domestic liturgy.

In accordance with the content of the subject matter to be discussed, this chapter will follow the usual life cycle.

Circumcision. The first religious obligation of every Jewish male is the rite of circumcision. Although the practice was certainly common before the time of Abraham, it was during his life that (according to the biblical account), this ceremony attained the status of a covenant, uniting the Jewish people with its God (Genesis 17:10). The punishment for failure to observe this rite is therefore *karet,* to be "cut off" from one's kind, understood by the rabbis to mean "excision at the hand of heaven from the community."

The ceremony itself has to be performed when the child is eight days old (his health permitting), even should that day coincide with a Sabbath or a festival. The operation itself is entrusted to a specially trained *mohel,* and is usually performed in the presence of the immediate family and friends. From amongst these, the child's godparents and his *sandak* ("holder," upon whose knees the child rests during the operation), are selected.

At the opening of the ceremony, the child is handed from his mother to his godmother and godfather and then to the *mohel.* Meanwhile, the congregation welcomes the infant by chanting *Barukh ha-Ba* ("Blessed be he that comes"); the Sephardim sing a *piyyut* in which those who keep the covenant are blessed. The *mohel,* having placed the child momentarily on a specially placed Chair of Elijah, then hands the child to the *sandak,* and performs the operation. Immediately thereafter, the father recites the benediction "Who has hallowed us by thy commandments and has commanded us to make our sons enter the covenant of Abraham our father." In Israel, this is followed by the *She-heḥeyanu* blessing. The congregated guests reply, "Even as this child has entered into the covenant so may he enter into the Torah, the nuptial canopy and into good deeds." The child is then handed to the father or an honored guest and the *mohel,* holding a goblet of wine, recites the benediction for wine and a second benediction praising God who established a covenant with His people. He then recites a prayer for the welfare of the child, during the course of which he also announces the child's name. The ceremony is followed by a festive meal at which special hymns are sung, and in the Grace after Meals blessings are recited for the child, the parents, the *sandak,* and the *mohel.*

Pidyon ha-Ben. Within less than a month of the normal time of the circumcision ceremony, the child—provided that he is a

ברית שלום

והוא תיקון המילה בפזמונה ושיריה
ורינה שם סדורי ברכותיה כלם
כתובים כאחד וסדורים יחד
פ ה
פ״ס ארו

firstborn—participates in a further religious rite, that of redemption. This, too, is of biblical origin, and is derived from the stipulation that the firstborn sons in Israel belong to the service of the Lord. Since, at a very early stage in Jewish history, only those males descended from the tribe of Levi were chosen to serve in the sanctuary and Temple, the obligation of the firstborn to perform such functions became inoperative. Nevertheless, the original biblical ordinance is commemorated in a ceremony during which all male firstborns not born to either a son or daughter of a *kohen* or *levi* are specifically "redeemed" from their obligations.

The redemption ceremony (*pidyon ha-ben*) is held in the presence of the *kohen* and invited guests, and takes place on the 31st day after the birth. This is due to the fact that the child is not considered as fully viable until he survives the first 30 days of his life. Even if circumcision has not yet been performed (for health reasons), there should be no delay. Only if the 31st day is a Sabbath or festival is the ceremony postponed to the following weekday. During the ceremony, the father presents his son, often on a specially embellished tray, to the *kohen* who asks him, in an ancient Aramaic formula, whether he wishes to redeem the child or to leave him to the *kohen*. In some sources the formula is given in Hebrew. The father, in reply, expresses the desire to keep his son, hands the redemption money to the *kohen*, and recites one benediction for the fulfillment of the commandment of redemption, and another of thanksgiving (*She-heheyanu*). The *kohen*, three times pronouncing "your son is redeemed," returns the child to the father. This dialogue is purely symbolic. A declaration by the father that he prefers the money to the child would have no legal validity. Finally, the *kohen* recites a benediction over a cup of wine, pronounces the priestly blessing on the child, and joins the invited guests at a festive banquet.

In Sephardi communities it is customary for the *kohen* officiating at the *Pidyon ha-Ben* to begin the ceremony by directing several questions to the mother of the child in order to determine that the child is indeed her firstborn son.

Fast of the Firstborn. A further reminder of the special position occupied by firstborn sons takes place every year on the 14th

Berit Shalom (The Covenant of Peace) is the name of a collection of *piyyutim* and hymns to be recited at the circumcision ceremony as well as the laws pertaining to the *mitzvah*. It was written on vellum in Pesaro, c. 1600. The silver double-cup (Augsburg, 1730) was specially created for use in the ceremony. Bernard Picart's engraving shows the ceremony of the redemption of the first born in what was obviously a well-to-do Dutch Jewish home.

of Nisan, the day before Passover. Ever since mishnaic times, it has been customary to celebrate that date as the Fast of the Firstborn (*Ta'anit Bekhorim*). Although the origins of the practice whereby firstborn males fast on the eve of Passover is obscure, it seems to be associated with the desire to express gratitude for the saving of the firstborn Israelites during the tenth plague in Egypt. Should the first day of Passover occur on a Sabbath, the fast is observed on the preceding Thursday.

In practice, the Fast of the Firstborn is today hardly observed. In most communities, the custom has evolved to complete the

Oppenheim's "Bar Mitzvah Speech" is a delightful family scene. The young man is declaiming with gusto and his elders are obviously enjoying it. In Jerusalem it has become very popular for the bar mitzvah boy to read his portion of the Torah at the Western Wall, often in addition to the synagogue ceremony. Both scenes shown here are common at the Wall on Mondays and Thursdays.

study of a Talmud tractate on the morning before Passover. Since the banquet which accompanies such occasions is considered to be a religious celebration (*se'udat mitzvah*), participation in this meal takes precedence over the fast. Most synagogues therefore arrange such a celebration in which firstborns participate.

Bar and Bat Mitzvah. In contrast to the ceremonies associated with the rites of circumcision and redemption, which are of ancient origin, the celebrations which mark the attainment of a child's religious and legal maturity have evolved during a much more recent period. Admittedly, as early as talmudic times Jewish law fixed the age of responsibility for boys at 13 and for girls at 12, considering this the time of their physical maturity. Thus the Mishnah states that until he is 13 years old, a son receives the merit of his father and is also liable to suffer for his parent's sin; after that he bears full responsibility for his own actions and is obliged to fulfill all the commandments (i.e. bar mitzvah, "son of the commandment"). However, mention of a specific ceremony to mark this event is not found before the 15th century. A special celebration to mark a girl's 12th birthday (bat mitzvah; lit. "daughter of the law"), was not apparently known before the 19th century.

Today, however, the attainment of religious maturity is marked by an elaborate series of ceremonies. In Orthodox circles it is also preceded by a period of intense preparation for the event. One striking example is the custom whereby the boy begins to put on *tefillin* every morning one month before his bar mitzvah. The most striking of the bar mitzvah celebrations themselves takes place in the synagogue, where the boy is called up to the reading of the Torah on the first possible occasion after his 13th birthday according to the Jewish calendar. This is the first public demonstration of his new role as a full member of the community. In modern times, it is to this occasion that the term bar mitzvah usually refers. Elaborate variations of this ceremony took root in many communities. In some cases, the boy himself reads the *maftir* portion and the *haftarah* on the Sabbath after (or, occasionally, before) his birthday; in others he reads the whole Sabbath Torah

In this marriage ceremony of Cochin Jews, no *ḥuppah* is used. Instead the bride and groom are wrapped in one *tallit* while the benedictions are recited. Otherwise, however, the basic elements of the marriage service are the same in all communities.

portion; in 17th and 18th century Worms those who possessed the necessary linguistic and vocal abilities also conducted parts or all of the service. Among the Jews of Morocco a special *piyyut* was recited when a bar mitzvah was called to the reading of the Torah, and in most congregations a special invocation is made at the end of the reading for the boy and his family.

When the boy has concluded the blessing after having been called to the Torah, his father then recites a short formula known as *Barukh she-petarani,* blessing God for relieving him of the responsibility of his son's conduct. In Reform congregations, this has been replaced by the *She-heḥeyanu* benediction. During the ensuing sermon, the rabbi of the congregation frequently stresses the new responsibilities which the young man has thereby attained.

It is after this synagogue ceremony that the bar mitzvah celebrations attain a domestic context. The boy's family often arranges a festive meal on either the afternoon of the Sabbath of the bar mitzvah, or on a conveniently close week-day (some authorities ruled that such a banquet was obligatory). On this occasion, it became customary for the boy to deliver a talmudic discourse, known to Sephardim as the *tefillin darashah.* Remnants of this practice are to be found in the general speech of thanks which many boys deliver during the course of the meal in the western hemisphere. Sons of traditional families, too, often take the opportunity of their talmudic discourse to thank their parents for their love and care. In Conservative, Reform, and some Orthodox synagogues, the boy recites a prayer before the Ark of the Law in place of the discourse.

A parallel ceremony for a girl, bat mitzvah, has recently become widely adopted. Forms of the ceremony differ widely. In some cases, the girl recites the *haftarah* and conducts specific prayers in the synagogue; in others the entire celebration is confined to the home or school. In many Israeli Orthodox synagogues the bat mitzvah is celebrated by calling the girl's father and brothers to the Torah; a special sermon is preached, and the girl is presented with a gift. In some congregations a collective ceremony is held when girls have reached the proper age. In recent times, the bat mitzvah has often been celebrated not as a religious ceremony but as a birthday celebration and family occasion.

CONFIRMATION. Reform congregations have instituted what is known as a Confirmation ceremony. This was originally in 19th century German Reform a substitution for bar mitzvah. The ceremony was held at a later age—16 or 17—on the grounds that before that age a young person cannot really understand the implications of the rituals. In modern times, especially in the U.S., confirmation has been adopted as a ceremony additional to bar mitzvah which is celebrated in a more traditional manner. The main intention of confirmation was to prolong the period of a child's Jewish education, and as such it is usually a ceremony with a "class" of young people being confirmed at the same time. The ceremony is usually held on or about Shavuot, the festival commemorating the giving of the Torah. The confirmands recite various sections from Scriptures and publicly declare their devotion to Judaism. The boys and girls frequently receive a special certificate, testifying their acceptance into the Jewish community.

Marriage. Neither the Bible nor the rabbis considered the sex act to be intrinsically sinful or shameful, but rather a legitimate human activity which, when performed properly achieves the status of a *mitzvah.* This view also fostered the attitude whereby marriage has become recognized as a state of perfection. In some cases the unison then achieved between man and wife has even been used to symbolize such other perfect relationships as that between God and Israel, or Israel and the Sabbath. It is hardly surprising, therefore, that the ceremony of marriage has become the occasion of a ritual which, in its elaboration, can be compared with almost no other in the entire Jewish liturgy.

ENGAGEMENT. In very early times, the marriage ceremony itself was preceded by a stylized form of engagement ceremony known as *shiddukhin*. Here, the terms of the marriage were formulated and sometimes reduced to writing. This ceremony is in only partial use today, and finds no liturgical expression. When it is performed, it is invariably immediately prior to the wedding ceremony itself. In Ashkenazi practice, the ceremony ends with the symbolic breaking of a plate.

THE AUFRUFEN. A custom which has retained its popularity somewhat longer is that whereby the groom is called to the reading of the Torah on the Sabbath prior to his wedding. This custom, known among Ashkenazim as *aufrufen*, is preceded in some communities by the recital of special hymns. The groom is similarly honored on the Sabbath following his wedding. In some communities, he is then seated in a place of honor with a ceremonial canopy spread over him. In Libya and Tunisia, a second Torah scroll is taken out and an additional section read in his honor. Traditionally, on the Sabbaths both immediately before and after his wedding, the bridegroom's right to be called to the reading of the Torah takes precedence even over a bar mitzvah. During his *aufrufen*, he is often showered with rice, wheat nuts and candy—a fertility symbol from which the modern confetti derives.

THE CEREMONY. Such symbolic gestures are paralleled during the wedding ceremony itself. This can be performed anywhere. In many communities—particularly Sephardi and Oriental—it is performed inside the synagogue. In other congregations it is performed in a wedding hall, or even out in the open. In order to avoid any irregularities which might possibly bring about legal complications, custom decrees that the ceremony be performed by a rabbi. His presence, however, is not essential and a ceremony performed correctly will be valid even if no clergyman is present. Nevertheless, the presence of an officiating person of some sort is required. This is in order to ensure that some direction is given to those bridegrooms who are unable to recite the necessary benedictions and formulas without some prompting. In order not to shame them, it has now become customary for an officiating person to recite these in all wedding ceremonies. It is also generally accepted that there shall be present at least a *minyan*, to ensure that the marriage ceremony receives maximum publicity.

The wedding ceremony itself consists of two distinct parts. The first is a formal act of betrothal (*erusin*). This begins with the writing of the marriage contract (*ketubbah*), in which the bridegroom stipulates the amount of money to be set aside for his wife should the marriage be dissolved. Once this has been signed and witnessed, the groom is led to the bride and lets down her veil over her face, at which time the rabbi or cantor pronounces the blessing invoked on Rebekah "O sister be thou the mother of thousands of ten thousands" (Genesis 24:60). This ceremony is known in Yiddish as *bedeken di-kale* (covering the bride) and is not practiced by Sephardi Jews. In some communities the *bedeken* ends with the bride's father placing his hands above her head as he recites the blessing "May God make thee as Rachel and Leah."

The groom is then led to the *ḥuppah* (canopy), to the accompaniment of music, by his and his bride's father (or two other male relatives or friends if he or the bride has been orphaned) and stands facing the direction of the Temple. There he is joined by the bride who is escorted by her mother and the groom's mother, usually to the accompaniment of a blessing of welcome chanted by the rabbi or cantor, the text of which is: "He who is supremely mighty; He who is supremely praised; He who is supremely great; may He bless this bridegroom and bride." It is customary among Ashkenazim for the bride to end the procession by being led in seven circuits around the groom, which is presumably to be associated with the magic circle to ward off evil spirits. The *erusin* proper begins with the rabbi's recital of the benediction over a glass of wine followed by the betrothal blessing (*birkat erusin*) which ends: ". . .who hallowest Thy people Israel by the rite of the nuptial canopy and the sacred covenant of wedlock." The groom and bride are then given to drink from the goblet, after which the groom places the ring on the forefinger of the bride's right hand. After doing so, he recites the marriage formula word by word after the officiating rabbi: "*Harei at mekuddeshet li betabba'at zo ke-dat Moshe ve-Yisrael* ("Behold, you are consecrated unto me by this ring, according to the law of Moses and Israel"). It is at this point in the ceremony that the *ketubbah* is read aloud and handed to the bride. In some communities

A paper plaque with the marriage benedictions (Czechoslovakia, 1771). This was used by the officiating rabbi and contains instructions on how to perform the ceremony. Issachar Ryback's "Wedding" (1917) is part of a cycle of Jewish ceremonies and depicts a typical Eastern European milieu.

(including many in the State of Israel), the *erusin* ceremony is then concluded when the groom crushes a glass underfoot. In other places, this is done only after the marriage ceremony, too, has been concluded. The breaking of the glass is generally understood to serve as a reminder, even on this happy occasion, of the sorrow which all Israel continues to experience since the destruction of the Temple.

THE SEVEN BENEDICTIONS. The second section of the wedding ceremony then commences. Known as *nissu'im* (marriage), it is the only portion of the ritual during which the bride and bridegroom are, in fact, customarily obliged to stand under the canopy. The symbolic bond thus created between them is then sanctified by the recital of the seven marriage benedictions. Beginning with the normal benediction over wine, these then go on to praise God "who has created all things to Thy glory"; to acknowledge that He is "the creator of man"; that He has made man in His image; to supplicate that God may "make Zion joyful through her children"; to recognize that He "makes a bride and bridegroom rejoice"; and to plead that there may soon be heard in the cities of Judah, and the streets of Jerusalem "the voice of joy and gladness, the voice of the bridegroom and the voice of the bride, the jubilant voice of bridegrooms from their canopies, and of youths from their feasts of song." Often, in order to honor several people with participation in the ceremony, each blessing is recited by a different guest. To the accompaniment of appropriate singing and dancing, the ceremony is then concluded with the drinking of the wine by the bride and bridegroom.

The same seven benedictions are recited at the conclusion of the Grace after Meals at the wedding banquet. This is itself introduced by a special invocation, beginning: "Banish, O Lord, both grief and wrath, and then the dumb shall exult in song." The only change in the seven wedding benedictions after the banquet is one of order: the blessing over wine is recited last, and not first. This is also the order followed at every meal of the bride and bridegroom during the subsequent festive week. The only stipulations made on these days are that this is not a second marriage for both members of the couple; that at least ten men are present at the meal; and that one of them has not been present at a previous recitation for the couple. The latter rule applies to all the seven days except the Sabbath, which is itself considered to be a "new face." If only three men are present, the last three wedding benedictions may be recited.

Prayers after Childbirth. Ancient biblical law stipulated the various sacrifices which a woman had to offer after giving birth to a child (Leviticus 12:6–8). In some communities, this practice is today commemorated by a special prayer of thanksgiving. In some congregations girl infants are named during this ceremony, although this is usually done on the Sabbath

after the birth when the father is called to the reading of the Torah.

The prayer of thanksgiving, as formulated by the Chief Rabbi of the British Empire, N. M. Adler, in 1880, consists of quotations from scriptural passages, interspersed with benedictions and prayers. Thus the mother, after reciting Psalms 5:8 and 116 pronounces the *Ha-Gomel* (thanksgiving benediction). The rabbi then responds "He who has shown you kindness, may He deal kindly with you for ever." The mother then concludes the ceremony by petitioning God for the health of her child and herself.

Burial and Mourning. The rabbis of the Mishnah instructed that a man should bless God on the occasion of a misfortune, just as he does at moments of joy. It is on the basis of the sentiments thus expressed, that the ritual and liturgy associated with death and mourning have developed.

The burial ceremony, although it must be performed as soon as possible after death, is necessarily preceded by a process of cleansing and washing the corpse (*tohorah*) and the continuous watching of it (*shemirah*) during which chapters of Psalms are recited. In the interval which thus occurs before burial, the mourner is designated the status of an *onen*. As such, he is exempted from fulfilling certain religious duties such as reciting the *Shema* and the daily prayers, or wearing the *tallit* and *tefillin,* so as to enable him to make burial arrangements. He must also eat in solitude and abstain from meat and wine. During the Sabbaths and festivals, however, the *onen* participates in the customary ceremonials such as *Kiddush*. Immediately prior to the funeral, the *onen* makes a rent in the lapel of an outer garment. This act, known as *keri'ah* ("tearing") is accompanied by the blessing "Blessed be Thou, O Lord, the righteous Judge." The *keri'ah* is subsequently exposed throughout the mourning period.

The Funeral. In ancient times, the burial ceremony itself was the occasion of several elaborate ceremonies. Most of these have either disappeared or been modernized. Thus, although the recital of Psalms in the home still precedes the burial act, the custom of having torchbearers, musicians and barefooted professional mourners in the funeral procession has been discontinued. So, too, has the dressing of the dead in costly garments of gold or silver. The funeral service, now often conducted in the vernacular, varies according to the age of the deceased. A male child who died before he was seven days old is circumcised and given a Hebrew name at the cemetery. Only two men and one woman participate in the funeral of children who die before they reach the age of 30 days, although children who have learned to walk and thus are already known to many people are escorted as adults. In such and normal cases, the coffin is carried on the shoulders of the pallbearers into the cemetery prayer hall (*ohel*) where the *Ẓidduk ha-Din* ("acknowledgment of the Divine judgment") beginning with the affirmation "The Rock, His work is perfect, for all His ways are judgment" is recited. In some communities, this prayer is recited after the coffin has been lowered into the grave, and on those days on which the *Taḥanun* is not said, Psalm 16 is substituted for *Ẓidduk ha-Din*. In the cemetery while the coffin is being borne to the grave, it is customary (except on those days when the *Taḥanun* is not recited) to halt at least three times and recite Psalm 91. In talmudic times, seven stops were made for lamentations and some Sephardi rites have the custom of seven *hakkafot* ("circumambulations") at the grave.

When the coffin is lowered into the grave, those present say, "May he (or she) come to his (or her) place in peace"; they then fill in the grave. As they leave, they throw grass and earth behind them in the direction of the grave, while saying, "Remember (God) that we are of dust." Prior to leaving the cemetery they wash their hands (in Jerusalem it is customary not to dry them afterward). In the *ohel,* Psalm 91 and the *Kaddish* are recited by the mourners. The participants at the funeral then recite "May the Almighty comfort you among the other mourners for Zion and Jerusalem" as they stand in two rows between which the mourners pass.

The precise order of the funeral service, as outlined here, varies from place to place and from community to community. In particular, many of the Sephardi customs are closer to those of talmudic times than those practiced by Ashkenazim. In Egypt, for instance, the funeral service was usually held in the synagogue. In Libya, bereaved sons did not go near the bier and did not enter the cemetery, but stayed at the entrance where they recited the *Kaddish* at the end of the ceremony. Moreover, certain burial practices are unique to Reform Jews (mainly in the U.S.), who also permit cremation.

THE MEAL. According to talmudic law, mourners are forbidden to eat of their own bread on the day of the funeral. On their return from the cemetery, therefore, their friends and neighbors prepare for them a meal known as *Se'udat Havra'ah* (Meal of Consolation). This the mourners eat while sitting on low stools and while wearing soft slippers, and after having recited the blessing *Barukh Dayyan Emet* which acknowledges God to be "the true judge."

SHIVAH. It is immediately after the burial, too, that the first week of mourning, known as the *Shivah* (meaning "seven") commences. Throughout this period (with the exception of the Sabbath and festivals when the mourning rites are discontinued), mourners are forbidden to perform manual labor, conduct business transactions, bathe or anoint the body, cut their hair, cohabit, wear leather shoes, wash clothes, greet acquaintances, study the Torah, or leave the house. In view of the latter stipulation, it has become customary for a *minyan* to gather for the daily prayers in the house of the mourner. Where this is not possible, the mourner may attend the synagogue for the purpose of reciting the mourner's *Kaddish* during the services.

In the house of mourning and in the mourner's personal prayers, a number of changes are made in the normal order of the services. Thus, the talmudic passage *pittum ha-ketoret* describing the compounding of the incenses for daily offering in the Temple, is omitted from the *Shaḥarit* by the mourner since he is forbidden to study Torah. Likewise, the mourner omits the recitation of *Eizehu mekoman,* the chapter of the Mishnah which describes the appointed places for the various animal sacrifices. The Priestly Blessing, which concludes with the greeting of peace, is omitted in the house of mourning because the mourner may not extend greetings. In Jerusalem,

Wilhelm Wachtel's "Funeral" (c. 1914) is leaving from in front of a bookstore. The artist succeeded in conveying an atmosphere of subdued grief, characteristic of a Jewish funeral.

however, it is recited. *Taḥanun,* too, is omitted because its theme, "I have sinned before thee," is deemed inappropriate for a mourner. Psalm 20 is omitted because its recital would intensify the mourner's grief during his "day of trouble," and the verse beginning, "And as for me, this is my covenant with them, saith the Lord" is omitted from the *U-Va le-Ẓiyyon* passage because the mourner does not desire a covenant which will perpetuate his unhappy situation. By contrast, however, Psalm 49 which declares that the injustices and inequalities of human existence are corrected in the hereafter is recited after the daily service in the house of mourning.

During the Friday evening service, the mourner omits the six Psalms recited before the *Ma'ariv.* He remains in the anteroom until the conclusion of *Lekhah dodi,* when he enters the synagogue. The congregation then rises and pronounces the traditional greeting extended to mourners: "May the Almighty comfort thee together with the mourners of Zion and Jerusalem." *Hallel* is not recited in the house of *Shivah* on Rosh Ḥodesh because it contains such verses as "The dead praise not the Lord, neither any that go down into silence" and "This is the day which the Lord hath made, we will rejoice and be glad in it." In most rites, however, it is recited when the mourners leave the room. If Rosh Ḥodesh coincides with the Sabbath, *Hallel* should be recited even if the services are

In contrast to Wachtel's "Funeral," Ryback's imparts a spirit of near-hysteria with its movement. The figure on the right is holding an alms-box, a common feature at burials since "charity saves from death."

being held in the house of mourning since no public display of mourning is permissible on the Sabbath. Finally the mourner is not called up to the reading of the Torah during the week of *Shivah* even should he be the only *kohen* or Levite in the congregation.

The period of the *Shivah* is followed by a second period of mourning lasting for another 23 days. Since the sum total of the two periods adds up to 30 days, the second is known as the *Sheloshim* (meaning "thirty" in Hebrew). During this time, the restrictions on the mourner's activity are relaxed. Nevertheless, he is still forbidden to attend places of public entertainment, to attend social functions, to embark on a business journey or to cut his hair. It has also become customary for mourners to change their synagogue seats during the weekday service. Moreover, throughout this period the mourner continues to recite the mourner's *Kaddish.* When mourning for parents, some of the above prohibitions remain applicable throughout the entire 12 months following the day of death. The *Kaddish,* however, is recited by one mourning a parent or child for only 11 months.

Reform Judaism has greatly modified these laws and customs. The week of mourning is often shortened, and frequently only a period of three days is observed. Practices such as the rending of garments, sitting on low stools, not wearing leather shoes, and not attending places of entertainment during the period of the 30 days or first year are not generally observed by Reform Jews. Some have the religious services in the home only for the first three days, while others have them only after returning home from the funeral.

Yahrzeit. The duty to mourn the departed is not restricted to the period immediately following death. Rather, the Jewish liturgy also makes provision for an annual commemoration of the event. This takes place on the anniversary of the Hebrew date of the death, a day which is popularly known as the *Yahrzeit*. There is an opinion that when three or more days elapse between death and burial, the first yahrzeit is observed on the date of the burial. Nevertheless, during subsequent years, *Yahrzeit* is observed on the anniversary of the date of the death.

As its name indicates, the practice of observing the *Yahrzeit* probably originated in medieval Germany. However, it soon spread to other regions. Indeed, it became so popular that this Yiddish word is often found in Sephardi religious works, in preference to the term *naḥalah.*

Detailed regulations have been laid down for the observance of family *Yahrzeits.* Where he is able to do so, the *Yahrzeit,* as the person observing it is also called, conducts the weekday service, and if not, recites *Kaddish.* If the Torah is read on that day, he is called to the reading of the Torah, otherwise he is called on the preceding Sabbath. A 24-hour memorial candle is lit for that day, as a symbol of the verse "the soul of man is the lamp of God" (Proverbs 20:27). Fasting is recommended as an act of piety but is not commonly observed.

Filial piety has made the *Yahrzeit* one of the most widely held observances in Judaism. Even in small communities where there is difficulty in assembling the necessary *minyan* for the congregational service, special arrangements are made for such worship when there is a *Yahrzeit.* Its observance is an act of pious commemoration and emphasizes faith in the immortality of the soul.

Tombstones. Ever since biblical times, it has also become customary to commemorate the dead by the erection of a *maẓẓevah* (literally "monument," meaning "tombstone"). The first record of such an act in Jewish history dates from the tombstone which Jacob set up for Rachel (Genesis 35:20). The practice has since become universal, and is regarded as a necessary mark of honor for the dead.

A special order of service for the consecration of the tombstone has therefore been drawn up. In Israel its main content is the reading of those portions of the alphabetical 119th Psalm which consitute the name of the deceased and the letters of the word *neshamah* ("soul"); in western countries it consists of a selection of appropriate Psalms and biblical passages; and in both cases it concludes with a memorial prayer and *Kaddish* by the mourners. In the Diaspora it is the custom to erect and consecrate the tombstone during the 12th month after death; in Israel on the 30th day. Ashkenazi tombstones are usually vertical; among the Sephardim they lie flat.

XII development of the liturgy

in the bible and second temple period

talmudic period

geonic period

liturgical rites

prayer books

The title page of Seligman Baer's *Avodat Yisrael*, Roedelheim, 1868. All his life, Baer remained in the humble position of a school teacher in a community school although he was one of the great masoretic scholars of his time, and his masoretic Bible was widely regarded as a masterpiece. His prayerbook was not only a scholarly feat but added dignity and decorum to Orthodox synagogue services throughout Western Europe. It is generally considered the standard prayerbook text.

Judaism is a complex religion which has been undergoing a process of development from its very beginning. This applies to the beliefs and practices of Judaism and how much more so to prayer, since it is central to the Jewish faith and reflects to a large degree its beliefs. Prayer—the idea and the form—has changed throughout the ages according to internal religious developments within Judaism and according to outside historical happenings. Thus, for example, the destruction of the Second Temple in 70 C.E. and the loss of national sovereignty has an enormous impact on the liturgy. And there can be no doubt that the invention of printing in the 15th century contributed greatly to the standardization and unification of the prayer texts. A more modern example is the establishment of the State of Israel. Even in the relatively few years that have passed since 1948, it is still possible to detect the harbingers of the major effect that the renewal of national sovereignty is going to have on the liturgy.

Jewish prayer, therefore, has always been in a state of flux. And so it should be because the liturgy is an organic body which must reflect the changing mentality of those who pray, i.e. the people and the changing conditions which surround them.

IN THE BIBLE AND THE SECOND TEMPLE PERIOD

The beginnings of the liturgy are obscure. The prayers found occasionally in the Bible are spontaneous reactions to personal events or experiences. Examples of these are the short prayers of Moses (Numbers 12:13), Jethro (Exodus 18:10) and Hannah (I Samuel 1:11), and the extended prayer of Solomon at the inauguration of the Temple (I Kings 8:15–24). The only fixed prayers required in the Bible are the confessions to be recited when bringing the first fruits (*Viddui Bikkurim*) and the tithe (*Viddui Ma'aser*) which have prescribed texts, and the prayer of the high priest which had no prescribed formula. The main form of worship in ancient times was the sacrifices offered in the biblical Tabernacle and, later, the two Temples. Pious individuals seem to have prayed thrice daily, and some chapters of the Book of Psalms may have served as texts for the levitical service twice a day in the First and Second Temples. There is no evidence, however, of communal prayer in the Temple. There was a short liturgy for the priests on duty which comprised a benediction, the recitation of the *Shema* and the Decalogue, three additional benedictions and the priestly blessing. The laymen present for the sacrifices participated in the ritual by prostrating themselves and at appropriate pauses, probably chanting such responses as "O give thanks unto the Lord, for He is good." This Temple ceremony might have been one of the sources from which the liturgy later developed.

The rise of the synagogue, the frequent fasts prescribed in times of drought for which a special liturgy was fixed in the Mishnah, and the *ma'amadot* institution contributed to the development of liturgy. The *ma'amad* consisted of representatives of the people, part of whom were present at the sacrifices and the rest assembled at home; both groups conducting prayers four times a day—*Shaḥarit, Musaf, Minḥah* and *Ne'ilat She'arim*. The hours later fixed for the *Shaḥarit, Minḥah* and *Ma'ariv* prayers were in accordance with the practices of pious individuals who fixed their prayer schedule according to the position of the sun. This subject is discussed in Chapter 6.

TALMUDIC PERIOD

In the tannaitic period there already existed a somewhat fixed order for prayers, which is found in the Mishnah and the Tosefta and whose composition is attributed to the men of the Great Synagogue. The original prayer formula, the *berakhah* ("benediction" see Chapter 2), with its wording *Barukh Attah Adonai* ("Blessed are Thou, O Lord") is recorded; it served both for prayers of adoration and of petition. The obligation derived from the Pentateuch, to recite the *Shema* twice daily (the recitation was by heart), with its benedictions (three in the morning and four in the evening); and the daily *Amidah* (see Chapter 5), comprising 18 benedictions and recited twice daily, are also recorded.

After reciting the obligatory service, private prayers including personal requests (known as *devarim;* also called *taḥanunim*) could be offered. The *teḥinnot* of a number of rabbis are pre-

"And she lifted up her voice and she wept" is perhaps the most sincere prayer imaginable. It was the prayer of Hagar, the concubine of Abraham, as her child, Ishmael, lay dying in the wilderness. Jean Baptiste Camille Corot's oil painting shows the angel coming in answer to her prayer.

יש מקומות שנוהגין
סדר המעמדות
באחד בתשרי

"There are places where they are accustomed . . ." is a common phrase in Hebrew prayerbooks. At the top of this page from the *Rothschild Maḥzor* (Florence, 1492) it introduces the custom of sounding the *shofar* during the month of Elul. At the bottom of the page, the "Order of the *Ma'madot*" starts.

served in the Talmud. Later, certain Psalms (6 and 25) were also used as *teḥinnot*. There is no evidence, however, that the Psalms were frequently used in the ancient liturgy. The early sources only mention the *Hallel* Psalms and the *Hallel ha-Gadol* in connection with special feasts.

The public reading of portions from the Torah and Prophets was already considered an old institution in mishnaic times. Some texts for these readings and the number of persons called to the reading were fixed. The public reading of the Aramaic translation (*Targum*) of the Torah was likewise a permanent practice in the tannaitic and amoraic periods, and it was still considered obligatory by Rav Amram Gaon in the ninth century. The old tradition which ascribes the Sabbath morning reading to Moses and the Sabbath *Minḥah* as well as the Monday and the Thursday reading to Ezra in the fifth century B.C.E., is indicative of the great antiquity of those readings.

During the amoraic period (third to sixth centuries C.E.) little change seems to have taken place in the liturgy. There may have been slight differences between the Palestinian and Babylonian rites in that the latter stressed the superiority of public worship and community prayer. All that is known from the sources about these periods concerns the structure and form of the liturgy, while almost nothing is recorded about the texts. Texts which do occasionally occur in the Talmud are the *Havdalah* prayer recited between the Sabbath and a festival following it, the seven marriage benedictions, the blessing of the New Moon and *Naḥem*, a special prayer for the Ninth of Av. These prayers, all essentially *piyyutim*, did not yet have a fixed formula at that time and variant readings of the same prayer were common. Ultimately, one of these readings received general acceptance, sometimes through a combination of two or more formulas. Tractate *Soferim* (compiled in the geonic period, sixth to 11th centuries C.E.) also contains very few prayer texts.

As early as the tannaitic period the service was elaborated with *piyyutim;* whole prayers were rendered poetically and existing ones were supplemented with poetic insertions. Consequently, the exact demarcation line between "ordinary prayer" and *piyyut* is blurred, and many of what were later considered ordinary prayers are actually piyyutic in form. The *piyyut* flourished mainly in Palestine; Babylonia was less productive and even resisted its adoption.

GEONIC PERIOD

By early geonic times, two different rites had already developed; the Palestinian and the Babylonian. The old Palestinian rite, which flourished until the 12th century C.E. at least, became known in modern times only after the discovery of the Cairo

Right: Majolica *seder* dish, Czechoslovakia, 19th century, showing the position of the items used during the ceremony. Cleveland, Ohio, Olyn and Joseph B. Horwitz Judaica Collection.
Below: *Seder* in an 18th-century Bohemian home. This illustration is the frontispiece to the *"Sister" to the Van Geldern Haggadah*, written and illuminated by the Moravian artist Moses Leib ben Wolf of Trebitsch, 1716–17. Cincinnati, Hebrew Union College.
Below right: Ceramic *seder* dish, Hungary, early 19th century. The center illustration shows a family at the *seder* table and around the borders are some of the benedictions said during the ceremony. Jerusalem, Sir Isaac and Lady Wolfson Museum, Hechal Shlomo.

Some circumcision scenes and appurtenances: A linen Torah wrapper made from a diaper on which a baby has been circumcised, South Germany, 1715. Ritual circumcision implements, including a silver and amber knife, Near East, 1819; silver foreskin bowl, Germany, 18th century; silver bottle, Italy, 18th-19th century; silver protective shield, France, 19th century. They are set against a book of laws and prayers for circumcision by Jacob Sofer ben Judah Loeb of Berlin, 1729. The circumcision of Isaac is shown in a detail from a full-page miniature in the *Regensburg Pentateuch*, Germany, c. 1300. Both the *sandak*, who is holding the baby, and Abraham who is performing the circumcision, are wearing medieval Jewish hats. Jerusalem, Israel Museum. A circumcision ceremony at Ramot Meir in Israel, 1972. Photo Werner Braun, Jerusalem.

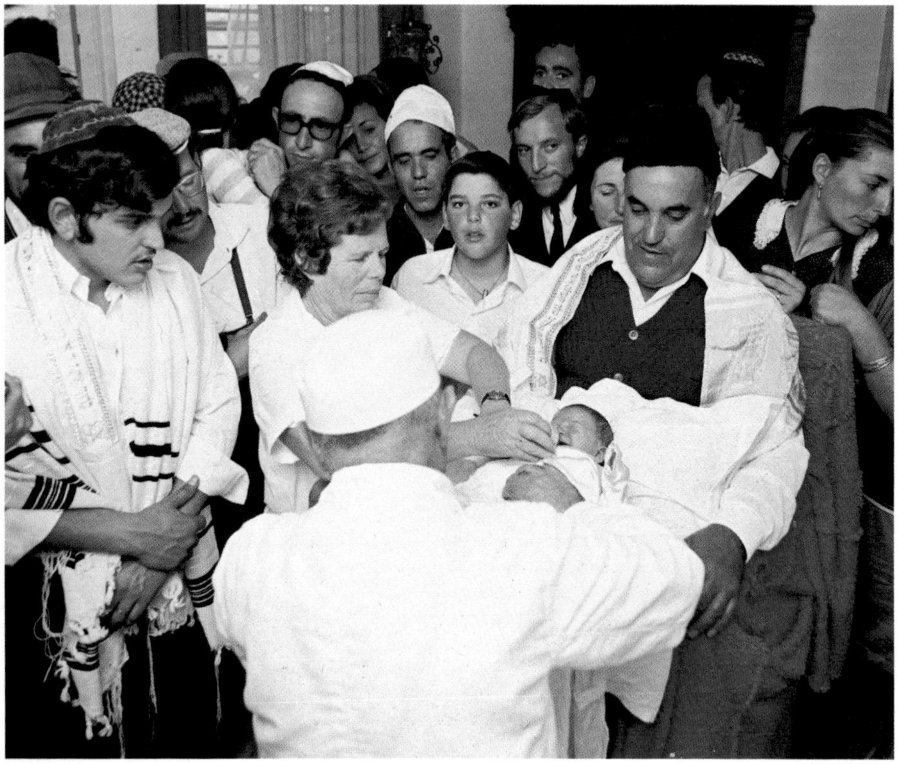

Right: China plate depicting a marriage ceremony, England, 1769. It forms part of a hand-painted coffee set designed as a wedding gift. New York, Jewish Museum.
Below: "Jewish Wedding" by Moritz Oppenheim, 1861, in which a *tallit* serves as the *ḥuppah* and the bridal couple have their belts symbolically joined together. On the steps stands a *badḥan* (jester) in his costume.
Below right: Wedding rings, 17th and 18th centuries. They are embellished with a house or a roof symbolizing the establishment of a new home. Jerusalem, Israel Museum.

"Rabbi with Torah" by Mane-Katz, 1960. Geneva, Oscar Ghez Collection.

A full page miniature from the *Darmstadt Haggadah* (15th-century Germany) illustrating the beginning of the *piyyut, Az Rov Nissim* recited at the Passover *seder*. The figures in the chambers are studying or praying.

Genizah in the 19th century. This was a storehouse for books and ritual objects that had become unusable and proved to be a veritable mine of information on the ancient Jewish world. While there are considerable differences between the Palestinian usage and the other known rites, the discovered texts do not always show whether they were destined for private or public prayer.

The old Babylonian rite is mainly known from geonic treatises; the oldest, the *Seder Rav Amram* (ninth century), comprises the text of the prayers together with respective halakhic prescriptions. The only earlier source is the responsum of Natronai ben Hilai concerning the 100 benedictions which a talmudic homily strongly recommends be recited daily.

The *Seder Rav Amram* was followed (a century later) by the *siddur* of Saadiah (Gaon) ben Joseph with prescriptions in Arabic which, despite some influences of Palestinian usage, is a good example of geonic prayer books; and later still by *Siddur Rashi* (without texts of prayers); *Maḥzor Vitry* (11th century, interpolated with insertions from 13th and 14th centuries); and Maimonides' *Sefer Tefillot* (part of *Mishneh Torah*). All these prayer books are discussed in the next chapter.

With the exception of the *Avodah* of the Day of Atonement, *azharot* for Shavuot, and *hoshanot* for Sukkot, the Babylonian rite adopted very little Hebrew poetry. In later times, however, when Babylonian communities were established in Palestine and Egypt, *piyyutim* were also introduced in those circles.

LITURGICAL RITES

All the various rites of the Jewish liturgy developed from those two ancient usages—the Palestinian and the Babylonian. According to some scholars their differences are mainly in the *piyyutim* adopted by the various communities, and they therefore tend to divide the rites into two groups: the Palestinian (comprising Italy, the Balkans, and the French-German countries) and the Babylonian (comprising the Spanish and Yemenite rites). This division may be justified from the historical point of view since the Jews of the first group, originating from the Byzantine Empire, accepted the Palestinian *piyyut* and retained

The *Apam* rite is very rare; it was used only in the three Italian towns of Asti, Fossano and Moncalvo. It has never appeared in a printed edition and those who used it prayed from handwritten prayerbooks. This example dates from 1702.

some of the original wording of regular prayers; the Jews of the second group did not accept the Palestinian *piyyut* and were later influenced by the liturgical poetry of the great Spanish Jewish poets. The division is, however, not justified from a textual point of view insofar as the statutory prayers are concerned. The wording and order of prayers in all known rites follow the *Seder Rav Amram,* i.e. the usage of the two great Babylonian academies, Sura and Pumbedita and, indirectly, the Babylonian Talmud. In contradistinction, the influence of the old Palestinian rite is hardly noticeable. Obviously, the rites themselves influenced each other, so that not a single rite remained in its original form.

At the same time it would also be incorrect to state that the various rites differ only in the *piyyutim* that they adopted. Distinctions in the regular prayers of the rites were introduced, such as variant readings in the text, which occurred even after the invention of printing which, generally speaking, unified the texts; the deletion or inclusion of certain passages; and differences in the order of the prayers in the ritual. All communities tended to shorten or omit entire *piyyutim,* or to combine various liturgical poems, even those of different authors. In some rites the opposition of the halakhic authorities caused the abolition of certain types of *piyyutim.*

Palestinian Group. The first ancient rite in what has become known as the "Palestinian" group is the Romanian (Greek) rite followed by the Jewish communities of the Byzantine Empire. In use in Greece and in European Turkey, at least until the end of the 16th century, and perhaps even later, it was superseded by the Sephardi rite. Besides slight changes in the order of certain sections and minor textual variations the *Maḥzor Romania* (as the prayer book of the rite is known) contains a large collection of *piyyutim* for *Shaḥarit; Ma'arivim* (*piyyutim* recited in the *Ma'ariv* service) for every festival (including the Day of Atonement); *kerovot* for fast days, Purim, the Day of Atonement, Rosh Ha-Shanah (in Mss. also for the other holidays and Ḥanukkah); and a large collection of *seliḥot* and *kinot.* Differences in the manuscripts and the printed editions show that the rite was edited in its final form at a comparatively late date.

The ritual of the Jews of Corfu is almost identical with the Romanian rite. The rite of the Jews of Kaffa (Feodosiya) and Karasubazar (Belogorsk) in the Crimea has, despite many elaborations of the texts, all the distinctions of the *Maḥzor Romania.* While their *siddur* was printed twice (last edition Kala, 1735), their *maḥzor* was never printed. One scholar lists 315 *piyyutim* from their *maḥzor.*

The Roman (Italian) rite, also called *Minhag ha-Lo'azim,* is in use in Rome, in the interior of Italy, in a few communities in Salonika and Constantinople, and also in the Italian synagogue in present day Jerusalem. Peculiar to this rite are: *le'eila le'eila* in the usual *Kaddish,* which in other ties is only added in the High Holy Day period; various textual changes in some

The great synagogue in Vilna as depicted in a lithograph by Yaacov Sher. The Jerusalem of Lithuania, as Vilna was known, was one of the most dynamic centers of Jewish life and scholarship until World War II. It maintained its opposition to Ḥasidism for generations and particularly objected to the changes the Ḥasidim introduced into the liturgy.

prayers; a special piyyutic version of the service for Friday evening and its *Amidah; kerovot* for the Day of Atonement and all the fast days, but not for Rosh Ha-Shanah and other festivals. A number of *piyyutim* had already been removed from the *maḥzor* before the invention of printing. The first edition of this rite was that of Soncino, printed at Cassalmaggiore, 1485–86.

The Northern French and Ashkenazi rites may be considered as one unit. They are known to have been followed as early as the tenth century at least. The rite of Northern France was never printed because it ceased to exist with the persecutions of the 13th and 14th centuries. It differs from the Ashkenazi rite only in certain additional *piyyutim;* a *kerovah* for the second day of Rosh Ha-Shanah, and some *ma'aravim* (two treatises of the 13th century, *Sefer ha-Maḥkim* and *Siddur Troyes,* record these peculiarities). Until the 1290 expulsion, English Jews also followed the ritual of Northern France. Part of this rite remained in use in three communities in Piedmont (Northern Italy): Asti, Fossano, Moncalvo (known by the initials of the Hebrew words as *Apam*) until modern times. These communities had accepted the Ashkenazi rite upon their establishment in Italy, but on the High Holy Days continued to recite the *piyyutim* of the French *maḥzor* from handwritten copies. The community of Asti continued to hold High Holy Day services in accordance with its ritual until about 1965.

THE ASHKENAZI RITE. The Ashkenazi rite, originally used by the German or German-speaking Jews, was the most widely followed and its *siddur* and *maḥzor* have been printed since the 16th century. Only fragments of the Palestinian texts have been retained. Most of the *piyyutim* are by Palestinian or German authors. The rite is now followed in Germany (from the Elbe River westward), Switzerland, Holland, Belgium, northern France, and in a number of communities of northern Italy.

During the Middle Ages, the Eastern European communities that followed the rite separated from the rest. This branch comprised the eastern part of Germany, Poland, Lithuania, Bohemia, Moravia, Hungary, and the rest of Austria, all of Russia, Rumania, and the rest of the Balkan countries, and later also included the Ashkenazi communities of Denmark, England, America, and Palestine. Differences between the two branches—the Western, called *Minhag Rainus* ("Rhine usage") in the Middle Ages; and the Eastern, called *Minhag Oystraikh* or *Minhag Peihem* ("Austrian or Bohemian usage"), today generally known as *Minhag Polin*—are hardly noticeable in the regular prayers, the main variances are in some special *piyyutim.* Different editions of *Minhag Ashkenaz* (Western) and *Minhag Polin* (Eastern) were published from the 16th century onward. The *seliḥot* pointed to local differences. Thirteen different sub-rites have been printed.

Until the 18th century, this rite was generally followed by all Ashkenazi Jews, but since the rise of Ḥasidism, the rite of Isaac Luria (*Nusaḥ ha-Ari*) was accepted in ḥasidic communities. Though retaining some of the Ashkenazi usage, *Nusaḥ ha-Ari* generally resembles the Sephardi rite (see below) and is therefore properly called *Nusaḥ Sefarad.* The *piyyutim* recited by the hasidic communities are, however, according to the Ashkenazi (Polish) rite. Through the negligence of printers, the texts of this rite were badly emended.

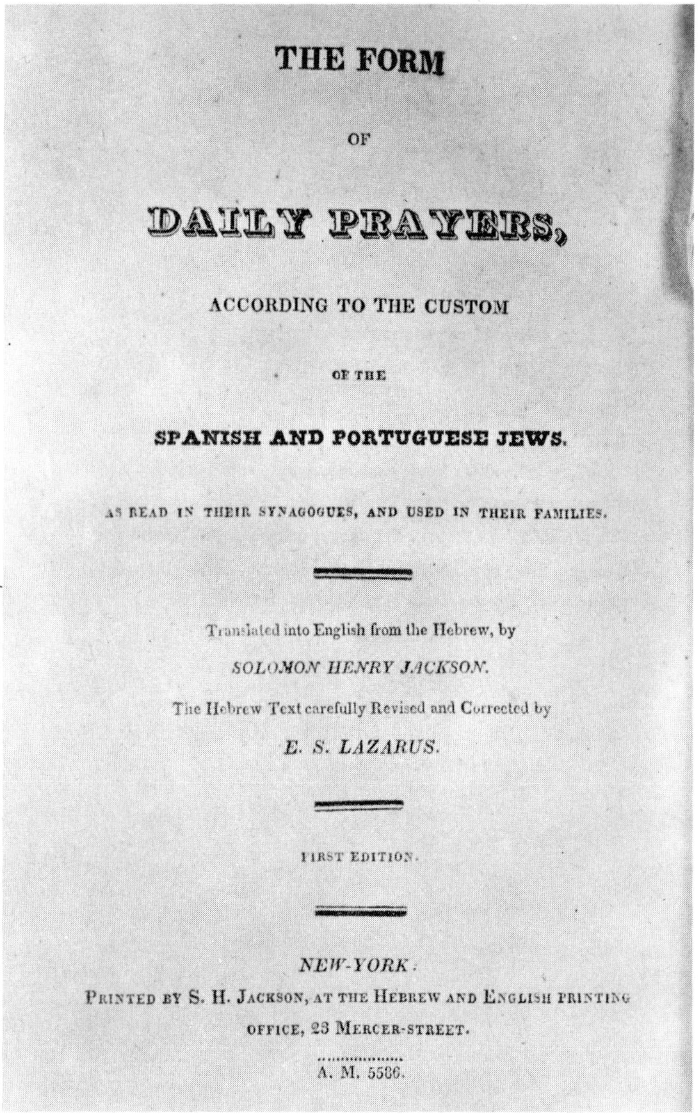
THE FORM

OF

DAILY PRAYERS,

ACCORDING TO THE CUSTOM

OF THE

SPANISH AND PORTUGUESE JEWS.

AS READ IN THEIR SYNAGOGUES, AND USED IN THEIR FAMILIES.

Translated into English from the Hebrew, by

SOLOMON HENRY JACKSON.

The Hebrew Text carefully Revised and Corrected by

E. S. LAZARUS.

FIRST EDITION.

NEW-YORK:

PRINTED BY S. H. JACKSON, AT THE HEBREW AND ENGLISH PRINTING OFFICE, 23 MERCER-STREET.

A. M. 5586.

Babylonian Group. The so-called "Babylonian" group is mainly represented by the Sephardi (Spanish) rite. Originally dominant in the Iberian Peninsula, after the Jewish expulsion it spread to North Africa, Italy, Holland, some communities in Germany (e.g. Altona, Vienna), England, the Balkans, and countries in the Near East, including Palestine. Later it reached North and South America and superseded the local rites of such communities as Greece and Turkey (*Maḥzor Romania,* see above), Persia, Aleppo, and Crimea. In the 16th century it was redacted and altered according to certain kabbalistic theories.

The Sephardi rite differs from the Ashkenazi in the order of the *Pesukei de-Zimra,* and in some text variations in the *Amidah* for weekdays and the Sabbath *Musaf.* The Sephardi (Castilian) rite has only a few *piyyutim* since most of them had been deleted by the time of David Abudarham (the famous 14th century liturgical commentator in Spain). Even for the Day of Atonement there are only one or two *piyyutim* for the introduction of the *Kedushah,* and the *seliḥot* are recited after the *Amidah.*

Both the rich literary output of the Sephardi poets and the characteristic form of the Sephardi *maḥzor* were preserved by the communities of North Africa where the Jews who were expelled from Spain had settled. The *maḥzorim* of Tunis, Algiers, and Oran-Tlemcen are very similar, containing *yoẓerot* and *kerovot* for Rosh Ha-Shanah, and the Day of Atonement, fast days, the four special Sabbaths, as well as the *tal* (dew) and *geshem* (rain) prayers. The community of Tripoli (its *maḥzor* was already printed in 1711 in Venice entitled *Siftei Renanot*) has an entirely different Day of Atonement liturgy in which the repetition of each *Amidah* contains a different *ma'amad* written by Isaac ben Judah ibn Ghayyat (11th century Spain). That *maḥzor* also has many *seliḥot.*

The *maḥzorim* of the rites of Catalonia and Aragon (identical with the Castilian rite in daily prayers) were printed several times (first editions: Catalonia (Salonika, 1627), Aragon (Salonika, 1629) for the Catalonian and Aragon Jews who settled in Salonika after the expulsion. The two *maḥzorim* are similar but differ from the rites of North Africa in *piyyut.*

The Provencal rite (southern France) is nearly identical with the Sephardi rite and was followed by the communities of Avignon, Carpentras, L'Isle sur la Sorgue, and Cavaillon until the 19th century. The text shows some additions due to the influence of the rite of northern France. The *maḥzor* of Carpentras, which abbreviated almost all the *piyyutim,* was printed in Amsterdam (1739–62, 4 vols.). The *maḥzorim* of L'Isle and Cavaillon, preserved only in manuscript, contain numerous *piyyutim* for festivals and Sabbaths, but only *kerovot* for the fast days, Rosh Ha-Shanah, the Day of Atonement, and the prayers for dew and rain. These *kerovot* were recited after the *Amidah* in accordance with the practice of the North African communities.

Minhag Teiman, the rite of the Jews of the Yemen who emigrated from southern Arabia, exists today only in Israel. It follows the *Seder Tefillah* of Maimonides which is based on the *siddur* of Saadiah Gaon, but shows the influence of Sephardi

Solomon Henry Jackson (died 1874) was the first Jewish printer in New York. One of his important productions was this prayerbook according to the Sephardi rite. In addition to printing and publishing it, he was also responsible for the English translation. It appeared in 1826.

elements. A small number of *piyyutim* such as *Avodah, hoshanot,* and *seliḥot* are taken from the Sephardi prayer book. The Yemenite liturgy was first printed in Jerusalem (2 vols., 1894) entitled *Tikhlal,* from which a handwritten (mimeographed) edition elaborated with many *piyyutim* was edited by J. S. Hobareh in 1964.

Lost Rites. Persecutions and migrations of Jews from country to country resulted in the disappearance of a number of rites, such as the old Palestinian, Romanian, Persian, and French rites. Besides the rites used by the few Italian and Yemenite communities, the Ashkenazi and Sephardi rites are the two most widely followed today. The need for a uniform rite, already foreseen in the 19th century, has been discussed in the last few years. Particularly in Israel, the need for a unified prayer book in the schools and army is felt, but until now no satisfying results have been achieved.

Other Rites. There are a number of rites which are difficult to categorize. Among them are the liturgy of the Persian Jews (preserved only in manuscripts and, as yet, insufficiently described); the rite of the Jews of Aleppo (*Maḥzor Aram-Zova;* printed Venice, 1523–27) whose High Holy Day prayers, very similar to those of the Persian prayer book, were also influenced by the Romanian and Roman rites; the liturgy of the so-called *Maḥzor Bilti Noda* ("Unknown Maḥzor"), a *maḥzor* for the Day of Atonement which, like the Tripoli *maḥzor,* contains the *piyyutim* of Ibn Ghayyat, but consists of an entirely different rite in the regular prayers—it apparently was printed as a supplement to the *Ḥizzunim* of the Jews of Sicily (Constantinople, 1585), which is the only work to provide information about the rite of this community after it settled in Salonika. It contains *piyyutim,* most of which are not included in other rites for many of the different Sabbaths and festivals, except for the Day of Atonement.

Reform. Dissatisfaction began to be felt with the traditional liturgy and the need to make it more relevant to the new conditions obtained after the Emancipation, especially in Western Europe, from the beginning of the 19th century. As a result there was a proliferation of new liturgies, based on the old but, as the Reformers saw it, having now a more refined, spiritual, and intellectual approach. The early Reformers were unduly influenced by the spirit of the times; they were eager to model Jewish prayer on the patterns of Protestant worship and keen to make the Jewish service "respectable" to the gentile neighbors. They had, however, real difficulties with some of the forms that had been handed down from the past and, since they disagreed with the Orthodox view which regarded the liturgy as sacrosanct, they were moved to introduce changes so that, as some of them were fond of saying, man might not speak lies to his Maker.

The Reformers felt the need to make the service more intelligible to the average worshiper. Less Hebrew was used; some of the traditional prayers were translated; and new prayers in the vernacular, as well as in Hebrew were introduced. The services were shortened by omitting some of the lengthier prayers, *piyyutim,* and study portions.

Other changes were governed by Western standards of decorum and by aesthetic considerations. For instance, the Torah, the prophetic readings and some of the prayers were declaimed rather than chanted as in the traditional mode. New melodies, influenced by the musical tradition of the West were introduced to the accompaniment of organ and choir. A determined effort was made to rid the service of such anachronisms as the *Yekum Purkan* prayer in Aramaic in which God is entreated to bless the exilarch and scholars of Babylon. Aramaic was generally abandoned in favor of Hebrew and this included in many congregations the famous Aramaic *Kaddish* prayer. Typical of the 19th century fastidiousness is the omission from the prayer service (even in communities which retained the account of the compounding of the incense) of the discussion found in the traditional liturgy, whether urine can be used in the mixture. The priestly blessing was generally omitted partly because it was held that the priesthood was an anachronism and partly because of the superstitions surrounding it (i.e., that anyone who gazes at the hands of the priests will become blind). On the other hand it became not at all unusual for the rabbi to adopt the priestly role by blessing the congregation with uplifted hands at the end of the service, an obvious imitation of church worship.

This synagogue scene painted by Alessandro Magnasco, one of the great 17th century Genoese painters, is really a caricature. Both he and some of his contemporaries painted fantastic representations of entirely imaginary synagogues with equally fantastic praying figures intended to represent praying Jews, but only in the remotest fashion. The painting shown here has an almost ghostly air.

There were moral objections to the few vestiges found in the traditional liturgy for the downfall of enemies (e.g. the *Av ha-Raḥamim* prayer). Many communities also omitted the *Kol* Nidrei (see chapter VIII) declaration on the eve of the Day of Atonement on the grounds that it lent credence to the accusation that the Jew's word was not his bond and the recitation of a bare juridical formula was historically and religiously an inappropriate beginning for the most solemn day in the Jewish calendar. Instead, "*O Tag des Herrn!*" an anthem by Leopold Stein, one of the early Reformers, was substituted, or *Kol Nidrei's* haunting melody was set to the words of a Psalm. The early morning benediction in which a man thanks God for not having made him a woman was omitted. The word *nokhri* ("stranger," "pagan") was substituted for *goi* ("gentile") in a similar benediction: "*who hath not made me goi.*" The statement that the "uncircumcised" do not rest on the Sabbath in the Sabbath morning prayer was changed so as to read the "wicked" do not rest.

Many changes were introduced on theological grounds. The most far-reaching one, which especially aroused the ire of the Orthodox, was the deleting of all references to the return to Zion. The Reformers believed that these references frustrated the universalistic aspect of Judaism and that the dispersion of the Jews was neither "exile" nor punishment for Israel's sins. Since the emphasis was placed on the messianic age rather than on a personal messiah, the necessary changes were introduced, e.g., instead of "He bringeth a Redeemer," "He bringeth redemption." Prayers for the peace of Israel were extended to embrace all mankind. Superstitious references were excised: e.g. the prayer for the sick in which the name of the sick person is changed so as to avert the evil decree; references to angels and demons. A theological question which greatly bothered not only the Reformers but some of the Conservatives and Orthodox as well, was whether a modern Jew could sincerely pray for the restoration of the ancient sacrificial cult. The tendency was either to omit references to it entirely or to change the wording so as to commemorate it historically rather than as a hope for the future (e.g. "and there our fathers offered. . ."). Most of these changes are still to be found in the Reform liturgy and some of them in the Conservative and Orthodox liturgies. In the Reform liturgy, however, there is a marked tendency to restore the prayers for the rebuilding of Zion.

PRAYER BOOKS

Books containing the texts of the customary daily prayers did not exist in ancient times. Sources from the tannaitic and amoraic periods take it as understood that prayers are recited by heart. In public prayer, the reader prayed aloud before the congregation, who responded "Amen" to the blessings. It was also considered forbidden to commit the text of blessings and prayers to writing ("writers of blessings are [like] those who burn the Torah"). After the completion of the Talmud, however, this prohibition was disregarded, and written prayer books undoubtedly existed as early as the geonic era (sixth to 11th centuries C.E.). In Babylonia it was permitted, at first, to use such prayer books only on the Day of Atonement, and on other fast days when the texts to be recited were lengthy and complicated, but later they were permitted generally. By the beginning of the eighth century this development was complete.

Siddur and Maḥzor. The book that included the regular prayers for the whole year was called *seder* (or *siddur*) *tefillah*—a name fixed by the *geonim* themselves—or, according to the cycle of the year, *maḥzor* (i.e. the cycle of prayers). Initially, there was no difference between the two names, which (in certain communities, until the present time) were used indiscriminately. In the course of time the additions for special days (i.e. the *piyyutim*) were also included. The present Ashkenazi custom (and, through its influence, that of some Sephardi communities as well) is to differentiate between the *siddur* (pl. *siddurim*)—containing only the regular prayers—and the *maḥzor* (pl. *maḥzorim*)—containing also the *piyyutim,* in most cases only those of the festivals. But this distinction came into being at a very late period, and is without foundation. The Jews of Yemen call their comprehensive *siddur, Tikhlal.*

Early Siddurim. Early traces of a set order of prayer are found in the second part of tractate *Soferim,* which is a compilation from the period of the *geonim.*

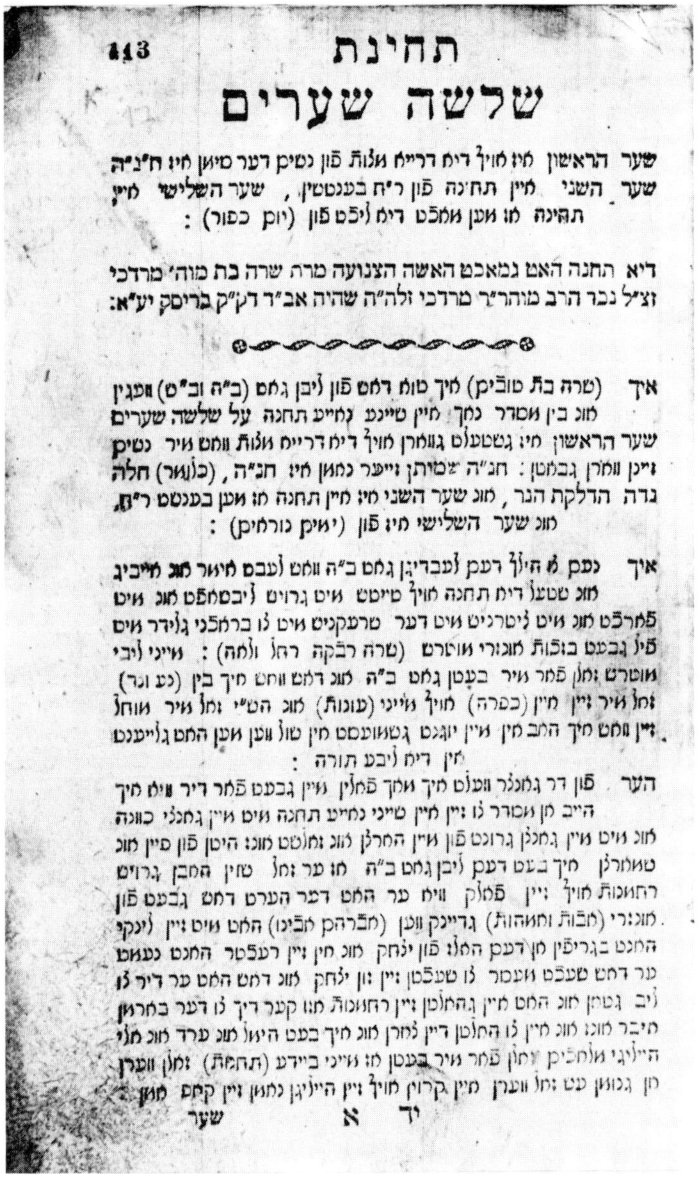

113

תחינת

שלשה שערים

Sarah Bas-Tovim was a 17th-century writer of *tkhines* (Yiddish prayers for women). Her prayer pamphlet *Shloyshe Sheorim* ("The Three Portals," 1838) deals with the three main *mitzvot* for women—*ḥallah, mikveh* and kindling the Sabbath and festival candles. Her *tkhines* taught ethics and commandments in rhymed verse and were exceedingly popular with Yiddish-speaking women from the time they first appeared.

SEDER RAV AMRAM. The first true prayer book, however, is the *Seder Rav Amram Gaon,* which dates from the ninth century. Compiled at the request of the Jews of Spain it contains the regular prayers, according to the order of the whole year—weekdays, Sabbath, New Moon, fast days, Ḥanukkah, Purim, and all the festivals. Each section is preceded by a summary of the relevant *halakhot*. The book concludes with benedictions and special prayers for occasions such as marriage, circumcision, redemption of the firstborn, and the burial service. Unfortunately this text of prayers cannot serve as an authentic source for the rite observed by the *geonim* since all the extant manuscripts of this *seder* differ greatly from one another. The probable reason is that the various copyists "corrected" the manuscript in accordance with their own rites.

SIDDUR RAV SA'ADIAH. One hundred years after the compilation of the *Seder Rav Amram Gaon,* the emerging prayer book attained a more definite form as a result of the work of the greatest scholar of Babylonian Jewry, Saadiah (ben Joseph) Gaon (882–942). He made a systematic compilation of the prayers for the whole year and an Arabic translation of the relevant halakhot. This became very well known in Egypt and in other countries where Arabic was the vernacular. With the passage of time, however, it was forgotten and was not published until recent times, when it appeared with a Hebrew translation, under the title *Siddur Rav Sa'adiah Gaon.* The only extant complete manuscript of this work apparently reproduces the rite of the Babylonian *geonim* (with some influence of the rite of Egypt). In contrast, the *Genizah* fragments of this *siddur* contain the text of the prayers in a different and adapted version. The logical, methodical order of this prayer book, however, which differs from the ordinary calendar order, was not generally accepted (except by Maimonides) and its order possibly explains its limited circulation. Nothing but fragmentary quotations to be found in halakhic literature survive from a prayer book compiled in the 11th century by Hai ben Sherira Gaon, a later Babylonian scholar.

SIDDUR RASHI. The work entitled *Siddur Rashi,* which emerged in the 11th/12th centuries from the school of Rashi (1040–1105; the leading Bible and Talmud commentator) does not contain the text of the prayers at all. It consists solely of the halakhic material, with full talmudic treatment. Similarly, the *Seder ha-Tefillot* that Maimonides (1135–1204; the leading halakhist) attached to his *Mishneh Torah* is not a true prayer book, but a collection of versions of prayers from which it is possible to compile a *siddur.* His manuscript apparently reproduced the rite current in Egypt in his time, which was very different from that of Spanish Jewry; it was also adopted in Yemen.

MAḤZOR VITRY. In contrast to these works, the *Maḥzor Vitry,* compiled in the 11th century by Simḥah ben Samuel of Vitry, a pupil of Rashi, is a prayer book in the full sense of the word. It contains the text of all the regular prayers, in accordance with the rite of northern France, which is similar to that of

This page from the *Leipzig Maḥzor* (13th-century Germany) is part of the morning service for Passover. The illustration is meant to represent the Egyptians pursuing the Children of Israel when the latter left Egypt. Although the Egyptians are dressed in medieval knightly armor, the chariot bears the crescent moon of Islam.

Germany. Each section is preceded by a detailed compilation of relevant laws. In the halakhic part of the work, which is mainly consistent with the *Siddur Rashi,* large sections were copied from the *Seder Rav Amram Gaon,* although later *geonim* were also cited. Besides the regular prayers, the *Maḥzor Vitry* includes only a limited number of *piyyutim,* mainly *ma'arivim* and *hoshanot;* added to it are the Passover *Haggadah* and the prayers for Simḥat Torah; it does not contain any *kerovot* (which were, however, already in use at that time), and thus cannot be regarded as a complete *maḥzor.*

This arrangement may have been the result of a certain logic for, beginning with the Middle Ages, two types of prayer books had evolved. One, which included the *kerovot,* was designed for cantors and was usually produced in a large format. The second, which was mostly copied in a small format for individual use, did not contain the *kerovot* but did (in Germany and France) include the *ma'arivim* and *hoshanot.* It is to the latter genre that the *Maḥzor Vitry* therefore belongs.

All of the above-mentioned prayer books, apart from a few differences in text, do not differ from one another in their scope. The sole difference is in the laws of the prayers, which some of them cite at length. In other cases, however, only the final rulings in each case were reproduced in place of the full talmudic explanation of the themes and the discussion of the various opinions found in the *Seder Rav Amram Gaon* and the *Maḥzor Vitry.*

Manuscripts From Other Rites. Prayer books of other rites have also been preserved in manuscript form from this period. These include those of the Jews of Italy (*Roman Maḥzor*) mainly in small folio format; of the Jews of the Balkans; and of the Jews of Spain, mostly in quarto. Among the Jews of Yemen (where there was no printing press at all) the writing of prayer books continued (mostly *Tikhalim* in small folio) until the beginning of the 20th century. This wealth of manuscripts, most of which are in the large libraries, has not yet been fully exploited for scientific editions and for research into the history of the text. No critical version of any of the well-known rites has yet been constructed out of the actual texts in the manuscripts.

Commentaries on the text of the prayers began simultaneously with the composition of the ancient prayer books. In the geonic prayer books there is as yet no explanation of texts of the prayers but the *Maḥzor Vitry* does contain explanations of a number of prayers, such as *Kaddish, Nishmat Kol Ḥai, hoshanot,* and the Passover *Haggadah.* The greatest rabbinic authorities participated in the exposition of the prayer books. These included men such as Rashi, Eliezer ben Nathan of Mainz (c.1090–1170), Ephraim ben Jacob of Bonn (12th century), Baruch the father of Meir of Rothenburg (12th century), Judah he-Ḥasid of Regensburg (c.1150–1217), Eleazar ben Judah of Worms (c.1165–1230), and Joseph Caro (1488–1575, the author of the major code, *Shulḥan Arukh*). Their comments were transmitted anonymously from place to place and passed into the customary manuscript expositions, and then into print in the margins of the *siddurim* and *maḥzorim.*

Printed Prayer Books. With the advent of printing, a wide variety of prayer books was produced. These included both *maḥzorim* for the whole year as well as *siddurim* in small format for individual use. Among the incunabula (books printed before 1500) there are already many prayer books. Prayer books of

סדר
תְּפִלּוֹת
כמנהג קהלות
קדש רומניא
נדפס בבירת זואן
דיגארה
באותיות בונבירני
בסכת חמשת לפים
ושלם מאות והרכעי'
וסטה לפק פה
ויניציאה

סדר הקונטירים

כולל בו הקידושין ופיוטים לשבת · סדר ההבדלה ופזמונים למוצאי
שבת · הדלקת נר חנוכה וסדר פורים · הגדה של פסח וקידושין
לימים טובים · סדר שבליל שמחת התורה קורין · וגם
נוסף על הראשונים · פיוטים וקידושין לחתנים · ופזמונים
שמזמרין בקול נאה ונעים · דבר יום ביומו כאלה
וכאלה רבים · כאשר עיני הקורא תחזינה מישרים ·
ובאופן שאין צריך לחזור הכל מסודרים ·
כמנהג קהלות הקודש שבמחוז ויניזין
דרים · ישמרם האל ויצילם לדורי
דורים :

נדפס במצות השותפים הצעירים ישעיה וידאל ומרדכי וינטורה ·
יצו המגיהים :

באויגניון
שנת
כה תברכו את בני ישראל לפרט קטן

the Roman rite were the first to be published (*Mahzor Roma*, Soncino-Cassalmaggiore 1485/86; *Siddur Katan* called "Sidorello," 1486), then those of the Spanish rite (*Seder Tefillot*, 1490). Printed Spanish and Portuguese books have survived in only fragmentary form. In the 16th century, prayer books were published in Germany and Poland (*mahzorim*, beginning with 1521, 1522, and *siddurim*, about 1508) and in Romaniot rite (*mahzorim* from 1510, *siddurim*, later still). Prayer books for the communities of southern France were not printed until the 18th century (*Mahzor Avignon* 1765–66, Carpentras 1739–62). The *Tikhlal* of the Yemenite Jews was not printed until the end of the 19th century (Jerusalem, 1894–98). Certain categories of prayers such as *selihot* and *kinot* for the Ninth of Av were printed very early in special editions (e.g. *selihot* according to the German custom, Soncino 1496; *kinot* for the Ninth of Av according to the Polish custom, Cracow 1584), although in the main they were also incorporated in the *mahzorim*.

Types of Prayer Books. In the course of time the following types of prayer book became established among Ashkenazi Jews: (1) *Ha-Mahzor ha-Gadol* in folio (also called *Kol Bo*), containing, according to the ancient custom, all the prayers of the year—weekday, Sabbath, festivals, and special days; (2) the so-called *Mahzor*, which included only the festival prayers, usually a separate volume for each festival; (3) the small *siddur*, containing only the regular daily and Sabbath prayers; (4) *Ha-Siddur ha-Shalem*, completed by the addition of the *yozerot* for the special Sabbaths, the *hoshanot*, *selihot* for fast days, *ma'arivim* for the nights of the festivals, and supplemented at times by the Book of Psalms and *ma'amadot*. The Sephardi Jews, on the other hand, arrived at the following subdivision: (1) *Tefillat ha-Hodesh*, comprising the prayers for weekdays,

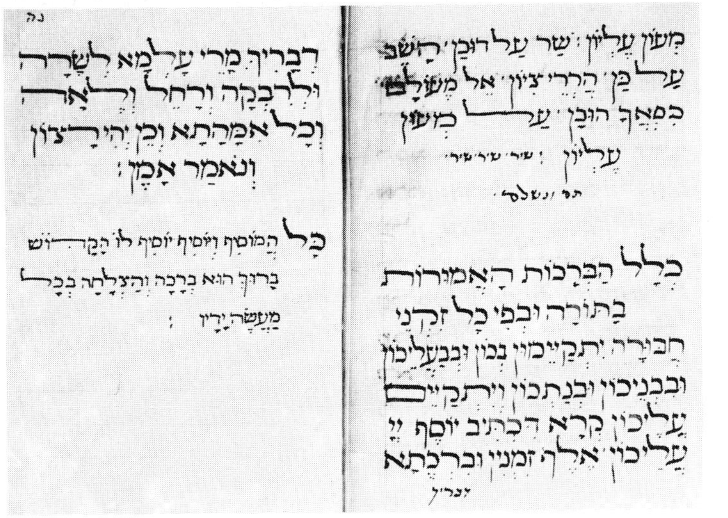

The plethora of different liturgical rites is amply illustrated in these three prayerbooks. On the far left is the title page of a prayerbook printed "in Bomberg letters" in Venice in 1586 according to the Romanian rite. Next to it is the title page of a prayerbook printed in Avignon in 1765 "according to the custom of the holy congregations that dwell in Comtat Venaissin." The third example was handwritten on rice paper in the 17th/18th century and is part of the service for Simḥat Torah according to the rite of the Jews of Cochin.

Sabbath, the New Moon, Ḥanukkah, and Purim; (2) *Mo'adim,* consisting of the prayers for the three pilgrim festivals; (3) *Rosh Ha-Shanah,* for the New Year; (4) *Kippur* for the Day of Atonement; (5) *Ta'aniyyot,* which also included the Ninth of Av and its *kinot.* Only the Jews of Italy and Yemen maintained the original form of the *Maḥzor ha-Shanah,* which contained all the prayers in cyclical order; they too however, published small *siddurim.*

TEXTUAL EDITIONS. The *siddur* used by Sephardi Jews was edited in the 16th century in accordance with the *kavvanot* appropriate to the prayers, stipulated by the kabbalist Isaac Luria (1534–1572; known as "Ha-Ari"). As a result, hardly any pre-Lurianic prayer books are extant. In many editions the divine names are made to conform with the Lurianic "intentions" by variations in voweling or by interlacing the Ineffable Name with various forms of the word *Adonai.* The text of the Ashkenazi *siddur* became a subject of study by several scholars, particularly between the 17th and 19th centuries. They published the prayer book in new editions or wrote books in which they justified or emended the text. Among these works are those by Naḥman Lieballer (Dyhrenfurth, 1690); Azriel and his son, Elijah of Vilna (*Derekh Si'aḥ ha-Sadeh,* Frankfort-on-Main, 1704); Solomon Zalman Katz Hanau (*Kunteres Sha'arei Tefillah* and *Beit Tefillah,* Jesnitz, 1725); Jacob Emden (Yavez; *Lu'aḥ Eresh,* an appendix to his prayer book, Altona, 1769); Mordecai Duesseldorf (*Kunteres Hassagot al Siddur Sha'arei Tefillah,* published after his death, at Prague in 1784); Isaac Satanow (*Va-Ye'etar Yizḥak,* Berlin 1785, who polemicized with all his predecessors); Judah Leib Ben Ze'ev (*Tikkunei ha-Tefillah,* published after his death with the edition *Tefillah Zakkah,* Vienna, 1816); Wolf Heidenheim (*Siddur Safah Berurah* with notes at several points, Roedelheim, 1806). In the course of time Heidenheim's *siddur* was more or less accepted as standard. All the scholarly disputes which these versions were designed to resolve turned on such grammatical niceties as the insertion of a *dagesh* or *meteg* and matters of pointing, and only very rarely on establishing the text. Heidenheim and his successors, particularly, preferred (to too great an extent) the language of the Bible to "the language of the scholars."

Critical treatment of the prayer book did not commence until the 19th century. It began with E. L. Landshuth who contributed a commentary, *Mekor Berakhah,* to the *Siddur Hegyon Lev* (published by Z. H. Edelmann, 1845). In this commentary he identified the sources of the prayers and tried to establish the date of their compilation and composition. This method was continued by W. Jawitz (*Mekor ha-Berakhot,* 1910), A. Berliner (*Randbermerkungen zum taeglichen Gebetbuch,* 2 vols., 1909–12), and S. Elbogen (*Der juedische Gottesdienst,* 1913, 1931[3]).

Commentaries. Commentaries to the prayer book have long been numerous. Those which were originally available only in manuscript form were later printed in the folio editions of *maḥzorim.* Some commentaries have a kabbalistic approach while others deal with explanations of the words and themes. The *Avodat Yisrael* (1868) compiled by Isaac Seligman Baer, contains sources of the prayers, many notes on grammatical topics, and comparisons of the texts of different rites, as well as a short exposition of the *seliḥot* and *yoẓerot.* This edition has been reprinted several times (the last occasion in 1937), and has been accepted as the standard prayer book text by most subsequent editions of the *siddur.*

The ancient connection between the text of the prayers and their laws was renewed in the 19th century. The *Derekh ha-Ḥayyim* (1828), written by Jacob Lorberbaum of Lissa and the *Nehora ha-Shalem* (1827) by Jehiel Michael of Michailishki (Vilna region), author of the *Korban Aharon* on the *maḥzor,* were then accepted into the prayer books; both have since been published innumerable times. The Sephardi Jews compiled similar editions for the use of their congregations. Thus H. J. D. Azulai's *Kesher Godel,* Leghorn, 1802, dealing with the laws of the prayers, and the anonymous *Shelemut ha-Lev* were added to their prayer books in the 19th century.

English Translations. Among the better-known translations of

עטרת צבי
שבתי צבי מלך ישראל
משיח אלהי יעקב
סדר הפטרות
כל השנה
כמנהג קהלות הספרדים
והאשכנזים
נדפסו מחדש והוגהו כדקדוק
נמרץ על ידי הסופרים בהירים
וידועים כטיב ההגהה בשלמות
באמשטרדם
במצות הה״ר שמואל ברוך
רוזא יצ״ו אתו את הברכה
בבית הה״ר דוד די קראשתו
תארתס יצ״ו
בשנת אשריך ישראל
מי כמוך עם נושע ב״י
היא השנה הראשונה לחדוש
הנבואה ומלכות

One of the most traumatic events for Jews in the Middle Ages was the appearance of Shabbetai Ẓevi as the messiah. During his meteoric rise to fame, Jews all over the world honestly believed that the messiah had come. The title page shown here is of a book which contains the *haftarot* for the whole year according to both the Sephardi and Ashkenazi rites. It was printed in Amsterdam in 1666 and under the crown at the top of the page it bears the text, "Shabbetai Ẓevi, king of Israel, the messiah of the God of Jacob."

the prayer books in English is the *Authorised Daily Prayer Book* (1890) by S. Singer. Although the minister of an Orthodox congregation, he was considered progressive in his religious views. He omitted some *piyyutim* from his work, and included a prayer for the welfare of the Royal family. It has been through many editions and by 1970 had sold nearly 500,000 copies (a revised edition was published in 1962). A companion to this prayer book was published by I. Abrahams (1914) and an annotated edition by Chief Rabbi J. H. Hertz (1941) with the addition of prayers for special occasions. In the U.S. another version with notes was edited by P. Birnbaum (*Daily Prayer Book* 1949, and many editions, and the *High Holyday Prayer-book* 1951, and many editions). The best-known modern Sephardi prayer book and *maḥzor* are those edited by David de Sola Pool, the U.S. rabbi and civic and communal leader.

Reform Prayer Books. Liturgical reform began in the practical sphere, with most attention being given to the external aspects of worship. During the initial stages, the aesthetics of the synagogue service occupied the minds of the early Reformers more than the doctrinal content of the prayer book. The major emphasis was placed on the form of worship rather than on more serious theological issues. In 1810 Israel Jacobson, a financier and philanthropist, provided a simplified, decorous service for boarding-school children in Seesen. The inauguration ceremony included the ringing of a bell and the singing of hymns in German. Jacobson himself conducted the festivities dressed in the robes of a Protestant clergyman. In 1815, he opened a synagogue in Berlin in which he installed an organ and instituted the confirmation ceremony (see page 236). Soon thereafter, I. S. Fraenkel and M. I. Bresselau produced the Hamburg *Gebetbuch* (*Sefer ha-Avodah, Ordnung der oeffentlichen Andacht,* first edition 1819). These early reformers did not ignore the scholarly contributions to the study of the liturgy already made by Wolf Heidenheim. Thus, the closing pages of the Hamburg volume contain learned notes citing dissenting views in older sources that might lend support to Reform. Not until several years later, however, did the burgeoning *Wissenschaft des Judentums,* as well as recent developments in Jewish theology, have an influence on the *siddur,* paying particular attention to the theological principles underlying the prayer text and making emendations accordingly. While the German Reform Rabbinical Conferences (1844–46) were in session, lending shape and direction to the amorphous variety of liturgical changes then in the making, the Berlin Reform community broke company and began to devise its own radical rite. Here, the predominant language of prayer was German, Hebrew being limited to a few selected biblical verses. When the congregation secured Samuel Holdheim, a radical reformer, as its spiritual leader, he was authorized to revise its liturgical manuals. There he introduced radical reform into the ritual. Services were conducted on both Saturdays and Sundays and after a while on Sundays only. At the same

A detail of the *Ma'ariv* service for festivals from an Italian manuscript *siddur* written in Bertinoro in 1390. Only the distinctive benediction of the festival is written in full, on the assumption that the user knows the standard benedictions by heart. No explanation has been put forward for the illustrations.

time, Holdheim brough classical and traditional forms and recent liturgical research into greater play, thus moderating the excesses of the Reform community's ritual. At the same time, D. W. Marks, a remarkably well-versed layman, edited *Seder ha-Tefillot—Forms of Prayer,* published in 1841–43. A spiritual offspring of the Hamburg *Gebetbuch,* this prayer book was used in the West London Synagogue of British Jews of which Marks was the spiritual leader. Although in the introduction the editor admits his debt to the scholarship of Zunz, Rapoport, and others, in fact he relied very little upon the content of their works. It is probably more correct to say that Marks derived from these learned men the encouragement and inspiration for his own original endeavors. Unlike its continental counterparts, *Forms of Prayer* evinces an almost Karaitic scriptural fundamentalism. Marks imitates his Hamburg predecessors, however, in the choice of some Hebrew prayers to be read in the vernacular, in shunning repetitions, in the offhand treatment of the *haftarah* (see page 99), in slight abbreviations of the standard text, and in a partiality toward Sephardi *piyyutim.* Apart from occasional pseudo-Karaizing, *Forms of Prayer* may be said to stand in the Orthodox tradition. Only infrequently did Marks contribute original Hebrew compositions. These works were often written in a felicitous classical style, as in his unique *Birkat ha-Mo'adim* which replaces the festival *Musaf* service.

Even though such Reform prayer books did radically alter the traditional liturgy, they did not introduce Reform principles into the body of the standard Hebrew text. The first to do so with any consistency was that compiled by Abraham Geiger, the founder and first director of the *Hochschule fuer die Wissenschaft des Judentums.* Historical consciousness and theological integrity were the hallmarks of Geiger's liturgical works (the first edition of his prayer book was published in 1854), and these became the major characteristics of the moderate Reform (Liberal) liturgy in Germany for nearly a century. Geiger's prayer book was the product of social and religious aims in conjunction with aesthetic considerations. He considerably shortened the order of prayer to enable worshipers to pray with devotion. He also established prayers for rain in summer, to suit conditions in Germany rather than in Ereẓ Israel. He also omitted portions from various prayers that he regarded as empty verbiage.

During the middle of the 19th century, German Jewish immigrants to the U.S. brought with them the liturgical reforms that were then emerging in Central Europe. The single formative influence to dominate all others was the Hamburg *Gebetbuch.* The principal U.S. prayer books of the day, Leo Merzbacher's *Seder Tefillah—The Order of Prayer for Divine Service* (1855), David Einhorn's *Olat Tamid—Book of Prayers for Israelitish Congregations* (1856) and Isaac M. Wise's *Minhag Amerikah—The Daily Prayers for American Israelites* (1857), varied in their degree of reform. In most cases, they revealed the tastes and talents of their authors and reflected the demands of their

In this small Jerusalem *bet ha-midrash* the *sheliaḥ ẓibbur* is standing in front of a very common type of prayer lectern. Besides the *shivviti* plaque, the lectern is also adorned with various liturgical instructions to the congregation. The photograph was taken on the 35th day of the *Omer,* as is evident from the paper hanging directly in front of the *ḥazzan.*
The miniatures in the *Dresden Maḥzor* (South Germany, c.1300) are zodiacal signs of the months of Tevet and Shevat. The text is one of the *piyyutim* incorporated in the Prayer for Dew.
Informal prayer has a place of importance in the Jewish liturgy. The photograph on the right was taken in the women's section of the Western Wall.

respective congregations. They all, nevertheless, bore the stamp of the Hamburg *Gebetbuch,* the parent Reform prayer book.

All of these rites were incorporated in the most important Reform work of the 19th century, *The Union Prayer Book of Jewish Worship—Seder Tefilot Yisrael* (first edition 1894–95). Of particular importance in the compilation of *The Union Prayer Book* were the transitional works of Adolph Huebsch (e.g. his prayer book for Congregation Ahawath Chesed (1889) in New York, translated by A. Kohut and Isaac S. Moses. Huebsch combined Goldheim's work with Wise's *Minhag*

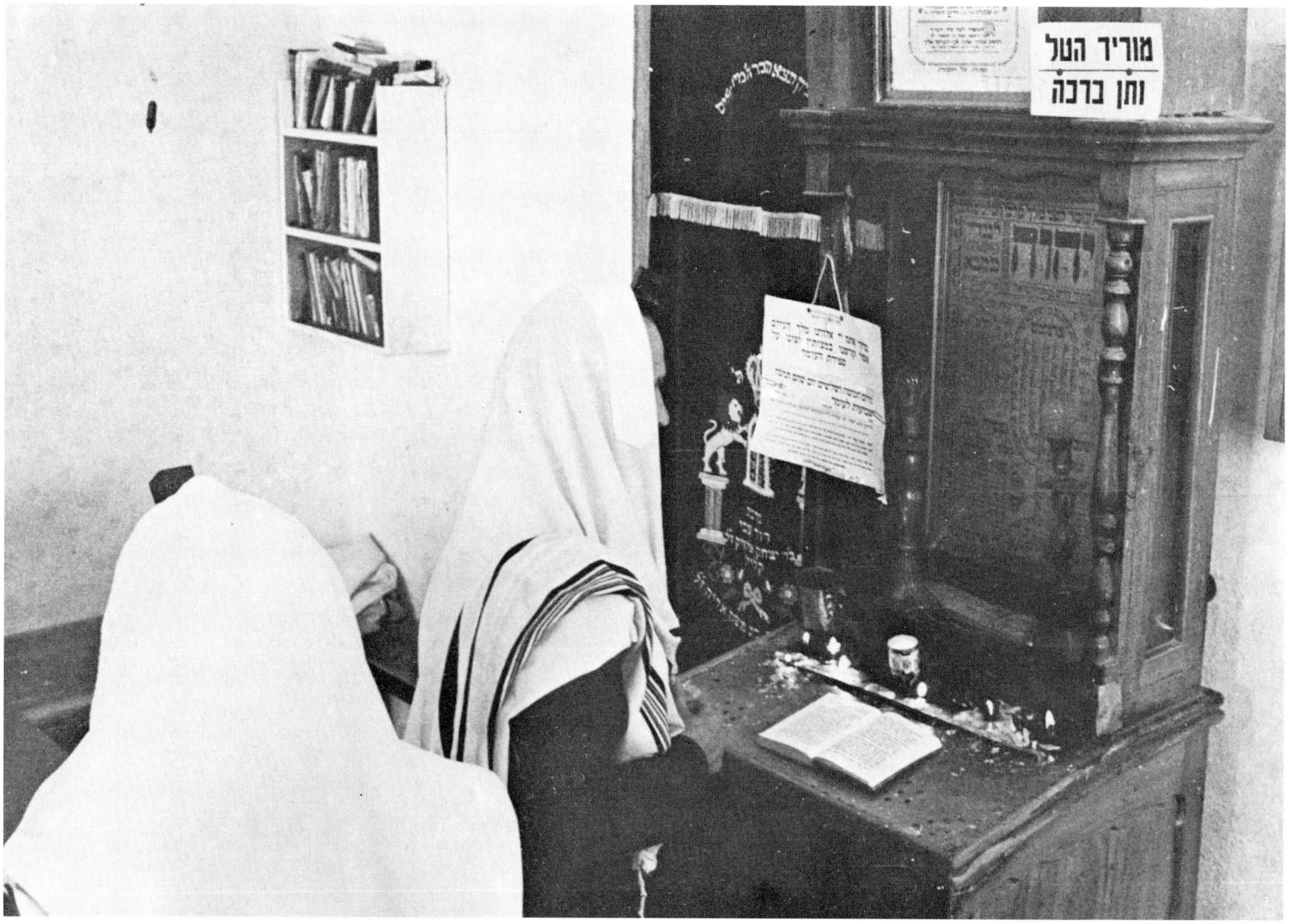

Amerikah; while Moses combined *Seder Tefillah, Olat Tamid,* and later, Huebsch's synthesis as well.

The end of the 19th century witnessed the writing of many new vernacular compositions. Some from predominantly English formularies, beginning with Joseph Krauskopf's *The Service Ritual* (1888) and *The Service Manual* (1892), Gustav Gottheil's *Morning Prayer* (1889), and Kaufmann Kohler's *Sabbath Eve Service* (1891), found their way into the *Union Prayer Book.* After much weighing and harmonizing of texts, the result was an abbreviated and simplified liturgy with both languages kept in balance, interspersed with prayers and reponses in the language of the country. The *Union Prayer Book* represents the cumulative efforts of the American Reform movement to achieve a uniform rite that would meet the needs of diverse congregations throughout the nation. The remarkable durability of the prayer book in its various editions testifies to the success of those efforts. Each edition mirrors changes in theological views and reflects the vicissitudes of the Jewish community both in the U.S. and abroad. The second edition (1922), for example, shows an increased interest in ceremonial life which hitherto had been substantially eliminated. Neither Merzbacher's volume nor Einhorn's contains the benedictions for the blowing of the *shofar* or the kindling of the Ḥanukkah candles, whereas the second edition of the *Union Prayer Book* readmits them. The greater quantity of Hebrew in the revised 1940 edition attests to a heightened ethnic consciousness. Jewish group solidarity is expressed by the inclusion of Hebrew

prayers from all eras and places, which enhance the diminished rabbinic *stammgebete* (regular prayers). This last edition is distinguished by variety and richness.

Outside U.S. in 20th Century. Reform in the U.S. was generally dependent upon Central European prototypes for doctrinal reformulations until the early 20th century, when American Reformers took the lead in liturgical renewal. Thus, Caesar Seligmann's *Israelitisches Gebetbuch* (1910) and the French Union Liberale Israelite's *Tefillot Kol ha-Shanah—Rituel des Prieres Journalieres* (1925), both of which take considerable liberties with the historical text and the directions for the performance of the ritual, were inspired by American models. While there is no direct imitation—distinctively European requirements having been considered—the desire to forestall monotony during the service by introducing variety and meaningful alternation of languages was substantially

"Moses before the Burning Bush," is the name the American artist, Milton Horn, gave to his bronze relief sculpture on the exterior of Temple B'nai Israel in Charleston, West Virginia. A very revolutionary aspect is the fact that God's Voice is given a vehicle in human form, namely the head rising out of the flames. The text underneath is God's answer to Moses' question, "When . . . they [the Israelites] ask me 'What is His name?', 'what shall I say to them?" *"Ehyeh Asher Ehyeh*—I am that I am."

derived from the U.S. The *Liberal Jewish Prayer Book* (1923–26) by Israel I. Mattuck, former U.S. Reforn rabbi and a founder of English Liberal Judaism, displays unique and wide-ranging literariness. (The same disposition toward variety is maintained in *Avodat ha-Lev—Service of the Heart* (1967). Largely influenced by the *Union Prayer Book* the emended West London Synagogue's *Seder ha-Tefillot—Forms of Prayer* (1931) exhibits renewed appreciation for both traditional rabbinic arrangement and religious liberalism in being shorn of its eccentric and ostensibly fundamentalist character. This is seen in the selection of benedictions for the weekday *Amidah,* in the choice of the *Aleinu* text, and the reinstitution of benedictions for rabbinic ordinances. The *Einheitsgebetbuch* (edited by C. Seligmann, I. Elbogen, and H. Vogelstein, 1929) deserves special mention not only because it appropriated a variety of texts from the *Union Prayer Book,* but, more significantly, because it succeeded in achieving unity among the Liberal congregations of Germany before World War II. This major accomplishment serves as a becoming *Memorbuch* to a decimated German Jewry.

Conservative and Reconstructionist Prayer Books. The Conservative and Reconstructionist manuals adhere to the classical outlines. Nevertheless, they too constitute a departure from traditional Judaism, representing what has been called "Reform from within." *Maḥzor le-Shalosh Regalim—The Festival Prayer Book* (United Synagogue of America, 1927), a Conservative publication, is closer to the enlightened Orthodoxy of Hermann Adler and Joseph H. Hertz, former chief rabbis of Great Britain, than to any publication of the moderate Reform or proto-Conservative movement such Benjamin Szold's and Marcus Jastrow's *Avodat Yisrael—Israelitish Prayer Book* (first edition 1865), or Aaron Wise's *Shalhevet Yah—The Temple Service* (1891). A reason for this may lie in the Conservative movement's loyalty to Solomon Schechter's motto "catholic Israel." Dependence upon the official British books can be seen in the use of the festival *piyyutim* and of the introductory memorial prayer at the memorial service. This anglophile penchant gave way approximately 20 years later to a more independent *Seder Tefillot Yisrael le-Shabbat u le-Shalosh Regalim—Sabbath and Festival Prayer Book* (Rabbinical Assembly of American and United Synagogue of America, 1946), wherein a minimum of textual reforms are permitted. With unity of Conservative congregations their overriding aim, the editors were determined not to add unnecessarily to the plethora of variations of controverted texts. Among the more innovative features of the *Sabbath and Festival Prayer Book* are the supplementary readings and explanatory notes at the end of the volume. The most far-reaching of the Conservative liturgical publications in hard-cover is the *Siddur li-Y'mot ha-Ḥol—Weekday Prayer Book* (1961). The editors introduce significant changes in wording to bring the prayers into closer harmony with the consensus of Conservative belief. Apart from obvious Zionist sentiment, the rewritten *Musaf* for the festivals and for Rosh Ḥodesh reads materially as a 19th-century German Liberal reconstruction. The Reconstructionist *siddurim* (*Seder Tefillot le-Shabbat—Sabbath Prayer Book,* 1945; *Maḥzor le-Yamim Nora'im—High Holy Day Prayer Book,* 1948; *Festival Prayer Book,* 1958; and *Seder Tefillot li-Y'mot ha-Ḥol—Daily Prayer Book,* 1963) also make extensive use of supplementary readings. They are distinguished from the Conservative prayer books by reference to such reconstructionist tenets as the denial of the idea of the Chosen People, and the diminution or deletion of supernatural and anthropomorphic references.

Abbreviated Prayer Books. Some modified and abbreviated prayer books have also been introduced by Orthodox congregations. This is particularly so of the special prayer books compiled for members of the Allied Forces during World War II by the chaplains to the services. Similarly, many special prayer books have been compiled for use in children's services. In this case, however, those for use in the Reform and Conservative rites are the most numerous. They include—in the Reform version—G. A. Rose, *Children's Services* (Rosh Ha-Shanah, Yom Kippur, 1926; Sabbath, 1937); and M. Marenof, *Religious Service for the Junior Congregation* (1949). Amongst the Conservative texts are: H. Chanover and E. Zusman, *A Prayer Book for Junior Congregations* (1959), and M. Silverman and H. E. Silverman, *Prayer Books for Summer Camps and Institutes* (1954).

אהיה
אשר
אהיה

index

C

D

L

M

n

O

p

Q

R

S

illustration credits

Jerusalem, Israel Museum Photo Archives, 1, 38 (right), 65 (bottom).
Kibbutz Ein Harod, Mishkan le-Omanut, 3, 11, 35, 40, 60, 150 (left) 151, 216, 239, 241, 242.
Florence, Fratelli Alinari, 4 (left).
Photo Arielli, Bat-Yam, 4 (right).
Jerusalem, Israel Museum, 5, 15, 23, 29, 33 (top, bottom), 41 (right), 59 (bottom), 61 (top), 62 (right), 69, 87, 88 (left), 95, 130, 144, 145 (right), 155 (right), 179, 198 (left), 206, 217, 221 (left), 238.
Photo David Harris, Jerusalem, 5, 23, 29, 33, 41, 61 (top), 70 (top), 87, 130, 142, 198, 201, 206, 221, 231, 238.
Photo Erich Hartmann, New York, 7.
Jerusalem, Jewish National and University Library, 8, 19, 63, 78, 79, 106, 124, 142 (right), 196 (right), 226, 245, 256.
Photo I. Zafrir, Tel Aviv, 9.
Jerusalem, Jewish National Fund Photo Archives, 10, 157.
Jerusalem, Israel Mehlman, 13.
Cecil Roth Collection, 16, 38 (left), 48, 73, 86, 98, 99 (left), 117, 129, 133, 135 (right), 142 (left), 155 (left), 156, 165, 180, 193, 185, 216, 232 (top), 233, 258, 259.
Photo David Posner, Jerusalem, 17, 20 (bottom), 62 (left), 121, 235 (right), 262, 263 (right).
Paris Rabbinical Collection, 18.
Berlin, Preussische Staatsbibliothek, 21.
Avigdor Herzog (ed.), *Renanot,* Song Sheet for Sacred Music, 22.
Munich State Library, 25 (left).
Manchester, John Rylands Library, 25 (right).
Jerusalem, Schocken Library, 26, 53, 135 (left).
Abraham Yaari, *Hebrew Printers' Marks,* Jerusalem (1943), 31, 57, 163 (right), 203.
New York, Women's League for Conservative Judaism, 34.
Government Press Office, Tel Aviv, 36 (left), 52, 65 (top), 89, 148, 150 (right), 152, 163 (left), 172, 191, 193, 194 (top), 197, 204, 235 (left).
David Davidowicz, *Synagogues in Poland and their Destruction,* Jerusalem (1960), 39.
Paris, Klagsbald Collection, 41 (left).
Amsterdam Rijksmuseum, 44.
London, the British Library Board, 46, 226 (top), 261.
New York, YIVO Institute of Jewish Studies, 49.
Sefer Kolo, Tel Aviv (1958), 51.
Philadelphia, Jewish Publication Society of America, 54, 55.
Photo Werner Braun, Jerusalem, 59 (top), 120, 129, 236.
Jerusalem, B. M. Ansbacher Collection, 61.
Photo Reuben Milon, Jerusalem, 62, 69, 155, 179, 238.
Courtesy Yigael Yadin, Jerusalem, 64.
Jerusalem, Jewish Agency Photo Service, 66.
Jerusalem, Sir Isaac and Lady Wolfson Museum in Hechal Shlomo, 67, 70 (top), 198 (right), 201.
Fribourg Synagogue, 68 (left).
Nuremberg, Hauptamt fuer Hochbauwesen, Photo Ferd. Schmidt, 68 (right).
New York, Union of American Hebrew Congregations, 70 (bottom), 96.
Jerusalem, Yad Vashem, 71 (left), 194 (bottom).
Jerusalem, Italian Synagogue Collection, 71 (right).
Copenhagen Royal Library, 75 (right), 221 (right).
Radom Memorial Book, Jerusalem (1961), 79.
Jerusalem, Keren Hayesod Photo Archives, 83, 208.
Los Angeles, Guggenheim Collection, 85.
Prague, State Jewish Museum, 88 (right).
Jewish Welfare Board, 91.
Photo Leon Alaluf, Santiago, 92.
Formerly Feinberg Collection, Detroit, 94.
Photo Alfred Bernheim, Jerusalem, 95.
Societe de Jesus, Provenance de Paris, 97.
A. Z. Idelsohn, *Melodien,* Vol. II (1922), 99 (right), 100.
Leipzig University Library, 107, 109 (right), 257.
Budapest, Hungarian Academy of Sciences, 109 (left).

Jerusalem, I. Ta-Shema, 111.
I. Singer (ed.), *The Jewish Encyclopedia*, Vol. XII, New York (1907), 112.
New York, Jewish Theological Seminary, 113, 138, 212 (right), 248.
Jerusalem, Society for Research on Jewish Communities, 114 (left), 187.
London, World Sephardi Federation, 114 (right).
L. Kolb, *The Woodcuts of Jakob Steinhardt*, San Francisco (1959), 118, 127.
Jerusalem, R. Posner Collection, 125, 140, 199, 228, 234.
Courtesy S. Bazak, Jerusalem, 131.
Strasbourg, Alsatian Museum, 132.
New York, Siegfried Bendheim Collection, 145 (left).
Avnet Collection, 159.
Sigmund Harrison Collection, Villanova, Pa., 161, 189, 225 (left).
Waltham, Mass., American Jewish Historical Society, 164, 252.
Amsterdam Nederlands Israëlitische Hoofdsynagoge, 171.
Paris, Mme. D. Kirszenbaum, Photo Marc Vaux, 175.
A. Z. Idelsohn, *Melodien*, Vol. VIII (1932), 176.
Paris, Bibliotheque Nationale, 178, 207.
Jerusalem, S. Gorr Collection, 182, 223.
Jerusalem, Ministry of Tourism, 190 (top).
Photo K. Weiss, Jerusalem, 190 (bottom).
New York, Oscar Gruss Collection, 199.
Photo Frank J. Darmstaedter, New York, 199.
New York, The Jewish Museum, 200, 225 (right), 230.
London, National Gallery, 205.
Tel Aviv, Ha'aretz Museum for Ethnology and Folklore, 210.
Formerly Letchworth, England, Sassoon Collection, 211.
Jerusalem, Israel Department of Antiquities and Museums, 213.
Leon, Spain, Library of San Isidoro, 214.
Abraham Yaari, *Bibliografyah shel Haggadot Pesaḥ*, Jerusalem (1960), 219.
Erlangen-Nuremberg, Universitaetsbibliothek, 222.
Lubavitch Foundation, *Challenge*, London (1970), 224.
New York, The Brooklyn Museum, 227.
Tel Aviv, I. Einhorn Collection, 231.
Hannover, Kestner Museum, 232 (bottom).
New York, Metropolitan Museum of Art, 247.
Darmstadt, Hessische Landes- und Hochschulbibliothek, 249.
Jerusalem, Scritti . . . Sally Mayer (1956), 250.
Z. Efron Collection, 251.
Cleveland Museum of Art, J. H. Wade Collection, 254.
Eẓ Ḥayyim Seminary and Library, Amsterdam, 260.
Dresden, Saechsische Landesbibliothek, 263 (left).

The last paragraph of the *Amidah* is from the translation by N. Glatzer, *A Jewish Reader*, New York, 1961.

NOTE

The editors of this work have borrowed extensively from the store of information contained in the *Encyclopaedia Judaica* (Keter Publishing House Jerusalem Ltd. 1972). At the same time, they wish to point out that the authors of the relevant articles in the *Encyclopaedia* are in no wise to be held responsible for any matter of fact or interpretation appearing in the present volume.